ADDRESSES
ON THE
GOSPEL OF LUKE

ADDRESSES ON THE GOSPEL OF LUKE

By H. A. IRONSIDE, Litt.D.

AUTHOR OF
LECTURES ON THE BOOK OF ACTS;
LECTURES ON ROMANS;
LECTURES ON THE REVELATION;
IN THE HEAVENLIES;
ETC., ETC.

LOIZEAUX BROTHERS
Neptune, New Jersey

FIRST EDITION, MARCH 1947
ELEVENTH PRINTING, DECEMBER 1978

PUBLISHED BY LOIZEAUX BROTHERS, Inc.
A Nonprofit Organization, devoted to the Lord's Work and to the Spread of His Truth

PRINTED IN THE UNITED STATES OF AMERICA

CONTENTS

Contents

PREFACE

This volume consists of the substance of a series of expository messages on the third Gospel, given on consecutive Lord's Days over many months in the Moody Memorial Church of Chicago. They were stenographically reported at the time, but considerable work was needed in the way of editing to make them presentable in book form.

Naturally, in a lengthy series such as this, with an ever-changing audience because of visitors added to regular attendants, much in the way of repetition was necessary in order to make things clear and lucid for those who had not heard the former messages. To a large extent these repetitions have been eliminated, except where such deletion would have destroyed the continuity of thought. It is hoped the careful reader will recognize the reason for occasional reiteration of certain truths or incidents mentioned. To have altered the whole structure of the discourses would have destroyed their colloquial character. Such as they are I give them to the public, Christian and otherwise, hoping the Lord will be pleased to use them for the blessing of souls and for His own glory.

H. A. IRONSIDE.

Chicago, Ill.

January, 1946.

ADDRESS ONE

THE GOSPEL OF LUKE: ITS THEME AND AUTHOR

✓ ✓ ✓

"Forasmuch as many have taken in hand to set forth in order a declaration of those things which are most surely believed among us, even as they delivered them unto us, which from the beginning were eye-witnesses, and ministers of the word; it seemed good to me also, having had perfect understanding of all things from the very first, to write unto thee in order, most excellent Theophilus, that thou mightest know the certainty of those things, wherein thou hast been instructed"—Luke 1: 1-4.

✓ ✓ ✓

IN taking up the study of any one of the Gospels it is always well to look at it in relation to the other three. We have four Gospels in the New Testament, and the questions are often asked, "Why are there four?" and "Why do they differ one from the others as they do?" and, "Would it not have been just as easy to have given us one continuous biography of Christ rather than four accounts, all written by different writers?" This was not God's desire. By giving us four different records written by four different men, we have a stronger foundation for our faith in the stories of the birth, life, death, and resurrection of our Lord Jesus Christ. We are told in Matt. 18: 16, "In the mouth of two or three witnesses every word may be established." God has given us this testimony not only from three, but four witnesses; each one written by the guidance of the Holy Spirit.

Another reason why He has given us the four Gospels is to present our Lord Jesus Christ in four different aspects. Matthew was chosen to present Him as the promised Messiah, the King of Israel. Mark presents Him as Jehovah's perfect, faithful Servant. Everywhere in Mark's Gospel we see active service to God and man. John presents Christ as the manifestation of Deity, the Eternal Son of the Father, who became Man to bring us salvation. He deigned to become flesh: "And the Word was made flesh, and dwelt among us, (and we beheld His glory, the glory as of the only begotten of the Father,) full of grace and truth" (John 1:14).

But when we turn to Luke, Jesus is presented as Man in all perfection, the "Son of Man." That is Luke's favorite expression. As we examine this book carefully, we shall see many evidences of this.

Luke dwells much on the prayer-life of Jesus Christ, and prayer, of course, is connected with His Manhood. Jesus never makes a move but He looks first to His Father in heaven. We see Him praying, praying, praying, as every important occasion arises.

In this Gospel we also see frequently the Lord Jesus Christ as a guest in the homes of various people. He sat with them and ate with them, and talked over their problems. No other Gospel presents Christ going out to dinner so often as Luke does. Jesus shares their joys and sorrows and partakes of the good things that are presented to Him. When you meet a man at the dinner-table you find out what he really is. I had read forty or fifty biographies of Martin Luther, but he always seemed to be a figure on a pedestal until I read "Luther's Table Talks." Then I felt that he and I were friends. I felt that I knew the man as I could not have known him otherwise. So these accounts of Christ at the dinner-table give us an understanding of His Manhood, which we would not get in any other way.

Luke was an educated man. He was a "beloved physician," and yet a very humble man. He never mentions himself, either here or in the book of Acts. He and Paul met at Troas on the second apostolic journey. After that, Luke was almost a constant companion of the apostle, but as you read the book of Acts from the sixteenth chapter on, you will notice that whenever Luke was with the company, he says, *we* or *us*. When he remains behind as Paul and the rest move on, he changes to *they* and *them*. When Luke joins them again he reverts to *we* and *us*. He was with Paul to the end. In his last letter from Rome, Paul writes, "Only Luke is with me." He was a widely traveled man, highly-educated, and was of a scientific mind and temperament. In all likelihood he was a Gentile. He may have been of Jewish descent, but his name is a Gentile name, and he writes for the information of Gentiles. His special object in writing this letter was to make clear to a Gentile the facts concerning the life, ministry, death, and resurrection of Jesus Christ. His friend, who is mentioned here in the prologue in verse 3, as "most excellent Theophilus," was possibly a governor of a Roman province. He uses the title given to a high Roman official. Theophilus was, we gather, a Gentile Christian who evidently held high position in the Roman empire, and Luke was an intimate friend of his. He wrote this Gospel to give Theophilus a clear understanding of what had taken place in Palestine.

Luke gives us a great deal of information that is not found in the other Gospels. It is he alone who relates the stories of the visits of the angel Gabriel to Zacharias and to Mary. No one else tells us of the song of Mary, and the prophecy of Zacharias. The birth of Christ in a stable is recorded only here, as also the angel's announcement to the shepherds. The presentation of the Child Jesus in the temple at Jerusalem, and the welcome given by Anna and Simeon, also are mentioned only here. The first meeting in Nazareth, as recorded in chapter four; the great draught of fishes; the interview with the woman of the city in the house of Simon the Pharisee, as found in chapter seven; the beautiful incident of Mary at the feet of Jesus; and the mission of the seventy (chap. 10) are found only here. Much of the material of chapters eleven to eighteen inclusive is told only by Luke, as also the story of Zaccheus. It is he alone who mentions the coming of the angel to our Saviour to strengthen Him in His Gethsemane agony. And had it not been for Luke, we would never have known of the penitent thief, nor of the visit of our risen Lord with the two disciples on the way to and in their home at Emmaus.

Then when we think of the parables, it is striking to note how many are only related in this Gospel. The story of the Good Samaritan, the rich fool, the barren fig-tree, the great supper (not to be confounded with the marriage of the king's son as given in Matthew) the lost coin, the prodigal son, the unjust steward, the story of Dives and Lazarus, the unjust judge and the widow, the Pharisee and the publican, and the parable of the pounds, are all given by Luke. The last-mentioned, while similar to the parable of the talents, is, nevertheless, quite a different story.

How much then we would be bereaved of, if Luke had not been moved by the Spirit of God to search out so many things that no other inspired writer has recorded. There is nothing redundant here. All is of great importance and cannot be overestimated, so far as its value to the Church of God is concerned, and also its importance in presenting the gospel of the grace of God in its manifold aspects.

The book divides itself into three parts: The first four chapters deal with the birth, baptism, and temptation of the Lord Jesus Christ. The second division, chapters four to eighteen, gives the opening up of the way of salvation and approach to God. The nineteenth chapter to the end gives us the story of the crucifixion and resurrection.

In each Gospel the crucifixion is linked with a different offering, as found in Leviticus 1 to 5. Matthew presents it as the trespass-offering. Mark gives us Christ as the sin-offering. John takes up Christ as the burnt-offering. Luke brings Him before us as our great peace-offering—Christ making peace between God and man by shedding His blood on the cross. The trespass-offering sets forth the death of Christ because of the sins actually committed against God and man. The sin-offering speaks of Christ dying for what we are, not only for what we have done. The burnt-offering speaks of Christ dying to glorify God. The peace-offering speaks of peace made by the shed blood of the Lamb of God.

In the book of Ezekiel we have the four faces of the cherubim—the lion, ox, eagle, and man. These answer to the four Gospels. In Matthew we have the majesty of the lion; in Mark the patient service of the ox; in John the penetrating eye of the eagle —the heavenly One; Luke shows us the face of the Man.

Luke was a careful and conscientious investigator. He sought out those who had known the Lord Jesus personally and learned the facts from their own lips. He was, of course, inspired by God, but the Spirit of God led him to make use of all reliable sources of information. Notice how he begins his book: "Forasmuch as many have taken in hand to set forth in order a declaration of those things which are most surely believed among us, even as they delivered them unto us, which from the beginning were eyewitnesses and ministers of the Word: it seemed good to me also, having had perfect understanding of all things from the very first,"—

Let us stop there for the moment. Luke was sure of his ground. He knew the certainty of the things of which he wrote. There were doubtless many uninspired records, now lost, setting forth much that was commonly reported concerning our Lord's life and ministry. These, however, were not authoritative; God would not leave us dependent upon untrustworthy records. Early in the next century, many such apocryphal Gospels appeared, none of which have the dignity, the transparency, the sanctity of the inspired Gospels. People talk of the "lost books" of the Bible, but this is all wrong. We have all the Bible God ever meant us to have, in the Old and New Testaments. The so-called "lost books" are unreliable and legendary.

Whether Mark and Matthew had written earlier than Luke we cannot say. If so, he did not copy from them. He wrote as divinely-directed, just as they did. John, we know, was not written until many years afterwards. It is the last of the Gospels in point of time. Luke was not seeking to cast doubt on any other apostolic record, but he wished Theophilus to have an altogether accurate account of "all that Jesus began to do and teach, until the day in which He was taken up" (Acts 1: 1), so he wrote as an independent investigator.

He speaks of those who were "ministers of the word." The last term may be either the word of the gospel, or perhaps we should capitalize it and read "the Word," thus referring to Him who, though the Eternal Word, became flesh for our redemption. Whether we think of Christ's servants as ministers of the written word or of the living Word, it comes to one and the same thing, for Christ is the theme of all Scripture. He is the gospel personified.

We may think of Luke as going to Palestine, seeking out the still-living friends of Jesus, interviewing them and so learning firsthand many facts concerning the Lord's words and ways that others were not led to put on record.

This is the only one of the four Gospels that gives us the wonderful account of the virgin birth of the Lord Jesus Christ, though it is corroborated by Matthew. Luke was a physician, and the facts brought out here are facts which could only be expected of a physician. He had exact knowledge of everything he wrote. He probably knew the virgin mother intimately and learned from her own lips the great mystery of the incarnation. In the same way he would learn of other facts. And so he wrote in order that Theophilus might "know the certainty of the things wherein he had been instructed."

May I say to the young people who are troubled with doubts as to these things: If one has an open mind and an honest heart, the Holy Spirit will reveal to him the truth of God's Word. Let me ask that you give special attention to the details Luke sets forth, and pray that the Holy Spirit of God will open the Word to you, as He did to this beloved physician, and to many millions since his day.

Let us notice carefully each verse of this section. To begin with, Luke tells us that many had taken in hand to set forth in order a declaration of those things which were most surely believed among the early Christians. Verse 1 says that already there had appeared numerous records purporting to give the life-story of Jesus, which have been lost to us. Perhaps both Matthew and Mark had already appeared, and as these were divinely given, they too have been preserved, with Luke, and John, which came later, to give us a fourfold view of our Lord's life on earth. In these records an orderly account had been given of those great facts upon which our Christian faith rests.

These things had been made known to him by those who were personally acquainted with the Lord, who had known Him from the beginning, for verse 2 states that, as in John's writings (1 John 1: 1, etc.), from the origin of the Christian testimony, God has given us, through reputable *"eyewitnesses, and ministers of the Word,"* a faithful account of those important events which mean so much for our heart's rest and confidence.

Luke insists that he had perfect understanding of all things from the very first. From verse 3 it is clear that he had made a very careful, independent investigation, as became a scientific man, questioning eyewitnesses and visiting the localities where Jesus had lived and wrought His works of power. The facts thus gleaned he desired to lay before his friend, the "most excellent Theophilus," as a result of which we have this precious portion of the Word of God. For the Holy Spirit used the pen of Luke to give what would be of permanent value not only to Theophilus, but to all people to the end of time.

Note the expression in verse 4, "The *certainty* of those things." The gospel rests upon these divinely-accredited certainties. It is not an imaginary system based upon weird and unproved legends, but a substantial and logical message resting upon an assured foundation of facts. The Gospels are true histories. Therefore the incidents they record actually occurred.

We need not fear to rest our faith upon this definite testimony which God has preserved for our instruction.

Address Two

THE COMING FORERUNNER

✝ ✝ ✝

"There was in the days of Herod, the king of Judaea, a certain priest named Zacharias, of the course of Abia; and his wife was of the daughters of Aaron, and her name was Elisabeth. And they were both righteous before God, walking in all the commandments and ordinances of the Lord blameless, and they had no child, because that Elisabeth was barren, and they both were now well stricken in years. And it came to pass, that while he executed the priest's office before God in the order of his course, according to the custom of the priest's office, his lot was to burn incense when he went into the temple of the Lord. And the whole multitude of the people were praying without at the time of incense. And there appeared unto him an angel of the Lord standing on the right side of the altar of incense. And when Zacharias saw him, he was troubled, and fear fell upon him. But the angel said unto him, Fear not, Zacharias: for thy prayer is heard; and thy wife Elisabeth shall bear thee a son, and thou shalt call his name John. And thou shalt have joy and gladness; and many shall rejoice at his birth. For he shall be great in the sight of the Lord, and shall drink neither wine nor strong drink; and he shall be filled with the Holy Ghost, even from his mother's womb. And many of the children of Israel shall he turn to the Lord their God. And he shall go before him in the spirit and power of Elias, to turn the hearts of the fathers to the children, and the disobedient to the wisdom of the just; to make ready a people prepared for the Lord.

"And Zacharias said unto the angel, Whereby shall I know this? for I am an old man, and my wife well stricken in years. And the angel answering said unto him, I am Gabriel, that stand in the presence of God; and am sent to speak unto thee, and to show thee these glad tidings. And, behold, thou shalt be dumb, and not able to speak, until the day that these things shall be performed, because thou believest not my words, which shall be fulfilled in their season.

"And the people waited for Zacharias, and marvelled that he tarried so long in the temple. And when he came out, he could not speak unto them: and they perceived that he had seen a vision in the temple: for he beckoned unto them, and remained speechless. And it came to pass, that, as soon as the days of

his ministration were accomplished, he departed to his own house. And after those days his wife Elisabeth conceived, and hid herself five months, saying, Thus hath the Lord dealt with me in the days wherein He looked on me, to take away my reproach among men"—Luke 1: 5-25.

❦ ❦ ❦

THERE is an interval, as you know, of about four hundred years between the book of Malachi, the last book of the Old Testament, and the Gospels of the New Testament. We speak of these sometimes as "the four hundred silent years" because in those years we have no record, so far as inspired history is concerned, of God's speaking audibly to man, either directly Himself or through angelic ministration. Of course, in the books sometimes called "Apocrypha" we do read of angels visiting men and prophets being raised up, but in the inspired Scriptures we have no record of anything of the kind during those four hundred years. They were years of waiting. The people of Israel had returned from captivity in Babylon about B.C. 536 to 445. God had spoken to His prophet Daniel, saying that at the end of a certain limited period—483 years to be exact, 69 periods of seven years each—the Messiah was to come, and the people were waiting for His coming. They knew that the time had almost expired, and one can understand the expectancy with which the Jews would go up to Jerusalem year after year to keep the feasts of the Lord, hoping that the promise would be fulfilled.

But nothing happened until a never-to-be-forgotten day when a priest named Zacharias was ministering in the holy place in the temple at Jerusalem. We read in verse 5: "There was in the days of Herod, the king of Judæa, a certain priest named Zacharias, of the course of Abia: and his wife was of the daughters of Aaron, and her name was Elisabeth." You will remember that, as recorded in 1 Chronicles, chapter 24, King David divided the priesthood of Israel into twenty-four courses, each course to serve two weeks at a time annually in the temple, and then give place to the next course. The course of Abia was the eighth. (In the Old Testament it is called Abijah, but it would be pronounced as it is spelled here in Luke.) Zacharias, then, belonged to this particular course, and he may or may not have served in the temple on previous occasions, but this day he was burning incense at the sacred altar, the golden altar in the holy place. We read of him and of his wife that, "They were both righteous before God, walking in all the commandments and ordinances of the Lord blameless" (verse 6). That is not to say that they were sinless, "for there is not a just man upon earth, that doeth good, and sinneth not," we are told; but *blameless* refers to motives. Their motives were right. They were seeking to obey God, to walk with God, and they had, in a sense, His approval except for one thing. It was a great reproach in Israel if a married woman did not give birth to a child; therefore, people must have wondered whether God was displeased with this couple, whether, after all, He did not look upon them with disfavor. But sometimes, you know, God does not do immediately that for which our hearts crave, and yet He has it in His own purpose to reward in due time.

The years went by and this couple were still childless, until now they were quite elderly, and had given up all thought that they might become the parents of a child. But we are told here that while Zacharias on that particular day "executed the priest's office before God in the order of his course, according to the custom of the priest's office, his lot was to burn incense when he went into the temple of the Lord" (vers. 9, 10). As he stood at the altar and sprinkled the incense upon the fire that was ever burning there, the multitude of the people gathered outside were bowed in prayer before God. It was a lovely picture of the fellowship of prayer. Zacharias here might really speak of our blessed Lord, who has entered into the Holiest above, ever living to make intercession for us, while we His people join in prayer down here.

As Zacharias was praying and the people were lifting up their hearts to God, suddenly the silence of four centuries was broken. We read: "There appeared unto him an angel of the Lord standing on the right side of the altar of incense" (ver. 11). It must have been a startling thing. No living Israelite had ever seen an angel. They had read of angelic appearances in years gone by, but they must have thought that perhaps all that was over forever and that none of them was ever likely to be so-visited. As Zacharias looked upon this glorious being, we are told, "He was troubled, and fear fell upon him" (ver. 12).

It was a customary thought among the Jews that it meant death to look either upon God or upon any heavenly representative. You remember in the Old Testament how when angels appeared to various ones they were filled with dread, and thought that it meant they were about to die. But the angel immediately quieted his mind. "The angel said unto him, Fear not, Zacharias: for thy prayer is heard; and thy wife Elisabeth shall bear thee a son, and thou shalt call his name John" (ver. 13). "Fear not!" This seems to have been a favorite expression on the lips of Gabriel, for farther down in the chapter the same angel is said to have appeared to the blessed virgin Mary, and we read in verse 30: "And the angel said unto her, Fear not, Mary: for thou hast found favor with God." Then in the second chapter and the tenth verse, where the angel host appeared in glory unto the shepherds tending their flocks on the hillside, we read: "The angel said unto them, Fear not: for, behold, I bring you good tidings of great joy." The gospel message is intended to take away all fear and to fill the heart with assurance, the knowledge of God's deep and abiding interest in His people.

So the angel quieted Zacharias' fears and gave him the promise, "Fear not, Zacharias: for thy prayer is heard; and thy wife Elisabeth shall bear thee a son." And the angel named the son: "Thou shalt call his name John" (ver. 13). What a wonderful thing for a heavenly messenger to give the name for a child! We have several instances like that in Scripture. God told Abraham that he was to call his son "Isaac." Here the angel named the child that he said would be born, "John." It simply means, "The grace of Jehovah."

This son who was to be born was to be the means of bringing joy and gladness to many people, and first of all to his own parents. "Thou shalt have joy and gladness; and many shall rejoice at his birth. For he shall be great in the sight of the Lord" (vers. 14, 15). You remember what the Lord Jesus Himself said of him later on; that "of those who were born of women there was none greater than John the Baptist. And yet he that is least in the kingdom of God is greater than he." This man was great, destined to be great, because he was to prepare the way for the coming of the King. He was to baptize the King and to present Him to Israel, but he himself was to go home to be with God, as a result of Herod's bitter cruelty, before he saw the new order fully established here in the earth. Therefore, the very least who now receives Christ and enters into the kingdom of God occupies a greater position than John the Baptist himself. He said, "The King is coming." We can say, "Thank God, He has come, and we are definitely linked up with Him."

John was to be a Nazarite. Long years before, when God gave the Law, He said that if any in Israel were especially devoted to the Lord, they were to keep away from anything that came from the vinetree. They were not even to touch dried raisins or any other product of the vine, because the vine itself was the symbol of joy, and these men gave up the joys of earth in order that they might be more wholly devoted to God Himself. Then there were other regulations laid upon them. They were not to become defiled by coming near any dead body. They were to grow long hair, indicating the place of dependence, until the days of their Nazariteship were fulfilled. Samson was to be a Nazarite from his birth, and he became weak when he allowed his long hair to be cut. John the Baptist also was to be a Nazarite from his birth. He was to be wholly devoted to the service of the Lord from the very beginning. But more than that, he was to be especially, singularly marked out and empowered by the Holy Spirit even from the moment he came into the world. We read: "He shall be great in the sight of the Lord, and shall drink neither wine nor strong drink; and he shall be filled with the Holy Ghost, even from his mother's womb. And many of the children of Israel shall he turn to the Lord their God" (vers. 15, 16).

God prepared him from his earliest days for the great mission that he was to fulfil. I think you will often find that when the Lord selects a man for some special work, He puts His hand upon him very early in life and impresses upon him the possibility and the joyful privilege of becoming His messenger to a lost and needy world. How many of God's servants who have had a great ministry throughout the years were called as little children, children of godly parents, and from their earliest days were made acquainted with the things of the Lord, exercised in regard to their responsibility to God, and then when there came the full, clear consciousness of salvation through faith in Jesus Christ, it seemed as though nothing could hold them back. Young as they were, they began proclaiming the unsearchable riches of Christ.

John, then, was called from his very babyhood to be Christ's servant, and the assurance was given: "Many of the children of Israel shall he turn to the Lord their God" (ver. 16). His coming had been foretold back in the book of Isaiah. The Holy Spirit definitely spoke of the coming of this one into the world. In the fortieth chapter, beginning with verse 3, we read: "The voice of him that crieth in the wilderness, Prepare ye the way of the Lord, make straight in the desert a highway for our God. Every valley shall be exalted, and every mountain and hill shall be made low: and the crooked shall be made straight, and the rough places plain: and the glory of the Lord shall be revealed, and all flesh shall see it together: for the mouth of the Lord hath spoken it" (vers. 3-5). This was a prophecy uttered seven hundred years before John's birth concerning the coming into the world of him who was to be the preparer of the Saviour's way.

And then Malachi, the last Old Testament prophet, speaks of him twice. In chapter 3, verse 1, God says through Malachi: "Behold, I will send My messenger, and he shall prepare the way before Me: and the Lord, whom ye seek, shall suddenly come to His temple, even the messenger of the covenant, whom ye delight in: behold, he shall come, saith the Lord of hosts." John the Baptist was that messenger, sent to prepare the way of the Lord. I might add that here you have clear, definite proof as to the Deity of our Lord Jesus Christ, because it was Jehovah whose way was to be thus prepared, and John came to prepare the way of Jesus. The Jesus of the New Testament is the Jehovah of the Old Testament. Then in the last chapter of Malachi, verse 5, we read: "Behold, I will send you Elijah the prophet before the coming of the great and dreadful day of the Lord: and he shall turn the heart of the fathers to the children, and the heart of the children to their fathers, lest I come and smite the earth with a curse" (vers. 5, 6).

This was prophetic of the ministry of John the Baptist. It was not exactly that Elijah himself was coming back from heaven to earth, but John was to come in his energy. Referring again to the first chapter of Luke, verses 16 and 17, we find that they emphasize the fact that John was the messenger of Jehovah. "And many of the children of Israel shall he turn to the Lord their God. And he shall go before Him in the spirit and power of Elias, to turn the hearts of the fathers to the children, and the disobedient to the wisdom of the just; to make ready a people prepared for the Lord." The reference is definitely to the prophecy given in Malachi.

You remember how later on, the apostles came to the Lord Jesus as He spoke of His second coming, and asked, "Why say the scribes that Elias must first come?" Jesus answered them, "Elias is indeed come, and they have done unto him whatsoever they listed"; and then He explained that John came in the spirit and power of Elijah. We have no other scripture intimating that Elijah is yet to come. He has already come in the person of John the Baptist. You may say, "Well, he is to come before the great and dreadful day of the Lord." Yes, and so he did! The great and dreadful day of the Lord is still in the future, and we have this dispensation of grace in between; but that is in accordance with all Old Testament prophecy. This present age is all hidden. It is the great parenthesis in God's plan. "He shall go before Him in the spirit and power of Elias, to turn the hearts of the fathers to the children, and the disobedient to the wisdom of the just"; that is, to call the people of Israel back to the testimony of the Word of God and to that law which had already been committed to their fathers.

When this announcement was made to Zacharias he was filled with amazement. See how human he is! He and his devoted wife had prayed for years, "O God, that it would please Thee to give us a son;" and they thought they prayed in faith, but the years had gone and no son had come into their home to brighten their lives. And now, when the angel appears and says, "You shall soon embrace a son, and you will call his name 'John'" Zacharias looked at the angel doubtfully. He forgot how he had prayed all these years. He forgot that God can be depended on to hear the prayer of faith, and he asked the angel: "Whereby shall I know this? for I am an old man, and my wife well stricken in years" (ver. 18). In other words, he is practically saying, "Well, what sign will you give me that this promise will be fulfilled? It is almost too much for me to believe. I can scarcely think that my prayer is really going to be heard. What sign will there be that God is going to do this for me?" The angel—may I say it reverently?—seemed to be just a little bit nettled over Zacharias' lack of faith.

I wonder if our God is not often grieved in the same way over our lack of faith! He gives us such great and precious promises, and we come to Him in prayer, and we spread out our needs before Him and He gives us His Word, and we find ourselves asking, "Whereby shall I know this?" Hath He spoken, and shall He not do it? That is all that is necessary for faith—the word of the living God. We do not need some other sign in order to make God's word more certain of fulfilment.

So the angel answered Zacharias and said: "I am Gabriel, that stand in the presence of God; and am sent to speak unto thee, and to show thee these glad tidings" (ver. 19). In other words, he is practically saying, "Zacharias, have you not failed to recognize who it is that has brought this message to you? I am the angel that stands in God's own presence—Gabriel, Gabriel who appeared to Daniel, Gabriel who unfolded the prophecy of the seventy weeks, who told of the glorious things yet to come." Now he says, "I am sent to speak unto thee, and to show thee these glad tidings." That ought to have been enough. "I have come direct from the throne as Jehovah's messenger. You ought to be ready to accept my word for it, but now you want a sign. I will give you a sign, a sign perhaps which you will not enjoy, but I will give you a sign since you are not willing to rest upon the naked Word of God." "Behold, thou shalt be dumb, and not able to speak, until the day that these things shall be performed, because thou believest not my words, which shall be fulfilled in their season" (ver. 20).

Unbelief shut Zacharias' mouth. The last words that came from his lips before the promise was fulfilled were these: "Whereby shall I know?" The first words that came from his mouth after the promise was fulfilled were words of praise and thanksgiving. Unbelief made him dumb: faith opened his lips again.

"The people waited for Zacharias, and marvelled that he tarried so long in the temple" (ver. 21). He was there, you see, at the altar of incense much longer than a priest ordinarily would be. He should have come out, according to the regular course of affairs, to bless the people; but he had remained there in the presence of God, although they did not understand it. So they marvelled that he tarried so long. "And when he came out, he could not speak unto them: and they perceived that he had seen a vision in the temple: for he beckoned unto them, and remained speechless" (ver. 22). He stood there and just made a sign, unable to speak. "He beckoned unto them, and remained speechless." Instinctively they realized that something amazing had happened, that he had seen a vision. Then we are told: "It came to pass, that, as soon as the days of his ministration were accomplished, he departed to his own home" (ver. 23).

He had to remain but the two weeks there in Jerusalem, and then he went back to his home and in due time God began to fulfil His promise. "And after those days his wife Elisabeth conceived, and hid herself five months, saying, Thus hath the Lord dealt with me in the days wherein He looked on me, to take away my reproach among men" (vers. 24, 25).

One can imagine how full her heart must have been as she realized that after all these years God was truly answering prayer, and she was to be the mother of this child who was destined to welcome the Messiah Himself when He came to Israel. Oh, that you and I might learn the lesson of faith, trust, confidence in God, a God whose hand is still stretched out, and who challenges us with the question, "Is anything too hard for the Lord?"

ADDRESS THREE

THE ANNUNCIATION

✝ ✝ ✝

"And in the sixth month the angel Gabriel was sent from God unto a city of Galilee, named Nazareth, to a virgin espoused to a man whose name was Joseph, of the house of David; and the virgin's name was Mary. And the angel came in unto her, and said, Hail, thou that art highly favored, the Lord is with thee: blessed art thou among women. And when she saw him, she was troubled at his saying, and cast in her mind what manner of salutation this should be. And the angel said unto her, Fear not, Mary: for thou hast found favor with God. And, behold, thou shalt conceive in thy womb, and bring forth a Son, and shalt call His name JESUS. He shall be great, and shall be called the Son of the Highest; and the Lord God shall give unto Him the throne of His father David: and He shall reign over the house of Jacob for ever; and of His kingdom there shall be no end. Then said Mary unto the angel, How shall this be, seeing I know not a man? And the angel answered and said unto her, The Holy Ghost shall come upon thee, and the power of the Highest shall overshadow thee: therefore also that Holy Thing which shall be born of thee shall be called the Son of God. And, behold, thy cousin Elisabeth, she hath also conceived a son in her old age; and this is the sixth month with her, who was called barren. For with God nothing shall be impossible. And Mary said, Behold the handmaid of the Lord; be it unto me according to thy word. And the angel departed from her"—Luke 1: 26-38.

✝ ✝ ✝

WHERE in all literature would you find anything more beautiful than this story? —a story which is all the more delightful because it is true. The world had been waiting for a number of millenniums for the fulfilment of the primeval prophecy that "the Seed of the woman should bruise the serpent's head." The expression there used is itself remarkable. Every other child born into the world, save our Lord Jesus Christ, has been distinctly the seed of the man. He alone was the Seed of the woman. Although truly the Seed of Abraham, through whom all nations of the world were to be blessed, and the Son of David, destined to rule in Zion and bring blessing to Israel and the nations, Isaiah predicted that He would be born of the virgin mother. Thus He was the Seed of the woman in an absolutely exclusive human sense. He had no human father.

Luke, who is always very particular about dates, tells us that it was in the sixth month that the angel Gabriel was sent from God into a city of Galilee named Nazareth, to reveal to a virgin of the house of David, espoused to a man named Joseph, who was also of David's line, that she was to be the destined mother of the Messiah. It was, of course, the sixth month after the announcement of the forthcoming birth of John the Baptist, which had been made to Zacharias in the temple.

In connection with this annunciation, let us notice four things, in particular: First of all, the angelic messenger himself. There are only two elect angels mentioned by name in Holy Scripture, Gabriel and Michael. Michael is the archangel. Men talk of archangels. Scripture never uses the plural in this case, but tells us of only one archangel, Michael, the great prince, who stands for the children of Israel; that is, he seems to be their protecting guide in large measure. Gabriel appears to be the messenger of the throne. It was he who revealed the counsels of God, in regard to the coming of Messiah, to Daniel. He told Zacharias that he was to be the father of John the Baptist. And here we see him appearing to Mary making known to her the glad message that she was chosen of God to be the mother of the Saviour. I might say that in the books known as the Apocrypha—which should never be included in the canon of Scripture—we do have names given to other angels, as for instance, Raphael and Uriel, but only the two I have mentioned are spoken of by name in the inspired writings.

Then, in the second place, notice who it was whom God chose to be the mother of the humanity of His blessed Son. She was a pure virgin of the house of David. Thus the One born of her would be in very truth great David's greater Son. It is very evident that Mary was chosen, not simply because she was a virgin, but because of her deep spirituality and her subjection to the will of God. When He chose a young woman for the high honor of becoming the mother of the Saviour, He did not take some frivolous worldly girl, living in carelessness and enjoying a butterfly existence. He chose a pious, lovely, young woman, who delighted in doing the will of God and ever sought to be subject to His Word.

Then note what is written concerning him who was to head up the little household in Nazareth. This virgin was espoused to a man evidently much older than she, whose name was Joseph, and he came also of David's lineage. In fact, according to Matthew's Gospel, it is evident that the throne rights were his, and yet he was living in obscurity, earning his way as a carpenter. Everything was out of order because Israel had drifted away from God. They were in subjection to the Roman authority, and the son of David moved about among them unknown and ignored. He was not himself to become the actual father of Jesus; but he was to be recognized legally as His father, because he married the virgin before her wonderful child was born, thus giving her the protection of his name.

In the fourth place, we note the colloquy between Gabriel and the Virgin Mary. Appearing suddenly before her, evidently in her own home—of which, however, we know absolutely nothing so far as the Scriptures are concerned, although tradition has invented a great many stories about that home which are absolutely unproven and therefore unreliable—the angel greeted her with these striking words: "Hail, thou that art highly favored, the Lord is with thee: blessed art thou among women." We, of course, have our conventional ideas of what an angel looks like. Scripture does not give us any very definite description of one of these heavenly messengers. In fact, their general appearance, according to the Old Testament, was that of men of noble and superior character. Though they do not actually possess material bodies, they can evidently assume them at will. We need not suppose that Gabriel appeared to Mary as a glorious, winged creature. That is largely artists' imagination. But whatever form he took, his declaration must have been an astonishment to the Virgin. We are told that "when she saw him she was troubled at his saying, and cast in her mind what manner of salutation this should be." Apparently stricken dumb for a moment by her amazement, she waited for further word from her heavenly visitor. Then, we are told, the angel said unto her: "Fear not, Mary, for thou hast found favor with God." "Favor" is "grace." Let us never forget that Mary, beautiful and lovely as she must have been, was nevertheless born of a sinful race and needed a Saviour. She acknowledged this in the Magnificat which she uttered later on, when she said, "My soul doth rejoice in God my Saviour." She had found grace with God. In other words, she was saved by His grace, sustained by His grace, and preserved by that grace to be the suitable mother for the Son of God in His humanity.

The angel Gabriel continued speaking: "Behold, thou shalt conceive in thy womb, and bring forth a Son, and shalt call His name Jesus. He shall be great, and shall be called the Son of the Highest: and the Lord God shall give unto Him the throne of His father David: and He shall reign over the house of Jacob forever; and of His kingdom there shall be no end." This was a full Messianic declaration in keeping with the many wonderful prophecies that had been uttered concerning the coming Redeemer centuries before.

It is important to understand that the Lord Jesus actually partook of the substance of the Virgin. Some have supposed that this could not be without His participating in sinful human nature. But the

Spirit of God took care of that, as we shall see further on. The important thing to notice here is that there was an actual conception, and that involved an absolute impregnation. Jesus, whose name means *Jehovah, the Saviour,* was to be actually of the Virgin's substance as to His humanity, with which His true Deity was to be united in such a way as to make one Person with two natures—the human and the divine. He was to be called *the Son of the Highest.* The Lord Jesus is the Son in several different senses. As to His Deity He is God the Son, one Person of the Trinity, co-equal with God the Father and God the Holy Spirit, from eternity. Having linked His Deity with our humanity in incarnation, He became as man on earth the Son of God or Son of the Highest, having no human father. Then again, in resurrection He is saluted as the Son of God, the firstborn from the dead. To Him the Lord God, the Eternal Father, will give the throne of His father David; that is, David was in this sense the father of Christ's humanity, which would not be true if Jesus had not been an actual partaker of the human nature of the Virgin, who came of David's line. As such He is destined to reign over the house of Jacob forever, and to establish that everlasting kingdom to which all the prophets give witness.

One can well imagine the perplexity and wonder of the blessed Virgin when this announcement was made. In her beautiful simplicity she asks, "How shall this be, seeing I know not a man?" It was not lack of faith that led to such a question. She does not here take her place with Zacharias, who inquired, "Whereby shall I know this, for I am an old man and my wife well stricken in years?" On his part it was unbelief that prompted the question. On the part of Mary it was the desire for enlightenment. The angel made all clear in his answer when he said, "The Holy Ghost shall come upon thee, and the power of the Highest shall overshadow thee. Therefore also that Holy Thing (or One) which shall be born of thee shall be called the Son of God." Unbelievers have said it is impossible to accept the Bible teaching of the virgin birth because it involves a biological miracle. What it really involves is the omnipotent power of God, and the reverent believer can accept this without hesitation.

Some opponents of the truth of the incarnation have even gone so far as to declare that the story of the virgin birth is not peculiar to Christianity, but that in the myths of the heathen gods we have many instances of virgin births. This, one can unhesitatingly deny. There is no comparison between the sweet, pure, lovely story that we have here, and the vile, lewd stories of the heathen mythologies. What some have presumed to call virgin births are the very opposite. In these stories certain gods are represented as lustful, licentious beings. They are pictured as falling in love with some earth-born maiden, assuming a human form in order to seduce her, as a result of which she becomes the mother of a demigod. Surely there is nothing in these corrupt tales that can be linked in any proper sense with the story of the virgin birth of our Lord Jesus Christ. Here we simply have the Holy Spirit of God producing, by divine power and creative energy, the body of the Lord Jesus Christ in the womb of the Virgin. When He came into the world He was to be known, therefore, as the Son of God. He who had been from eternity God the Son, became in grace as Man, the Son of God, that He might be our Kinsman-Redeemer.

In order to confirm the faith of Mary, Gabriel then gave her the surprising information that her aged cousin Elisabeth had also conceived a son in her old age—though this was according to the natural order—and that it was now the sixth month with her, who was called barren. The explanation of all this is given in verse 37, "For with God nothing shall be impossible."

In charming simplicity and in marvelous devotion to the will of God, Mary answered, "Behold the handmaid of the Lord; be it unto me according to thy word." How much she, as a young virgin, understood of the shame to which she would be subjected by an unbelieving world, because of the peculiar circumstances in which she was soon to be found, we do not know, but she accepted all as from God and bowed in submission to His will. Remember, she was already engaged to be married. She must have wondered how she could ever explain what was soon to transpire, to Joseph. We know from Matthew's Gospel something of the grief and perplexity that Joseph himself actually went through when he learned that his affianced bride was already pregnant. Her condition apparently suggested a sad deviation from chastity, for which, according to the law, she could have been stoned to death. But Joseph loved her and was studying how he might hide her away privately until her child was born, in order that she might not be put to public shame or exposed to danger of death. But the angel messenger appeared to him in a dream, clearing up the mystery, and he accepted his responsibility in a wonderful way.

Mary must have foreseen some of these things, but doubtless did not enter fully into what she would be called upon to pass through. But since God had revealed His mind, she was ready to accept His will without rebellion or hesitation. In this she became an example to us all. The only truly happy life is a life lived in subjection to the will of God. To be able to say from the heart, "Be it unto me according to Thy word," means lasting blessing and abiding communion with God.

Having made known his mission, the angel, we are told, departed from Mary and left her to await the fulfilment of his words.

Address Four

THE MAGNIFICAT

✓ ✓ ✓

"And Mary arose in those days, and went into the hill country with haste, into a city of Juda; and entered into the house of Zacharias, and saluted Elisabeth. And it came to pass, that, when Elisabeth heard the salutation of Mary, the babe leaped in her womb; and Elisabeth was filled with the Holy Ghost: and she spake out with a loud voice, and said, Blessed art thou among women, and blessed is the fruit of thy womb. And whence is this to me, that the mother of my Lord should come to me? For, lo, as soon as the voice of thy salutation sounded in mine ears, the babe leaped in my womb for joy. And blessed is she that believed: for there shall be a performance of those things which were told her from the Lord. And Mary said, My soul doth magnify the Lord, and my spirit hath rejoiced in God my Saviour. For He hath regarded the low estate of His handmaiden: for, behold, from henceforth all generations shall call me blessed. For He that is mighty hath done to me great things; and holy is His name. And His mercy is on them that fear Him from generation to generation. He hath showed strength with His arm; He hath scattered the proud in the imagination of their hearts. He hath put down the mighty from their seats, and exalted them of low degree. He hath filled the hungry with good things; and the rich He hath sent empty away. He hath holpen His servant Israel, in remembrance of His mercy; as He spake to our fathers, to Abraham, and to his seed for ever. And Mary abode with her about three months, and returned to her own house"—Luke 1: 39-56.

✓ ✓ ✓

WE can well understand the emotions that would fill the heart of the blessed Virgin Mary after this interview with the angel. When she knew within herself that the angel's words were in course of fulfilment, she must have been greatly moved as she meditated on the marvelous mystery which had been revealed to her. She—an unmarried young woman who had lived a life of perfect physical purity — to become the mother of a child! How would she ever be able to explain things to those of her acquaintance who would naturally question the story she had to tell of the angel's visit and the message he brought. Perhaps it was such thoughts as these that led Mary to go up into the hill country with haste, into a city of Juda, and there visit her cousin Elisabeth; for although Elisabeth's circumstances were altogether different from those of Mary, still the supernatural entered into her condition too; and we can well believe that the elder woman would have much to say to the younger woman that would be a comfort and help to her. In fact, Elisabeth's first words of greeting must have thrilled the soul of Mary and confirmed the angel's words, as Elisabeth exclaimed, "Blessed art thou among women, and blessed is the fruit of thy womb. And whence is this to me, that the mother of my Lord should come to me?" Here was absolute faith, not only in the purity of Mary but also in the words of Gabriel, that the mysterious child to be born would be none other than God manifested in the flesh. Just imagine how cheered Mary must have been by such a greeting. Then as Elisabeth went on to express her further approval and to pronounce a blessing upon her young cousin because she had believed the word of the Lord, there must have been double assurance, for, apparently, she had not said one word to Elisabeth concerning her condition before the elder woman exclaimed there should be a performance of those things which were told her from the Lord.

When at last Mary opened her mouth, it was to praise the Lord in a beautiful psalm which compares favorably with any of those written by divine inspiration by David, the sweet Psalmist of Israel. Unquestionably, Mary herself was inspired to utter these words. They are of great value to us, not only because of their poetic beauty and their high devotional character, but also because they give us to know on what Mary, herself, rested for her own salvation. Romanists may declare that she was born without inbred sin and therefore did not need a Redeemer, but she herself says, "My soul doth magnify the Lord, and my spirit hath rejoiced in God my Saviour." Notice those last three words, *God my Saviour!*

Mary, then, lovely as she was; beautiful in character, perhaps beyond any other young woman of her day, yet realized that in herself she was a sinner who needed a Saviour, and she found that Saviour in God Himself. She took no credit to herself for any extraordinary righteousness that lifted her above other people, but she went on to acknowledge, "He hath regarded the low estate of His handmaiden." Realizing that everything was of grace, she could rejoice in the loving-kindness shown her.

It is well that we Protestant Christians should note carefully her next words: "Behold, from henceforth all generations shall call me blessed." Because, in the Roman Church, Mary is given a place far beyond any that is accorded to her in the Word of God, we are inclined to fear that we might honor her too much if we speak of her as the "Blessed Virgin." We have warrant for calling her blessed in her own words as here given. She was indeed marvelously blessed above all other women and we need not fear to acknowledge it. Since our Lord Himself chose Mary to be the means whereby He came into the world as a little Babe, why should we hesitate for a moment to speak of her as the Blessed Virgin?

She attributes everything to the goodness of God as she exclaims, "For He that is mighty hath done to me great things; and holy is His name." She shows an understanding of God Himself far beyond her years or her station in life. It is evident that she had been divinely taught, and that to a very remarkable degree. Her last words indicate that she had often meditated on the lowly condition of her people and the oppression that they were enduring, and she recognized in her unborn child the promised Messiah who was to deliver Israel from their afflictions and visit with judgment their Gentile oppressors. Note her words: "He hath showed strength with His arm; He hath scattered the proud in the imagination of their hearts. He hath put down the mighty from their seats, and exalted them of low degree." Had things been normal in Israel, her home would have been a palace instead of a peasant's cottage; Joseph, her betrothed, would have been recognized as a prince of David's royal house, and would not have had to earn his living as a carpenter; but how wonderfully God has exalted the lowly in bringing them into this blessed and remarkable relationship with Himself.

A divine principle is expressed in ver. 53, that runs throughout all Scripture and characterizes God's dealings with men in all dispensations, "He hath filled the hungry with good things; and the rich He hath sent empty away." The trouble with men generally is that they do not realize their need; they are not aware of their lost condition, and so, they do not turn to God for deliverance. They attempt to feed their souls with the husks of this world, and have not yet learned how futile is such an effort, and how impossible it is to satisfy a soul made for eternity with temporal things; and, because of their fancied wealth, they turn away from eternal riches and continue in their sins. Just as men recognize their need; as soon as they begin to hunger and thirst after righteousness; as soon as they recognize their spiritual poverty—as soon as they realize all this, they find in God One who meets every need. May we not well cherish in our hearts the blessing that belongs to the poor in spirit: that is, to those who have no spiritual assets in which to trust, but who come to God as poverty-stricken sinners to receive of the bounty which He delights to bestow. Scripture speaks of His riches in four different ways: we read of the riches of His mercy, the riches of His grace, the riches of His love, and the riches of His glory. All these are for those who come to Him acknowledging their poverty and need, and who are ready to receive at His hand the bounty which He delights to bestow.

The spirit of prophecy enables one to speak of the things which are not as though they are; and in the closing verses of the Magnificat, Mary does this very thing. She already sees by faith the fulfilment of all God's promises in connection with the restoration of Israel, and their further blessing in the kingdom promised by the prophets. She exclaims, "He hath holpen His servant Israel, in remembrance of His mercy. And He spake to our fathers, to Abraham, and to his seed for ever." There is something beautiful and sublime about the way in which this lovely young woman lays hold of the promises of God and counts on Him to fulfil them to the letter. May the same faith and comfort be ours!

We are told that for three months Mary abode with her cousin Elisabeth, and then returned to her own home in Nazareth. This was before the birth of John the Baptist, so she was not with Elisabeth when that event took place. Nazareth was in the northern part of the land of Palestine, and the prophet Micah had declared that Jesus was to be born in Bethlehem. It might seem as though there were little likelihood that this prophecy would be fulfilled, but we shall see later how God wrought in order to bring it about.

Address Five

THE PROMISE FULFILLED

✓ ✓ ✓

"Now Elisabeth's full time came that she should be delivered; and she brought forth a son. And her neighbors and her cousins heard how the Lord had showed great mercy upon her; and they rejoiced with her. And it came to pass, that on the eighth day they came to circumcise the child; and they called him Zacharias, after the name of his father. And his mother answered and said, Not so; but he shall be called John. And they said unto her, There is none of thy kindred that is called by this name. And they made signs to his father, how he would have him called. And he asked for a writing table, and wrote, saying, His name is John. And they marvelled all. And his mouth was opened immediately, and his tongue loosed, and he spake, and praised God. And fear came on all that dwelt round about them: and all these sayings were noised abroad throughout all the hill country of Judaea. And all they that heard them laid them up in their hearts, saying, What manner of child shall this be! And the hand of the Lord was with him. And his father Zacharias was filled with the Holy Ghost, and prophesied, saying, Blessed be the Lord God of Israel; for He hath visited and redeemed His people, and hath raised up an horn of salvation for us in the house of His servant David; as He spake by the mouth of His holy prophets, which have been since the world began: that we should be saved from our enemies, and from the hand of all that hate us; to perform the mercy promised to our fathers, and to remember His holy covenant: the oath which He sware to our father Abraham, that He would grant unto us, that we being delivered out of the hand of our enemies might serve Him without fear, in holiness and righteousness before Him, all the days of our life. And thou, child, shalt be called the prophet of the Highest: for thou shalt go before the face of the Lord to prepare His ways: to give knowledge of salvation unto His people by the remission of their sins, Through the tender mercy of our God; whereby the dayspring from on high hath visited us, to give light to them that sit in darkness and in the shadow of death, to guide our feet into the way of peace. And the child grew, and waxed strong in spirit, and was in the deserts till the day of his showing unto Israel" —Luke 1: 57-80.

FIRST of all, our attention is directed to the fulfilment of the promise regarding the birth of John the Baptist. Nine full months before, the angel Gabriel had appeared to Zacharias when he was ministering in the temple in Jerusalem, and notified him that he and his aged wife Elisabeth were to be the parents of a child who was to prepare the way for the promised Messiah. It seemed almost unbelievable, and Zacharias asked the question, "How can these things be?" The angel said, "You will be dumb until they are performed." Zacharias left the temple that day unable to speak, and during all these waiting months he had been dumb until God fulfilled the promise. Elisabeth's full time came that she should be delivered. She brought forth a son. Her neighbors, her cousins and others, heard how the Lord had showed great mercy toward her, and they came together to rejoice with her. God, in a wonderful way, had visited this family. Now a name was to be chosen for the new-born babe. Some of you parents remember how you thumbed through the list of names in the back of the dictionary trying to find one that would be outstanding! With others, it was already settled for you. You had long ago declared the little one must bear the name of grandma or grandpa, or some other relative. But often children are born and live for months before they get a name that is thought suitable. In this case, they came together to give the name to the child. He was presented for circumcision and given the name that they thought he would bear, that of his own father, Zacharias.

But the mother said, "He shall be called John." It happened that there was no John in that family. They said to her, "There is none of thy kindred called by that name." But the angel had told Zacharias before the child was born that he was to be called John. John means "the grace of the Lord," and his birth was a definite evidence of the grace of the Lord to his family. They turned to the father and they made signs to him, asking him how they should call the child. He, unable to speak, called for a tablet, and wrote upon it, "His name is John." Notice that—not, "He shall be called John," but "His name *is* John." He had been named already! He was named by the angel long before, and Zacharias simply kept that in mind. They were amazed. They could not understand it. The moment that Zacharias thus ratified the word of the angel his mouth was opened, and his tongue loosed, and he spake and glorified God. Unbelief had closed his lips; faith opened them. Unbelief made him dumb; faith enabled him to speak and to praise God. And we are told that fear came on all that dwelt round about. People felt there was something strange, something mysterious about all this. Undoubtedly, this was a child who was to have some very remarkable destiny. All these sayings were noised abroad, throughout all the hill-country of Judaea, and they that heard them laid them up in their hearts, and they asked, "What manner of child shall this be?" They could see that the hand of the Lord was upon him, thus far, in connection with the fulfilment of the promise in the birth of the child and the name that he was to bear.

Now the rest of our passage has to do with the prophecy of Zacharias. Many years had gone by since God had spoken through the prophets. But now, in a special way He opened the lips of Zacharias, the father of this remarkable child, and enabled him to speak prophetically. Zacharias was filled with the Holy Ghost. To prophesy is not only to be able to foretell coming events, but to give the mind of God in relation to the present or future. We see both here. Zacharias did see things to come, and he realized something of the remarkable place this child of his was to have. Then, he also spoke of the spiritual benefits to result from his ministry. "Blessed be the Lord God of Israel," he exclaims, "for He has visited and redeemed His people." It is remarkable how faith enables one to speak of the things which are not, as thought they are. Zacharias said, "God has visited and redeemed His people." They were not yet redeemed; that is, not actually, but he could speak in faith. He was certain that since the promise had been fulfilled in regard to the birth of this child that the promise of redemption for Israel, through the coming Saviour, was just as certain of fulfilment.

What is redemption? It is deliverance from bondage. It is to buy back that which has been forfeited. Not only Israel, but the nations of the Gentiles were in bondage to sin and they needed to be redeemed. They had forfeited all title to blessing, and they needed to be redeemed, and our blessed Lord Jesus, was coming to redeem them. He said, "The Son of Man came not to be ministered unto, but to minister, and to give His life a ransom for many." Do you know the redeeming power of the Lord Jesus Christ? He redeems not only from the judgment due to sin, but He also redeems from the power of sin itself. He sets free from sin's bondage those who put their trust in Him. Zacharias looked on in faith to the time when all this would be true for Israel and the nations. "He hath visited and redeemed His people, and hath raised up a horn of salvation for us in the house of His servant David." God had promised long before that the Messiah was to come through David's line, and Mary was a daughter of the house of David. Through her the child was to be born who was to bring salvation, and Zacharias could speak of this as though it were already accomplished, because his unbelief was gone and he had absolute confidence in the word of God. All this, he says, is, "As He spake by the mouth of the holy prophets, which have been since the ages began."

The word "world" here is not simply the *cosmos*—the ordered world—but the ages of time. From the very beginning God had been speaking of this coming One. From the Garden of Eden right on, He had been telling of the coming Saviour, and now He was soon to appear. His forerunner had already arrived. God had given His word and He sealed His word with an oath; and so He was about to perform the mercy promised to the fathers, and to remember His holy covenant, "the oath which He sware to our father Abraham." We are told in

Genesis that when God made the covenant with Abraham, He said, "In thy Seed shall all nations of the earth be blessed," and He confirmed it with an oath, and because He could sware by no greater He sware by Himself. He is the only one who has a right thus to sware. This was in connection with the Old Testament, and now the precious blood of Christ has sealed the New Covenant. We know that the Almighty will never go back on His covenant; so our Lord Jesus Christ came as the promised Seed of Abraham, and through Him already blessing untold has gone out to Jew and Gentile, but the promises are by no means fulfilled in their entirety. When they are, all Israel, as a nation, shall be saved, and shall turn to the Lord for redemption; and all the Gentiles shall own His authority, and righteousness will cover the earth as the waters cover the great deep. Then the entire universe shall be subjected to the Lord Jesus Christ.

It was to this that Zacharias looked on—"that He would grant unto us, that we, being delivered from the hand of our enemies, might serve Him without fear, all the days of our life." As far as Zacharias was concerned, he expected the fulfilment of all this. Yet nineteen hundred years have gone by, and we see the people of Israel today suffering more from their enemies than perhaps they have ever suffered down throughout the centuries. One might have a tendency to feel that God's Word has failed; that its prophetic declarations have not been fulfilled, and that there is something wrong. There is nothing wrong with the Word of God. The wrong is here.

God sent the Saviour. He came unto His own and they received Him not. Jew and Gentile are both guilty and united in rejecting the Saviour that God had promised. The Lord Jesus said, "Think not that I have come to send peace upon earth. I tell you nay, but rather a sword." He predicted, "Nation shall rise against nation and kingdom against kingdom," and there will be warfare and destruction through the world until the day of His return. When He comes back the second time, then these prophecies are going to be fulfilled. They might have been fulfilled before if men had received him. But they would not open their hearts to Him. Now He does speak peace to all those that trust Him; and in the midst of a war-torn world those who have received him in faith know the meaning of the words, "Thou wilt keep him in perfect peace whose mind is stayed on Thee, because he trusteth in Thee." There is no peace for the world because it has rejected Christ. But there is lasting peace for those who trust Him, even in the midst of the most dreadful circumstances. What He promises in regard to Israel will some day be fulfilled, "That He would grant unto us that we, being delivered out of the hands of our enemies, might serve Him without fear, in holiness and righteousness before Him all the days of our life." Neither Jew nor Gentile can expect God's deliverance unless there is a real heart-turning to Him. That is the trouble with the world today. Men would like God to intervene for them. They would like Him to come in and show mercy, but they are not willing to honor

Him by bowing before Him in repentance and seeking to live for His glory. When God shall deliver Israel, it will not only mean that they will be set free from their enemies and be restored to their own land, but that they may serve Him without fear and walk before Him in holiness and righteousness all the days of their lives. Oh, that there might be a great turning to God today! Oh, that throughout this nation and the other nations of the world there might be a recognition of the sinfulness of our departure from God, that we might return to Him, confessing our failure, owning our guilt, and trusting the Saviour He has provided, and then seeking to walk before Him in holiness and righteousness. Then we might expect God to come in and give marvelous deliverance. There will be no lasting peace for the world unless the nations bow in repentance before God and get right with Him; and so far as we understand the prophetic Word, that will never be until our Lord Jesus, the rejected Prince of Peace, returns again in person to this scene.

And now, in the last part of his prophecy, Zacharias turns to the little unconscious babe lying there, either in his crib or in his mother's arms, and he says, "And thou, child, shalt be called the prophet of the Highest." What a privilege this was to be! The Lord Jesus said afterward of those that were born of women there was not a greater than John the Baptist. And so Zacharias recognized that he was to have the high honor of being the prophet of the Highest. "Thou shalt go before the face of the Lord to prepare His way." He was really quoting here from the Old Testament. There we read that John was to go before the face of Jehovah to prepare the way. He went before the face of Jesus to prepare the way. The Jesus of the New Testament is the incarnate Jehovah of the Old Testament. John was to go before the face of Jehovah to prepare His way, to give knowledge of salvation unto His own people. It seems to me we sometimes underrate the work of John the Baptist. We think of him simply as the one who came to prepare the way of the Lord, and we forget that he also presented a message of grace, a definite proclamation of the gospel. It was he who said, "Behold the Lamb of God, which taketh away the sin of the world." Could you get a clearer gospel message than that anywhere? That is the gospel of the grace of God in all its simplicity. It was given to John to point the Saviour out, not merely as the King of Israel, not merely as the One who was to fulfil the promises and reign in righteousness over all the world, but as the One who was to provide salvation for sinful men. It is only through Him salvation comes "to give knowledge of salvation unto His people by the remission of their sins." When John baptized it was for remission of sins. His baptism was the recognition on the part of the people that they were sinners and deserved to die. As they went down into the waters of baptism they were saying as it were, "We ought to die for our sins." But John told of One who was coming to pay the penalty for those sins, and the people believed the message, and so rejoiced in the knowledge of forgiveness. "To give knowledge of salvation unto His people for the remission of their sins through the tender mercy of our God, whereby the dayspring from on high hath visited us." How beautiful the language Zacharias uses! He speaks of the grace of God thus being manifested to sinful men like the rising of the morning sun after the darkness of the night, "to give light to them that sit in darkness and in the shadow of death." That was the condition of the world all about him when Zacharias spoke these words; and that is the condition of a large part of the world today, and that is why we are entrusted to send the gospel out to the very ends of the earth, that men and women everywhere may hear it—that it may give light to those in darkness, in the very shadow of death. We read, in regard to those that turn away from God, who live for self and sin, "The way of peace have they not known;" but John the Baptist was to go before the face of the Lord to proclaim the testimony God had given, in order to guide the feet of the people into the way of peace. The servant of God who points men and women to Christ is showing them the way to peace, for, "Being justified by faith we have peace with God."

Our minds are naturally curious and there are a great many things of which we have no record in the Gospels concerning which we would like information. We would like to know something of the training of this child. We would like to be permitted to look behind the scenes and see sometihing of the home-life of John the Baptist as a little child and as a youth growing up. We would like to know what led him, eventually, into the wilderness, and how God spoke to him. But the Lord has not been pleased to gratify our curiosity in regard to these things. He tells us all that is important for us to know, and the rest He leaves. We shall find them out by-and-by when we get home to heaven.

But the story of John the Baptist's early life—the whole story—is given in one verse (ver. 80): "And the child grew, and waxed strong in spirit, and was in the deserts till the day of his showing unto Israel." Only a little less than four lines in my Bible, but they cover, perhaps, some twenty-five or twenty-eight years of life, and they picture for us very graphically a child growing up before the Lord devoted to Him, strong in spirit, spurning the evil, choosing the good; and then, when the divine call came, going apart from the rest of the world, alone out there in the desert where he might commune with God, where he could better hear His voice and be instructed by Him, in order that when the appointed time came he might appear before the people of Israel as the messenger of Jehovah, who had come to prepare the way of the Lord.

Address Six

THE BIRTH OF THE SAVIOUR

✝ ✝ ✝

"And it came to pass in those days, that there went out a decree from Caesar Augustus, that all the world should be taxed. (And this taxing was first made when Cyrenius was governor of Syria.) And all went to be taxed, every one into his own city. And Joseph also went up from Galilee, out of the city of Nazareth, into Judaea, unto the city of David, which is called Bethlehem; (because he was of the house and lineage of David:) to be taxed with Mary his espoused wife, being great with child. And so it was, that, while they were there, the days were accomplished that she should be delivered. And she brought forth her first-born son, and wrapped him in swaddling-clothes, and laid him in a manger; because there was no room for them in the inn. And there were in the same country shepherds abiding in the field, keeping watch over their flock by night. And, lo, the angel of the Lord came upon them, and the glory of the Lord shone round about them: and they were sore afraid. And the angel said unto them, Fear not: for, behold, I bring you good tidings of great joy, which shall be to all people. For unto you is born this day in the city of David, a Saviour, which is Christ the Lord. And this shall be a sign unto you; Ye shall find the babe wrapped in swaddling-clothes, lying in a manger. And suddenly there was with the angel a multitude of the heavenly host praising God, and saying, Glory to God in the highest, and on earth peace, good will toward men. And it came to pass as the angels were gone away from them into heaven, the shepherds said one to another, Let us now go even unto Bethlehem, and see this thing which is come to pass, which the Lord hath made known unto us. And they came with haste, and found Mary, and Joseph, and the Babe lying in a manger. And when they had seen it, they made known abroad the saying which was told them concerning this Child. And all they that heard it wondered at those things which were told them by the shepherds. But Mary kept all these things, and pondered them in her heart. And the shepherds returned, glorifying and praising God for all the things that they had heard and seen, as it was told unto them"—Luke 2: 1-20.

THE incarnation of our Lord is not merely a doctrinal tenet about which theologians of different schools may hold various views; it is a glorious reality, a wondrous fact, apart from which there could be no salvation for sinful men. "When the fulness of the time was come, God sent forth His Son, made of a woman, made under the law, to redeem them that were under the law, that we might receive the adoption of sons" (Gal. 4: 4, 5). The miraculous birth of our Saviour is one of the foundation stones of our Christian faith. It is the companion truth to that of His expiatory sacrifice on the cross. Because of this, it will generally be found that he who denies the one denies the other. Too much importance cannot therefore be attached to the historic fact that Jesus was born of a virgin mother and that the "Child . . . born" was the "Son . . . given" (Isa. 9: 6). He who deigned to enter human conditions by the birth in Bethlehem is the One "whose goings forth have been from of old, from everlasting" (Mic. 5: 2). To deny this is to repudiate the truth of the gospel, apart from which there is no hope for a lost world.

This passage connects very definitely with a prophecy which was given some 700 years before the events took place, which is found in the fifth chapter of the book of Micah. Micah was contemporary with Isaiah, and both prophets predicted the coming of the days of the Messiah, our Lord Jesus Christ. In the fifth chapter of Micah, second verse, we read, "But thou, Bethlehem Ephratah, though thou be little among the thousands of Judah, yet out of thee shall come forth unto Me, Him that is to be ruler in Israel; whose goings forth have been from of old, from everlasting." It is rather interesting to note the next verse. You might expect the prophet to declare that immediately all Israel would recognize as their Messiah and find redemption through, Him; but we read "Therefore will He give them up, until the time that she which travaileth hath brought forth: then the remnant of his brethren shall return unto the children of Israel."

How little chance there seemed, to almost the very last, of any possibility of the fulfilment of verse 2. It was given, as I have already said, 700 years before the Lord Jesus Christ was born. The Holy Spirit definitely indicated the place where he must be born—Bethlehem, a city of Judaea. It was David's city. It was not a very large city, but it is the most beautiful city, to my mind, in all Palestine. For over a thousand years since the days of the first crusade Bethlehem has been a Christian city, at least in name. It has not been given over to Mohammedanism, but has been a recognized Christian community. The prophet said that the Messiah must be born there, and he declared that this mysterious Child was to be One "whose goings forth have been from of old, from everlasting." The psalmist says, "From everlasting to everlasting, Thou art God."

This child, then, would be both God and Man—God and Man united in one Person, never again to be separated. This is the mystery of the incarnation.

Such was Micah's declaration, but it seemed until a very, very short time before the actual event took place, that the prophecy could not be literally fulfilled. Almost up to the very last Mary was dwelling in the city of Nazareth, in the northern part of the land. In those days when one could only travel on foot, or on the back of an ass or a camel, it took a long time to get from Nazareth to Jerusalem. It is very different today. We made the journey from Nazareth to Jerusalem in about eight hours, and we stopped over at a number of places en route, but that was by automobile. It was not possible to travel that quickly in those days. There was Mary at her home in Nazareth, expecting almost daily the birth of the wonderful Babe, the secret of whose conception she alone thoroughly understood, and yet the prophecy said, "He must be born in Bethlehem." I wonder if Mary ever thought of the words of Micah. I wonder if Joseph was concerned. Did Joseph know that the child must come into the world at Bethlehem? At any rate, they seemed to make no preparation for it. Then we are told it came to pass in those days that there went out a decree from Caesar Augustus, that all the world should be taxed. He was the ruler of the ancient world. He had his throne in the city of Rome. And here was the prophecy which said that the Messiah must be born in Bethlehem, and there was Mary waiting in Nazareth. So God put it in the heart of the emperor, that everybody must go to his own city, the city where he was born, in order to be enrolled for the taxing. This was God's way of bringing Mary and Joseph to Bethlehem on time, in order that His Word might not fail. We are told this taxing was first made when Cyrenius was Governor of Syria. The critics, those who try to find fault with the Bible and question its inspiration, used to point to this second verse and say, "Now you have positive proof that the Gospel of Luke could not have been divinely inspired because you have an inaccuracy. Cyrenius ruled over Syria something like 6 A.D., really ten years after the actual birth of Christ, because He was born four years before the change of the calendar from B.C. to A.D." These objectors said Cyrenius was Governor of Syria, which included Palestine, a number of years, on from A.D. 6. This taxing could not have taken place in his time if it took place at the time when Christ was reputed to have been born. God has been answering the critics in a very wonderful way in our day. The spade of the archaeologist has been turning up a great many remarkable things that have demonstrated the truth of the Bible. One of the leading archaeologists of the day wrote recently, "I am acquainted with practically all the results of archaeological discovery for the last hundred years, and I have not discovered any that cast doubt on the Scripture, but hundreds of things have proved its statements to be absolutely accurate."

I have jotted down an item which I took from one of the records. "It has been thought that Luke confused this census with that under Cyrenius, at 6 to 7

A.D., when he became Governor the second time. Luke refers to that also in Acts 5:37 as 'the days of the taxing.' " But we know that Cyrenius had been Governor of Syria before that, under the reign of Augustus, from B.C. 12 on to B.C. 3. It was during this period that the census was taken, to which Luke refers here in his Gospel. Men are too short-sighted and know too little, to find fault with the Bible. Just give us the opportunity to get more facts, and the Bible will always prove triumphant in every controversy. God had so ordered things that this enrollment had to take place, and that meant that Joseph and Mary must go to Bethlehem.

We read in verse 4, "And Joseph also went up from Galilee, out of the city of Nazareth, into Judaea, unto the city of David, which is called Bethlehem; (because he was of the house and lineage of David)." So it was that while there the days were accomplished that she should be delivered. Thus you will see God had set the whole world in motion—millions of people going to their own cities to be enrolled for the taxation, in order that one prophecy in the Old Testament might be fulfilled on time, and that Christ might be born in Bethlehem of Judaea. They were not looking for Him down there. There was no welcome. Though Joseph was of the lineage of David and though Mary was a daughter of the house of David, there was no blare of trumpets when they arrived. There was no reservation for them in the local inn. We read there was "no room for them in the inn." I suppose hundreds of people were crowding into Bethlehem. The wealthy would make reservations ahead and preempt the good places to stay. I can imagine Joseph and Mary coming, tired and worn after that long journey, and saying to the innkeeper, "Have you a comfortable place?" The innkeeper would say, "You didn't make any reservations. All the rooms have been taken." You can imagine there would not be much attention paid to this poor carpenter. Yet God had made provision. There was one place, if there was no room for His Son to be born in the inn, there was a place in a stable among the cattle. So we read, "She brought forth her first-born Son, and wrapped Him in swaddling-clothes, and laid Him in a manger; because there was no room for them in the inn." Do not think of the stable in which He was born as what we would call a stable today. It would not be a wooden barn but a cave cut in the limestone. When they show this place to people in Bethlehem today they say, "This is the cave in which Christ was born." We could see where the sheep and goats and oxen had been kept; and passing through a kind of a catacomb-like lane, we got into another cave where Jerome spent so many years while he translated the Bible into the Latin from the Greek. According to his own record, he said that his cave was right close by the one where Jesus Himself had been born. They will show you the cave today. It was in some such cave-stable that our blessed Lord was born. They took the little One and they wrapped Him in swaddling-clothes, and for a cradle they put Him in a manger from which the cattle were accustomed to get their food.

Think of God's blessed Son: become Man for our redemption! Born in a stable! and cradled in a manger! We find all heaven was stirred. In these early chapters of Luke you get one song after another. You have the song of Elisabeth, the song of Zacharias, and the song of Mary, and here you get the song of the angel. I know we do not actually get the word "song" here. It does not actually say the angel sang. But I am sure that the ordinary speech of the angels would be sweeter and more melodious than any song that anybody could sing on earth. All heaven was moved. We are told, "There were in the same country shepherds abiding in the field, keeping watch over their flocks by night, and lo, the angel of the Lord came upon them, and the glory of the Lord shone round about them, and they were sore afraid." They had heard of angels appearing in time past. But 400 years had gone by since the last of the prophets, and there was no authentic record of angels being seen on earth until Gabriel appeared to Zacharias in the temple. Now all heaven was illuminated and a majestic being was actually visible to mortals. They were sore afraid; but the angel said unto them, "Fear not; for, behold, I bring you good tidings of great joy which shall be to all people." What a message—FEAR NOT! Gabriel twice before had used these same words, and this may have been Gabriel again. "Fear not; for behold, I bring you good tidings." That is what the gospel is. The word means "good tidings." Our English word "gospel" is just a slightly changed form of the old Anglo-Saxon *Gudspel,* which means "good tidings." So the angel came to preach the gospel, and that word rings all through the Word of God. The gospel was preached to Abraham, and to the people of Israel. The gospel was preached all through the time or ministry of John the Baptist, and the gospel is being proclaimed today in the power of the Holy Ghost, sent down from Heaven. It is God's message about His blessed Son. There is only one gospel. Paul says, "Though we or an angel from heaven preach any other gospel, let him be accursed." This was an angel from heaven. If there be any who preach any other gospel than that which we have preached, let them be accursed. It is God's good news about His blessed Son. It takes on different forms at different times. It was the gospel of the Kingdom, specifically, when our blessed Lord and the early apostles gave it forth.

Since Christ ascended to heaven, the message has been sent down to earth, that a Saviour is seated at God's right hand. This tells of a finished work. It is called the "glorious gospel," because it leads to the glory, and the "everlasting gospel," for it is the gospel for all ages. The gospel will be the joy of our hearts for all eternity. It is all summed up in those wonderful words of John 3: 16, "For God so loved the world, that He gave His only begotten Son, that whosoever believeth in Him should not perish, but have everlasting life."

There are good tidings of great joy for all people, not just for the elect, not just for a limited number, but for *all* people. All men everywhere are invited to put their trust in the Saviour whom God has sent into the world. We have the definite announcement of the Lord's birth as given by the angel, "Unto you is born this day in the city of David a Saviour, which is Christ the Lord. . . . And this shall be a sign unto you; Ye shall find the babe wrapped in swaddling-clothes, lying in a manger."

Then we read that "suddenly there was with the angel, a multitude of the heavenly host, praising God and saying, 'Glory to God in the highest, and on earth *peace,* good *will* toward men'." It seems strange—doesn't it?—to hear those words ringing down through the ages, when you think of the awful condition which prevails in the earth today. Look where you will; there is no peace. Look at the lands abroad; there is war. Look out over our own land; it is strife between Capital and Labor—between different groups. There is misery and wretchedness everywhere—unrest on every hand; and yet the angel said, "Peace, goodwill toward men." Ah, but that peace was dependent upon receiving the Saviour whom God had sent into the world. Alas, men rejected Him. They refused Him, and that is why the world remains in its unhappy condition.

According to Micah, the Messiah is coming back again, when the rest of Israel shall return to their God.

The shepherds did not stop to question, but we read, "It came to pass, as the angels were gone away from them into heaven, the shepherds said one to another, Let us now go even unto Bethlehem, and see this thing which is come to pass, which the Lord hath made known unto us." I like the simplicity of their faith. They did not say, "Let us go and see *if* this thing has come to pass." They said, "Let us go and see this thing which *has* come to pass." They were persuaded even before they saw. They hastened and came and found Mary and Joseph, and the Babe lying in the manger; and when they had seen it they made known the saying which was told them concerning this Child. The first evangelists of the new age were these simple shepherds who went out saying, "He has come," and "We have seen Him. He was born in Bethlehem. We saw Him there lying in a manger." They went forth proclaiming the advent of our blessed Lord Jesus Christ, and all they that heard it wondered at those things which were told them by the shepherds.

Think of the virgin mother—what it must have meant to her! There she lay in the palace of straw! There—on the floor of the stable—there was the little Babe in the manger where she could just reach it with her delicately-shaped fingers; and all the time she was thinking what a wonderful message had come to her some months before, and now was the fulfilment. What does it all mean? Little could she see the wonderful results that would be manifested down through the ages, but she knew that God had come in, in grace, and visited His people. We read that "Mary kept all these things, and pondered them in her heart, and the shepherds returned, glorifying and praising God for all the things that they had heard and seen, as it was told unto them."

How our hearts rejoice in this story. We have read it over and over again, but it is always new;

is it not? The sweetest story ever told—the coming to earth of our Lord Jesus Christ. No room for Him in the inn. Is there room in your heart? Have you made room for Him? Have you received Him? Have you trusted Him? If you never made room for Him before, won't you say now,

> "Come in, my Lord, come in,
> And make my heart Thy home,
> Come in and cleanse my soul from sin,
> And dwell with me alone."

He wants to come in, and He will come in if you will open the door.

Address Seven

THE PRESENTATION IN THE TEMPLE

⸙ ⸙ ⸙

"And when eight days were accomplished for the circumcising of the Child, His name was called JESUS, which was so named of the angel before He was conceived in the womb. And when the days of her purification according to the law of Moses were accomplished, they brought Him to Jerusalem, to present Him to the Lord; (as it is written in the law of the Lord, Every male that openeth the womb shall be called holy to the Lord;) and to offer a sacrifice according to that which is said in the law of the Lord, A pair of turtle doves, or two young pigeons. And, behold, there was a man in Jerusalem, whose name was Simeon: and the same man was just and devout, waiting for the consolation of Israel: and the Holy Ghost was upon him. And it was revealed unto him by the Holy Ghost, that he should not see death, before he had seen the Lord's Christ. And he came by the Spirit into the temple: and when the parents brought in the Child Jesus, to do for Him after the custom of the law, then took he Him up in his arms, and blessed God, and said, Lord, now lettest Thou Thy servant depart in peace, according to Thy word: for mine eyes have seen Thy salvation, which Thou hast prepared before the face of all people; a light to lighten the Gentiles, and the glory of Thy people Israel. And Jeseph, and His mother marvelled at those things which were spoken of Him. And Simeon blessed them and said unto Mary, His mother, Behold, this Child is set for the fall and rising again of many in Israel; and for a sign which shall be spoken against: (yea, a sword shall pierce through thy own soul also;) that the thoughts of many hearts may be revealed. And there was one Anna, a prophetess, the daughter of Phanuel, of the tribe of Aser: she was of a great age, and had lived with an husband seven years from her virginity; and she was a widow of about fourscore and four years, which departed not from the temple, but served God with fastings and prayers night and day. And she coming in that instant gave thanks likewise unto the Lord, and spake of Him to all them that looked for redemption in Jerusalem"—Luke 2: 21-38.

THERE are really five parts in this section. First, we have the actual presentation of the Lord in the temple, to do for Him according to the law. As a Jewish child the ordinance of circumcision had been performed upon Him when He was eight days old. At that time His name was definitely called Jesus, as the angel declared should be the case before His birth. It is important to remember that this very name signifies not only His Saviourhood, but also His Deity, for it actually means "Jehovah the Saviour." That was the name given to Him before He was born, and confirmed to Mary before He was presented in the Temple. How blessed to know Him as that! God Himself came down in grace, linked His Deity with our humanity, in order to perfect our redemption. We have something that is rather pathetic and deeply interesting to me, in the offering that Mary and Joseph brought. According to the law, after a child was born and a certain number of days had elapsed, a secrifice was to be brought in recognition of the Lord's goodness to the parents, and also in recognition of the fact that even little children, as sweet and comparatively innocent as they are, come of a sinful race and need a Saviour. According to the law, that sacrifice might be of various animals. It might be a lamb out of the flock, or a kid of the goats, or, the Word says, if they were not able to bring a lamb or a kid, they might bring two turtledoves or two young pigeons. Here we have a most significant thing. When Mary and Joseph came to offer this sacrifice in connection with the presentation of our blessed Lord Jesus, their wonderful adorable Babe, we read that they brought a pair of turtledoves. They could not bring the higher-priced offerings. They were numbered among the poor of Israel. That gives us some conception of the place our Saviour took in grace—He who was higher than the highest. He who created all things came into this world and took His place in a family so poor that they were not able to bring a lamb out of the flock, but they brought the offering of the very needy—two turtledoves.

Next we have the recognition of the Saviour by Simeon and the prophecy concerning Him. We are told that, "There was a man in Jerusalem whose name was Simeon, and the same man was just and devout, awaiting the consolation of Israel." There were, doubtless, many of the Jews at this time who recognized the fact that the great time-prophecy of Daniel 9 had almost run out and that very soon the promised Messiah, the King and Saviour of Israel, must appear in accordance with the Word of God; and so they waited for Him. I wonder how many of us are waiting for His second coming. The years have gone since He went away. He said, "If I go to prepare a place for you I will come again, and receive you unto Myself." The Thessalonian believers "turned to God from idols to serve the living and true God and to wait for His Son from heaven." Are we numbered among those who are waiting for the Lord Jesus—waiting for Him to return again; waiting for Him to call His Church to be with Himself, and then to be manifested in glory for the full blessing of Israel and the nations? Just as this little remnant in Israel was waiting for Him to come the first time, so we should be waiting for Him to appear the second time, apart from the sin question, unto our complete and final salvation.

This man, Simeon, an aged man, was waiting for the consolation of the coming of the Messiah, and it was revealed to him by the Holy Spirit that he should not taste of death until he had seen the Lord's Christ; that is, until he had seen the Messiah that Jehovah had promised. As Mary and Joseph came into the Temple bringing the little child in their arms, Simeon entered also, and when the parents presented the Child Jesus, Simeon saw Him immediately and said, "That is the One," and without a moment's hesitation he went to Mary and took the child in his own arms and blessed God and said, "Now, Lord, let Thy servant depart in peace according to Thy Word, for mine eyes hath seen Thy salvation." That for which he was waiting had now actually been fufilled. The Spirit made it clear to him, and he said, "This is what I have waited for. This is what I wanted, and I now have that for which I longed, and I am ready to go home. Let me now depart in peace, for mine eyes have seen Thy salvation." Notice the last expression—God's salvation is bound up in a Person. When he saw Christ he said, "I have seen Thy salvation." If you would ever see God's salvation you must see the Lord Jesus Christ. If, when you look by faith upon Him, when you behold Him as the One who was sent by the Father, who came to this world in grace, and gave Himself a ransom for our souls—when you can see Him you are beholding God's salvation. So, if you would know God's salvation you must receive Christ.

Then Simeon goes on to prophesy. He says, "Mine eyes have seen Thy salvation, which Thou hast prepared before the face of all people, a light to lighten the Gentiles and the glory of Thy people, Israel." You might have expected Simeon to reverse that expression, for it was prophesied in the Old Testament that the Messiah was coming first to bring blessing to Israel and then, through Israel, to the Gentile world. Simeon realizes and recognizes that there is a break in God's way in dealing with men; so he puts the Gentiles first, and then Israel. The Spirit of God knew that when our Lord Jesus Christ came that first time in lowly grace, His own people would refuse Him. They would turn away from Him. They would not receive Him as their Messiah. So their hour of blessing was to be deferred. But he said, "He shall be a light to lighten the Gentiles," and that explains why it is that, though Israel refuses to own our Lord Jesus Christ as their Saviour, He has been manifested to untold millions of Gentiles who have recognized and trusted in Him. Has God lost His interest in Israel? No; for the present time blindness, in part, has happened to Israel until the fulness of the Gentiles comes in. When the work among the Gentiles is completed, then He is going to take up Israel again in a marvelous way. So Simeon says, "He is a light to lighten the Gentiles, and the glory of Thy people,

Israel." What a day it will be when Israel returns to the Lord, and when they shall recognize in Him the One whom their fathers rejected—the Saviour that God had promised, whose finished work on the cross alone redeems!

Then notice in the third place, the special word for Mary, the mother of our blessed Lord. Simeon said unto her, "Behold, this Child is set for the fall and rising again of many in Israel; and for a sign which shall be spoken against." How this must have confirmed to the blessed mother of our Lord the words spoken by the angel before His birth. It was all so strange and mysterious, but when this aged Spirit-controlled servant of God definitely said to her, "This child is set for the fall and rising again of many in Israel," it would confirm what had already been revealed to her. What does he mean by the fall and rising again? You will remember, Jesus said He was the stone of salvation, but He said, "Whosoever shall fall upon this stone shall be broken." Israel stumbled over the lowly Jesus. He was a stumbling-stone and a rock of offence to both the houses of Israel; so He was set for the fall of many in Israel; but, on the other hand, down through the centuries thousands upon thousands have turned to Him, as many did in the days immediately following His resurrection—three thousand at Pentecost, thousands more afterward, untold myriads down through the centuries since. Vast numbers from Israel have turned to God and found in the Lord Jesus their Saviour, and by-and-by the nation as a whole will be converted. So, this Child was set for the fall and rising again of many in Israel, and for a sign that should be spoken against. Oh, the bitter things, the blasphemous things that have been said concerning the Lord Jesus Christ! When people reject the Lord Jesus Christ there is no saying to what length they will go to bolster up their false beliefs.

Then Simeon turned directly to Mary and said to her, "Yea, a sword shall pierce through thine own soul also, that the thoughts of many hearts may be revealed." I wonder if these words did not come back to Mary as she stood by the cross and saw her blessed Son nailed to the tree, as she looked upon the thorn-crowned head, as she saw blood spurting from every wound, as she saw the hands that had been pressed upon her brow so many times nailed upon that cross, and those feet that had gone about, carrying their blessed Owner on errands of love and mercy, spiked to that tree. Her sorrows must have been deep indeed, and yet she knew that all was foreknown of God, and that it was her appointed destiny to bring into the world the Saviour who was thus to give His life a ransom for all.

The next thing we notice is that in verse 36, God gives further confirmation. This time an aged woman appears on the scene, a prophetess, named Anna, the daughter of Phanuel. She had lived with an husband seven years from her virginity, we are told, and was a widow of about eighty-four years, so she must have been above a hundred years of age. She was one of the remnant in Israel, waiting for the coming of the Messiah. She departed not from the Temple, but served God with fastings and prayer night and day. She, coming in that instant, suddenly recognized the Babe as the Saviour, and she gave thanks likewise unto the Lord, and she spake of Him to all them that looked for redemption in Jerusalem. This aged woman, becomes one of the first evangelists of the new age, saying, "I have seen the Saviour. He has come—the One who is to bring redemption."

The closing part of our passage has to do with the Childhood of our blessed Lord. When they had performed all things according to the law of the Lord they returned into Galilee, into their own city, Nazareth, and the Child grew and waxed strong in spirit. It is a lovely picture of this Child growing up in the seclusion of the home and glorifying God, His Father, in all things. There was nothing abnormal about Him. He was not doing wonderful and remarkable things. If you want signs and wonders the "Apocryphal Gospels" will give you all kinds of things attributed to our blessed Lord. It is told how, when He was a little boy, He went to school and the teacher started to teach Him the alphabet. The teacher said, "Say *Aleph,*" and He repeated it. Then the teacher told Him to say *Beth.* He replied, "No, I will not say *Beth* until you tell me what *Aleph* means." The teacher lifted up his hand to strike Him and his hand became paralyzed. That is the kind of Jesus the Apocryphal Gospels tell us of.

There is nothing like that in God's Holy Word. This is a beautiful, perfectly normal Child growing up in a lowly home where God is revered, and feeding upon the Word of God until the hour when He was to go forth on His great mission to redeem the world. Those hidden years were the suitable preparation for His future ministry.

Address Eight

THE BOY CHRIST AMONG THE DOCTORS

✝ ✝ ✝

"Now His parents went to Jerusalem every year at the feast of the passover. And when He was twelve years old, they went up to Jerusalem after the custom of the feast. And when they had fulfilled the days, as they returned, the Child Jesus tarried behind in Jerusalem; and Joseph and His mother knew not of it. But they, supposing Him to have been in the company, went a day's journey; and they sought Him among their kinsfolk and acquaintance. And when they found Him not, they turned back again to Jerusalem, seeking Him. And it came to pass, that after three days they found Him in the temple, sitting in the midst of the doctors, both hearing them, and asking them questions. And all that heard Him were astonished at His understanding and answers. And when they saw Him, they were amazed: and His mother said unto Him, Son, why hast Thou thus dealt with us? behold, Thy father and I have sought Thee sorrowing. And He said unto them, How is it that ye sought Me? wist ye not that I must be about My Father's business? And they understood not the saying which He spake unto them. And He went down with them, and came to Nazareth, and was subject unto them: but His mother kept all these sayings in her heart. And Jesus increased in wisdom and stature, and in favor with God and man" —Luke 2: 41-52.

✝ ✝ ✝

IT has not pleased God to give us very much information in regard to the early life of His beloved Son, as Man here on earth. Uninspired writers have tried to fill the gap by producing imaginary stories of the Childhood, and Youth, and Manhood of Jesus. There are weird myths stating that He went off to India as a young man and there sat at the feet of Hindu yogis, and learned the art of healing, and such like rubbish. We may be sure none of these things is true. Our Lord Jesus lived a normal life as a boy, growing up in a beautiful Jewish home where the Word of God was adored and loved.

As a young man He worked at the carpenter's bench with His foster-father, Joseph, and inasmuch as Joseph disappears from the picture in a little time and never seems to appear again, we are forced to the conclusion that he must have died while our Lord was quite a young man. That would bring Him to the place where He would be the head of the family, and caring for His mother and His younger brothers and sisters, for the Scriptures speak of His brothers and sisters. God never seeks to gratify mere curiosity.

We would like to know more of those hidden years at Nazareth. We would like to know more of the early days of our blessed Lord. We just have enough to let us know that He was a subject Child, and that His heart was always open to the voice of God, His Father. Here we get a little light on the habits of the family that help us to understand just what kind of a group it was. His parents went to Jerusalem every year at the feast of Passover. Long years before, God had commanded in the law that His people should go up to the place where He set His name from year to year, to keep the Passover feast, and it was His thought that every Passover might be a lesson to the children.

You remember that when the children asked, "What mean ye by these things?" they were told how their fathers had been slaves in the land of Egypt, and how God had delivered them and brought them out of the house of bondage. The parents were to explain the meaning of the Passover lamb, and though, perhaps, they realized it not, it was a picture of redemption.

One can think of our blessed Lord as a mere child taking the place of a little Jewish boy in that home, looking up into the eyes of His dear mother and saying, "What mean ye by these things?" Then as Joseph went on to explain, He would know far better than Joseph the real meaning of the Passover rites. He knew that He was the true Passover Lamb. He had come from heaven in order to give His life a ransom for many. He knew that the blood of the Passover lamb typified His own precious blood soon to be shed for the world's redemption, and yet, perhaps all this knowledge did not come to Him as a child immediately, for we are told that Jesus increased in wisdom as He increased in stature and in favor with God and man. The mystery of His incarnation is beyond our keenest comprehension. As the Eternal Son of God we hear Him saying to the Father, "Lo, I came to do Thy will, O My God. Yea, Thy law is within My heart." Voluntarily He left the throne of glory for the manger of Bethlehem. As God, of course, He knew all things, and yet as Man He chose to grow in wisdom as He grew in stature. It is a mystery. We cannot understand how He, who was the Eternal Wisdom, could yet learn from the Word of God. When we turn back to the prophet Isaiah we hear Him say, "He wakeneth morning by morning, He wakeneth Mine ear to hear as the learned." Our Lord Jesus, as a little child, grew and studied the Word of God. Later He fed on the Word of God. It was His constant delight and joy. All these different circumstances must have spoken to His heart as He knew He was the One who had come to fulfil every one of the types and shadows of the Law.

It is wonderful to contemplate that lovely family on its way to Jerusalem year after year, and that little Child Jesus toddling along beside, or His mother cuddling Him in her arms as she rode upon an ass.

Then, when He was twelve years old, the visit to Jerusalem had special significance for Him. When He was twelve they came up to Jerusalem after the custom of the feast. It was the rule in Israel, when a child reached the age of twelve, to bring him to the temple, and there he went through certain ceremonies something like that of confirmation in some of our churches. From that time on he was recognized as the son of the Law. A child was not supposed to be on his own responsibility until he reached the age of twelve. His parents were responsible for him until that time, but when he became twelve years of age he accepted his own responsibility, and it was now put up to him that he was to obey God and keep His Law and seek His favor. So our Lord Jesus at twelve years of age took His place as the son of the Law. He was a true Israelite and He came to fulfil everything in the Law of Moses according to the will of God.

On this occasion something occurred that may have a very serious lesson for us. When the Passover feast was ended and the people were leaving the city and wending their way back to their various homes, the family to which our blessed Lord belonged and many of their friends and relatives passed through the gates of the city and took the road to the north. Joseph and His mother did not inquire whether the young lad Jesus was with them. They took that for granted. No word was told Him that they were going, and He was not under responsibility to leave with them. There was something else upon His heart and mind that God the Father had revealed definitely to Him. They took the northern route, and went on a whole day's journey supposing Him to be in the company. Then, when they undertook to camp for the night, they sought Him everywhere and He wasn't there.

Our friend, Gipsy Smith, has often preached a very great sermon on the subject, "The Lost Christ," and pointed out how possible it is to take it for granted that Jesus is in the company, and yet to be without Him. It is never true that the Lord Jesus Christ leaves those whom He has saved by His grace. It is never true that, having taken anyone up in His loving-kindness, He later forsakes them, but it is sadly true that Christians may go on taking it for granted that they are in fellowship with Him when actually they have drifted away from Him in heart. They are not enjoying

His presence, and they hardly realize their loss. I wonder if there are not some of us here today who have had that experience. It is so easy to go on in an outward form of religiousness and not really enjoy the presence of Christ. It is possible to sit at the table of the Lord and to be conducting services for the Lord, and yet not have the presence of the Lord with us, and it is possible to go on, day by day, thinking everything is all right when in reality things are very, very wrong because we are out of touch with Him. We are not enjoying communion with Him. So it was with this group, awakened at last to realize that in some way or other they had missed Him. They took the long road back to Jerusalem, no doubt inquiring of friends if they had seen Him. When they got to the city three days went by before, at last, they found Him in the Temple. One would have thought they would have gone there first. That was His Father's house. There He had professed His allegiance to the Lord God, because the One in whose name it was dedicated was so precious to His youthful heart.

When the parents came they found Him sitting in the midst of the doctors, both hearing them and asking them questions. Now notice this: There is no evidence of undue precocity and He is not an impertinent child. He is not sitting in the midst of the doctors teaching them, nor leaving His place as a child to try to instruct these older people. He has all the marks of a humble child. He is listening to them, hearing what the elders have to say, and asking them questions. They too, evidently, ask Him questions. When they did He answered modestly and so wonderfully that they were amazed.

We read, "And it came to pass, that after three days they found Him in the temple, sitting in the midst of the doctors, both hearing them, and asking them questions. And all that heard Him were astonished at His understanding and answers." They did not know that this Child was "over all, God blessed for ever," who had taken our humanity in order that He might fulfil all that was written of Him in the Law. They did not realize that the Messiah for whom they had long waited was there in their midst. They said, "We have never seen a child like this before. He seems to know God so intimately. He knows the Scriptures so well—not merely the letter of the Law, but the spiritual meaning of it." So they looked one upon the other in amazement as they heard His questions and listened to His answers.

In this as in all else the Lord Jesus has left young people an example that they should follow. He left us an example of a Man who went around doing good. Consequently when He was reviled He reviled not again, and when He suffered He threatened not. We have an example as a Child, that children who have been brought to know their God and Father may follow in His steps. Young folk, let me impress upon you the importance of familiarizing yourselves with God's blessed Word. What you learn of this blessed Book in childhood will abide with you through the years. Some of us have proven that. We took it as the man of our counsel in our early days when we read it over and over again, and how much it has meant to us throughout the years. In the desire to get an education and to become familiar with the events of the day do not so give yourselves to other books that you neglect the Word of God. Feed upon His Word. See that you get some of it every day for your own soul. Don't be content to read a chapter at a time, but meditate when you read, and ask God to open it up to you by the Holy Spirit, and as you thus feast upon the Word you, too, will increase in wisdom, and in stature and in favor with God and man. You will be able, some day, to astonish those who do not know the secrets of the Lord, by your calmness, your restfulness of spirit in the midst of all the strife of earth, as you depend upon the living Word of God.

Mary and Joseph came to the temple and there they found Jesus, the Boy Jesus, sitting in the midst of the doctors, interested as they discussed together the things of the Scriptures, and when they saw Him they were amazed, and His mother said unto him, "Son, why hast Thou thus dealt with us? behold, Thy father and I have sought Thee sorrowing." You cannot blame her for the seeming reproach in her words. She had never known Him to be disobedient. He was perfect in all His ways. This was the first time perhaps that anything had occurred that had perplexed her in the bringing up of this Child, this Holy One. Mary speaks of Joseph as His father because he took a father's place, but actually God was His only Father. "And He said unto them, How is it that ye sought Me? wist ye not that I must be about My Father's business?" "Did I ever say anything that would warrant your losing faith in Me? Could you not trust Me? Could you not count upon My doing the thing that was right?" I wonder if that was not to remind her of that great mystery of twelve years back, when she, a virgin, had become the mother of a Child who had no human father. She knew that He was the Son of God. She knew that His first allegiance was to God the Father. Why did she not understand? There is just a gentle reprimand here that might seem unkind if we did not understand who He was. It was He who was both God and Man in one glorious Person. We read in verse 50, "And they understood not the saying which He spake unto them." It was something utterly beyond their comprehension.

Then, we have the next part of His life, up to the time of the beginning of His public ministry, brought before us in just two verses. These two verses are all that God has been pleased to tell us of the hidden years before He came forth to proclaim His Messiahship. "And He went down with them, and came to Nazareth, and was subject unto them." There again, what an example He sets to Christian young people of all ages. Oh, how much insubjection there is today. God's Word has said, "Children, obey your parents, for this is right." It is the first commandment with a promise. Children are to honor their parents although sometimes the parents are not very deserving of honor, but the children at least should try to cover the failures of their parents and to give them what honor they can, but oh, how children today dishonor their parents! How much disrespect there is! How much disobedience there is! In the old days it was "Children, obey your parents." Now it is largely, "Parents, obey your children." I was in a home not long ago and the folks were getting ready to go out on a little trip. The mother was downstairs in the car, and the daughter was calling upstairs to the father. I think she felt she ought to apologize to me, and she said, "I hope you won't misunderstand, but, you know, I have the most awful time training father to do as he is told." That is just a picture of the times. Instead of children doing as they are told, they are seeking to force the parents to obey the children. But how different the example set here by our blessed Lord, this holy Youth growing up there in Nazareth. He was subject unto His parents. We are told His mother kept all these sayings in her heart. She was pondering day by day as she noticed the development of this wonderful Child, as she thought of the angel's message of the miraculous birth and of some things that had transpired since. She was trying to peer into the future, wondering what was to be the destiny of this marvelous Being, of this One who was to be in her care.

The last verse gives us the end of what the Scriptures reveal concerning His early years: "And Jesus increased in wisdom and stature, and in favor with God and man." In all this He is an example to us. If we would grow in grace as we grow in years we need to feed on the Word of God and to spend much time in communion with our Heavenly Father by prayer and meditation. In Hebrews 5: 11-14 the inspired writer bewails the sad fact that so many of God's children make such slow progress in the spiritual life. After years of Christian profession they are still as babes in Christ, unable to appropriate and to digest the deeper spiritual truths of the Scriptures, but are such as need to be fed upon the milk of the Word. Paul speaks in a similar way to the Corinthian believers (1 Cor. 3: 1, 2). One evidence of spiritual babyhood is the tendency to quarrel over trivial questions, and to follow after human leaders instead of being subject to the direction of the Holy Spirit. Babies are inclined to be quarrelsome and self-willed. Some Christians manifest the same childish characteristics. Those who go on with the Lord and grow in grace and in the knowledge of Christ become increasingly like their Master. In this, as in all else that pertains to life and godliness, our blessed Lord as Man on earth was our example. While Jesus was the Incarnate Son, yet as a youth in the home at Nazareth "He increased in wisdom" as He grew in stature, and men marveled at the grace that was seen in His holy ways.

ADDRESS NINE

THE BAPTISM OF JESUS

✝ ✝ ✝

"Now in the fifteenth year of the reign of Tiberius Caesar, Pontius Pilate being governor of Judaea, and Herod being tetrarch of Galilee, and his brother Philip tetrarch of Ituraea and of the region of Trachonitis, and Lysanias the tetrarch of Abilene, Annas and Caiaphas being the high priests, the Word of God came unto John the son of Zacharias in the wilderness. And he came into all the country about Jordan, preaching the baptism of repentance for the remission of sins; as it is written in the book of the words of Esaias the prophet, saying, The voice of one crying in the wilderness, Prepare ye the way of the Lord, make His paths straight. Every valley shall be filled, and every mountain and hill shall be brought low; and the crooked shall be made straight, and the rough ways shall be made smooth; and all flesh shall see the salvation of God. Then said he to the multitude that came forth to be baptized of him, O generation of vipers, who hath warned you to flee from the wrath to come? Bring forth therefore fruits worthy of repentance, and begin not to say within yourselves, We have Abraham to our father: for I say unto you, That God is able of these stones to raise up children unto Abraham. And now also the axe is laid unto the root of the trees: every tree therefore which bringeth not forth good fruit is hewn down, and cast into the fire. And the people asked him, saying, What shall we do then? He answereth and saith unto them, He that hath two coats, let him impart to him that hath none; and he that hath meat, let him do likewise. Then came also publicans to be baptized, and said unto him, Master, what shall we do? And he said unto them, Exact no more than that which is appointed you. And the soldiers likewise demanded of him, saying, And what shall we do? And he said unto them, Do violence to no man, neither accuse any falsely; and be content with your wages. And as the people were in expectation, and all men mused in their hearts of John, whether he were the Christ, or not; John answered, saying unto them all, I indeed baptize you with water; but One mightier than I cometh, the latchet of whose shoes I am not worthy to unloose: He shall baptize you with the Holy Ghost and with fire: whose fan is in His hand, and He will thoroughly purge His floor, and will gather the wheat into His garner; but the chaff He will burn with fire unquenchable. And many other things in his exhortation preached he unto the

people. But Herod the tetrarch, being reproved by him for Herodias his brother Philip's wife, and for all the evils which Herod had done, added yet this above all, that he shut up John in prison. Now when all the people were baptized, it came to pass, that Jesus also being baptized, and praying, the heaven was opened, and the Holy Ghost descended in a bodily shape like a dove upon Him, and a voice came from heaven, which said, Thou art My beloved Son; in Thee I am well pleased"—Luke 3: 1-22.

✝ ✝ ✝

THIS passage brings before us the baptism of John, the baptism to which our blessed Lord Himself submitted.

Perhaps there is no person portrayed by the pen of inspiration less understood than John the Baptist. Our Lord Jesus said of him that of all those born of women there had never been a greater than he, but yet he that is the least in the kingdom of heaven is greater than John the Baptist. He stood at the door inviting people to enter. He never got in himself. He did not belong to the new dispensation in its fulness, but he showed the way to others; so in the sense of privilege, those who are in the kingdom of heaven are greater than he. But Jesus said that of all the prophets none was greater than John. Abraham was not greater. Moses was not greater; David was not; neither were Isaiah nor Jeremiah greater. John the Baptist in some way outshone them all. He was chosen by the Spirit of God to prepare the way for the coming of the Lord Jesus Christ and to seek to bring men and women to an attitude of soul where they would be ready to receive the Saviour when He appeared before them.

In telling the story, Luke is very specific. He writes as a careful historian. He gives us dates that any readers of his own time would have been able to verify, and that we ourselves to some extent are able to verify today. He tells us exactly when John the Baptist began his ministry. It was in the fifteenth year of the reign of Tiberious Caesar, Pontius Pilate being governor of Judaea, and Herod, tetrarch of Galilee. This was a grandson of the infamous Herod who was responsible for the slaughter of the babes in Bethlehem. His brother Philip was tetrarch of Ituræa and of the region of Trachonitis, and Lysanias was the tetrarch of Abilene. John got into trouble later on because of the fact that Herod lured away his brother Philip's wife, and took her to himself. Then we are told that Annas and Caiaphas were high-priests in Judaea. We might ask, According to the Old Testament Scriptures how could there be two high-priests? There was to be only one high-priest at a time and then he was to be succeeded by his son. But at this time everything was out of order and the high-priesthood was a political plum bought and sold by the Roman conquerors who gave the office to the highest bidder. Annas was retired later on, and his son-in-law, Caiaphas, had the position. But they were both recognized as high-priests.

It was at this time, when Israel was in dire confusion, that the Word of God came to John the Baptist. Thirty years or more had gone by since his birth. We know nothing of his early training. We are not given any particulars as to how the

Lord made Himself known to him, and gave him to realize that he was appointed to be the herald of the coming of the Saviour. Evidently for sometime he had been dwelling in the wilderness. Many of God's servants had graduated from the university of the wilderness! Moses was given a post-graduate course there for forty years. Much of David's training was given him in the wilderness. Take Elijah the Prophet—what lessons he had to learn out in the desert! And our blessed Saviour Himself spent forty days in the wilderness of Quarantana.

John the Baptist suddenly appeared in the region around Jordan, and we are told he was preaching the baptism of repentance for the remission of sins. He was not telling people that if they would be baptized their sins would be remitted. There is no such doctrine as that in Scripture. When we read of being baptized for the remission of sins it means that by baptism one confesses that he deserves to die. When John the Baptist called upon the people to be baptized confessing their sins, he was telling them that they were lost, that they deserved to die, that they could not make atonement for their own sins; but he told them of One who could. Some people imagine that John knew nothing of the grace of God. They forget that his real message was this: "Behold the Lamb of God, which taketh away the sin of the world." Who said that? John the Baptist. That is the gospel of the grace of God. Did John the Baptist preach the gospel? Yes! He told men that only through the Lamb of God, the Lord

Jesus, would their sins be remitted. He stood there in the Jordan valley and he drove home to the people their sins. We are told that those who believed his words justified God, and were baptized of him in the Jordan, confessing their sins. Their baptism was the outward acknowledgment of their lost condition. All this was in accordance with prophecy.

We are referred to Chapter 40 of Isaiah where God says, "Comfort ye, comfort ye My people, saith your God." The prophet looks up and asks, "How will I comfort them?" The voice of God says, "Cry that all flesh is grass and all the goodliness thereof is as the flower of the field." If God is going to comfort men they must first own their utter good-for-nothingness in His sight. To bolster men up in their own self-righteousness by trying to make them believe they have ability in themselves whereby they may save their own souls, is simply misleading men, and those who so preach will be responsible for soul-murder. The true servant of God is to put before men their lost condition in order that they may see their need of a Saviour. So Isaiah tells us that one was coming into the world with a message like this: "Every valley shall be filled, and every mountain and hill shall be brought low; and the crooked shall be made straight, and the rough ways shall be made smooth; and all flesh shall see the salvation of God." There is beautiful poetry in the Bible. He means that God's messenger was to go forth before the face of the coming Messiah as a leveler, to bring all men to one common plane, the recognition of their sinnership: "All have sinned, and come short of the glory of God." John was to bring this to the hearts and consciences of Israel in order that they might realize how badly they needed the Saviour who was about to come.

"Then said he to the multitude that came forth to be baptized of him, O generation of vipers, who hath warned you to flee from the wrath to come?" In the great audience he saw many who were really unreal. They were there sight-seeing. They had heard of the strange, weird, desert-preacher, and they wanted to find out what he was doing. So John turned to them and said, "All of you who have never been born of God, who are not honest with God, and do not want to be honest with God, who warned you to flee from the wrath to come?" John says, "If you profess to be the people of God evidence this in your lives. Bring forth fruits worthy of repentance." Do not misunderstand me. He was not saying they could be saved by anything they might do. They were in the place of covenant relationship with God. They professed to be the seed of Abraham, and yet their lives were bringing disrepute upon the very name they bore. Whatever you profess to be, evidence it in your lives. Repent. What is repentance? It is self-judgment. It is a complete change of mind and attitude. If you have repented, if you have faced your sins before God, if you know deliverance from them as shown by new lives, you are a truly repentant people. Do not fall back on natural relationship. It would be a small thing for God to raise up children from the stones unto Abraham. The mere fact that you are

Israelites does not mean that you are children of God. It is just another way of saying what Jesus said to Nicodemus later on, "You must be born again."

Then John adds, "And now also the axe is laid unto the root of the trees: every tree therefore which bringeth not forth good fruit is hewn down, and cast into the fire." In many places today you will hear beautiful, eloquent sermons that really would amount to this: "The axe is laid to the *fruit* of the tree." In other words, men are told, "Give up your bad ways. Give up your evil behavior. Everything will be all right and you will be saved by reformation. You will be saved by ethical culture. You will be saved by character. That's all you need." Imagine an orchardist trying to make a bad tree produce good fruit by cutting off all the imperfect fruit! The next crop will be just more bad fruit. The more you keep cutting it off the more bad fruit there will be. It won't change the nature of the tree at all. The apple-tree isn't an apple-tree because it bears eatable apples. It bears good apples because it is a good apple-tree. A crab-apple tree isn't bad because it bears crab-apples. It bears crab-apples because it is a crab-apple tree. A man isn't a sinner because he sins. He sins because he is a sinner. That's the trouble with him. That's why he needs to be born again. That's why John the Baptist came saying, "Cut it down completely. Let there be a new thing altogether." The axe is laid to the root of the trees; every tree therefore that beareth not good fruit shall be hewn down, and cast into the fire." Nothing you can do as a natural man will enable you to bring forth fruit to God. The apostle Paul preached the same doctrine that John the Baptist preached. He told the Ephesian elders that throughout his ministry. He preached "repentance toward God and faith in the Lord Jesus Christ." Repentance means that the natural man takes God's side against himself. God says, "All have sinned." Man says, "I'm not a sinner." The penitent confesses he is a sinner. He acknowledges his sin. He confesses his guilt. There is a Saviour for sinners. That's the gospel. "This is a faithful saying and worthy of all acceptation, that Christ Jesus came into the world to save sinners." But it is only the repentant one who cares anything about his Saviour.

When men do not realize their lost condition, they do not care. But when the Holy Spirit of God awakens a man to see his need, he is ready for Christ. When John the Baptist's ministry takes effect, and when men realize the axe is laid to the root of the tree, and they come down before God and take sides with God, they say, "Tell me about the Saviour," and then the further message of John the Baptist fits in, "Behold the Lamb of God, which taketh away the sin of the world."

When John saw the people were repentant he baptized them and they confessed their sins. He expected them, however, to give some evidence of their sincerity. "If you have two coats look around for a fellow who doesn't have one, and if you have more food than you need, divide with somebody else." There are many professing Christians who could not stand that test. One evidence that a man is truly repentant toward God is that he has real concern for his fellow-men who are in worse circumstances than he is himself. So John says, "Show yourself by your concern for others. To the publicans, that is, the tax-collectors, who inquired, "What shall we do?" He said, "You be careful now. Don't you gouge the people. Don't you take any more than you should—exact no more than is appointed you." That would be the evidence of a repentant tax-collector. Even Roman soldiers came to John asking, "What shall we do?" He replied, "Don't swagger so much, and don't act as if you are so important. Don't trample on the rights of any man! Do violence to no man! Serve your country, and try and let it go at that. Don't lord it over other folks." Understand, not as a means of salvation, but as an evidence of repentance. This would show that they were genuine.

The people were greatly interested and they wondered whether John himself might be the promised Messiah, but he said, "No, I am not He. I indeed baptize you with water; but One mightier than I cometh, the latchet of whose shoes I am not worthy to unloose: He shall baptize you with the Holy Ghost," or, He is going to baptize you with fire. Do not make the mistake that some people do—as though the baptism of fire and of the Holy Ghost are the same thing. The baptism of the Holy Ghost is something which every believer enters into, but the baptism of fire is the baptism of judgment which all men must know who reject the salvation that God has provided. See what he says about that: "He will truly purge His floor. He will gather the wheat into His garner"—that is the redeemed—"but He will burn up the chaff with unquenchable fire"—those are the unreal.

Herod heard about this. He wanted to see the strange desert-preacher. We are told he sent for him and he liked to hear John talk. There was something about that earnest man that appealed to the poor, wretched, godless Herod, and he was stirred. But when John spoke out plainly concerning Herod's adulterous relation with his brother's wife, Herod was angry. John said, "It is not lawful for thee to have her." Herod said, "I didn't ask you to come and tell me how to live. I don't believe in preachers interfering in personal affairs. Keep out of this." But John refused to keep out of it. Herod said, "Off to jail with you," and that was the end of John the Baptist, so far as his ministry was concerned. Herod liked to hear him preach as long as he did not touch the sin of Herod's own life. There are many people like that. They can enjoy fervent, earnest preaching as long as it is directed to somebody else, but when it comes home to them it is too personal. They don't like it.

Before John was put into prison something very important happened. When all the people were baptized it came to pass that Jesus also was baptized. He came to John, and He stepped down to the waters of Jordan. John drew back as he recognized Him, and said, as it were, "I cannot baptize you in repentance. You have nothing to repent of. I have need to be baptized by you." But Jesus replied, in effect, "John, you baptize Me. I know that I am not a sinner, but I see these sinners being baptized, and I am going to take My place with them. I am here today to pledge Myself to fulfil every righteous demand of the throne of God on their behalf." It was His pledge to go to the cross and die for sinners. So John baptized Him. When I see my Lord going down into Jordan I say, "There He is promising to go to the cross and die for me." He came forth from the waters, and the Spirit descended like a dove upon Him, and a voice was heard saying, "Thou art My beloved Son; in Thee I am well pleased."

At the very time when He had pledged Himself to fulfil all righteousness on behalf of sinners which involved His being made sin for them God the Father signified His delight in Him and declared Him to be the Holy One who glorified Him in all His ways.

Address Ten

THE GENEALOGY OF JESUS

ɫ ɫ ɫ

"And Jesus Himself began to be about thirty years of age, being (as was supposed) the son of Joseph, which was the son of Heli, which was the son of Matthat, which was the son of Levi, which was the son of Melchi, which was the son of Janna, which was the son of Joseph, which was the son of Mattathias, which was the son of Amos, which was the son of Naum, which was the son of Esli, which was the son of Nagge, which was the son of Maath, which was the son of Mattathias, which was the son of Semei, which was the son of Joseph, which was the son of Juda, which was the son of Joanna, which was the son of Rhesa, which was son of Zorobabel, which was the son of Salathiel, which was the son of Neri, which was the son of Melchi, which was the son of Addi, which was the son of Cosam, which was the son of Elmodam, which was the son of Er, which was the son of Jose, which was the son of Eliezer, which was the son of Jorim, which was the son of Matthat, which was the son of Levi, which was the son of Simeon, which was the son of Juda, which was the son of Joseph, which was the son of Jonan, which was the son of Eliakim, which was the son of Melea, which was the son of Menan, which was the son of Mattatha, which was the son of Nathan, which was the son of David, which was the son of Jesse, which was the son of Obed, which was the son of Booz, which was the son of Salmon, which was the son of Naasson, which was the son of Aminadab, which was the son of Aram, which was the son of Esrom, which was the son of Phares, which was the son of Juda, which was the son of Jacob, which was the son of Isaac, which was the son of Abraham, which was the son of Thara, which was the son of Nachor, which was the son of Saruch, which was the son of Ragau, which was the son of Phalec, which was the son of Heber, which was the son of Sala, which was the son of Cainan, which was the son of Arphaxad, which was the son of Sem, which was the son of Noe, which was the son of Lamech, which was the son of Mathusala, which was the son of Enoch, which was the son of Jared, which was the son of Maleleel, which was the son of Cainan, which was the son of Enos, which was the son of Seth, which was the son of Adam, which was the son of God"—Luke 3: 23-38.

WE come now to consider the genealogy of our Lord Jesus Christ. Those who read their Bibles with any degree of care have often noticed the two genealogies of the Saviour—the one given in the first chapter of the Gospel of Matthew, introducing the New Testament record, and the other given here in the third chapter of the Gospel of Luke.

In the Old Testament we have a great many genealogical tables. In the Book of Genesis we have ten of them, and in other Old Testament books, notably First Chronicles, we have a great many. God had a purpose in preserving these lists. They may not seem very interesting to us. Oftentimes those of us who read our Bibles through regularly year by year, are tempted to pass them over as of no real spiritual value, and yet every little while we find some bright jewel flashing out in the midst of a chapter of the utmost unpronounceable names for some of us. We may be sure there was a very special purpose for preserving them, and it was this: God had said, "The sceptre shall not depart from Judah, nor a lawgiver from between his feet, until Shiloh come; and unto Him shall the gathering of the peoples be." Shiloh is a name for our Lord, Jesus Christ, Israel's Messiah, the Prince of Peace, for Shiloh means "peace." And God saw to it that the genealogical tables were preserved from Adam right on down through Abraham and on to David, and then from David to the coming into the world of our Lord Jesus Christ, in order that His title to the throne of David might be definitely proven.

Now there are those who reject the Saviour as the Messiah, as many for instance in Israel do, who are still looking for a Messiah, and expect that sometime, perhaps very soon, perhaps in the more distant future, the Old Testament prophecies concerning the coming of Jehovah's Anointed into the world will have their fulfilment. If Jesus is not the Messiah there are no records left whereby it would be possible for them to trace out the genealogy of any one who might come in the future professing to be the true Son of David, who was destined to fulfil the promises made to the people of Israel and to rule over the Gentile world. There is no way now by which they could prove that any future Messiah was really the promised Saviour. The genealogies have all been lost. We have nothing beyond that which is given us here in the Bible. After the coming of the Lord Jesus Christ no other records were preserved that would enable anyone to trace out the genealogy of a future Son of David, if He were yet to arise. So God had a special reason for preserving the genealogical lists until His Son should actually be born into the world of a virgin, as predicted. After that there was no special reason to keep the records, so they were lost.

When you turn back to Matthew's Gospel you find that Joseph is the son of a man named Jacob, not Heli; and from Heli back to David you have an altogether different line from what you get in Matthew. Surely here is a contradiction in the

Bible! Surely this proves that, after all, the Bible cannot really be inspired of God, that it only consists of mere human records and it is not trustworthy! That's the way men have reasoned. When we look into it carefully I think the mystery is cleared up. It is remarkable that God has preserved the key to the mystery in the last book on earth in which we might have expected to find it.

After the fall of Jerusalem, the Jews, in order to keep before their people the great teachings of the past, combined many things in a series of volumes called "The Talmud," and today the orthodox Jews give far more attention to the study of the Talmud than they do to the Holy Scriptures themselves, though I was very glad to see in a Jewish magazine that some of the leading rabbis of this country are urging the Jewish soldiers to familiarize themselves with the Old Testament, to read it carefully. We rejoice in this because we know that if people read the Old Testament carefully and thoughtfully, many of them will be brought to the Light of the New Testament. The Old Testament points people to the Christ revealed in the New Testament. In the Jewish Talmud, written just a few years after the death of our Lord Jesus Christ, we are told that Jesus was the illegitimate son of Mary of Bethlehem, the daughter of Heli. That clears the mystery for us here.

Women's names are dropped out of this genealogy, but here we are told that Joseph was the son of Heli. This genealogy then is clearly the genealogy of Mary. Heli was the father of Mary, and Joseph by marrying Mary became the son of Heli. Married folks have two sets of fathers and mothers, do they not? You husbands speak of the bride's parents as father and mother, and the bride speaks of the husband's parents as father and mother. So it was in the old days in Israel. When a man married a maiden of a certain family, her father and mother were recognized as his father and mother. So Joseph was actually the son of Jacob, but through marriage to Mary he was the son of Heli, and Mary herself was the daughter of the house of David.

The reason for giving us the two genealogies seems to be this: In the first chapter of Matthew we have the genealogy of the King. Matthew deals particularly with the Messiahship of Jesus. It was written to prove that He was the promised King of Israel. Joseph, who married Mary before the actual birth of Jesus and took her under his protecting care, was himself lineally descended from David, through King Solomon; and had conditions been right in Israel, Joseph possibly would have sat upon David's throne. Instead of being Joseph, the carpenter, he would have been Joseph, the King of the Jews, but on account of the failure and sin that had come in, David's family had been set to one side and, we find, were in very poor circumstances. Nevertheless, the royal line ran on as God saw it, and Joseph was the last of the royal line of David, and by marrying Mary, her son Jesus, being born after she entered into wedlock, became the legal heir to the throne of David. That's why we have this genealogy in the Gospel of Matthew—to prove that Jesus is the legal heir to the throne of David.

The blood of Joseph did not run in the veins of Jesus, and according to the prophets, the Messiah Himself is to actually come through David's line. He is to be the Son of the house of David. He is called David's Son. Luke shows that this too was fulfilled, for we find as we go down through this genealogy that Heli, the father of Mary, came from a Davidic line, but the line through which she came was that of another son of David. Heli was a lineal descendant of David's son, Nathan. So the blood of David flowed in Mary's veins. Therefore, when our Lord Jesus Christ was conceived by the Holy Ghost in the womb of the blessed Virgin Mary and born of her, he was actually a son of David. Do I say a son of David? He was *the* Son of David, the One who transcended every other, the One who is to confirm the sure mercies of David, and bring in everlasting blessing for the world — "Great David's greater Son!"

So God has been very careful here to give us these two genealogical lists, to show us that the Lord Jesus is the rightful King. Through Joseph He is entitled to the throne, and then through Mary He is an actual Son of David. There are no mistakes in God's books. We may often come across things in the Bible that we find difficult to understand, but we can be very sure of this: If we only had a little added information, if we only had fuller knowledge, God's Word would always be shown to be right. There are no mistakes here. "All Scripture is given by inspiration of God, and is profitable for doctrine, for reproof, for correction, for instruction in righteousness: that the man of God may be perfect, throughly furnished unto all good works" (2 Tim. 3:16,17).

You remember, back in the Book of Psalms, the Lord speaks of one particular Person that would be before Him, He said, "It shall be said, This and that man was born in her, but the Lord shall count, when He writeth up the people, that this Man was born there," and this Man is God's Messiah, the Saviour of Israel and of the world.

When we come to look at these two genealogical lists as given in Matthew and Luke we are at once struck by their differences, and many have supposed that the one is contradictory of the other. In Matthew's Gospel we have a list beginning with Abraham and culminating in Joseph, the foster-father of Jesus. We read, in the very opening of Matthew's Gospel of the generations of Jesus Christ, the Son of David, the Son of Abraham. Now, Matthew is the Jewish Gospel. Do not misunderstand me when I say that. I do not mean that it has no word of authority for the Gentiles, but I mean that it was written specifically for the Jewish people in order to prove to them that Jesus of Nazareth was the Messiah promised in the Old Testament. The Messiah was to be the Seed of Abraham, through whom all nations of the earth should be blessed, and He was to come in the direct line of David. So in this first chapter we have the generations of Jesus Christ, Son of David, Son of Abraham, and beginning with Abraham we go right on to Joseph. In verse 16 we read: "And Jacob (that is, Joseph's father,) begat Joseph the husband of Mary, of whom was born Jesus, who is called Christ." Then the Scriptures carefully show us that Mary was already with child by the Holy Spirit before Joseph gave her the protection of his name and took her to be his wife. This table in Matthew's Gospel is definitely the genealogy of Joseph. It gives us the line from Abraham to Joseph. It is divided into three parts of fourteen generations each. Actually, when you go back to the Old Testament you find that there were quite a number of other names that came in along the way, but for certain reasons God dropped out various ones. He dropped out three kings of Judah because they came of the race of that vile woman Jezebel. For other reasons He dropped different ones out of the list, and He focuses our attention on three groups of fourteen each.

In the last instance, however, we seem at first sight to have only thirteen names. We read in verse 17: "So all the generations from Abraham to David are fourteen generations; and from David until the carrying away into Babylon are fourteen generations, and from the carrying away into Babylon unto Christ are fourteen generations." Notice again in the 16th verse: "Jacob begat Joseph." That's the twelfth generation. "The husband of Mary, of whom was born Jesus"—that's the thirteenth generation. "Who is called Christ"—that's the fourteenth generation, for when He comes the second time He will be recognized as the Christ, the Messiah of Israel.

In this list given by Matthew we have four women referred to beside Mary herself. Ordinarily it was not customary for the Jews to include any reference to women in their genealogies, and the four women mentioned in this list are the very four which one who was jealous of the purity of the Hebrew strain would have left out. There was Tamar, whose history was one of the most wretched stories in the Bible. There was Rahab, the harlot of Jericho. There was Ruth, a Moabitess, outside the covenant of promise altogether. There was Bathsheba who had been the wife of Uriah, with whom David sinned so grievously. Why are these four women's names listed here? Surely to show us that "where sin abounded grace did much more abound!" All of these women, three of whom were great sinners, are found in the line from which our Saviour came. The other one was an outcast and a stranger of Moab, of whom the Lord had said, "The Moabite shall not enter the congregation of the Lord unto the tenth generation." This outcast is brought in to tell us that Jesus is not only the Messiah of Israel, but He is the Saviour of all sinners, of all nations who will put their trust in Him.

Now, when we turn over to the Gospel of Luke and we look at the genealogy there, we find it is quite different. "Jesus began to be about thirty years of age." A Levite was thirty years of age when he began to serve. With our Lord Jesus it presents a new dispensation. He has now reached the age when He is about to enter upon His public ministry, "being as was supposed, the son of Jeseph." Notice that Luke has been very careful in the previous chapters to show us that the Lord Jesus was not the son of Joseph, that He had no human father. On the other hand, he recognizes that people supposed that He was the son of Joseph. So he mentions that here. Joseph, he says, was the son of Heli.

I said earlier that Matthew wrote especially for the Jews; therefore the genealogy tracing Christ from Abraham down—from Abraham and Solomon to Joseph.

Luke wrote for the Gentile world, and he is concerned not simply in proving that Jesus is the Son of David, nor yet that He is the Seed of Abraham, with all that implies, but He also undertakes to show that He has become, in grace, one with the entire human race. He is the Son of Man, and so the genealogy is traced back not to David or Abraham, but to Adam himself, and from Adam to God.

The Scriptures speak of the first man—Adam. There have been those who have suggested that there might have been some pre-Adamic race in this world, but God's Word says, "The *first* man, Adam, was made a living soul." Adam was not born into the world. He was created. God fashioned his body of the dust of the earth. Do you really believe that? I believe it, and in any case—if it was not in the Bible—I would believe it because of the fact that when the body dies it goes back to dust again. God took from the dust of the earth and formed the body of a man, and then God breathed into that man the breath of the spirit of life, and man became a living soul. So Adam could be called, in this sense, the son of God. God is the Father of spirits, "the God of the spirits of all flesh." There is a sense in which it is perfectly right to speak of the Fatherhood of God and the brotherhood of man. There is another sense in which it is wrong. As created originally, Adam was the son of God. God was his Father by creation, but sin came in and man became alienated from God. All men are now born in sin. There is a universal brotherhood of man, but it is a brotherhood of sinners. "All have sinned and come short of the glory of God." When people are born again, when they are regenerated, then they enter into a new relationship. They are in a new sense the children of God. God is their Father, and they that believe are all brethren in Christ. The heathen had the conception of man coming originally from God. They said, you remember, in the poem that Paul quoted, on Mars' hill—"We are also His offspring." But oh, how man has dishonored God. How far away we have gotten from Him! Therefore the need of regeneration.

It is not for us today to pride ourselves on being children of God by natural birth and to claim God as our Father simply by creation. We are alienated from the life of God through the ignorance that is in us. In order now to be able to look up to heaven and call God our Father and in order to enter the new brotherhood that has been established by grace, we must be born again. How does that new birth take place? We are told of our Lord Jesus, "He came unto His own, and His own received Him not;

but as many as received Him to them gave He the power to become the children of God, even to them that believe on His name, which were born not of blood, nor of the will of the flesh, nor of the will of man, but of God." It is when we receive Christ, when we trust Him as our Saviour, that we become children of God. This does not mean that we are put back to the place that Adam was in before his fall—created in righteousness, created in innocence he fell into sin. In the old creation he was put to the test, and when he went down the whole creation went down with him. But now Christ, the last Adam, has met all the claims that God had against sinful men by His sacrifice on Calvary. He has been raised in triumph from the dead, and He has become the head of a new race, a new creation. Those who put their trust in Him are not put on trial as Adam was before he sinned, but they are now raised up together and seated together in Christ, in heavenly places. This is our glorious calling, and so for us there is no interest except an academic one in the matters of genealogy.

We are told in 1 Tim. 1:4: "Neither give heed to . . . genealogies." We do not base anything on our earthly genealogy. We rest everything on the fact that we have been regenerated by the Word and Spirit of God. God has preserved the genealogies of His Son in order that we may have a clear and faithful record, and see His identification with David and Abraham, and with Adam as the Son of Man who has "come to seek and to save that which was lost;" as the Seed of Abraham, through whom all nations of the earth shall be blessed; as the Son of David, who shall yet sit upon the throne of His father David and reign in righteousness over all this universe when it has been turned back to God. How we can thank Him for the perfection of His Holy Word!

Address Eleven

THE TEMPTATION OF JESUS

"And Jesus being full of the Holy Ghost returned from Jordan, and was led by the Spirit into the wilderness, being forty days tempted of the devil. And in those days He did not eat anything: and when they were ended, He afterward hungered. And the devil said unto Him, If Thou be the Son of God, command this stone that it be made bread. And Jesus answered him, saying, It is written, that man shall not live by bread alone, but by every word of God. And the devil, taking Him up into an high mountain, showed unto Him all the kingdoms of the world in a moment of time. And the devil said unto Him, All this power will I give Thee, and the glory of them: for that is delivered unto me; and to whomsoever I will give it. If Thou therefore wilt worship me, all shall be Thine. And Jesus answered and said unto him, Get thee behind Me, Satan; for it is written, Thou shalt worship the Lord thy God and Him only shalt thou serve. And he brought Him to Jerusalem, and set Him on a pinnacle of the temple, and said unto Him, If Thou be the Son of God, cast Thyself down from hence: for it is written, He shall give His angels charge over Thee, to keep Thee: and in their hands they shall bear Thee up, lest at any time Thou dash Thy foot against a stone. And Jesus answering said unto him, It is said, Thou shalt not tempt the Lord thy God. And when the devil had ended all the temptation, he departed from Him for a season"—Luke 4: 1-13.

WE have two separate accounts of the temptation of our Lord Jesus in the New Testament, Matthew and Luke both relating His experiences at that time. It has often been noticed that the order of the tests is not the same in each of these Gospels. This does not, however, imply any contradiction, but simply that in the one Gospel, Luke, we evidently have the moral order of the temptations, and in Matthew the historical. We are told that our blessed Lord was "tempted in all points like as we are, apart from sin." Actually there are only three points on which anyone can be tempted. All temptation appeals either to the lust of the flesh, the lust of the eye, or the pride of life. That is, there is the fleshly, the aesthetic, and the spiritual or intellectual temptation. It was in this way that Eve was tempted in the garden of Eden, and she capitulated on all points. She saw that the fruit of the tree was good for food; that was an appeal to the flesh: that it was pleasant to the eye; that was an aesthetic appeal: then that it was to be desired to make one wise; this, of course, was an appeal to spiritual pride. Our Lord resisted on every point and so demonstrated the fact that He was the sinless One.

He was born into the world as the holy One, and holiness repels evil. In Adam unfallen, we see humanity innocent; when fallen, humanity sinful. In our Lord Jesus Christ we have humanity holy. The question is often asked, "Could our Lord have sinned? If not, why the temptation, and what was the virtue in His standing?" The answer is clearly this: He was not tempted to find out if He could sin, but to prove that He was the sinless One. It was like the acid test for the gold, which demonstrates the purity of the metal. We need to remember that the Lord Jesus was God and Man in one Person. He was not two persons in one body. It is unthinkable that he could sin so far as Deity is concerned. God cannot be tempted with sin. Had He been only a man He might have been put on trial like Adam and failed. But because He was God and Man in one Person He could not sin. There was, of course, in Him no evil nature, but there was none in Adam before he yielded. If our Lord had inherited fallen human nature, if there had been in Him any tendency to sin, He would have needed a Saviour Himself. Because He was the absolutely sinless One He could offer Himself a ransom for our souls and so bring fallen humanity back to God.

We are told in the Epistle to the Hebrews that He suffered being tempted. On the other hand, Peter tells us, "He that hath suffered in the flesh hath ceased from sin." These two passages bring out most vividly the difference between Christ and us. We suffer by resisting temptation and so are enabled to cease from sin, but temptation caused Him the keenest suffering. As the holy One He could not endure this contact with Satanic suggestion without suffering inward distress.

We are told that "Jesus, being full of the Holy Spirit, returned from Jordan; and was led by the Spirit into the wilderness." This in itself is most suggestive. Acknowledged by the Father as His beloved Son in whom He had found all His delight, sealed by the Holy Spirit and thus marked out as the Messiah, the Anointed of Jehovah, He was led by the Spirit into the wilderness of Quarantana, according to accepted tradition, in order that, through the temptation, it might be demonstrated that He was in very truth the holy One, who was thus suited to offer Himself a sacrifice on behalf of those who are unholy.

Standing in the ruins of the recently uncovered city of Jericho and looking up upon the bare, desolate mount of Quarantana, in the wilderness of Judaea, my own heart was deeply stirred some years ago, as I thought of my blessed Lord spending forty days there with the wild beasts of the wilderness and without food. What a contrast to Adam the First, who was placed in a garden of delight, with every creature subject to his will and provided with everything needful to sustain and strengthen him physically! Jesus stood every test, fasting in a wilderness among the wild beasts because He, the Last Adam, the Second Man, was God's blessed, Eternal Son become flesh for our redemption.

We are told definitely that He was forty days tempted of the devil. Let me emphasize that. There are those today who deny the personality of the devil. They say that all the devil there is, is the evil of a man's own heart, his own wicked desires, his own evil thoughts. In one great religious system, which has been taken up by multitudes, the teaching is current that if you just cut the letter "D" out of the word "Devil" you will find what that word really represents. The devil is simply the personification of evil. Actually, they tell us, there is no personal devil. Have you ever thought what that implies? First of all, it implies this: all the wickedness, all the vile iniquity, all the abominable filth and the dreadful corruption that have characterized the most vicious men and women during the millenniums of history have come from their own hearts without any tempting spirit to incite to these excesses. That is the worst indictment of the human race that anyone ever dreamed of bringing against mankind: It implies that man's heart, in itself, is so utterly evil that it needs no outside incentive to produce the unbelievable vileness which has polluted the pages of human history. Surely, no stern, hyper-Calvinist of Reformation days ever brought as strong an indictment against humanity as that! And yet, because error is never consistent, the very people who teach this tell us that all men are children of God by natural birth, and deny the necessity of redemption and of regeneration!

But then there is more than this to be considered. The denial of the personality of the devil is positive blasphemy against our Lord Jesus Christ. Here we are told that He was led into the wilderness to be tempted of the devil. Dare we say that this means He was to be tempted by His own evil thoughts, by the wickedness of His own heart? We have already seen that there was no wickedness there. He was the pure and sinless One. Yet He was tempted of the devil. He Himself tells us elsewhere that the devil abode not in the truth, that he is a liar from the beginning, a murderer, and that there is no truth in him. Note these personal pronouns. Our Lord Jesus recognized in Satan a sinister personality, the foe of God and man.

The question may be asked, "Why, then, did God create such an evil being? Why did He ever bring a devil into existence?" He did not create him as an evil spirit but as a pure and innocent angel. He abode not in the truth. Like all the other angels, he was created in innocence, but temptation came, the temptation to exalt himself, and so he fell and became the enemy of God and man. His judgment has already been declared, but before it is carried out God has chosen to permit him a certain measure of power and liberty in order that men may be tested to find out whether they prefer Satan's service or whether to live in loving devotion to the God who created them. You may take your choice, but if you choose Satan as your master here you must share his doom for eternity, for hell was prepared for the devil and his angels, that is, his messengers.

Now notice the order of the temptations as here given. Satan came to Jesus when He was hungry, when physically He was weakest. This was the opportunity to present to Him the appeal to the lust of the flesh, if there had been anything in Him contrary to the holiness of the Godhead. So the devil said to Him, "If Thou be the Son of God, command this stone that it be made bread." To have yielded would have been to accept a suggestion from Satan and thus to take Himself out of the hand of God. There was not the slightest tendency to do this. Jesus met the tempter with Scripture, saying, "Man doth not live by bread only, but by every word that proceedeth out of the mouth of God doth man live." There is something more important than bread to sustain the body, and that is the Word that sustains the spirit. So the Lord Jesus repudiated the suggestion of the devil. He had no word from the Father commanding Him to change stones into bread. He would not put forth such power in obedience to Satan.

Alas, how often have we who profess His name failed in similar circumstances. We have reached the place of grave extremity in some experience of life. Satan presents an opportunity to prosper through doing something that is a little bit off-color and that is not quite in keeping with the full Christian profession. How many a child of God has failed right there and has allowed himself to take up with something which even the world recognizes as shady or crooked, in order that he might procure more of the bread that perishes, only to find out at last that he breaks his teeth upon the very stones which he attempted thus to change into food. That is not God's way. He does not call upon His people to make bread out of stones. He feeds us both naturally and spiritually as we labor day by day for that which is for our blessing. There is something more important than bread, and that is to do the will of God.

The second temptation was the attempted appeal to the lust of the eye. From a great and high mountain in marvelous vision Jesus looks over the whole world. Satan shows Him all the kingdoms of the earth in a moment of time. He declares that all this belongs to him; he is the god of the world; he is its prince; men have surrendered it to him, and he says, "To whomsoever I will give it. If Thou wilt therefore worship me all shall be Thine." It was the offer of the kingdom without the cross; but there was no inward response on the part of the Saviour. He had come into the world not only to rule as King, but first to give His life a ransom for many, and

Satan's suggestion make no impression upon Him whatever. He replies, "Get thee behind Me, Satan, for it is written, Thou shalt worship the Lord thy God, and Him only shalt thou serve." He recognizes at once who the tempter is, calls him by name, spurns his suggestion and again triumphs through the Word.

The day will yet come when the kingdoms of this world shall become the kingdom of our God and His Christ. In that day Satan himself will have to acknowledge that "Jesus Christ is Lord to the glory of God the Father." All created intelligencies will prostrate themselves before Him, even though many of them will do it with weeping and gnashing of teeth because of the rebellion of their hearts.

The third test was an endeavor to appeal to the pride of the natural heart, something of which our blessed Lord knew nothing. He could ever say, "I am meek and lowly in heart." We are told that Satan brought Him to Jerusalem and set Him on a pinnacle of the temple and said unto Him, "If Thou be the Son of God cast Thyself down from hence." Impudently he quoted Scripture, a portion of the Ninety-first Psalm, as an assurance that if our blessed Lord did this He would be held up by angel hands and would not suffer death. Cunningly he omitted the most important part of the passage.

Try to imagine just what was here suggested. Think of a great throng of people gathered in the temple courts, and our Lord looking down upon that worshipping multitude from one of the highest heights of that noble building. Remember He has come to present Himself as the Messiah of Israel. Now Satan pretends to co-operate with Him and suggests: "Here is your opportunity to prove to the people that you are really the Son of God and their promised Messiah. Leap off the pinnacle of the temple: let them see you being sustained in mid-air by angelic hands. Then they will know that you are what you profess to be." It did indeed seem from a natural standpoint to offer a remarkable occasion for the Lord to demonstrate His Messiahship. Notice exactly how Satan misquoted Scripture to back up his suggestion. He said, "It is written, He shall give His angels charge over Thee, to keep Thee, and in their hands they shall bear Thee up lest Thou dash Thy foot against a stone." Our Saviour recognized the misquotation at once and saw through the Satanic suggestion as an appeal to spiritual pride. The devil said, as it were, "I am only asking you to do what Scripture warrants: leap from the pinnacle of the temple and count upon God to fulfil His own Word and to protect you from harm." But if we turn back to the Ninety-first Psalm we will find the passage actually says, "He shall give His angels charge over Thee to keep Thee *in all Thy ways."* These last four words Satan cunningly omitted. It could never be part of the holy ways of the Son of God to try to put His Father to the test in such a manner as that suggested by Satan. Jesus, however, did not argue the question with the devil. He just met him with another saying of God. He answered, "It is said, Thou shalt not tempt the Lord thy God." That is, it is never right to do anything just in order to see whether God will keep His Word or not. It is never necessary to do that. He can always be depended on to do as He has said. Had it been part of the ways of the Son of God as planned by the Father that He should leap from the pinnacle of the temple and be supported by angelic hands, Jesus would not have needed to get instruction from Satan. He came to do the Father's will, and in doing that will He could always depend on the Father's sustaining power.

As an illustration of tempting God, let me refer to some strange things that have taken place recently in our Southern Mountains. There is a sect of fanatical people down there who have sought to test God on a promise given by the Lord to His apostles that they should be able to tread upon serpents, and that the bite of a serpent would not harm them. So in weird meetings conducted by these ignorant people, many of whom could not read or write, the teaching was given out that if one was really a Christian the bite of a rattlesnake could not hurt him, as God had promised protection. A number of instances have occurred wherein live rattlesnakes were brought into the meetings and certain leaders actually permitted these writhing reptiles to bite them, and hoped thereby to demonstrate their invulnerability to serpent poison. Several died because of it, others suffered terribly, but were eventually freed of the poison through proper treatment. The Government had to interfere because of the folly of this sect. It was all a matter of trying to put God to a test, and, of course, God would not respond to anything of the kind.

But now contrast with this that which happened to the apostle Paul on the island of Melita. As the shipwrecked sailors were warming themselves around a fire, there came out a viper and fastened itself upon Paul's arm. The people expected him to fall down dead, but he threw the reptile off into the fire and was himself unharmed. God kept His Word, but Paul did not attempt to put Him to a test.

And so in our Lord's temptation in the wilderness, Satan endeavored to trap Him on every point, but He proved Himself to be the holy One in whom was no inward desire to yield to any other direction than that given Him by the Father. Satan failed to make any impression whatever on the Son of God, and then we read, "He departed from Him for a season." He returned again from time to time and sought through enraged and fanatical unbelievers to put Him to death before the cross, and in Gethsemane, and again when our Saviour was actually nailed to the cross, Satan sought once more to thwart the purpose of God, only to be defeated each time.

The great lesson for us is that our Lord Jesus, who was tempted in all points like as we are, apart from sin, lives in the glory today and is able to exert His mighty power on our behalf and to succor us when we are tempted. Whatever the trial or test we may have to face, let us remember that He stands ready to come to our relief, to give to us strength through the power of the Holy Spirit, that we may resist temptation and not dishonor our God and Father through our failures.

CHAPTER TWELVE

"THE ACCEPTABLE YEAR OF THE LORD"

✝ ✝ ✝

"And Jesus returned in the power of the Spirit into Galilee: and there went out a fame of Him through all the region round about. And He taught in their synagogues, being glorified of all. And He came to Nazareth, where He had been brought up: and as His custom was, He went into the synagogue on the sabbath day, and stood up for to read. And there was delivered unto Him the book of the prophet Esaias. And when He had opened the book, He found the place where it was written, The Spirit of the Lord is upon Me, because He hath anointed Me to preach the gospel to the poor; He hath sent Me to heal the brokenhearted, to preach deliverance to the captives, and recovering of sight to the blind, to set at liberty them that are bruised, to preach the acceptable year of the Lord. And He closed the book, and He gave it again to the minister, and sat down. And the eyes of all them that were in the synagogue were fastened on Him. And He began to say unto them, This day is this scripture fulfilled in your ears. And all bare Him witness, and wondered at the gracious words which proceeded out of His mouth. And they said, Is not this Joseph's son? And He said unto them. Ye will surely say unto Me this proverb, Physician, heal Thyself: whatsoever we have heard done in Capernaum, do also here in Thy country. And He said, Verily I say unto you, No prophet is accepted in his own country. But I tell you of a truth, many widows were in Israel in the days of Elias, when the heaven was shut up three years and six months, when the great famine was throughout all the land; but unto none of them was Elias sent, save unto Sarepta, a city of Sidon, unto a woman that was a widow. And many lepers were in Israel in the time of Eliseus the prophet; and none of them was cleansed, saving Naaman the Syrian. And all they in the synogogue, when they heard these things, were filled with wrath, and rose up, and thrust Him out of the city, and led Him unto the brow of the hill whereon their city was built, that they might cast Him down headlong. But He passing through the midst of them went His way"—**Luke 4: 14-30.**

IN this portion of Scripture we have the account of the Lord's return visit to the city of Nazareth after He laid aside His carpenter's apron and His artisan's tools, and went forth, first to be baptized by John in the Jordan, to be sealed by the Holy Spirit for His specific work, and then to go through His temptation in the wilderness. After a short stay in Jerusalem, He returned to His own hometown. The people had heard a great deal about Him. They had heard of marvelous signs and wonders following His ministry in other places, and they were in great expectation, hoping to see something remarkable done by Him when He appeared among them. We are told that He entered into the synagogue, as His custom was. There is something about that which might speak to everyone of us. The Lord Jesus grew up in that city of Nazareth. When He dwelt there, as a young man, it was His custom to attend the services in the place where the Word of God was read and expounded, and where the people gathered together for prayer. I fancy there must have been many things about the synagogue service which often offended His spirit. Many of those who participated must have greatly misunderstood the real meaning of the Word of God. But to Him the synagogue represented the authority of God in that city. So it was His custom to wend His way there from sabbath to sabbath.

I think some christian people need to have their consciences exercised more than they are, in regard to gathering together with God's people, where the

Word of God is appreciated and where they come together to sing His praises and to pray. A man said to me once, "If I could find a perfect Church I would attend there." I replied; "My dear friend, don't. If you find a perfect Church don't join it, because if you did it would be imperfect the moment you got into it." There is no such thing as a perfect Church, but we can thank God for the places where people meet to hear the Word of God, and to join in praise and prayer. We need to remember the words, "Not forsaking the assembling of yourselves together, as the manner of some is, but exhorting one another." We need to do this "so much the more as we see the day approaching!"

Jesus could always be depended upon, as a Boy and as a Youth, to be in His place in the synagogue, as divine service was being carried on. So the people knew that He would be there on this given sabbath day, and they gathered to hear Him. He was evidently accustomed to participate publicly in the service. As soon as He entered, we read, "There was delivered unto Him the book of the prophet Esaias. And when He had opened the book, He found the place where it was written, The Spirit of the Lord is upon Me." It would seem as though it was an ordinary thing for Him, when He attended the synagogue service, to take the sacred scroll, and to turn from one passage to another and expound them to the people. So now, as He entered on this particular sabbath-day, the one who had charge of the scrolls turned to Him and inquired what portion of the Scriptures He would like to read. He asked for the Book of the prophet Esaias, and He turned to this particular section and He read, "For the Spirit of the Lord is upon Me, because He hath anointed Me to preach the gospel to the poor; He hath sent Me to heal the brokenhearted, to preach deliverance to the captives, and recovering of sight to the blind, to set at liberty them that are bruised, to preach the acceptable year of the Lord," and He closed the Book. There might not be any special significance in that. He reads His text, He rolls up the scroll, and He is now about to expound it. But the remarkable fact is this: He broke off His reading in the middle of a sentence. He stopped at a comma. If you will turn to this passage in Isaiah 61:1, 2, you will find that it reads as follows: "To preach the acceptable year of the Lord, and the day of vengeance of our God." The Lord Jesus did not read those last words. Why? Because He had not come to proclaim the day of vengeance of our God. He had come to do all that is written of Him in the other part of the passage.

He had come to preach the gospel to the poor. Oh, I like that! It is a striking fact that in every land where the gospel has gone it has been largely the poor who have rejoiced in its message. You remember, it is written, "He hath filled the hungry with good things, and the rich He hath sent empty away." "How hardly shall they that have riches enter into the kingdom of God!" The trouble is that when men have an abundance of this world's goods they are so taken up with them that they are not concerned about spiritual riches. But it is the poor, the needy, the struggling, who love to hear the gospel message. When Jesus was here, the common people "heard Him gladly." It was the rulers, the self-righteous leaders, who had no sense of their sinfulness, and no realization of their need, and who could not appreciate Jesus. They had no concern about His message. But the poor—they loved to listen to Him. Thank God, though nineteen centuries have gone by since He left this scene, the gospel still is preached to the poor. If the time ever comes when we are not interested in the poor, and do not care for the poor, and draw away from the needy, "The Glory is Departed" will be written over the doors of the church.

We read of the poor in this world rich in faith. Those who do not have earthly wealth are rich often in spiritual things in a way that others who are in better circumstances are not. You remember that little poem:

"In the heart of London city
 'Midst the dwelling of the poor,
These bright golden words were uttered,
 'I have Christ, what want I more?'
He who heard them ran to fetch her
 Something from the world's great store.
'It was needless,' died she saying,
 'I have Christ, what want I more?' "

Christ is a substitute for everything, but nothing is a substitute for Christ. Jesus was always interested in the poor, and He is interested in the poor today. He came to preach the gospel to the poor, and He says, "The Lord has sent Me to heal the broken-hearted." In that He expresses His Deity, for it is God only who can heal broken hearts. No man can do it. The best man you ever knew couldn't heal a broken heart. It would not be of any use to send your broken-hearted friends to the most spiritual ministers of Christ, and saying, "These men will be able to make you whole again." We have no ability to heal broken hearts, but we can point people to One who can. How many broken-hearted men there are! Dr. Joseph Parker, one-time minister of the London City Temple, was once addressing young preachers, and he said to them, "Young gentlemen, always preach to broken hearts, and you will never lack for an audience." There are so many of them everywhere. Hearts are bleeding and broken all around us. Jesus came to heal the broken-hearted, and if you who read these words are broken-hearted people, let me say to you, you wrong your own souls if you do not bring your burdens to the feet of Jesus. An old chorus says,

"You've carried your burden,
  You've carried it long!
Oh, bring it to Jesus—
  He's loving and strong!
He'll take it away
  And your sorrows shall cease,
He'll send you rejoicing,
  With His heavenly peace."

Then He came to preach deliverance to the captives, not exactly to open all prison doors and let people out of jails and penitentiaries, but to deliver men from the captivity of sin and free those who are bound in chains of habit which they could not break. He is doing that today. He is freeing men from the power of sensuality, from unclean living, from evil tempers and vile dispositions, that bind folks as chains bind men in prison-cells. And He came to give the recovery of sight to the blind. When He was here on earth He touched the blind and His glory shone through their darkened lids, and lighted them forever. Though we may not see Him now by the natural eye, and He is not perhaps working the same kind of miracles which He did when He was here on earth, those who are blind spiritually, those who have had the understanding darkened, and have not been able to comprehend spiritual realities, when they come to Him the scales fall from their eyes, and He gives them light, and they are able to say with that delivered man of old, "There are many things I do not know or understand, but one thing I know, that whereas I was blind, now I see." Oh, what a wonderful thing it is when Jesus touches blind eyes!

Then "He came to set at liberty those that are bruised." We have been bruised by Satan. The very humanity in which we live has been bruised by the fall, but He came to set at liberty them that are bruised, to enable the lame to walk, and the dead to live and to rejoice in His saving grace.

He closed with the words, "To preach the acceptable year of the Lord." The *acceptable* year of the Lord—what is that? It is the time when God is looking in grace upon poor sinners. It is the time when the gospel is going out to lost men and women.

He says, "Now is the acceptable time. Now is the day of salvation."

Does some one say in his heart, "Oh I would like to be a Christian, I would like to know the healing power of Jesus, but I'm afraid the time has not come yet. I do not feel the proper moving of the Spirit. I am not certain that I would be welcome. I must await God's time?" That is an illusion of the enemy. God's time is now. It is He Himself who says it. "*Now* is the accepted time." "Come *now,* and let us reason together . . . though your sins be as scarlet, they shall be as white as snow; though they be red like crimson, they shall be as wool." "Today if you will hear His voice, harden not your hearts." There is no reason why any anxious soul should go on in sin for another hour, because God is waiting to be gracious. This is the acceptable year since Jesus came to reveal the Father's heart, since He came to die on the cross for our sins. God sent the message out to the world that all may come and find peace in Him. This is still the acceptable time. It will not last forever. It has lasted now for nearly two thousand years, since Jesus came and read this Scripture. He said He came to preach the acceptable year of the Lord. He did not read, "And the day of vengeance of our God." Jesus did not read that because the time had not come for the vengeance of our God to begin, and it has not come yet. But listen to me! It may come soon! It may not be long now ere the Lord Jesus will descend from heaven with a shout, with the voice of the archangel and with the trump of God; and the dead in Christ shall rise first: then we which are alive and remain shall be caught up together with them in the clouds, to meet the Lord in the air." Then the day of vengeance of our Lord will begin for this poor world. Then the book of doom will be opened, the trumpets of judgment will be sounded, and then the vials of wrath will be poured out upon this guilty world. This whole dispensation of the grace of God in which we live, the Lord Jesus puts into a comma. That is why He did not read on to "the day of vengeance of our God." I plead with you to avail yourselves of the grace of God before He arises in judgment to shake terribly this world and shut the door. Today the door is wide open, and He says, "Whosoever will may come."

Our Lord Jesus read this scripture and then He closed the Book. He rolled up the Scroll and gave it again to the minister, and He sat down. He rose up to read the Word and sat down to teach it. And He began to say unto them, "This day is the scripture fulfilled." That is, He applied the scripture to Himself. "The Spirit of the Lord is upon Me"—upon Jesus. It was He who had come in actual fulfilment of this Old Testament prophecy. In the Old Testament, in the Book of the prophet Isaiah we have this wonderful prediction of the Messiah who is coming. The Lord Jesus Christ took these same words and read them, and He applied them to Himself, to the amazement of His hearers. To apply them to Himself is one thing and to prove it quite another, but He proved it by what He did. He did the very thing that these words said He would do, and He has been doing it all through the centuries since. Millions have tested Him for themselves. They have come to Him. They have come with their sins. They have come to be delivered from their chains of evil habits, and they have put their trust in Him, and they have found He is able to do what He said He would do.

As He declared, "This day is this scripture fulfilled in your ears." We are told that all bare Him witness, and wondered at the gracious words which proceeded out of His mouth. And they said, "Is not this Joseph's son?" They had never heard anything like this before. None of the Scribes ever said anything like this. None of them ever dared to apply such a prophecy to themselves. He was actually the son of the blessed Virgin Mary, but so far as they knew He was the son of Joseph, who had taken His mother under his protective care. So they said, "Is not this Joseph's son?" He knew what they were thinking. And He said unto them, "Ye will surely say unto Me this proverb, "Physician, heal Thyself; whatsoever we have heard done in Capernaum, do also here in Thy country." But He added, "No prophet is accepted in his own country." He knew the unbelief that controlled their hearts, so that they had no desire to turn to God in repentance. So He used two illustrations saying, "I tell you of a truth, many widows were in Israel in the days of Elias, when the heaven was shut up three years and six months, when great famine was throughout all the land; but unto none of them was Elias sent, save unto Sarepta, a city of Sidon, unto a woman that was a widow. And many lepers were in Israel in the time of Eliseus the prophet; and none of them was cleansed, saving Naaman the Syrian." Naaman the Syrian was a Gentile, and that stirred them. They did not like His speaking in this way. As though God was just as much interested in needy Gentiles as in Jews! Yes, He is just as much interested in all the needy, for "all have sinned, and come short of the glory of God." He is the same Lord over all.

When Jesus presented these two instances of God's grace going out to the needy Gentiles they were filled with wrath and they rose up and they thrust Him out of their city.

A few years ago I went along the path they took, and I could visualize the synagogue and the crowd rushing around Jesus and saying, "We do not care anything about what You say. Out You go!" They crowded Him out unto the cliff at the edge of the city, and their object was to cast Him down headlong! "But He, passing through the midst of them, went His way." How did He escape? Was it a miracle? I think it was. He simply passed through and they could not see where He had gone, so they were unable to cast Him over the cliff. His hour had not come. He had come into this world to die on Calvary's cross, and no power of men or of the devil could put Him to death until that hour when He was to yield Himself a ransom for sinners, upon the tree. Till then all their power was in vain.

Address Thirteen

JESUS AT CAPERNAUM

✓ ✓ ✓

"But He passing through the midst of them went His way, and came down to Capernaum, a city of Galilee, and taught them on the sabbath days. And they were astonished at His doctrine: for His word was with power. And in the synagogue there was a man, which had a spirit of an unclean devil (demon), and cried out with a loud voice, saying, Let us alone; what have we to do with Thee, Thou Jesus of Nazareth? Art Thou come to destroy us? I know Thee who Thou art; the Holy One of God. And Jesus rebuked him, saying, Hold thy peace and come out of him. And when the devil had thrown him in the midst, he came out of him, and hurt him not. And they were all amazed, and spake among themselves, saying, What a Word is this! for with authority and power He commandeth the unclean spirits, and they come out. And the fame of Him went out into every place of the country round about. And He arose out of the synagogue, and entered into Simon's house. And Simon's wife's mother was taken with a great fever; and they besought Him for her. And He stood over her, and rebuked the fever; and it left her: and immediately she arose and ministered unto them. Now when the sun was setting, all they that had any sick with divers diseases brought them unto Him; and He laid His hands on every one of them, and healed them. And devils (demons) also came out of many, crying out, and saying, Thou are Christ the Son of God. And He rebuking them suffered them not to speak: for they knew that He was Christ, And when it was day, He departed and went into a desert place: and the people sought Him, and came unto Him, and stayed Him, that He should not depart from them. And He said unto them, I must preach the kingdom of God to other cities also: for therefore am I sent. And He preached in the synagogues of Galilee"—Luke 4: 30-44.

✓ ✓ ✓

THE greater portion of this section consists of one day's work on the part of our blessed Lord Jesus Christ, in the city of Capernaum, at the northern edge of the Sea of Galilee. It is called elsewhere "His own city." After He gave up His work in the carpenter shop and went out on His great mission to proclaim the gospel of the kingdom to a waiting people, a people who had been expecting that kingdom for so long, He removed from Nazareth to Capernaum, and made that the center from which He traveled back and forth to the various parts of the land. So on this occasion He returned to Capernaum, and He taught them, we are told, on the Sabbath days. By the term "Sabbath-day," we are not to understand our Sunday, but the Jewish Sabbath, the seventh day. That was the day on which the people laid aside their usual employment and gathered together in their synagogues to hear the Word of God and to offer prayer. Our Lord took advantage of that day and joined with them. It had been His custom always to do this, and there in the synagogue on the Sabbath-days He ministered the Word of God. We are told that the people were astonished at His doctrine, for His word was with power. There was a divine energy about Him that appealed to them. They had never heard another like Him. You remember sometime afterward when officers were sent to arrest Him, they returned without Him and were asked, "Why have you not brought Him?" Their answer was, "Never man spake like this Man." There was something so compelling about the message of the Lord Jesus Christ, that it moved the hearts even of His enemies. His word was with power.

It was not only the power of His Deity, but it was also the power of the Holy Spirit, for our Lord Jesus chose, as Man on earth, not to act according to His own Deity, but to be led, and guided, and controlled by the Holy Spirit. Therefore, in the power of the Holy Spirit He preached the gospel of the kingdom.

On one particular occasion we read that in the synagogue there was a man who had a spirit of an unclean demon, and cried out with a loud voice. We should change the word *devil* in the Authorized Version to *demon,* because of the well-recognized fact that according to Scripture there is only one devil, Satan, who is called "that old serpent, the devil"; but there are a great many demons. These demons, evidently, were spirits led by Satan in his great rebellion, and he is called "the prince of the power of the air." So we gather that these demons are not yet confined in hell, but with their master, Satan, they have access to men, and on certain occasions they can actually indwell and dominate men, or even where they do not indwell them, are able to impress them for evil, and lead them into ways contrary to the will of God. Here was a case of a man who was actually possessed with a demon. Just as in our dispensation of grace Christians are indwelt by the Holy Spirit of God, and so act under His control as they yield obedience to Him, so it was possible for men to be indwelt by one of these evil spirits and act as under that control. When this man, in whom the evil spirit was, saw the Lord Jesus Christ there in the synagogue he cried out, "Let us alone. What have we to do with Thee, Thou Jesus of Nazareth. Art Thou come to destroy us? I know Thee who Thou art—the Holy One of God."

There is something very striking here. Men, ordinarily speaking, did not know Him. "He came unto His own, and His own received Him not." Those who should have known Him, those who should have recognized Him as having been sent by the Father, failed to understand who He was. The demon knew because Jesus has absolute authority over the unseen world. This is the only world in which anyone dares to flaunt His will, or deny His Deity. Everybody does His will in heaven. Everyone knows Him there, and all the lost have to be subject to Him in the under-world. Even demons have to recognize His authority. So this evil spirit called out, "I know who Thou art—the Holy One of God." But Jesus did not desire a testimony of that kind; so He rebuked him, saying, "Hold thy peace, and come out of him," and immediately in response to the word of the Lord Jesus the evil spirit, dominating the man, threw him in convulsions on the ground, and then came out of him and no longer hurt him.

All this took place in the synagogue at Capernaum. When I was visiting Palestine some years ago, I think the greatest thrill I had, next to visiting "the place called Calvary," and the garden tomb just outside the Damascus gate of Jerusalem, was when standing on that very platform of the synagogue in Capernaum where this event and other events recorded in the Gospel took place. It was at Capernaum, we are told, that a Roman centurion built the Jews a synagogue, and for many, many centuries Capernaum had been entirely hidden from view. Archaelogists were unable to identify its site, until some years before the First World War a group of German monks built a monastery on a hill north of the Sea of Galilee, and when the World War broke out they were interned within the monastery grounds and were not permitted to leave until the war was over. While interned, in order that they might keep physically fit, they began to dig about on the hill where their monastery stood, and soon they began uncovering great blocks of limestone. The work went on with great interest, and by-and-by they uncovered an ancient synagogue. There was the entire floor, the great stones of the side walls, and the platform and pillars that had once upheld the roof. Now they have restored a great part of that synagogue, set up those pillars in place again, and though, of course, the roof is not on, you can enter the building, can look out over the vast floor capable of seating several hundred people, and you can stand on the platform back of the stone reading-desk. As I stood there with one of the monks by my side and my wife and daughter on the other side, how sacred a spot it seemed! I knew that my feet were standing on the very place where my blessed Lord had stood so long ago. They were able to identify it as the synagogue of Capernaum by this: They found on the great stones of the foundation all kinds of Hebrew signs. For instance, you can see cut in the stone Aaron's rod, and the golden bowl that was placed in the ark, the five-pointed star of Solomon and the six-pointed star of David, the olive, the fig, and vine-leaves which are used as symbols of Israel, and a great many other signs that were distinctly Jewish, and yet the synagogue itself is definitely Roman in architecture. But there is only one Roman sign to be seen. That is the great eagle. Evidently some Jew who revolted at this had chiseled off most of the eagle. The Jew did not like the sign of the eagle on a synagogue devoted to Jehovah. There is little question but that it is the synagogue built by the Roman centurion, that the Jews might have a suitable place of worship. There it is, bearing silent testimony to the Word of God. As I stood there at the reading-desk, I could look down, and I said to the monk, "Somewhere near there was that man with the unclean spirit. I can almost imagine I see him rising to his feet, and hear him screaming, 'Let us alone, what have we to do with Thee, Jesus of Nazareth? Art Thou come to destroy us?'" The monk said, "And Jesus rebuked him." I said, "Yes." So we went on, mentioning one thing after another that had taken place in that synagogue.

It is a very real thing when you read the Bible in the light of what you can see, even in present-day Palestine. You realize how wonderfully accurate everything is. When this man, then, was delivered from the power of the evil spirit, the people assembled there were stirred greatly. They were all amazed and spake among themselves, saying, "What a word is this! for with authority and power He commandeth the unclean spirits, and they come out. And the fame of him went out into every place of the country round about." Notice one thing about the miracles of our Lord. He never wrought a miracle for self-aggrandizement. He never exercised His marvelous power merely in order to draw attention to Himself. In other words, He was not like the so-called magicians among the heathen who do all sorts of wonders to amaze and dazzle people. Jesus never wrought a miracle of any kind except for the benefit of others.

It was so in delivering this man from the power of the unclean spirit. It was so great a miracle that the audience was stirred and they began to spread His fame abroad. But He went out of the synagogue on the same day and went down into the city. He entered into the house of Simon Peter, the fisherman, who lived there also. Simon's wife's mother was taken with a great fever, and they besought Him for her. Some people have forgotten that Simon Peter ever had a wife. He was not a celibate clergyman! His mother-in-law lived with them. He was doubtless deeply concerned because she had taken ill, and they called to Jesus, and they besought Him for her. Oh, how often in these records we find people going to the Lord Jesus about others. And He invites us to do the same, and to bring to Him those who are sick, and those who are needy, and those who are distressed. He loves to answer prayer today as He did so long ago. They pleaded with Him to do something for Simon's wife's mother, and He went into the sick room. He stood over her and rebuked the fever and it left her. There is an added word in one of the other Gospels I like so much. It says, "He touched her hand, and the fever left her." He stood over her and rebuked the fever, and He put His hand upon that hot fevered hand of the patient, and immediately there came a calmness, a sense of quietness and coolness. In the same wonderful way the Lord Jesus loves to minister to our fevered, restless hearts today. Oh, how many of us, in a certain sense, are like this poor woman. We are all distracted and upset and disturbed by existing conditions. What a blessed thing it is when Jesus comes to the bedside, when Jesus draws near, and when He rebukes the fever, when He touches the hand, and the fever dies away.

We are told that immediately she arose and ministered unto them. This is quite natural when one has experienced the delivering power of our Lord Jesus Christ. How the heart delights then to do something for Him and for others. This good woman no sooner is healed, no sooner realizes that she is well, than she says, "Now, I want to serve Him who has done this thing for me, and I want to serve those who are dear to Him and to me." So she ministered unto them.

Have you felt a touch of His healing hand? Has His voice rebuked the fever of sin that once raged in your very being? Is it your delight now to serve Him? Are you among those who are glad not only to avail themselves of His delivering power, but are now concerned about giving Him the service of a grateful heart? Are you putting yourself out for the blessing of other people? This is the test of real conversion. You can tell a person who has experienced the saving power of the Lord Jesus

Christ by the manifestation of a desire to please Him, a desire to do His will, to glorify Him, to make Him known to others, and to bring them into contact with Him.

Every time the Lord wrought a work of power like this upon the body of some dear needy soul, the word of it went abroad to encourage others to come to Him. It is the same today. When the Lord Jesus works in great grace, saving one from the life of sin, bringing him to know God and giving him the power to live a new life to His glory, how it appeals to other people! I do not think there is anything that has such a tendency to draw folks to any place where the Word of God is preached as the word going forth that people are being saved, that men and women are being delivered from their sins, that God is working miracles among them. Oh, that we might see more of that here—the saving power of our Lord Jesus thus manifested!

In this instance we are told that as the sun was setting, and the day drew to a close, a day in which He had been so busily engaged in alleviating woes, that multitudes were brought to Him, and He laid His hands on them and healed them. Nobody ever came to Him in the days of His flesh, seeking deliverance from any ailment, but He met them in grace and delivered them. Somebody might say, "Well, how is it that now sometimes when we are sick, we come to Him, and we do not receive that for which we ask?" We need to remember that those mighty signs and wonders that He wrought when He was here on earth were the witnesses given to Israel to His Messiahship. He did them not only to help those who came to Him, but also to bear testimony to those who saw and heard, that He was indeed the promised Saviour. You will remember that the prophet of old declared that in His day the tongue of the dumb should be made to sing; the lame should leap as a hart; the eyes of the blind should be opened; the ears of the deaf unstopped, and that sorrow and sickness should flee before Him. These were the outward evidences that He was what He professed to be, the Messiah of Israel. Now that He has gone back to glory He has not given the definite promise that He will heal diseased bodies, but He has promised that He will always deliver sin-sick people that will come to Him. He says, "Him that cometh to Me, I will in no wise cast out."

Every miracle that He wrought was in someway a picture of what sin does to men and women and how they are delivered. Take, for instance, the man who was possessed with a demon. He is just a picture of people all about us controlled and dominated by Satanic power, driven by habits and passions from which they cannot deliver themselves. This woman, with a fever raging in her veins, is a picture of the feverishness of sin, from which the Lord gives complete freedom.

They came to Him from all quarters and He healed them. We are told that demons also came out of many, crying out and saying, "Thou art Christ the Son of God." They knew Him. They recognized Him. They understood who He was.

Men might deny Him, but the demons could not. He rebuked them because He did not want their testimony. "And He rebuking them suffered them not to speak: for they knew that He was Christ."

Then we are told that when it was day He departed. When the morning dawned, He left Capernaum and went out into a desert place, and people sought Him there, and came to Him and begged Him not to depart from them. It is beautiful to see this. At this time, at least, He was appreciated, and the people wanted Him to remain. There may have been some selfishness in that. But they recognized His power and they desired Him to stay in their city. He said, "I cannot confine Myself to one place. I must preach the kingdom of God to other cities also." He went on from place to place, and preached in the synagogues of Galilee. Thus He was being accredited to the people of Israel as the promised One for whom they had waited so long. Oh, what a joy it is to realize that although now He is hidden from the eyes of men, yet His power is just the same! If I am addressing any who are in trouble, or sorrow, or distress, who are bound by chains of sin, or controlled by the power of habit; if you will only come to Jesus, though He is now in heaven and seated at the right hand of the Father, you can reach out the hand of faith and feel the touch of His hand of healing. He will give deliverance to all who call upon Him in faith.

Address Fourteen

FISHERS OF MEN

✝ ✝ ✝

"And it came to pass, that, as the people pressed upon Him to hear the Word of God, He stood by the lake of Gennesaret, and saw two ships standing by the lake: but the fishermen were gone out of them, and were washing their nets. And He entered into one of the ships, which was Simon's, and prayed him that he would thrust out a little from the land. And He sat down, and taught the people out of the ship. Now when He had left speaking, He said unto Simon, Launch out into the deep, and let down your nets for a draught. And Simon answering said unto Him, Master, we have toiled all the night, and have taken nothing: nevertheless at Thy word I will let down the net. And when they had this done, they inclosed a great multitude of fishes: and their net brake. And they beckoned unto their partners which were in the other ship, that they should come and help them. And they came, and filled both the ships, so that they began to sink. When Simon Peter saw it, he fell down at Jesus' knees, saying, Depart from me; for I am a sinful man, O Lord. For he was astonished, and all that were with him, at the draught of the fishes which they had taken: and so was also James, and John, the sons of Zebedee, which were partners with Simon. And Jesus said unto Simon, Fear not; from henceforth thou shalt catch men. And when they had brought their ships to land, they forsook all, and followed him"—Luke 5: 1-11.

✝ ✝ ✝

FISHERS of men! We hear a great deal about that nowadays. This is the first occasion on which our Lord Jesus Christ called men to that high calling. I want you to notice it particularly. We read, "And it came to pass, that, as the people pressed upon Him to hear the Word of God, He stood by the lake of Gennesaret." The lake of Gennesaret is the same as the Sea of Galilee, or the Sea of Tiberias. It is a fresh-water lake, not very large, but very beautiful. One who has seen it can readily visualize what this first verse brings before us. In many places the hills seem to roll gently down to the lake itself, and there is just a very narrow beach so that one standing there would find himself crowded back to the water as people thronged toward him. On the other hand, the people could stand or sit up along the hillside and listen very readily as one spoke to them, either from the shore itself, or as our Lord did, from a boat. Everything about the Sea of Galilee fits in perfectly with the picture that we have in the New Testament. There is one thing that is indisputable: The New Testament was clearly never written by men who simply imagined the stories that they tell. They knew what they were talking about. Every detail of the picture is exact. Luke, himself, perhaps was not among those who had heard the Lord Jesus preach, but he said he had accurate knowledge of all things from the first, and he must have visited the Sea of Galilee. He must have looked over all the country round about, or he could not have given such accurate descriptions of the various places that he mentions in his Gospel. He is recognized, even by unbelievers, as one of the most careful geographers as well as one of the most accurate historians extant.

It is a great moment in one's life when he hears the call to a life of service, in devotion to the Lord Jesus Christ and for the blessing of a lost world. To respond to that call in loving obedience is to enter upon an altogether new and blessed experience, where one lives and moves on a higher plane than ever before. This is something more than conversion or even than consecration. For all who are saved have been born from above and all such are consecrated by God Himself to glorify Him and to do His will in this scene. But to some there comes a higher calling—a summons to leave all in the way of occupation with temporal things and to go forth at His bidding to represent Him as His ambassadors. His anointed ministers, to whom is committed in a special way the great task of "taking men alive" and then leading them on in the knowledge of Christ. That many imagine they are "called to the ministry" who are unfitted in every way for such high and holy service is very true, and often more evident to others than to those who are thus self-deluded. But when the Lord truly calls one to go after Him in full-time service, He fits that one for the work which He intends him to do. Possibly, there were never four men who gave less promise of marked ability as preachers of the Word than the fisherman quartet here; yet each of these was chosen by Jesus to fill a special place, and two of them were destined to become known as among the greatest missionary-preachers and teachers of all time. We know very little of Andrew, and James was martyred very early (Acts 12:1, 2), but Peter and John were granted many years of devoted service and their written ministry has edified untold millions.

The Lord Jesus was standing upon the shore. The people were thronging down to hear Him, crowding Him back toward the blue waters of the Sea of Galilee or the Lake of Gennesaret, as here called. Then Jesus turned about and He saw two fishermen's boats in the lake, close to the shore, but the fishermen were gone out of them and were washing their nets. Jesus knew the owners of these boats, and He felt perfectly free to ask for the use of one of them. He entered into one belonging to Simon Peter and asked him to thrust out a little from the land. This was not the first time the Lord had contacted Simon Peter, neither was it the second nor third. We read of the first definite instance in John, chapter one, where two of the disciples of John the Baptist heard their master say, "Behold the Lamb of God," and they left John and followed Jesus. They spent all the rest of the day with Him, listening to the wonderful words that fell from His holy lips, and then immediately became exercised about bringing others to Him. We read that one of the two who heard John speak was Andrew, Simon Peter's brother—"And he first findeth his own brother Simon, and brought him to Jesus." There is something about the actual arrangement of the Greek text there that has led scholars to believe that it really means this: He was the first of the two to find his brother, implying that John himself found his brother James on that occasion and brought him to Jesus also, but John modestly hides himself and speaks only of that which his friend Andrew did. Andrew found his brother Simon and brought him to Jesus. The Lord Jesus welcomed him and gave him that new name "Peter." From this time on Peter was numbered among those who are recognized as disciples of the

Lord Jesus, but the disciples of Christ were not necessarily separated from their secular employment. Many delighted to listen to His messages and were taught by Him, and it was later that He separated a little group of twelve, and another group of seventy to go out preaching. So Peter at first continued in his daily work as a fisherman. He was engaged in this occupation when the Lord Jesus asked for the use of his boat. He entered into Simon's boat and when He had done so, Jesus sat down in the boat and taught the people.

It is easy to visualize that scene. There were the crowds of people on the hillside. Here is the Lord Jesus sitting in the boat and as He addresses the throng, His voice carries in the clear air to the last one on the hill. He instructs them concerning the kingdom of God, and I can fancy Simon Peter sitting there with all the sense of ownership, thinking, "This is my boat, and Jesus is here talking to these people. I am so glad to see them listening to Him." The Lord said some pretty serious things. Peter would be looking around and thinking like so many folks today, "I am glad to see so-and-so here; I hope he is taking this in, and I hope so-and-so is getting what she needs." But apparently Peter was not taking in anything. He was just allowing it all to go to the rest of the folks. The Lord Jesus recognized his true state, and his need for something to probe his conscience. So He said unto Simon, "Launch out into the deep, and let down your nets for a draught." Simon was bewildered and surprised. Jesus was not a fisherman. He was a carpenter, and He had not lived in a town on the lakeside. He lived in Nazareth, some miles away from the lake, and He could not be expected, if He were only a man, to know the right time or the right conditions for fishing. So Peter explains in the next verse that they had been out all night long fishing, and had gotten nothing. So he was amazed when Jesus said to him in broad daylight, probably with the sun shining brightly down, "Launch out into the deep, and let down your nets." You can imagine an experience like this for Peter, and he, saying to himself, "If the fish were not there in the night, certainly they will not be in the sunshine. There is no use expecting to take any fish at this time of day. I know the conditions here too well for that." Of course, our modernistic ministers and preachers have tried to explain the situation like this: they tell us that Jesus happened to look about and saw a school of fish, and instead of saying to Peter, "Look, there is a school of fish," He thought it was a good opportunity to make Peter think He was working a miracle and so He said, "Let down your nets for a draught." This is an endeavor to make our blessed Lord appear a mere charlatan. But the Lord Jesus wanted to reach the conscience of Peter, so He did something that would make him realize he was in the presence of God Himself.

"Let down your nets for a draught." Simon Peter says, "Master, we have toiled all the night, and have taken nothing." It had been a most disappointing night. But then, instead of saying it is useless to let down the nets today, he says, "Nevertheless at Thy word I will let down the net." Jesus did not say, "Let down the net." Jesus said, "Let down the nets," to prepare for a great draught. Peter said, "Well, Lord, we will let down one net anyway." Of course, he felt it was a poor time to fish and he did not expect to get anything, but since Jesus said so, he let down a net. When they had done this they caught a great multitude of fishes, and their net brake. Maybe, if they had let down the nets, that which was used would not have broken so easily. One was not sufficient to hold the great draught of fishes rushing into it, and when they realized that they would not be able to handle this great catch themselves they beckoned unto their partners who were in another ship. I suppose that would be James and John, for they seemed to be working together. They beckoned unto their partners that they should come and help them, and they came and they filled both the ships so they began to sink. I saw a number of ship-loads—boat-loads—come in to Tiberias from the Sea of Galilee, but I never saw such a catch as this threatening to sink the boat. I remember, as they were bringing in a great lot of fish, I was quite surprised, and I said to one of the fishermen, "What do you call these fish?" and he said, "*Poisson St. Pierre*"—St. Peter's fish. I said, "Are these some of the fish that Peter caught?" He said, "No; but these are some of the children of the fish he didn't catch!" His name, though, is linked with them to this day.

They got such a multitude of fish that the boats were almost sinking as they drew them to land.

Simon Peter was so stirred by what had taken place that he recognized the fact that no one but the Creator of the fish could ever have commanded the treasures of the deep to come into his net that way. He realized in a moment that he was in the presence, not only of the greatest prophet that had ever risen in Israel; not only of the greatest teacher that had ever come to mankind; not only of the most remarkable miracle-worker that the Jews had ever seen—he was in the presence of God! He fell down at the feet of Jesus, saying, "Depart from me, for I am a sinful man, O Lord." When one is brought consciously into the presence of God, it always has the effect of making him realize his own unworthiness and sinfulness. When Job came into the presence of God he said, "I have heard of Thee by the hearing of the ear, but now mine eye seeth Thee. Wherefore I abhor myself, and repent in dust and ashes." Yet he was the best man living in his day, a man whose outward life was perfect and upright, and a man who feared God; but in the presence of the Lord, with the infinite holiness of God revealed to him, he felt he was but a poor sinner. Isaiah had the same experience. He was one of the most noble and eloquent of all the prophets, a man used of God to preach to others. Yet when he was in the temple one day and God was manifested to him, he cried out, "I am undone; because I am a man of unclean lips." He heard the seraphim surrounding the throne of God, singing, "Holy, Holy, Holy, is the Lord of hosts; the whole earth is full of His glory!" He recognized in a moment that there was a holiness of which he knew nothing and to which he, in himself, could never attain; but when he confessed his sinfulness and said, "I am a man of unclean lips, and I dwell in the midst of people of unclean lips," one of the seraphs took a coal from off the altar and touched his lips, saying, "Thine iniquity is taken away, and thy sin purged."

And now, Simon Peter here, active, energetic, and who had been with the Lord on a number of occasions; who had listened to His teaching and seen His miracles, now, apparently for the first time, recognized Him as God manifest in the flesh; and the result was a complete breakdown on his own part, and he cried, "I am a sinful man, O Lord!" I wonder if we have all broken down like that before God? The thing that is most natural to the heart of man and most hateful to God, is pride. "Most men," we are told, "will declare to every one his own goodness, but a faithful man who can find?" Speak to the average man about his hope of heaven and he will tell you, "Yes, I do expect some day to arrive there." He does trust that eventually he will find his home in that city of the saints; and you ask, "On what ground do you expect to be there?" Almost invariably he talks to you about his efforts to do good; his attempt to obey the Golden Rule and to love God with all his heart, and to love his neighbor as himself, and that he has never been guilty of any serious offenses. He bases his hope on his own merits. But God's Word says, "By the deeds of the law there shall no flesh be justified in His sight." Whenever you find men or women talking about their own righteousness, bolstering themselves up by the records of their own good works you may be sure they have never actually been in the presence of God. Simon Peter exclaims, "I am a sinful man; depart from me," as much as to say, "I recognize I am not fit to associate with a Holy One such as Thou art." Yet he clings to Him and says, as it were, "You will have to send me away, if You do not want me with You." And our Lord never sends any sinner away. If you come, recognizing your guilt and confessing your sin, you may be sure He will receive you.

The Lord Jesus, instead of driving Peter away, said unto him, "Fear not; from henceforth thou shalt catch men." In other words, "The very fact, Simon, that you have recognized that in yourself you are a poor sinful man makes you fit to go forth and become a blessing to others. You are going to have a higher calling, Peter. You are not going to spend the rest of your life on the Sea of Galilee fishing, but you are going out at My command to win souls, to bring others to a saving knowledge of the God of all grace; from henceforth thou shalt catch men." Or, as He puts it in another Gospel, "Follow Me, and I will make you fishers of men."

Now do not misunderstand. I do not suppose that the Lord Jesus says exactly those words to everybody. He does not call everybody to give up their temporal employment, and go forth in the ministry of the gospel, or to go out as missionaries to distant lands. But He does call everybody to be devoted to Himself and if devoted to Him, whatever your calling in life, whatever your station, however you may be occupied, you will be enabled to glorify Him, and though it may not be for you to do the work of an evangelist, though it may not be for you to go out as an apostle as Peter did, you will be able to influence others by your life, a life lived for God, which is the best testimony any one can give to the saving grace of God. Fear not. It is true you are a sinner in yourself, but if your trust is in Christ and you are resting in Him who died to save you, in Him who shed His blood to put away your guilt, you can go forth in confidence to serve. "From henceforth thou shalt catch men."

God could have sent angels into this world to carry the gospel of His grace to lost men, and I am sure there is not an angel in heaven who would not gladly leave the glory and come down into this world and go up and down among the nations to tell the wondrous story of Christ, who died and rose again. But Christ did not commit to them this precious ministry. He has entrusted it to saved sinners—to you and to me, who, through His grace, know Him as our Redeemer. God give us to be faithful in making known the message to those round about us. We may have to do it in a very quiet way. It may be just a little word here and there. It may be just a short gospel message; it may be a brief testimony that will tell of the saving grace of Christ. All of these may be used as the hooks wherewith we catch men and bring them to know the Lord Jesus Christ for themselves.

This was a crisis in the life of the Apostle Peter,

or I should say, the fisherman Peter. It marked the break between his life as a fisherman and that which was to prepare him for the apostleship, for we read, "When they had brought their ships to land, they forsook all, and followed Him." Never again was Peter to be engaged in the fishing-business for a living. There was one time, you remember, after the resurrection, when he was still in a somewhat bewildered state, following his denial, that he went down to the Sea of Galilee, and was fishing; and again the Saviour appeared and again a great multitude of fish came into his net, but from that time on we never read of Peter taking up a net again. He devoted his life entirely to carrying the gospel message to a lost world. "They forsook all, and followed Him." I take it that "they" here included, at least, the four men—Peter, Andrew, James, and John. This was really their induction into the apostolate. They gave up their temporal employment and from this time on they were associated with Jesus as He went from place to place, preaching the gospel of the kingdom. So, after three-and-a-half years of association with Him they were prepared, when the Holy Spirit came at Pentecost, to go forth declaring the gospel of His grace in power; so that multitudes, both of Jews and Gentiles, were saved. In this way they proved the truth of the Lord's words, "From henceforth thou shalt catch men." I cannot conceive of any higher calling on earth than that of being used of God to bring precious souls to Himself. Who would shrink from such service when commissioned by so wondrous a Master! To be a fisher of men is one of the greatest privileges one can enjoy.

ADDRESS FIFTEEN

A LEPER CLEANSED

✓ ✓ ✓

"And it came to pass, when He was in a certain city, behold a man full of leprosy: who seeing Jesus, fell on his face, and besought Him, saying, Lord, if Thou wilt, Thou canst make me clean. And He put forth His hand, and touched him, saying, I will: be thou clean. And immediately the leprosy departed from him. And He charged him to tell no man: but go, and show thyself to the priest, and offer for thy cleansing, according as Moses commanded, for a testimony unto them. But so much the more went there a fame abroad of Him: and great multitudes came together to hear, and to be healed by Him of their infirmities"—Luke 5: 12-15.

✓ ✓ ✓

IN this wonderful miracle of our Lord—a miracle duplicated many times in His ministry on earth—we find Him dealing with a man afflicted with leprosy, which is used in Scripture to illustrate the disease of sin. There are four things to be said of leprosy that are all true of sin. First, it is a constitutional disease; secondly, it is a loathsome disease; thirdly, it is an infectious disease; and lastly, so far as human power of healing was concerned, in the days of old, it was an incurable disease. In our day, science has discovered ways to cure it if taken in time, and to alleviate the suffering of those who have been ill longer. But in Bible times, no such method was known. God alone could undertake for the leper; that is what made the miracle of the Lord so significant.

Leprosy is a constitutional disease, and in that it pictures man's sinful state by nature. You see, the trouble with all mankind is not that they become sinners by sinning, but they sin because they are sinners. We are are born in sin and are shapen in iniquity. The virus of sin is in our being, from the moment we draw our first breath. We readily disobey God and go from one sin to another because of the sinful nature with which we are born. We do not all sin in exactly the same way, but the Scriptures say that "all have sinned, and come short of the glory of God."

I remember reading some years ago in a Medical Journal of a dance which was held in the city of Calcutta, India, where there were many beautiful ladies, noblemen, people of wealth and culture. One young woman, the belle of the evening, was dancing with a Scottish doctor. He said, when he brought her back to her seat, "May I have a word with you? I hope you won't take offense. I couldn't help but notice it, but upon your shoulder there is a certain spot. Has it been there long?" The young lady's face colored. "Yes, doctor; it appeared some months ago, and it has bothered me considerably." He said, "I wish you would come down and see me tomorrow. I would like to call in a specialist along a certain line and have him look at this spot." The young lady was rather frightened, but she did as he asked, and the next day after a thorough examination of the spot, she received word that she had the disease of leprosy. One little spot upon her shoulder and yet the disease was working within, and soon it would be manifested more and more, and that beautiful body would be marked and scarred.

Isn't that just like sin? And yet so often it seems to be such a little thing to begin with; some habit which one knows is not right, so insignificant, and it grows and grows until at last sin is manifested in all its terrible corruption. A little sin leads to something worse, and it increases until it is emphasized in the whole life and is a spiritual form of leprosy.

Leprosy is one of the most loathsome of all diseases, and sin is loathsome. It is the most loathsome thing in the entire universe of God. It is the one thing which has blighted the whole universe, broken millions of hearts and brought dishonor to God, the One who created the world. There is nothing in His sight so hateful as sin. We are told in the book of Proverbs that "fools make a mock of sin, but among the righteous there is favor." Many are the foolish, careless, frivolous folk, who say, "A short life and a merry one," and, "We might as well get all the enjoyment we can and indulge in every evil." They do not seem to realize the loathsomeness of sin.

Leprosy is an infectious disease. One might easily pass it on to others by contact with them; and that was why the leper, whence once discovered, was sent away from his friends and family. He had to dwell apart in the wilderness. The Old Testament regulations were very strict. He had to present himself before a priest to be examined, and if found to be leprous he was obliged to remain without the camp, far from the dwellings of healthy folk. He had to put a cover on his upper lip and cry, "Unclean, unclean." That is God's picture of the sinner. Separated from others, you see, because he might infect them. Those who live in sin are continually infecting others, for "one sinner destroyeth much good." Yet in every heart is this virus working until checked by divine grace.

Leprosy was an incurable disease in olden times, and sin is incurable so far as human help is concerned. Scientists and philosophers have tried to evolve plans and schemes which might rid the human race of sin, but today, in spite of all their work and effort, sin reigns and ruins as heretofore. We are as wicked a people as mankind has ever been. No cure has been invented but the divine one,—the mighty power of the gospel of the Lord Jesus Christ.

There was no possibility of mistaking this case. Leprosy was openly manifested. Some men's sins are open. In some men the sins are not so evident. We have no difficulty in recognizing that broken-down drunkard as a sinner; the licentious man's evil habits soon become evident to all. Some are able to keep their sins covered, like a leper covering his body with beautiful clothing. But God sees and knows all our wickedness and is going to deal with every man according to His Word.

However, no matter how sinful or vile we have become; no matter how polluted or unclean our hearts may be, there is healing and cleansing if we will but come to our blessed Lord who is as ready today to deliver from sin and its guilt and power, as He was to heal and save those who came to Him of old. No case is too bad for Christ. George Whitefield used to cry out sometimes, "My friends, Jesus will take even the devil's castaways." This expression gave great offence to Lady Huntingdon, who was a warm friend of Whitefield's as also of the Wesley's, but she thought the expression savored of irreverence and was not becoming on the lips of a gospel preacher. She is reported to have taken Whitefield to task for it, and he listened humbly and then sometime later asked one who had been converted through his ministry to go and see Lady Huntingdon and give her the story of his conversion. He told her how he had been down in the very depths of sin, a drunkard and a blasphemer, until at last he felt the only thing left was suicide. He would rather risk unending misery in the world to come than continue in the awful wretchedness which sin had brought into his life here. And so with this in mind he was on his way early one morning to throw himself into the River Thames and end it all, as he thought, when passing by Moorfields, he saw a great throng gathered at that early hour, and found they were listening to the great field-preacher, George Whitefield. Drawing near to the outskirts of the crowd, he heard the stentorian voice of the evangelist exclaim, "My friends, Jesus will take even the devil's castaways." It went home to his heart and he came to Christ. As Lady Huntingdon listened to the story, tears filled her eyes, and when she met Whitefield again she said to him, "Do not be afraid to tell them that Jesus will take even the devil's castaways."

We are told here that Jesus put forth His hand and touched the leper. Had He been but an ordinary man, such contact would have made Him ceremonially unclean, but instead of that, the leper was immediately cleansed, and the Lord Jesus commanded him to go to the temple and offer for his cleansing according as Moses had given instruction. This instruction is found in the fourteenth chapter of the book of Leviticus. Perhaps never before had any priest in Israel for hundreds of years had a cleansed leper come to him in order that this service might be carried out. Jesus said it was to be for a testimony unto them; and how much it must have meant when a man thus healed came to the priest and asked him to examine him carefully, and then to offer the sacrifices as prescribed in this chapter. In the thirteenth chapter of Leviticus we read how the priests were to diagnose cases of leprosy and undoubtedly they had to refer to this portion of the Word many, many times, for there were large numbers of lepers in Israel in those days. But possibly the fourteenth chapter was practically a dead letter, as there had never been an occasion for any of them to carry it out. What a testimony it must have been then when this leper, and in the months to follow many others, came to the temple in order to be officially pronounced clean and restored to the congregation of the Lord. One is not surprised to turn to the book of Acts later on and read, "A great company of priests were obedient to the faith." They had known so many cases of the power of the Lord Jesus to heal that they must have realized, particularly after they learned of His resurrection from the dead, that He was in very truth the promised Messiah of Israel.

ADDRESS SIXTEEN

HEALING AND FORGIVENESS

"And He withdrew Himself into the wilderness, and prayed. And it came to pass on a certain day, as He was teaching, that there were Pharisees and doctors of the law sitting by, which were come out of every town of Galilee, and Judaea, and Jerusalem: and the power of the Lord was present to heal them. And, behold, men brought in a bed a man which was taken with a palsy: and they sought means to bring him in, and to lay him before Him. And when they could not find by what way they might bring him in because of the multitude, they went upon the housetop, and let him down through the tiling with his couch into the midst before Jesus. And when He saw their faith, He said unto him, Man, thy sins are forgiven thee. And the scribes and the Pharisees began to reason, saying, Who is this which speaketh blasphemies? Who can forgive sins, but God alone? But when Jesus perceived their thoughts, He answering said unto them, What reason ye in your hearts? Whether is easier, to say, Thy sins be forgiven thee; or to say, Rise up and walk? But that ye may know that the Son of Man hath power upon earth to forgive sins, (He said unto the sick of the palsy,) I say unto thee, Arise, and take up thy couch, and go into thine house. And immediately he rose up before them, and took up that whereon he lay, and departed to his own house, glorifying God. And they were all amazed, and they glorified God, and were filled with fear, saying, We have seen strange things today"—Luke 5: 16-26.

THOSE were very busy days for our Lord as He went from place to place manifesting His mighty power and ministering so graciously. In verse 16 we read, "He withdrew Himself into the wilderness and prayed." I do not know of anything that so emphasizes for us the reality of the humanity of our Lord as the fact that He felt the *need* of praying and withdrew Himself to pray. He who was God, He who heard the prayers of others, came down here as man and took the place of the dependent One and lifted His heart to the Father in earnest prayer. It is a good thing for us all to retire into the wilderness and pray. As we enter more into the life of prayer, we will find renewed strength and courage for our daily tasks.

"And it came to pass on a certain day, as He was teaching, there were Pharisees and doctors of the law sitting by, which were come out of every town of Galilee, and Judaea, and Jerusalem: and the power of the Lord was present to heal them." He went into one home and many gathered about, and others stood in the doorway and openings as He ministered the Word to all those who were near enough to hear. While the meeting was going on, there came four men bearing on a bed a poor neighbor of theirs, a paralyzed man, "a man which was taken with a palsy": But they could not get in through the door because of the crowd. They might have said, "Well, we will have to try some other time. We can't get through that crowd now." This is probably what you and I might have said. We would have gone away to wait for some more convenient season. I like the earnestness of these men. They wanted to bring this man into contact with the Lord, and so they took him up to the housetop and let him down through the tiling.

The roofs in the Orient were flat, as you can see them today in many places in Palestine and Syria, and in other lands of the East. These men lifted their poor paralyzed friend up onto the roof, and then they removed the mud hardened by the sun and lifted up the tiles and when they had a space large enough for the couch to go through, they put ropes underneath it and let him down through the roof into the midst before Jesus.

I can imagine the people there wondering what was happening when the pieces of mud and tiling fell through; and then when this couch was let down, they no doubt said something about spoiling the roof and were provoked at the interruption of the meeting.

Palsy pictures the helplessness of the sinner. This man was hopelessly ill. Perhaps he had lain on that couch for years and the outlook as far as he was concerned was absolutely dark. There seemed to be no possibility of a cure. How like that is to the case of the poor helpless sinner! Many know they are sinners but do not realize that they are absolutely helpless to relieve their condition.

We are not only utterly weak because of sin and cannot do a thing to save ourselves, but we are beyond all human help. No one else can deliver us, no matter how good or how well-meaning he may be. If we are ever saved at all it must be through the interposition of One who is more than man. Apart from Christ, there is no possibility of deliverance.

But this man had some friends who were interested in him. It is a great thing to have a friend concerned about you. It is a great thing when some unsaved one has some believer interested in him. Oh, unconverted man or woman, it means a lot to have someone praying for you! Husband, you may not realize it, but it is a wonderful thing to have a praying wife; wife, it is a wonderful thing to have a praying husband. Friend, it means a great deal if there are friends interested enough to pray for you. You should thank God when people are interested enough to pray for you. Some resent it, but why should anyone be angry because others are enough concerned to pray for them?

This man had friends and they determined if it was at all possible they were going to get him to Jesus. Christian, have you someone on your list of whom you are saying in your heart, "I must get him to Jesus"? These four men were not discouraged because of difficulties, but they brought their friend to Jesus even though they had to tear up part of the roof to do it. Can't you picture them bringing him down the road and saying, "When we get him to Jesus, we know something will happen." They might have said—but they did not—"Look at that crowd of people, there is not much hope today;" or, "Look at the crowds, but perhaps when they see the condition of this man, our friend, they will make way for him." But no one wanted to make way, and they could not get their friend in through the doorway where Jesus was.

They might have reasoned, "It isn't the Lord's time; we will have to wait until the Lord is more willing to do something for him," and so have gone back home and missed a blessing for him and for themselves. But these tremendously earnest men were determined to bring their friend to Jesus, and so they said, "There is another way; we will try the roof." I think as the Lord was teaching, the folks must have been astonished as they saw the four eager faces of these men peering through the opening and then the couch being let down. They might even have said that the preaching of Jesus was more important than bothering with a paralytic like that! These men were so definitely interested; and we may well imitate their example. Some may have suggested, when they first went to get their sick friend to take him to Jesus, that it was of no use. But they were not discouraged. They knew that Jesus had healed others and they were insistent that he must come to Jesus also and prove what He could do. The sick man may have said, "All right; if you can get me there, I will go." We often hear seeking souls exhorted to "pray through" in order to be saved, but it is the sinner's friends who need to pray through in order that he may be led to trust the Lord Jesus Christ and be saved.

No matter what the others may have thought, the heart of Jesus was delighted. It is always a joy to Him when He finds folks who are really in earnest. "When He saw their faith"—I think it means the faith of the four men and the faith of the sick man also; for it was faith that made him willing to come. The evidence of their faith was seen in what they did and by their earnest desire to get their friend to the feet of Jesus. "When He saw their faith, He said unto him, Man, thy sins are forgiven thee." He saw that this man's spiritual need was greater than his physical need. The spiritual need is always greater. "Seek ye first the kingdom of God, and all these things shall be added unto you." Many will say, "I wish you would pray that I might be healed of my sickness." But few realize the need of pardon for sin.

Get right with God first—know His saving help first of all. So often people think of just one particular evil habit. They say, "I wish you would pray that I might have victory or be delivered from this evil habit." But they do not seem to realize that our Lord Jesus does not specialize in merely fixing people up, but in giving them pardon for their sins and imparting a new life.

Jesus looked at the man and said, "Man, thy sins are forgiven thee." Surely that was good news. Did you ever hear Him say that to you? You would not hear an audible voice, but we find it in His Word. He says to you who believe in Him, "Thy sins are forgiven thee." The only way you can be sure of this is by taking Him at His Word.

How did this man know his sins were forgiven him? Because Jesus said so. If people asked this man how he knew this, he could have replied, "I rest in His Word, and I trust Him." Have you trusted His Word? But my! How this angered the legalists! They thought that one had to buy and pay for everything. They thought that God does not do anything for you unless you pay for it, and that salvation has to be earned by something that you do for God. They did not understand grace, and asked, "Who is this which speaketh blasphemies? Who can forgive sins, but God alone?" What they didn't know was that it was God in flesh standing in the midst of them who had said, "Man, thy sins are forgiven thee." If Jesus had been only man, then it would have been blasphemy, but because He was God manifest in the flesh, He could say that and not blaspheme. No one needed to tell Jesus what these men were thinking, and so He answered them saying, "What reason ye in your hearts? Whether is easier, to say, Thy sins be forgiven thee; or to say, Rise up and walk?" One was as difficult as the other. There was no use for them to say to anyone, "Thy sins be forgiven thee," for they had no such authority. Neither could they give strength to palsied limbs.

Jesus said, "But that ye may know that the Son of Man hath power upon earth to forgive sins," He saith unto the sick of the palsy, "I say unto thee, Arise, and take up thy couch, and go into thine house." He did this that they might know that He was not speaking lies; that they might know that He had the authority to forgive sins.

The Lord Jesus met the spiritual need first, and then demonstrated His divine power by healing the man's bodily disease. He forgave him first and then healed him. We read, "And immediately he rose up before them and took up that whereon he lay, and departed to his own house, glorifying God." I don't believe he walked like an ordinary man. I can imagine him leaping for joy as he hastened to demonstrate what Jesus had done for him. I think I see this man going to his home and saying, "Oh, friends, what do you think? I have been to Jesus and He has forgiven all my sins and healed my disease." What a testimony! What a living proof of the Deity and compassion of the Saviour!

ADDRESS SEVENTEEN

THE CALL AND RESPONSE OF MATTHEW

✝ ✝ ✝

"And after these things He went forth, and saw a publican, named Levi, sitting at the receipt of custom: and He said unto him, Follow Me. And he left all, rose up, and followed Him. And Levi made him a great feast in his own house: and there was a great company of publicans and of others that sat down with them. But their scribes and Pharisees murmured against His disciples, saying, Why do ye eat and drink with publicans and sinners? And Jesus answering said unto them, They that are whole need not a physician; but they that are sick. I came not to call the righteous, but sinners to repentance. And they said unto Him, Why do the disciples of John fast often, and make prayers, and likewise the disciples of the Pharisees; but Thine eat and drink? And He said unto them, Can ye make the children of the bridechamber fast, while the bridegroom is with them? But the days will come, when the bridegroom shall be taken away from them, and then shall they fast in those days. And He spake also a parable unto them; No man putteth a piece of a new garment upon an old; if otherwise, then both the new maketh a rent, and the piece that was taken out of the new agreeth not with the old. And no man putteth new wine into old bottles; else the new wine will burst the bottles, and be spilled, and the bottles shall perish. But new wine must be put into new bottles; and both are preserved. No man also having drunk old wine straightway desireth new: for he saith, The old is better"—Luke 5: 27-39.

✝ ✝ ✝

WE have really three distinct narratives in these verses but they are all linked together; the last two spring out of the first. The Lord Jesus passing by the custom office saw a publican, named Levi, sitting at the receipt of custom: and He said unto him, "Follow Me." Levi is the author of the first Gospel in the New Testament and in that record uses his other name, "Matthew." The author of this Gospel gives him his Hebrew name.

They use the word "publican" in Great Britain for one who keeps a tavern. In the Bible, it refers to a tax-collector, one who was enriching himself by oppressing his own people. Under the Roman Government in Palestine, the chief publican was generally a Jew who purchased the office from the Government and farmed the taxes for his own benefit. Matthew belonged to this group. Someone has said that he was probably the man who taught Peter to swear! I cannot say this was true, but I can understand people saying that. Twenty per cent of all the fish which were taken out of the lake were collected as taxes at the port of Capernaum. How that would rile Peter to have to give up the best of his catch, and so it possibly did start him swearing! Matthew was therefore of unsavory reputation among his own countrymen.

I do not know how frequently he saw and heard Jesus and beheld His works of power, but he was familiar with His ministry, and so when the Lord Jesus called him, saying, "Follow Me," Matthew left all, and rose up and followed Him. That does not mean that he left everything immediately, but that he turned over all the accounting and satisfied the Roman Government and said to them, "I have heard the voice of Jesus of Nazareth, and henceforth I give Him my life and all that I have."

For Matthew, following Jesus meant that he must give up all dishonesty and selfishness. Jesus said, "If any man will come after Me, let him deny himself, and take up his cross, and follow Me." What is your response to this call? When Matthew heard the call, he wound up his business and recognized Jesus as the Lord of his life. Then, ere he left all for good, he made a great feast. I suppose he was a comparatively wealthy man, and he called a big company of those whom he knew well, and they all sat down at the feast together. He invited Jesus and His disciples also, and they came. To the Pharisees it seemed strange that Jesus would accept such an invitation.

They were more concerned about the details of the law than they were about the souls of men. They found fault with the Lord because He healed on the Sabbath day, and associated with publicans and sinners; but these despised people were the very folk that He came from heaven to save. Jesus said, "I came not to call the righteous, but sinners to repentance."

There is a Saviour for you if you are lost. If you are not lost, if you have always done the best you could and obeyed the law and kept the Golden Rule maybe you can get along without Jesus! But if you are a poor sinner, and if your heart is black from sin, you are the very one that Jesus is seeking. He longs to have you know Him.

One thing of which you may be sure: He was not having a jolly time with them. One of the great curses today is the devil's mission of amusement!

Have you ever thought of what the word "amusement" means? *Muse* means "to think," and the *a* is "the negative," so *amuse* means "not to think." David said that while he was musing the fire burned. The devil finds all sorts of things to amuse the people in order to keep them from thinking and facing the realities of eternity.

Jesus did not meet with Matthew's friends in order to amuse them. He was speaking faithfully and earnestly about things pertaining to the kingdom. Always serious, He was there to save them and bring them to God. These scribes and Pharisees looked on to criticize. They were just as bad as those whom they despised, in the sight of God. The Lord heard them murmuring and said to them, "They that are whole need not a physician; but they that are sick. I came not to call the righteous, but sinners to repentance."

There are some folk who are never happy without a doctor, but ordinarily people do not want the doctor if they are well, only when they are sick. So when people know that they are sinners, thank God, there is a Saviour to save them!

Someone may say, "I am too great a sinner to be saved." But you can never be too great a sinner for the Lord Jesus to save. Paul said, "Christ Jesus came into the world to save sinners; of whom I am chief." The chief has already been saved and is in glory, so any other sinner may be saved if he wills. "Whosoever will may come."

I was having a meeting for boys and girls and I held my New Testament up and asked, "Who would like to buy this for $1.75?" No one had the money to buy it. Then I announced, that "whosoever" would come up and claim the New Testament might have it freely. A little fellow looked up and finally came out in the aisle and said to me, "I will take the Testament, please." I said that I would give it to "whosoever" will, and the little fellow realized that "whosoever" included him.

If you are ready to take your place among the "whosoevers," there is salvation for you. Levi took that place and trusted Jesus before he followed Him. You are not saved by following Jesus, but you are saved by trusting Him. That is what Levi did.

The scribes and Pharisees could not enter into the joy of the feast. They said, "Why do the disciples of John fast often, and make prayers, and likewise the disciples of the Pharisees; but Thine eat and drink?" In other words they were saying unto Jesus, "Your disciples are too happy, and John's and ours are more sober." Jesus replied, "Can you make the children of the bridechamber fast, while the bridegroom is with them?" That is, as long as He was there, why should they not rejoice?

Then He spoke a parable unto them in order to show them that they should not piece things together which are not suitable. "No man putteth a piece of a new garment upon the old; if otherwise, then both the new maketh a rent, and the piece that was taken out of the new agreeth not with the old." You would rather find a piece of cloth that is similar. The piece that was taken out of the new is not in harmony with the old. You are not to try to mix the grace of the gospel with the cold legality of Judaism.

The law was given by Moses, but grace and truth came by Jesus Christ. The law comes from God to man, and says "This do" and "Thou shalt not do." Grace declares the salvation of God which is apart from human merit.

"And no man putteth new wine into old bottles, else the new wine will burst the bottles, and be spilled, and the bottles shall perish. But new wine must be put into new bottles; and both are preserved." He was speaking of leather bottles made of the skins of animals. You put new wine into new bottles and when fermentation begins, the bottles will give. You can't take the living truth of the gospel and put it into the ordinances of the law. If you try to confine it in them it will burst all bounds. "No man also having drunk old wine straightway desireth new: for he saith, The old is better." And so these Pharisees would go away saying, "We are satisfied with the old wine," and legalists and worldlings are like that today. They are apparently content with what they are trying to enjoy down here and do not care for that which God offers them in Christ Jesus. You remember that fable of Aesop's, in which he tells of an eagle flying in the heavens, who looked down into a well and saw a stork feeding on frogs. The eagle asked the stork why he did not come up there where he was, and the stork asked him if there were any frogs up there. The eagle replied that there were no frogs there but told him how beautiful it was to fly up into the open heaven. The stork replied, "You can keep your heaven, and I will keep my frogs."

Men say today, "You may have your Christ and your heaven, and we will keep the things of the world." These poor legalists said the same thing. Is that what you are saying? God give you to rest in Christ as your Saviour if you have not done it before!

ADDRESS EIGHTEEN

JESUS REBUKES LEGALITY

"And it came to pass on the second sabbath after the first, that He went through the corn fields; and His disciples plucked the ears of corn, and did eat, rubbing them in their hands. And certain of the Pharisees said unto them, Why do ye that which is not lawful to do on the sabbath days? And Jesus answering them said, Have ye not read so much as this, what David did, when himself was an hungred, and they which were with him; how he went into the house of God, and did take and eat the show-bread, and gave also to them that were with him; which it is not lawful to eat but for the priests alone? And He said unto them, That the Son of Man is Lord also of the sabbath. And it came to pass also on another sabbath, that He entered into the synagogue and taught: and there was a man whose right hand was withered. And the scribes and Pharisees watched Him, whether He would heal on the sabbath day; that they might find an accusation against Him. But He knew their thoughts, and said to the man which had the withered hand, Rise up, and stand forth in the midst. And he arose and stood forth. Then said Jesus unto them, I will ask you one thing; Is it lawful on the sabbath days to do good, or to do evil? to save life, or to destroy it? And looking round about them all, He said unto the man, Stretch forth thy hand. And he did so: and his hand was restored whole as the other. And they were filled with madness; and communed one with another what they might do to Jesus"—Luke 6: 1-11.

WE have really two incidents here which took place a week apart. Both have to do with the same general subject; that is, the legalistic attitude of certain of the leaders in Israel in regard to the sabbath, and the manifestations of our Lord's grace. These men make a burden of the very thing that God has given them for the comfort and blessing of His people, while that which He commended as of more value than any ordinances was ignored completely. God gave the sabbath to Israel for blessing, and commanded that on that day they should not do any work. But one class of people flaunted the Word of the Lord and went to the fields and their business and used the sacred hours of the sabbath in order to enrich themselves. Then there were the rigid legalists who looked upon the sabbath as though it had more or less to do with the salvation of their souls. If they kept it they would be saved, and, if not, they would be lost, and so they added to the Word of the Lord restrictions without number until it was almost impossible for a man to keep in mind all these rules. It is almost amusing to read the Talmud and note these absurd regulations.

Our Lord disregarded these man-made rules. God made the sabbath to be a delight, a means of joy and gladness and help for His people, not linked with hard and fast rules difficult to observe, that they might obtain merit, but because He knew the need of the human body and mind for rest. Then, too, it was His joy to have His people gather together on that day and worship Him. We today are not under these ancient laws of the sabbath. We read in Col. 2: 16, "Let no man therefore judge you in meat or in drink, or in respect of an holy day, or of the new moon, or of the sabbath days: which are a shadow of things to come; but the body is of Christ." We have the Lord's Day instead.

The sabbath was a shadow of things to come. Man toiled for six days and rested on the seventh. Men toil on through life until they know Christ and enter into rest in Him. The sabbath is a type of Christ, and of the rest He gives.

New Testament believers are taught to observe the first day of the week out of love, recognizing the fact that God has honored it above every other day in bringing His Son back from the dead on the first day of the week. "This is the day that the Lord hath made; let us rejoice and be glad in it." People who spurn the privileges of the Lord's Day, think nothing of buying and selling, whether necessary or not, and doing their own pleasure on that day, are wronging their own souls. Many professed Christians make it the one day of the week when they can enjoy a game of golf or go on an excursion, instead of valuing the opportunity to use the day to meet with fellow-believers for worship, prayer, and testimony.

Here we are told that our blessed Lord and His disciples were walking through the corn-fields in the countryside. It means wheat, not corn, as we know it. As they walked through the fields of wheat, His disciples plucked the ears and began to eat, rubbing the kernels out in their hands. According to the law of Moses, one might pluck the corn and eat as he went through the fields, but he was not to put the sickle in it. So the Lord and His disciples availed themselves of this privilege. They were rubbing out the kernels of wheat and eating them, but certain of the legalists, the scribes and the Pharisees, who were watching them, said to the Lord, "Why do ye that which is not lawful to do on the sabbath day?" Had the Word of God prohibited it? Why did they use this term, "not lawful"? This was according to tradition. Our Lord answered them by referring to an incident that had occurred many years before. David was fleeing from Saul to escape from his jealous rage. David and they which were with him became an hungred and went to the house of God and asked the priest if he had any bread and he replied that there was none except the showbread. David asked for some of that in order to satisfy his hungry men. The priest complied, and David and his men ate of that bread. Jesus said to them, "Have ye not read so much as this, what David did, when himself was an hungred, and they which were with him; how he went into the house of God, and did take and eat the showbread, and gave also to them that were with him; which it is not lawful to eat but for the priests alone?" The point the Lord Jesus was emphasizing is this that man is more important in the eyes of God than any ritual observance. And yet how slow we are to realize this! David and his men were suffering, and Jesus commends the high priest for giving them the showbread. Our God is a lover of men, and He has given to His people ordinances that they might be used as a blessing, and not made into a burden. "And He said unto them, That the Son of Man is Lord also of the sabbath." In other words, He was the One who had given the sabbath. These people were finding fault with Him, the Son of Man, the Lord of the sabbath. Here was God manifest in the flesh standing among them, yet they knew Him not.

The second incident was of similar character. "And it came to pass also on another sabbath, that He entered into the synagogue and taught: and there was a man whose right hand was withered." The one incident occurred outside in the wheat-field and this one in the synagogue. He saw a man with a withered right hand. Jesus always sees the one who is in need. He never overlooks one in distress, always sympathizes with any one who is in trouble. The Sadducees and Pharisees saw this man also. I can imagine they said among themselves, "This is the sabbath day, and if He dares to heal that man on the sabbath we can brand Him as a sabbath-breaker." You know when people get taken up with some little religious niceties they can be as cruel as savages. These legalists would rather have left this man in his wretched condition than have him healed on the sabbath. So they watched to see what Jesus would do. He knew their thoughts, of course He did, and that speaks of His Deity. He read their inmost thoughts. He knew all that was running through their minds. And so He turned to the man saying, "Rise up, and stand forth in the midst." I think I can see that poor fellow standing there with such an expectant expression on his face! Is Jesus going to do something for him? The Pharisees and scribes and priests are all watching Him, and Jesus turns to them, and says, "I will ask you one thing: Is it lawful on the sabbath days to do good, or to do evil? To save life, or destroy it?" The legalists did not dare to reply. They stood there with downcast but angry eyes, and then the

Lord Jesus said to the man, "Stretch forth thy hand. And he did so: and his hand was restored whole as the other." In a moment new life and strength came into the hand. One would have thought that the most hard-hearted man there would have shouted praise to God, but instead these zealots were filled with anger. They wanted to get rid of Him, because He had broken their regulations and did not fit in with their legal standards. They did not realize that He was manifesting the love and graciousness of God. So they would have destroyed Him, but nobody could kill Him till the time came for Him to lay down His life on the cross.

Instead of arguing with these men, He left them and went out in the mountain to talk with God, His Father, to commune with Him whose will He had come to do.

ADDRESS NINETEEN

JESUS COMMISSIONS THE TWELVE

✓ ✓ ✓

"And it came to pass in those days that He went into a mountain to pray, and continued all night in prayer to God. And when it was day, He called unto Him His disciples: and of them He chose twelve, whom also He named apostles; Simon, (whom He also named Peter) and Andrew his brother, James and John, Philip and Bartholomew, Matthew and Thomas, James the son of Alphaeus, and Simon called Zelotes, and Judas the brother of James, and Judas Iscariot, which also was the traitor"—Luke 6: 12-16.

✓ ✓ ✓

WE read frequently in this Gospel of the times that our Lord spent in prayer. This is in keeping with its special character as portraying the perfect Manhood of Him who was also God the Son. As Man, He felt not only the need of, but the desire for these seasons of communion with His Father. On this occasion, before choosing the twelve who were to represent Him as His apostles, He spent the entire night on a mountainside, alone with God the Father.

It was not as though He were presenting His own needs to God. It was rather that He was communing with the Father concerning these men, whom He was about to appoint to their high offices, and praying for divine blessing upon them. He ever lived in obedience to the Father's will, and did nothing except as directed of Him.

If He, the Sinless One, the Divine Man, recognized the place and value of prayer in this way, how much more should we, who are so conscious of our frailty and sinfulness, and so ignorant of what is best for us, spend much time in prayer, seeking wisdom for the path and grace to help in every hour of need. Prayer is not just asking of God. It is talking to God. It involves worship, thanksgiving and communion, as well as supplication and intercession.

On the morrow, following the night of prayer, Jesus called twelve men from the larger group that followed Him, whom He set apart in a special way that they might be with Him and be trained to go forth as His representatives. To them He gave the name of "apostles." An apostle is a sent one; literally, a missionary. But the apostleship of the twelve involved more than this. They were specially commissioned to represent Christ as His ambassadors, first to the lost sheep of the house of Israel, later to the great Gentile world. Judas, we know, failed in this, but Matthias was chosen to take over his office. Paul was an apostle of a new order, with a special commission for the present age only.

The twelve were separated from temporal employment, and as they went about with their Master they learned to rely on God for sustenance and to share the hardships into which Jesus had entered voluntarily, as a Servant of God and man. Their training was preparatory to the greater mission upon which they were to enter after the death and resurrection of their Lord.

Let me stress one thing in connection with them that is often overlooked. They were a band of comparatively young men. John, we are told by one of the early Church Fathers, was an adolescent when called of Jesus to follow Him. The others, too, were either very young or just in the prime of life. The artists generally represent most of them as elderly men from the beginning of their association with Jesus. But the fact that, except as their lives were cut short by martyrdom, they continued as witnesses for Christ for many years after the new dispensation began, is proof that they were far from being advanced in age when they first gathered about the Saviour. This is suggestive: Youth is the time to yield oneself to Christ for life-service. Too many wait until the flower of life is past before giving heed to the divine call and accepting the cross, with all that it implies. The earlier one is saved and surrendered to the Lord, the more he may be permitted to accomplish for God. Consider the many who heard and heeded the call, while young, to follow Jesus. Think of the young Martin Luther, the college students, John and Charles Wesley, George Whitefield and their associates, the youthful D. L. Moody, the sixteen-year-old Chas. H. Spurgeon, the earnest lad, Wm. Booth, and a host of others who might be named, all illustrating the old couplet which declares that,

> "Youth is the time to serve the Lord,
> The time to assure the great reward."

Let us examine this list of young men chosen to be Christ's apostles. Every name is interesting and suggestive as we recall what Scripture tells us concerning its bearer.

First, we have impetuous, but devoted Simon the fisherman, whom Jesus named Peter: the rock-like man, a stone to be builded upon Christ, the great foundation Rock on whom the whole Church was to rest. He was a man of contradictions, which is to say, that like all true believers, he had two natures. Sometimes we see the flesh in activity, and more often, the spirit. Though he denied his Lord on the night of the betrayal and mock trial before Caiaphas, he became valiant for the truth after the Pentecostal enduement, and eventually, in old age, about A. D. 69 or 70, sealed his testimony by a martyr's death.

Andrew, Peter's brother, excelled as a personal worker. It was he who led Peter first to Christ. We do not get much information about his later ministry in Scripture, but wherever he is mentioned he is seen as a helpful man, serving in a humble capacity. According to early Church records, he too was martyred, nailed on a cross.

James and John, the sons of Zebedee, like the two mentioned above, were fishermen. Jesus designated them "Boanerges," that is, Sons of Thunder. This suggests that they were stormy, energetic young men, very different, so far as John is concerned, to the almost effeminate character generally given him by the artists. James was the first of the twelve to be put to death for the gospel's sake, "slain with the sword" by Herod's order. John lived to be over ninety years of age, and though suffering much for Christ, died a natural death at Ephesus.

Philip and Bartholomew (also called Nathaniel) are linked together. They were friends before they knew the Lord and closer comrades afterwards.

Matthew was, as we have seen, a tax-collector under the Roman Government, with his office in Capernaum. He there left all to follow Christ, and probably devoted his wealth to the cause in which he was enlisted.

Because of his attitude following the resurrection, we often call Thomas, the Doubter. But he was more than that. He came to conclusions slowly, but he was faithful and devoted and was ready to go to Judaea with Jesus and die with Him if necessary. He seems to have carried the gospel to India. To this day, there is a church of many members in that land, who call themselves Christians of Saint (or, holy) Thomas.

Of James, the son of Alpheus, we do not know very much. He and his brother Judas (not Iscariot) were cousins of Jesus after the flesh. Judas may be the author of the Epistle that we know as Jude, but the James who wrote the Epistle bearing his name seems to have been a brother of Jesus, an overseer of the church in Jerusalem. Elsewhere this Judas is called Thaddeus.

Simon Zelotes, or the Canaanite, was formerly a member of a secret order that had as its object the overthrow of the Roman Government and the deliverance of the Jews from that authority. He turned from this to Christ as the true Deliverer of Israel.

To all eternity, the last of the group will be known as "Judas the traitor." Of him our Lord declared, "Good were it for that man if he had never been born!" He was apparently the only Judean of the company, a man of Kerioth, as Iscariot means. He was probably the most cultured of the twelve and their trusted treasurer, but he proved recreant to this responsibility and went down to eternal infamy as the one who fulfilled the prophecy of Zechariah, selling the Shepherd of Israel for thirty pieces of silver.

The question is often raised as to why Jesus chose Judas and what his actual relation to Him was. We need to remember that our Lord takes men on their profession of faith in and loyalty to Himself, and then gives them the opportunity to demonstrate the true character of that profession. Judas was, like many in Israel, looking for the Kingdom to be set up in power, and he was possibly sincere in his attachment to Jesus as the Man of the hour. But though a trusted follower, appointed to be the treasurer of the little group of disciples, he was never intrinsically honest (John 12:6; 13:29) and at heart was described by Jesus at last as a devil (John 6:70). Three years of association with Christ failed to lead to a true appreciation of His Person and to bring him to heart-allegiance to Him as his Lord. It is a solemn warning of the danger of confounding mere profession with real possession of salvation.

As we consider these men, what lessons they bring before us. May it be ours to emulate their virtues and to avoid their faults!

ADDRESS TWENTY

CHRIST'S ETHICAL TEACHING

✝ ✝ ✝

"And He came down with them, and stood in the plain, and the company of His disciples, and a great multitude of people out of all Judaea and Jerusalem, and from the sea coast of Tyre and Sidon, which came to hear Him, and to be healed of their diseases; and they that were vexed with unclean spirits: and they were healed. And the whole multitude sought to touch Him: for there went virtue out of Him, and healed them all. And He lifted up His eyes on His disciples and said, Blessed be ye poor: for your's is the kingdom of God. Blessed are ye that hunger now: for ye shall be filled. Blessed are ye that weep now: for ye shall laugh. Blessed are ye, when men shall hate you, and when they shall separate you from their company, and shall reproach you, and cast out your name as evil, for the Son of Man's sake. Rejoice ye in that day, and leap for joy: for, behold, your reward is great in heaven: for in the like manner did their fathers unto the prophets. But woe unto you that are rich! for ye have received your consolation. Woe unto you that are full! for ye shall hunger. Woe unto you that laugh now! for ye shall mourn and weep. Woe unto you, when all men shall speak well of you! for so did their fathers to the false prophets"—Luke 6: 17-26.

✝ ✝ ✝

IN considering the Gospel of Luke we have come now to what answers to the similar sermon on the mount, which is given more thoroughly in the Gospel of Matthew. Luke gives us a brief account, whereas in Matthew's Gospel there are three chapters of the sermon on the mount.

All down through the centuries right-minded people have recognized the fine moral tone and deep spirituality of the sermon on the mount. Generally speaking, that sermon has given us the highest ethical teaching in the world. It is the heart of Christ's instruction. However, when you examine it carefully, you will find that it is not the gospel at all, for the gospel is the declaration of God concerning His blessed Son. In the sermon on the mount, we do not have any reference made to the work of our Lord Jesus Christ, but it is a message to the disciples from Christ as to how they who profess to know Him should behave. It gives us the principles that will ever characterize His kingdom.

That kingdom is to be set up here eventually. The sermon on the mount sets forth the principles that should control the disciples during the time of His absence, while still rejected by the world. It would be foolish to say that it only applies to the millennium, because it predicates conditions which will not prevail then. There will be no such circumstances in the millennium, as people being called upon to suffer for righteousness' sake. Here, however, the Lord Jesus speaks of blessings which belong to them in a special way. In that day of triumph Christ's authority will be recognized everywhere. This sermon gives the principles that should actuate and motivate the disciples while they are waiting for their Master to return in power and glory.

There are many who say that it does not apply at all to us today. But we need to realize that everything that is spiritual in any age applies to the people of God in this dispensation as well as in any other period. "All Scripture is given by inspiration of God and is profitable" for our guidance as we go through this godless world, while waiting for our Lord's return. Therefore, I cannot ignore any part of the Scripture if I want to be a well-furnished man of God today, living to His glory. What about the law? Do we not recognize the fact that believers are delivered from the law and are under grace? Yes, the curse of the law is what we have been freed from. But the Epistle to the Romans, which tells us that the law of the Spirit of life in Christ Jesus hath made us free from the law of sin and death, also declares that the righteousness of the law might be fulfilled in us, who walk not after the flesh, but after the Spirit. Everything of a righteous character which the law requires of man will be fulfilled in the lives of godly men and women today.

It is well to remember, as one has said, that, "Some things are right because they are commanded; other things are commanded because they are right." The law said, "Thou shalt not steal." But it is always wrong to steal. It was just as wrong to steal in the days from Adam to Noah and from Noah to Moses, as after the law was given. Everything that was morally right in any age applies to us today. Therefore, when it comes to the ethical and spiritual instruction given in the sermon on the mount, we are not to ignore or seek to set it aside.

Now a word or two as to the circumstances under which this sermon was preached. In Matthew 5, we read that Jesus went up into a mountain and sat down. But Luke tells us that "He came down with them and stood in the plain, and the company of His disciples, and a great multitude of people out of all Judaea and Jerusalem, and from the sea coast of Tyre and Sidon, which came to hear Him, and to be healed of their diseases." While standing in the plain, He gives this sermon on the mount. There have been some who have been quick to say that there is a discrepancy here. Matthew says "mountain" and Luke says "plain." A few years ago it was my privilege to stand with some members of my family at the foot of that mountain, near Capernaum. You can see a road ascending until it comes to a broad tableland and then goes up higher and higher until it reaches the peak. Our Lord went up first "into the mountain," that is, to the very top. Then in the morning He came down to the plain. "And it came to pass in those days that He went out into a mountain to pray, and continued all night in prayer to God. And when it was day, He called unto Him His disciples; and of them He chose twelve, whom also He named apostles; and He came down with them and stood in the plain . . ." And turning to His disciples, while the multitude listened, He spoke to them. There is no contradiction here. The only trouble is that if one does not understand the circumstances he jumps at conclusions. One has well said that the more he studied the Word of God the more he came to the conclusion that no one knows enough to charge that Word with inconsistencies. This is just one such instance.

Now the Lord, having gathered His own about Him, "lifted up his eyes on His disciples and said,

Blessed be ye poor: for your's is the kingdom of God." This is not mere temporal poverty. He is not saying that men should just be content to be poor, but He is comforting those who are poor by telling them that though they may be poor in this world, they may be rich in faith. It is a remarkable fact that in some way or other the followers of the Lord Jesus Christ are almost always poor. Our Lord said, "The foxes have holes and the birds of the air have nests, but the Son of Man hath not where to lay His head." The followers of the Lord Jesus, in a large measure, have been among the poor and lowly, but oh, how much the grace and love of Christ has meant to them. How many a lowly and humble home has been brightened by the fellowship of the Lord Jesus Christ. He is not saying a word against rising up from poverty, but is encouraging those who are poor in purse and poor in spirit by assuring them of part in the kingdom of God. It is in Matthew's account that we find Jesus emphasizes, not simple poverty as to material means, but says, "Blessed are the poor in spirit." What does this mean? It is to be without spiritual assets. It is to acknowledge that in yourself you have absolutely nothing to satisfy God, but when you trust His grace then you can say that yours is the kingdom of God.

"Blessed are ye that hunger now: for ye shall be filled." Matthew says, "Blessed are they that hunger and thirst after righteousness." If you feel a great yearning in your soul for something that you have not found in this world, you may take heart and turn to Him who supplies the living bread, which satisfies the hunger of all who put their trust in Him. "Blessed are ye that weep now: for ye shall laugh." And oh, how many of God's people have had to go through trial and distress! Savonarola said, "A Christian's life consists in trial and distress, doing good and suffering evil." As you try to follow your Lord in a world like this, many a tear will roll down your face. Your Saviour was a Man of tears, a Man of sorrows and acquainted with grief, but "for the joy that was set before Him He endured the cross, despising the shame, and is now set down at the right hand of the throne of God." All the suffering the people of God will ever know is right here on earth, for they will have joy forever with Him in the world beyond. But those who seek to find their joy here without Christ will have sorrow and grief in the world beyond.

Then Jesus gives a word to those who are suffering for His name's sake: "Blessed are ye, when men shall hate you, and when they shall separate you from their company and shall reproach you, and cast out your name as evil, for the Son of Man's sake." You would not like to give up that beatitude, would you, Christians? You would not want to lose the good of it. Thank God, it is always true until Jesus establishes His kingdom and authority over all the world.

> "Life with trials hard may press me,
> Heaven will give me sweeter rest."

This is the only world in which we can have that privilege of suffering for His name's sake. Let our hearts cry out, "Beautiful cross, wonderful cross! I will embrace it." Jesus said that "whosoever cometh after Me, let him take up his cross and follow Me."

And now we have the four woes: "Woe unto you that are rich! for ye have received your consolation." Even as, on another occasion, the Lord speaks of the once-rich man, suffering in Hades, who had received his good things in this life and now his day was past. When death comes, such are poorer than the poorest.

"Woe unto you that are full! for ye shall hunger." Those who gorge themselves with present worldly enjoyments, ignoring the more important spiritual realities, will find themselves left in a state of bitter disappointment and unsatisfied yearning when life's short day is ended.

"Woe unto you that laugh now! for ye shall mourn and weep." To live for pleasure and seek after folly and carnal mirth in a scene where there is so much reason to be serious and sober-minded, means to face an eternity of tears and mournings as one realizes the sadness of wasted talents and opportunities.

"Woe unto you, when all men shall speak well of you! for so did their fathers to the false prophets." To be highly esteemed by worldlings indicates that one is just part of the world, and the world loves its own; but Jesus said that if we follow Him we need not wonder that the world will hate us, for they hated Him before they hated us. It is no evidence that a man is going on with God because he has the good-will of unspiritual and Christless people. The world delights in those of its own kind. We who are Christians have been called out from this world to the One whom they reject. God give us grace to enter more and more into fellowship with our blessed Lord, who is still in the outside place!

Address Twenty-one

THE BOOK OF THE GOLDEN RULE

"But I say unto you which hear, Love your enemies, do good to them which hate you. Bless them that curse you, and pray for them which despitefully use you. And unto him that smiteth thee on the one cheek offer also the other; and him that taketh away thy cloke forbid not to take thy coat also. Give to every man that asketh of thee: and of him that taketh away thy goods ask them not again. And as ye would that men should do to you, do ye also to them likewise. For if ye love them which love you, what thank have ye? for sinners also love those that love them. And if ye do good to them which do good to you, what thank have ye? for sinners also do even the same. And if ye lend to them of whom ye hope to receive, what thank have ye? for sinners also lend to sinners, to receive as much again. But love ye your enemies, and do good, and lend, hoping for nothing again; and your reward shall be great, and ye shall be the children of the Highest: for He is kind unto the unthankful and to the evil. Be ye therefore merciful as your Father also is merciful. Judge not, and ye shall not be judged: condemn not, and ye shall not be condemned: forgive, and ye shall be forgiven: give, and it shall be given unto you; good measure, pressed down, and shaken together, and running over, shall men give into your bosom. For with the same measure that ye mete withal it shall be measured to you again"—Luke 6: 27-38.

DO not these words seem rather strange to come to us in a day like this when so-called civilized nations are in sanguinary warfare and death prevails almost everywhere?* Of course, we have to remember that our Lord Jesus Christ was speaking to His own disciples. We do not have here, and we might as well frankly face it, instruc-

* Written during the 2nd World-War.

tion for the nations of the world as to how they are to carry on their affairs of government. We find if we go through the Book that, when nations forget God, He uses other nations to punish them. The principle of government runs all through the Bible and it does not conflict with the plan of grace.

We have noticed already that the Sermon on the Mount is not the gospel. It gives us the principles of the kingdom of God, principles which should govern the lives of God's children at all times. There are some who would ignore what we have here. They insist that it was given to the disciples in Israel and it will only come into effect again just before the coming of Christ at the Second Advent. That is sophistical reasoning. In view of the fact that we are told that the righteousness of the law is fulfilled in us who walk not after the flesh but after the Spirit, how can we think for a moment that the principles laid down here for the disciples have no application for us? Christ is still the absent One, and we are here where we are bound to be misunderstood and will have to suffer if we bear His name. That is just what our blessed Lord emphasized in His address. "But I say unto you which hear, Love your enemies, do good to them which hate you." Now there is a direct challenge to everyone as individuals. I put the question to you as I put it to my own heart. Do we professed Christians love our enemies? That is the command of the Lord Jesus Christ. If we love our enemies, we will not be glad when they suffer, and certainly we will endeavor to make things no worse for them. He is speaking here of disciples, not of national affairs. If there were Christian nations they would be responsible to live according to such principles. But there are no nations which honor the Lord Jesus Christ completely and yield to His commands. The Christian sailor or soldier needs not to hate his enemy though he serves his country in battle.

Chiang Kai-Shek has sought to maintain an attitude of forbearance and love even toward those who have brought travail to his nation. A missionary tells us how his heart was stirred as that great Chinese leader prayed, "O God, keep me from ever hating the Japanese!" It took grace to pray like that. How often we have heard of Christian soldiers with no hatred in their hearts against their enemies. Yet how often we find even professing Christians with a spirit of malice and hatred toward each other. Nothing is such a hindrance to the work of the Lord as this. We need to remember that Christ has said: "With what measure you mete, it shall be measured to you again." "But I say unto you which hear, Love your enemies, do good to them which hate you." To obey these precepts is to manifest the spirit of Christ. This is love in activity. It was fully displayed in our blessed Lord, who laid down His life for those who were His enemies and who hated Him without cause. When we are born from above (John 3:3), we receive the nature which is divine, and so are enabled in our measure to walk in love toward all men, no matter how injurious and hateful their behavior toward us may be.

Then our Lord continues: "Bless them that curse you, and pray for them which despitefully use you." This is faith's resource. None are so vicious or depraved but what there is a possibility that they may be reached and softened by means of the throne of God. We touch that throne by prayer. Blessing those who curse us, we intercede with God on their behalf. Again our Lord sets us the example, He who prayed, "Father, forgive them; for they know not what they do" (Luke 23: 34).

When somebody has been very unkind, instead of meeting him in the same way, get down on your knees and plead for his blessing, and when the Spirit of God speaks to him, his attitude will change. Try it and see. Go alone into the presence of God and ask Him to speak to those hearts in divine love. Pray for those against whom you have been cherishing ill feelings. "And unto him that smiteth thee on the one cheek offer also the other; and him that taketh away thy cloke forbid not to take thy coat also." This is one of the verses that I find a great many of my brethren delight to pass on to the remnant of Israel! It may prove a little inconvenient now, but the Lord meant us to take His words literally. He gave to His disciples an example. He bore reproach uncomplainingly and committed Himself to Him that judgeth righteously. Men maltreated Him most cruelly. They dragged Him out to Calvary and nailed Him to the cross. He might have called on God to visit judgment upon them, but He cried out, "Father, forgive them; for they know not what they do." If someone smites us on one cheek, are we willing to endure it and even to face further ill-treatment for Him? "And him that taketh away thy cloke forbid not to take thy coat also." We need not try to press this too literally. Our Lord Himself, when smitten on the one cheek, is not said to have challenged His persecutor to smite the other. It is rather the spirit of retaliation which is here rebuked. The disciple of the Lord Jesus is to be content to suffer wrongfully. Even if sued at the law, he is to be ready to give more than can be legally demanded. It is a standard too high for the unregenerate man, and seldom reached by those who profess to be followers of Christ.

That is manifest grace and it is supplied by Christ. "Give to every man that asketh of thee: and of him that taketh away thy goods ask them not again." The Christian is to be constantly on the giving side and he does not have to be too particular to see that men deserve everything that they ask from Him. Do you deserve everything that God gives you? Have we not all been ungrateful for what He has given? This does not mean that we can always give everything that others ask for, but the point is that we are to have the attitude of giving, to be ready to assist and help rather than to oppose.

Observe it is not said that we are to give *what* every man asks. To do so would often mean to work injustice on others, as for the head of a family to give to beggars what his own household, for whom he is responsible to care (1 Tim. 5:8), might sorely need. There are times when it is better to give faithful advice than to bestow alms. But if one's goods are taken by force, we can be content to let them go when assured we possess the true riches that shall never pass away.

Now comes the golden rule—"And as ye would that men should do to you, do ye also to them likewise." It has often been said that the Lord Jesus Christ was not original in giving this rule, that it is found in other and older literature of the world. The great Chinese teacher, Confucius (King Futsze), said, "What you would not have others do to you, do not you to them." That is negative. Our Lord Jesus makes it positive. "And as ye would that men should do to you, do ye also to them likewise." Here is benevolence in activity, here is goodness positive, not negative, even looking for an opportunity to emphasize the love and kindness of God to men and women in need all about one, this high standard is only found here in the Book of God.

You can search the literature of the world before Christ came, and you will not find it anywhere. This golden rule was first proclaimed by the blessed Son of God. The Bible is the Book of the golden rule.

Do not make a mistake and think this is the way of salvation. My dear friends, if you had to wait until you obeyed the golden rule, you would never become a Christian. You need to acknowledge that you have sinned against God, and when you trust Christ and accept Him as your Saviour, you become a Christian. Then you are to own Him as your Lord. He will enable you to live out the golden rule. "And as ye would that men should do to you, do ye also to them likewise."

In the next part of our passage, the Lord Jesus shows how men profess to be His disciples and yet rise no higher than the world in practical behavior. "For if ye love them which love you, what thank have ye? for sinners also love those that love them." If you only love them that love you what credit is that to you? "And if ye do good to them which do good to you, what thank have ye? For sinners also do even the same." "And if ye lend to them of whom ye hope to receive, what thank have ye? for sinners also lend to sinners, to receive as much again." The Lord ridicules those who pretend to be the children of God when they have not reached any higher, so far as practical behavior goes, than those who make no profession at all. We are not to try to overcome evil with evil; but overcome evil with good. Then you are manifesting the spirit of Christ. "But love ye your enemies, and do good, and lend, hoping for nothing again; and your reward shall be great, and ye shall be the children of the Highest: for He is kind unto the unthankful and to the evil." This is one of the hardest lessons we have to learn. But by obedience to these words, we will be emphasizing our relationship to God our Father, for He is kind to the unthankful and to the evil. "Be ye therefore merciful, as your Father also is merciful."

Then our Lord says something which many of us have never considered. We know that it is in the Bible and yet it has so little influence on our lives: "Judge not, and ye shall not be judged: condemn not, and ye shall not be condemned: forgive, and ye shall be forgiven." I wonder who of us can take a test like that and say, "Not guilty!" How quick we are to judge others—to judge people's motives, to imply evil where it may not exist. How often are judgments unkind and untrue! "Judge not," our Lord Jesus said, and we pay so little attention to it. "Judge not, and ye shall not be judged: condemn not, and ye shall not be condemned: forgive, and ye shall be forgiven." The poet says, "To err is human, to forgive, divine." Forgive and you shall be forgiven. "Give, and it shall be given unto you; good measure, pressed down, and shaken together, and running over, shall men give into your bosom. For with the same measure that ye mete withal it shall be measured to you again." God is ever a Giver and we are called to be imitators of Him. Let us not be self-centered, always looking for recognition. True joy is found in ministering to others. "It is better," said Jesus, "to give than to receive."

If we manifest the fruit of the Spirit, which is love, we shall find that even unsaved and godless men will begin to recognize the fact that we really belong to Christ. It is amazing how grace can overcome evil and sin. You cannot lose if you spend your life giving, but if you spend it by taking in and taking in, you will lose out completely. How many folks are like the Dead Sea. For many centuries the River Jordan has been pouring fresh water down to the Dead Sea, and yet it remains as it has been for centuries. There is no outlet, it has been "taking in" all the time. If you want to know the secret of a happy life, you will find it in obeying the Lord's word, "Give, and it shall be given unto you."

In God's government, He will see to it that we are treated at last as we treat others. The generous heart will receive generously in return. No one ever loses by loving, nor becomes poor by giving, for he has the blessing of those needier than himself.

Christ's instruction was given for the guidance of His disciples. It is a mistake to suppose that in the teaching of our Lord we have a system of ethics designed to curb the evil propensities of natural men and so raise them to a higher spiritual plane. Nothing will do this but the new birth. When men are born of God, they find in the instruction of Jesus, the principles that guide in living the new life. But we need to remember there must be a life by which we live before we can live the life.

ADDRESS TWENTY-TWO

SECURE AND INSECURE FOUNDATIONS

✓ ✓ ✓

"And He spake a parable unto them, Can the blind lead the blind? Shall they not both fall into the ditch? The disciple is not above his master: but every one that is perfect shall be as his master. And why beholdest thou the mote that is in thy brother's eye, but perceivest not the beam that is in thine own eye? Either how canst thou say to thy brother, Brother, let me pull out the mote that is in thine eye, when thou thyself beholdest not the beam that is in thine own eye? Thou hypocrite, cast out first the beam out of thine own eye, and then shalt thou see clearly to pull out the mote that is in thy brother's eye. For a good tree bringeth not forth corrupt fruit; neither doth a corrupt tree bring forth good fruit. For every tree is known by his own fruit. For of thorns men do not gather figs, nor of a bramble bush gather they grapes. A good man out of the good treasure of his heart bringeth forth that which is good; and an evil man out of the evil treasure of his heart bringeth forth that which is evil: for of the abundance of the heart his mouth speaketh. And why call ye Me, Lord, Lord, and do not the things which I say? Whosoever cometh to Me, and heareth My sayings, and doeth them, I will show you to whom he is like: he is like a man which built an house, and digged deep, and laid the foundation on a rock: and when the flood arose, the stream beat vehemently upon that house, and could not shake it; for it was founded upon a rock. But he that heareth, and doeth not, is like a man that without a foundation built an house upon the earth; against which the stream did beat vehemently, and immediately it fell; and the ruin of that house was great"—Luke 6: 39-49.

✓ ✓ ✓

IN accordance with our Lord's customary method of instruction, He reverts to parabolic teaching in closing this great discourse. How vivid is the picture brought before our eyes as we hear him say, "Can the blind lead the blind? Shall they not both fall into the ditch?" Could one more aptly set forth the sad results of following unenlightened human teachers instead of being guided by the plain Word of the Lord? It is noticeable that in the First Epistle to Timothy, the sixth chapter, the apostle Paul stresses the importance of taking heed to the words of our Lord Jesus Christ which set forth the teaching that is according to godliness. These words are found in the four Gospels, where we hear the Lord Himself speaking to His disciples. Yet frequently we are told that this instruction is no longer binding upon Christians today, since the fuller revelation of the mystery of the One Body has come in. The sad results of accepting such views are soon seen. Those who set them forth prove to be in very truth blind leaders, and those who accept them blind disciples, and both alike stumble and fall into the ditch of Antinomianism on the one hand or of hard legality on the other. It is well to weigh carefully these words of the apostle, which I quote in full:

"If any man teach otherwise, and consent not to wholesome words, even the words of our Lord Jesus Christ, and to the doctrine which is according to godliness; he is proud, knowing nothing, but doting about questions and strifes of words, whereof cometh envy, strife, railings, evil surmisings, perverse disputings of men of corrupt minds, and destitute of the truth, supposing that gain is godliness: from such withdraw thyself. But godliness with contentment is great gain."

The Master, our blessed Lord, has laid down principles upon which His disciples should order their lives. If we would attain to spiritual perfection we cannot afford to ignore what He has thus set before us. Verses 41 and 42 are almost humorous in the way they ridicule the folly of one attempting to set his brother right, who is himself far from walking in paths of rectitude. "Why beholdest thou the mote that is in thy brother's eye, but perceivest not the beam that is in thine own eye?" In the *Koine,* as set forth in the recently discovered records in Egypt, this very word is used by a young man who writes to his mother, speaking of the suffering he has endured because of a beam having gotten under his thumb-nail. It is clear that by *beam* he really means a splinter, but this splinter seemed so large that he used the term *beam* to describe it. Undoubtedly, this is what our Lord has in mind. Who, with a splinter in his own eye, can properly discern the condition of a brother's eye? If I am under the power of sin myself I am in no condition to reprove another. What I need to do is to get right myself and then I can help an erring brother. To take the other attitude is to brand oneself a hypocrite—professing one thing and living another. And so the Lord insists that the beam be cast out first from one's own eye, and then we shall be able to see clearly to take the mote out of our brother's eye.

In many places in Scripture, man is pictured as a tree. In the Psalms, the righteous is seen as a palmtree or an olive, beautiful and verdant; whereas the wicked are set forth under the picture of an evil tree, eventually to be cast into the fire. The Lord uses the same figures in the next two verses: a good tree brings forth good fruit; a corrupt tree brings forth evil fruit. A man is not a sinner because he sins. He sins because he is a sinner. When one is born of God sin becomes hateful to him and he seeks to order his life in righteousness. So he brings forth fruit unto God. In this way every tree is known by its own fruit. Men do not expect to gather figs from thorn-trees, nor grapes from bramble-bushes. Each bears according to its kind. The man who is yielded to the Lord and seeks to walk in accordance with His Word will bring forth out of the good treasure of his heart that which is good, to the glory of God and the blessing of mankind; while a man inherently evil, who has never been regenerated, will, out of the evil treasure of his heart, bring forth that which is evil. It is the heart that makes the man. "Out of the abundance of the heart the mouth speaketh." To profess allegiance to Christ and to call Him Lord while walking in disobedience to His Word, is both folly and hypocrisy. We sing sometimes, and rightly:

"If He is not Lord of all,
Then He is not Lord at all."

How we need to remember this! His Word should dominate and control in every aspect of our lives.

We are all familiar with the parable with which our Lord closes this discourse. He likens the man who hears His Word and obeys it to one who undertook to build a house, and in order that it might be secure, he digged deep and laid the foundation on a rock. Christ Himself is that Rock. It is only as we build on Him that we are secure. Graphically, the Lord pictures the house built on such a foundation as weathering the most violent storm. He says that when the flood arose, the storm beat violently on that house and could not shake it because it was founded on a rock. So it will be with everyone who has trusted Christ as Saviour, and then seeks to walk in obedience to His revealed will.

The disobedient, self-centered man, who hears the Word of Christ, but does not yield his heart to the Saviour, does not trust and obey Him, is likened to a man who, without laying any foundation, built his house upon the earth. When the storm arose and the stream beat violently upon it, it fell, and the ruin of that house was great because it had no secure foundation. The parable explains itself. It needs no illumination of the Spirit of God to make the meaning clear. All that is required is an active conscience and a desire to be right with God. May this be true of all to whom this message comes.

ADDRESS TWENTY-THREE

TWO NOTABLE MIRACLES

"Now when He had ended all His sayings in the audience of the people, He entered into Capernaum. And a certain centurion's servant, who was dear unto him, was sick, and ready to die, and when he heard of Jesus he sent unto Him the elders of the Jews, beseeching Him that He would come and heal his servant. And when they came to Jesus, they besought Him instantly, saying, That he was worthy for whom He should do this: for he loveth our nation, and he hath built us a synagogue. Then Jesus went with them. And when He was not far from the house, the centurion sent friends to Him, saying unto Him, Lord, trouble Thou not Thyself: for I am not worthy that Thou shouldest enter under my roof: wherefore neither thought I myself worthy to come unto Thee, but say in a word, and my servant shall be healed. For I also am a man set under authority, having under me soldiers, and I say unto one, Go, and he goeth: and to another, Come, and he cometh; and to my servant, Do this, and he doeth it. When Jesus heard these things He marvelled at him and turned Him about, and said unto the people that followed Him, I say unto you, I have not found so great faith, no, not in Israel. And they that were sent, returning to the house, found the servant whole that had been sick. And it came to pass the day after, that He went into a city called Nain; and many of His disciples went with Him, and much people. Now when He came nigh to the gate of the city, behold, there was a dead man carried out, the only son of his mother and she was a widow; and much people of the city was with her. And when the Lord saw her, He had compassion on her, and said unto her, Weep not. And He came and touched the bier: and they that bare him stood still. And He said, Young man, I say unto thee, Arise. And he that was dead sat up and began to speak. And He delivered him to his mother. And there came a fear on all: and they glorified God, saying, That a great prophet is risen up among us; and, That God hath visited His people. And this rumor of Him went forth throughout all Judaea, and throughout all the region round about. And the disciples of John showed him of all these things"—Luke 7: 1-18.

IN this wonderfully precious seventh chapter of Luke we have four very striking illustrations of the grace of God in Christ overleaping all boundaries and flowing out to meet the needs of troubled hearts. The centurion was a Roman, not one of the lost sheep of the house of Israel, to whom Christ was sent (Matt. 15:24). The widow's son was already dead and the body was being carried to the burial-place. Only divine power could avail. All human hope was gone. The bewildered disciples of John were troubled because the Kingdom did not immediately appear. In grace Jesus showed them the signs of the Kingdom so as to confirm their faith and that of their teacher, now in prison. Last of all, the poor woman who found forgiveness at His feet was a sinner of the streets, despised by the self-righteous, but just the one for Jesus, who had come, not to seek out the righteous, but to seek and to save that which was lost (Luke 19:10). It is abounding grace throughout—grace that delights to give, and asks nothing in return, but which produces gratitude and loving service on the part of the recipient.

Jesus never wrought miracles to gratify curiosity or to compel the amazement and admiration of carnal worldlings. Every putting forth of His power was with the distinct objects in view of glorifying God and ministering to human need. His heart of compassion went out to men in their sorrows and distresses, and it was His joy to speak the word of healing and to deliver the troubled soul. He could not be indifferent to what sin had wrought, and so

He came to destroy, or undo, the works of the Devil (1 John 3:8). He did not come to destroy men's lives, but to save them (Luke 9:56), that men might be at their very best for God.

When we speak of anything as miraculous, we mean that it is beyond the power and ability of the natural man. A miracle is the putting forth of supernatural power, and as found in Scripture, is always to alleviate human sorrow or distress and as a manifestation of divine authority. Jesus was accredited as the Son of God and the Messiah of Israel by the mighty works which He performed.

In the present portion we have, first, the healing of a Roman centurion's servant (vers. 1 to 10); and then the raising up from death of the son of the widow of Nain (vers. 11 to 18). We shall consider these in their order as here set forth.

We are told that as Jesus entered into Capernaum, after preaching the great sermon, a portion of which is preserved for us in the previous chapter, and a fuller record given in Matthew 5 to 7, He was met by a deputation of Jewish elders, who came to Him on behalf of a military officer, a centurion, whose servant (to whom he was greatly attached), was seriously ill. Matthew tells us the centurion himself came (Matt. 8:5), but we can readily understand that the elders presented his case to the Lord, as representing him. The discrepancy exists only in the minds of men who seek for some fancied evidence that Scripture is not wholly inspired by God. The case was urgent. The young man was already in a dying condition.

The elders pressed the claim of the centurion by declaring "He was worthy for whom He should do this: for he loveth our nation, and he hath built us a synagogue." It is significant that in recent years a synagogue of evident Roman construction but with distinctly Jewish ornamentation has been uncovered among the ruins of Capernaum. It is a thrilling sensation to stand on the dais in that ancient building and reflect that possibly one's feet are resting on the very stones where the holy Saviour's feet once stood! This was my privilege some years ago.

A centurion was a captain of one hundred men, in the Roman army. This officer had a servant, a bondsman, whom he loved and who was at the point of death. It is evident that this centurion was a true believer in the Lord Jesus Christ. He had heard of Him through his friends and, probably, had listened eagerly to His gracious messages. He had witnessed His works of power and he was convinced that Jesus was more than man. Though himself of a more exalted station in life than Jesus, he nevertheless recognized Christ's superiority, and so he sent messengers pleading for mercy and help, not arrogantly demanding attention. His faith was a cup of joy pressed to the lips of the blessed One who was despised and rejected by so many whom He sought in love to save.

Jesus immediately started for the centurion's home, but on the way was met by other messengers, who, speaking on behalf of their soldier friend, said, "Lord trouble not Thyself; for I am not worthy that Thou shouldest enter my house." Note the difference. The elders said: "He is worthy." He himself insisted: "I am not worthy!" He was one who had taken his due place of repentance as an unworthy sinner before God. Realizing something of the true nature and character of Jesus he said, "Wherefore neither thought I myself worthy to come unto Thee; but say in a word, and my servant shall be healed." As a military man he explained that he could speak with authority and his soldiers would be obedient. Surely Jesus could speak in the same way and rebuke the disease that threatened the life of his servant!

Such an expression of trustful confidence gladdened the heart of our Lord. He marvelled at the man's simple faith—a faith such as He had not found in Israel. Nothing glorifies God like confidence in His Word. In response to the centurion's faith, the apparently dying man was instantly restored. This was faith indeed! He did not feel that the personal presence and touch of Jesus was needed to heal the dying servant. He recognized the fact that "where the word of a king is, there is power" (Eccles. 8:4), and he was sure that Jesus had that authority, and that a word from Him would bring health to the one who was so ill.

Faith's reward is sure. When the messengers returned to the house, they found the servant well, and inquiry proved that the change for the better had come at the very time when Jesus spoke the word (Matt. 8:13).

But a greater evidence of His power was soon to be given. On the following day Jesus went with

His disciples to the nearby city of Nain, the ruins of which are still to be found in Galilee. A large throng followed them, doubtless stirred by what had taken place the day before, and hoping to see some other great wonder wrought by Jesus; nor were they disappointed. As the crowd drew near the village, they saw a funeral procession wending its way to the cemetery. They soon realized it was the funeral of a young man, whose widowed mother was the chief mourner. As Jesus drew near, His tender heart was filled with compassion as He beheld the evidences of her grief. He bade her cease weeping; then touching the bier on which the corpse lay, He said with authority, "Young man, I say unto thee, Arise!" Immediately, in response to that voice which shall one day awaken all the dead, the young man opened his eyes. Life returned to that cold body. To the amazement of all, he sat up and began to speak. How graphically Luke describes it all, and what a stirring of heart there must have been in the breasts of the many on-lookers as Jesus "delivered him to his mother." Who can dry tears like Jesus? Some day He will wipe away all tears from the eyes of His redeemed (Rev. 21:4), for He is God as well as Man. When He bade the widow dry her tears, He did not merely seek to soothe, but He was about to work a miracle that would fill her heart with unexpected joy.

It was such a demonstration of divine power as they had never known before and they glorified God, declaring that a great prophet had risen up among them.

The news of this mighty miracle went abroad through all Galilee and Judaea, even coming to the ears of John the Baptist, who was pining in prison because of his faithfulness in rebuking King Herod's wickedness.

Thus God had borne witness to the claims of His Son, who in grace had come into the world to be the Saviour of sinners.

It has pleased God to honor our faith, because faith is that which honors Him. Faith takes Him at His word, and counts the things which are not as though they were (Rom. 4:17). But it is not faith that does the work. It is but the means which God uses to unloose His unlimited power. Faith is the hand which lays hold of Omnipotence. As Man on earth, our Lord was the pattern Man of faith and He taught faith to others. He chose, in this scene of His humiliation, to live in daily dependence upon the living Father (John 6:57). Thus the works of power He wrought were those which the Father gave Him to do (John 14:10). In rebuking disease and death, and in saving from sin those who sought His grace, He was manifesting the heart of God toward a needy world. His concern for the life and health of mankind was but the expressed desire of God the Father, that all men who believe in Him might be at last delivered from the effects of sin. It is not always His will to grant perfect health now, but faith can firmly trust Him in every circumstance.

ADDRESS TWENTY-FOUR

CHRIST'S ENDORSEMENT OF JOHN THE BAPTIST

✝ ✝ ✝

"And John calling unto him two of his disciples sent them to Jesus, saying, Art Thou He that should come? or look we for another? When the men were come unto Him, they said, John Baptist hath sent us unto Thee, saying, Art Thou He that should come? or look we for another? And in that same hour He cured many of their infirmities and plagues, and of evil spirits; and unto many that were blind He gave sight. Then Jesus answering said unto them, Go your way, and tell John what things ye have seen and heard: how that the blind see, the lame walk, the lepers are cleansed, the deaf hear, the dead are raised, to the poor the gospel is preached. And blessed is he, whosoever shall not be offended in Me. And when the messengers of John were departed, He began to speak unto the people concerning John, What went ye out into the wilderness for to see? A reed shaken with the wind? But what went ye out for to see? A man clothed in soft raiment? Behold, they which are gorgeously apparelled, and live delicately, are in kings' courts. But what went ye out for to see? A prophet? Yea, I say unto you, and much more than a prophet. This is he, of whom it is written, Behold, I send My messenger before Thy face, which shall prepare Thy way before Thee. For I say unto you, Among those that are born of women there is not a greater prophet than John the Baptist; but he that is least in the kingdom of God is greater than he. And all the people that heard Him, and the publicans, justified God, being baptized with the baptism of John. But the Pharisees and lawyers rejected the counsel of God against themselves, being not baptized of him. And the Lord said, Whereunto then shall I liken the men of this generation? And to what are they like? They are like unto children sitting in the marketplace, and calling one to another, and saying, We have piped unto you, and ye have not danced; we have mourned to you, and ye have not wept. For John the Baptist came neither eating bread nor drinking wine; and ye say, He hath a devil. The Son of Man is come eating and drinking; and ye say, Behold a gluttonous man, and a wine-bibber, a friend of publicans and sinners! But wisdom is justified of all her children" —Luke 7: 19-35.

DURING the early part of our blessed Lord's ministry, John the Baptist was arrested by order of King Herod because of his faithfulness in seeking to press upon the conscience of that wicked monarch his vileness and corruption, particularly in connection with his adulterous relation with his brother's wife, Herodias. For months John was allowed to languish in prison.

According to tradition, this was the castle of Machaerus, a stronghold in the wilderness of Judaea overlooking the Dead Sea. There is no positive proof, however, that John was there incarcerated. Machaerus is quite a distance from Tiberias, where Herod held his court and where John was brought to be beheaded. At any rate, wherever he was confined, it must have been for him a strange ending to his great ministry. He who had been used to speak to thousands and who had presented the Lord Jesus to them as the promised Messiah, the Son of God, the Lamb of God who taketh away the sin of the world, now seemed to be neglected and forgotten. Doubtless, there would come to him from time to time rumors of the great miracles that Jesus did, and reports of His discourses, but there was nothing to indicate that He was actually presenting Himself to Israel as the promised Messiah. Whether John himself began to entertain doubts as to this, or whether it was simply his disciples who were perplexed, we cannot now say, but we are told in this passage that John called unto him two of the disciples, and sent them to Jesus, inquiring "Art Thou

He that should come, or look we for another?" Could it be that Jesus, like John himself, was simply another forerunner of the true Messiah, or was He actually the promised King, and was there some reason for which He refrained from asserting His authority? These were the problems involved in John's inquiries.

When these men came to Jesus, they asked Him according to John's instructions. We do not read that He gave any immediate answer, but He permitted them to look on as He healed many of various diseases and plagues and cast out demons. He also gave sight to some that were blind. These were the visible tokens of His Messiahship and should have counted far more than any words in proving that He was truly the expected One. After John's disciples observed the evidences of His power, Jesus told them to return to John and tell him of the things they had seen and heard: how that "the blind see, the lame walk, the lepers are cleansed, the deaf hear, the dead are raised, to the poor the gospel is preached." What more could Messiah do so far as ministering to the needs of men? Jesus added, "Blessed is he whosoever shall not be offended in Me." That is, He meant those who would not be stumbled by His failure to assert Himself in the way that many in Israel expected Messiah to do.

No sooner had the messengers of John left than the Lord began to speak to the people concerning His forerunner. In a most appreciative way He insisted on the greatness of the ministry of this devoted man. There is something here that should be very precious to our hearts. We are all inclined, at times, to feel that we have been neglected and forgotten, and the Lord does not always speak words of endorsement directly to us, but we may be assured of this: if we have sought to be faithful to Him, He always approves us before His Father and the holy angels. John himself could not hear what Jesus said to the multitude. If he could have done so, it would, no doubt, have been a great encouragement to him, but he was left in ignorance of this for the time, in order that his faith might be more firmly established.

The Lord inquired, first of all, "What went ye out into the wilderness for to see?" And then suggested an answer to the question. "A reed shaken with the wind?" John surely was not that. He was a strong, fearless messenger of the truth, not turned aside by any opposition. "But," continued the Lord, "what went ye out for to see? A man clothed in soft raiment?" Was John like many of the leaders in Israel, one who looked upon his office as a lucrative profession and profited by it, and so lived in luxury, and dressed magnificently in order to impress the people? Such men had access to kings' courts and were honored by enjoying the favor of rulers. But it was otherwise with this wilderness preacher. Again the Lord puts a question. "But what went ye out to see? A prophet?" Immediately He adds, "Yea, I say unto you, and much more than a prophet." A prophet is one who speaks directly for God. He is not merely one who foretells future events, but he is one who speaks forth divine truth in the energy of the Holy Spirit. This indeed characterized John the Baptist.

The Lord then definitely identified John as the one whose coming was predicted in Isaiah 40:3. He declared, "This is he of whom it is written, Behold, I send My messenger before Thy face, which shall prepare Thy way before Thee." Whatever John's doubts or those of his disciples may have been, if any, as to the Person and ministry of the Lord, because He did not immediately ascend David's throne, Jesus Himself leaves no possible doubt in the minds of those who were prepared to receive His Word, as to the identity of John himself.

He was the one whose coming had been foretold over seven hundred years before he appeared. It was given to him to herald the advent of Israel's Messiah, God's Son, the world's Redeemer.

Because of this special privilege granted to John, the last of the prophets, Jesus added, "I say unto you, Among those that are born of women there is not a greater prophet than John the Baptist." Isaiah, Jeremiah, Ezekiel, Daniel, and all the rest of the prophetic brotherhood, looked forward to the coming of Messiah, but it was given to John alone to actually present Him to Israel and proclaim Him definitely as the long-expected Deliverer.

John was the last of the Old Testament prophets. We are told elsewhere, "The law and the prophets were until John." Following him we have the bringing in of the acceptable year of the Lord, the presentation of Christ Jesus as the only Saviour, who came to establish the kingdom of God on earth. It was given to John to direct people to the King and to stand, as it were, at the open door of the kingdom and invite people to enter; but he did not live himself to go into the new dispensation and so become a member of that kingdom in the form in which it has taken since Christ came into the world. And so Jesus said, "He that is least in the kingdom of God is greater than he."

We need to remember that the terms "the kingdom of God," as used here, and "the kingdom of heaven," as used in Matthew, refer at times to two different aspects of the kingdom. They speak primarily of heaven's rule established on earth. That kingdom was offered to Israel, but rejected by them. Nevertheless, the authority of the Lord was recognized and has been recognized by millions since, and these enter into the kingdom of God in its present spiritual and mystical form. John will have his part in the coming age in the manifested kingdom, but he had no part in the kingdom as now set up in the hearts of men, while the King is on the Father's throne, awaiting His own second advent.

We have the results of John's ministry set forth in verse 29, where we are told that "all the people that heard him, and the publicans, justified God, being baptized with the baptism of John." That was a baptism unto repentance. It was the acknowledgement on the part of the baptized that they were sinners and deserved to die. In making this acknowledgment they justified God. Baptism itself had no part in their salvation. That could only be through the Lord Jesus Himself, whose great atoning work John proclaimed when he exclaimed: "Behold the Lamb of God that taketh away the sin of the world." John never taught that baptism, as such, could take away sin. His baptism was only the outward acknowledgment of the fact that men were sinners and needed a Saviour. Great multitudes in Israel listened to John with appreciation and exercise of conscience, and so received the testimony of God against themselves and humbly owned their lost condition by being baptized of John. But it was otherwise with the majority of the leaders. The Pharisees and lawyers, we are told, rejected the counsel of God against themselves, being not baptized of him. These proud, haughty legalists refused to take the place of lost, needy sinners, and so, would not stoop to a baptism which spoke of the necessity of repentance.

In the verses that follow, 31 to 35, the Lord draws a vivid contrast between the conscience-searching ministry of John the Baptist and the message of grace, which He came to proclaim. He likens the men of the generation to children sitting about in the market-place. One group of them are trying to arouse the others to take part in some childish games. First they say, as it were, "Let us play wedding," and they attempt a merry tune upon their pipes, but the others refuse to dance. Then the first group say, "Well, if you will not play wedding, let us play funeral." And so they pipe out a doleful elegy. But the others refuse to mourn. The ministry of John was more like the latter. He came with a very solemn message, calling upon people to recognize the seriousness of their condition as sinners needing a Saviour, but the Pharisees and those of their group turned away with a sneer and said, "He hath a demon." Jesus came with a more joyous message, mingling with publicans and sinners, as He proclaimed that grace and truth which offered salvation to all who would trust in Him; but the legalists turned coldly away, declaring Him to be a gluttonous man and a wine-bibber, a friend of publicans and sinners. But Jesus said, "Wisdom is justified of all her children." That is, in the wisdom of God there is a time to stress the importance of repentance; there is also a time to stress the preciousness of the grace of God, and He will be glorified in both messages and in whatever servants He uses to give them forth.

ADDRESS TWENTY-FIVE

CHRIST AND THE SINFUL WOMAN

"And one of the Pharisees desired Him that He would eat with him. And He went into the Pharisee's house, and sat down to meat. And, behold, a woman in the city, which was a sinner, when she knew that Jesus sat at meat in the Pharisee's house, brought an alabaster box of ointment, and stood at His feet behind Him weeping, and began to wash His feet with tears, and did wipe them with the hairs of her head, and kissed His feet, and anointed them with the ointment. Now when the Pharisee which had bidden Him saw it, he spake within himself, saying, This Man, if He were a prophet, would have known who and what manner of woman this is that toucheth Him: for she is a sinner. And Jesus answering said unto him. Simon, I have somewhat to say unto thee. And he saith, Master, say on. There was a certain creditor which had two debtors: the one owed five hundred pence and the other fifty. And when they had nothing to pay, he frankly forgave them both. Tell Me, therefore, which of them will love him most? Simon answered and said, I suppose he, to whom he forgave most. And He said unto him, Thou hast rightly judged. And He turned to the woman, and said unto Simon, Seest thou this woman? I entered into thine house, thou gavest Me no water for My feet: but she hath washed My feet with tears, and wiped them with the hairs of her head. Thou gavest Me no kiss: but this woman since the time I came in hath not ceased to kiss My feet. My head with oil thou didst not anoint: but this woman hath anointed My feet with ointment. Wherefore I say unto thee, Her sins, which are many, are forgiven; for she loved much: but to whom little is forgiven, the same loveth little. And He said unto her, Thy sins are forgiven. And they that sat at meat with Him began to say within themselves, Who is this that forgiveth sins also? And He said to the woman, Thy faith hath saved thee; go in peace"—Luke 7: 36-50.

HOW God delights to emphasize His grace to great sinners! It was always a matter of distress to the Pharisees that the Lord Jesus showed such a deep interest in those who were despised and outcast because of their wicked lives.

His heart went out to them. He came not to call the righteous, but sinners to repentance. I remember hearing a great evangelist say many years ago, "Oh, how hard it is to find sinners; I would be willing to go any distance to find a sinner who recognizes his need of a Saviour." We read in Proverbs 20:6, "Most men will proclaim every one his own goodness: but a faithful man who can find?" If you try to talk to most men about the Saviour and their need of Him, they will begin at once to tell you of their own merits. They try to make out a good case for themselves, covering their sins and insisting on their goodness.

In the Word of God, you will find that as long as people try to justify themselves, God cannot help them. But when they recognize their need and own their guilt, He can save them.

I have drawn attention before to the fact that in this Gospel we read of several instances where the Saviour dined out. Luke, who is presenting Jesus as the perfect Man, shows Him to us at the dinner-table. There is no place where a man relaxes and manifests his true character as when he is at the table with good friends around him and good food before him. Our Lord did not turn down invitations, even though He knew there was some ulterior motive in inviting Him. So here He accepted this Pharisee's invitation and went to his house for dinner, and had hardly reclined at the table before this interesting situation took place.

We need to remember that it was not customary for the Jews to sit up at the table in chairs like we do. The table itself was generally in the shape of a horseshoe and the guests reclined at the outside of the table, on couches. One took his place and reclined, supporting himself on his right elbow, and served himself with his left hand. Thus, servants passing about could readily wash the feet, which were farthest from the table.

Right there outside the door, a poor woman is looking in. I have no question but a number of those in the house knew who she was. She had no character, was despised by everyone, and yet she wanted to see Jesus and to seek relief from her burden of sin. Her heart was distressed and she longed for deliverance and for cleansing. We look down, perhaps, on those in sin and say, "Thank God we are not like them." But we little realize how close some of them are to the kingdom of heaven; closer than those who are self-righteous. She was an immoral woman. All down through the centuries respectable people have looked down on her kind as they looked down on her. But we need to remember that there never was a fallen woman unless some man had caused her wretched condition. He who is responsible for the poor woman's condition is accepted as a member of good society, while she who has fallen is outside. Jesus said the publicans and harlots would go into the kingdom of heaven before the hard-hearted Pharisees.

I imagine this woman was thinking, "If I could only get to Jesus, He would understand, He would know how to deal with me." Possibly, the servants were keeping their eyes on her. But she was waiting and watching and perhaps the moment the servants' backs were turned, in she slipped and there she is down on her knees at the couch where Jesus' exposed feet were. She burst into tears, and realizing her need of cleansing, she began to wash Jesus' feet with her tears and to dry them with her beautiful hair. With that lovely hair, which perhaps had lured others into her house of shame, she was now wiping the feet of Jesus. Impulsively she began to kiss His feet. This annoyed the Pharisee. Jesus perceived the thoughts of this man. "Now when the Pharisee which had bidden Him saw it, he spake within himself, saying, This Man, if He were a prophet, would have known who and what manner of woman this is that toucheth Him; for she is a sinner." I wonder how he knew so well. He knew her character. He knew the life she had lived. The Pharisee would have passed her by. Jesus did not shrink from her. He never does from any sinner. He did know what manner of woman she was who touched Him. But that was why He welcomed her. He came to redeem sinners. It rejoiced His heart when such came to Him in repentance.

He read every one of Simon's thoughts, and He knew all her thoughts. She was thinking, I am not worthy to come here, and yet He will surely do something for me. Jesus turned to Simon and just as though Simon had spoken out, He answered him: "Simon, I have somewhat to say unto thee." And Simon said, "Master, say on." Jesus answered, "There was a certain creditor which had two debtors: the one owed five hundred pence, and the other, fifty." Five hundred pence does not mean very much to us if we think of it in our own pennies, but according to the standards of those days it meant a great deal of money. There are some men who realize that they are great sinners and have broken the law of God and they feel hopeless—these are the five-hundred-pence sinners. But there are others who say that they are not very wicked, they know they have not always obeyed the law of God, but did not intend to do wrong; they have failed here and there, but in the main they are very good. These are the fifty-pence sinners.

A Sunday School teacher was speaking to her class of two kinds of sin—sins of commission and omission, and we are responsible for both. She asked, "What are sins of commission?" The children replied, "They are sins we commit." Then she inquired, "What are sins of omission?" One boy answered, "They are sins we meant to commit, and forgot to." That is not it. But every time you fail to do the thing you know you should do, this is as truly sin as the evil things you did. The fifty-pence sinners have nothing to pay, nor have the five-hundred-pence sinners. Whether you realize it or not, whether you are a great sinner, or, as you imagine, you are not much of a sinner, the fact remains, that, "There is no difference, for all have sinned and come short of the glory of God." How could you make up for your sins? That lie you told! You can never undo it! That time you took the name of God in vain! You can never atone for the wrong you did to God, and His Name. That time you fell into some great moral evil! You can never make that right, either toward God or to the one with whom you sinned. You have nothing to pay. You owe so much and you have nothing with which to pay it and you cannot settle it. What are you going to do about it? Jesus went on to say, "When they had nothing to pay, he (to whom they were indebted) frankly forgave them both." That is just a picture of the grace of God in Christ. Through the work of Jesus on Calvary, God is able to forgive every sinner who comes to Him in repentance.

A story is told of an eccentric Irish nobleman who some years ago became converted, and whose salvation was the wonder of the countryside. He was so filled with the sense of the grace of God that he began to go around preaching, and people called him "the crazy nobleman." On one occasion he posted notices to this effect, that he would be in his office from ten to twelve on a given day, and he would be prepared to settle the debts of everyone of his tenants who would come to him. Some of the folks could not read it and would ask someone else to read it to them. Many would not believe it. So they talked about it, and the days went on and finally that certain day arrived, and the people went down to his office. At ten o'clock sharp, the carriage pulled up in front of his office, and the nobleman got out and entered it with his secretary. Outside, the tenants talked among themselves as to whether he really meant it. They could hardly believe him. About half-past eleven o'clock, an old man and his aged wife came hobbling along, and the old man had a number of bills in his hand, and he asked, "Is it true that his lordship said he would pay our debts?" They replied, "Why don't you go in and try it?" He was so anxious to be free of debt that he decided to do so. He and his wife went in to see if his lordship would pay their debts. Outside, people waited anxiously to see what would happen as he handed his bills to the landlord. His lordship told his secretary to total them up and give him a check. "Oh, my lord, thank you so much! I am over eighty years old, and now my wife and I can die with our debts paid. Now we must go out and tell the rest." But the nobleman replied, "You took my offer by faith and because you believed me your debts are paid. The rest must do the same." They outside waited and wondered why the old people did not come out. Finally twelve o'clock struck, the door opened and the nobleman stepped out, and the old couple followed. The others asked the old man if he had his debts paid. He said, "Yes." Then they all crowded about pleading to have theirs paid also. But the nobleman said, "My friends, I gave you the opportunity to come, and I would have paid everything, but you would not believe me, so now you will have to pay them yourselves." He then used this illustration as a basis to preach the gospel to them. If you will not come to Christ, then there is no one to blame but yourselves if you have to face that dreadful accounting day of judgment.

"And when they had nothing to pay, he frankly forgave them both. Tell Me, therefore, which of them will love him most? Simon answered and said,

I suppose that he to whom he forgave most. And He said unto him, Thou hast rightly judged." Jesus said, "Yes, you have answered well. You are like that fifty-pence sinner, you did not think you had done much wrong, but when I came to your house, you did not do the things for Me that are done in ordinary homes. You did not have a servant wash My feet. But this woman since the time I came in hath not ceased to wash My feet with her tears. You gave Me no kiss, but this woman hath not ceased to kiss My feet. Wherefore, I say unto thee, Her sins, which are many, are forgiven; for she loved much: but to whom little is forgiven, the same loveth little." "And He said unto her, Thy sins are forgiven." Why were they forgiven? Because she washed the feet of Jesus? Because she wiped them with her hair? No, not at all. She did these things because she came to Him in repentance and this was an expression of her love for Him.

"And He said unto her, Thy sins are forgiven." Who can forgive sins but God only? "Who is this that forgiveth sins also?" they questioned among themselves. They did not understand that He was God manifested in the flesh. Ignoring them, Jesus turned to the woman and said, "Thy faith hath saved thee; go in peace." I think I see her hurrying back to her home, and saying to herself, "I must get everything cleaned up now. I must get those dirty pictures off the wall, and those vile books out of the place!" Perhaps some one saw her and noticed the different expression on her face and the change in her demeanor, and inquired the reason.

She would say, the old life was ended and a new life was beginning.

That is what Jesus does for sinners. If you have never trusted Him before, will you trust Him now? Take Him as your Saviour and you will hear Him say to you, "Your sins, which were many, are all forgiven."

Address Twenty-six

THE SOWER AND THE SEED

"And it came to pass afterward, that He went throughout every city and village, preaching and showing the glad tidings of the kingdom of God: and the twelve were with Him. And certain women, which had been healed of evil spirits and infirmities, Mary, called Magdalene, out of whom went seven devils, and Joanna, the wife of Chuza, Herod's steward, and Susanna, and many others, which ministered unto Him of their substance. And when much people were gathered together, and were come to Him out of every city, He spake by a parable: A sower went out to sow his seed: and as he sowed, some fell by the way side; and it was trodden down, and the fowls of the air devoured it. And some fell upon a rock; and as soon as it was sprung up, it withered away, because it lacked moisture. And some fell among thorns; and the thorns sprang up with it, and choked it. And other fell on good ground, and sprang up, and bare fruit an hundredfold. And when He had said these things, He cried, He that hath ears to hear, let him hear. And His disciples asked Him, saying, What might this parable be? And He said, Unto you it is given to know the mysteries of the kingdom of God: but to others in parables; that seeing they might not see, and hearing they might not understand. Now the parable is this: The seed is the Word of God. Those by the way side are they that hear; then cometh the devil, and taketh away the Word out of their hearts, lest they should believe and be saved. They on the rock are they, which, when they hear, receive the Word with joy; and these have no root, which for a while believe, and in time of temptation fall away. And that which fell among thorns are they, which, when they have heard, go forth, and are choked with cares and riches and pleasures of this life, and bring no fruit to perfection. But that on the good ground are they, which in an honest and good heart, having heard the Word, keep it, and bring forth fruit with patience"—Luke 8: 1-15.

THIS parable of the Sower and the Seed should be both a warning and an encouragement to all who endeavor to labor in the gospel: a warning against the folly of taking at face value every profession of faith in Christ, but an encouragement when many who profess prove unreal, as we remember that even when the divine-human Preacher was the Sower of the gospel seed there were many who heard in vain and who never brought forth fruit unto perfection. It is our business to sow under all circumstances (Eccles. 11: 6), knowing that the seed is incorruptible (1 Pet. 1:23), and that, though many give but momentary thought to the message, it will accomplish the purpose of God (Isa. 55: 11), and that all who hear in faith will be saved (John 5: 24).

The Word tests as well as saves. Where the heart is occupied with other things—such as the cares of this world or the deceitfulness of riches—there will be little appreciation of that message which speaks of another scene altogether and of riches that can never pass away. Where possible, the preacher is to break up the fallow ground and sow not among thorns (Jer. 4: 3). On the other hand, he is to be instant in season and out of season (2 Tim. 4: 2) even though this involves some seed falling upon hard, unprepared hearts, only to be devoured by the birds of the air, fit pictures of Satan and his demon host, who are ever on the alert to hinder the progress of the gospel, because they know that if men believe the message they will be saved. It is well, too, for those who profess faith in Christ to test themselves and make sure that their's is a faith that works by love and not mere empty credulity.

The first three verses of this portion of Scripture serve as an introduction to that which follows and give us the circumstances of Christ's setting forth the truth of God in this parable form. We are told that the Lord Jesus went about preaching and showing the gospel. He was declaring the gospel by word of mouth; He was showing the gospel by manifestation of the marvelous things that were accomplished in those who believed. That is what God is doing today.

The word of the truth of the gospel is likened to a seed because it is a living thing. It is the means God uses to produce the new birth (Jas. 1:18). The Holy Spirit causes it to fructify in the heart of the believer and so it produces fruit unto life eternal. This is not true of the proclamation of mere human theories or doctrinal systems. The preaching of the Christ has power. It is the dynamic of God unto salvation to all who believe (Rom. 1:16).

Oh, what a wonderful testimony this brings before men and women. It is our privilege not only to preach the gospel but also to show forth the power of it in redeemed lives. Here is the testimony of some who had been healed of evil spirits. They had been actually under the power of demons who had controlled and spoken and acted through them. The Lord had set them free. Mary Magdalene is mentioned first, "out of whom went seven devils." The word should be demons—"out of whom went seven demons." There is only one devil. We do not know what kind of a woman she was. There is no reason to believe that she was an unchaste woman. A great many people have tried to identify her with the woman spoken of in Luke 7, but there is no proof of this. She had been a demon-controlled woman, and she found deliverance when Jesus set her free. Then we read of Joanna, the wife of Chuza, Herod's steward, who gladly turned her back upon her place in society to become a simple, humble follower of the Lord Jesus Christ. Susanna and many others also became followers of Him, and ministered unto Him of their substance. Our Lord was a carpenter and doubtless helped to support His mother until the day when He went forth to carry out His Father's ministry. From that time on He deigned to be sustained by the gifts of those who followed Him.

When the Pharisees came one day and asked, "Is it lawful to give tribute to Caesar?" instead of drawing out a coin from His pocket, He had to ask for someone to show Him a penny. He entered into our poverty in order that He might sympathize with us. He and His disciples needed food and clothing. Where did the money come from? These dear devoted women ministered unto Him of their substance. Judas was trusted to handle the money for the group as they went about doing their work of ministry.

"And when much people were gathered together, and were come to Him out of every city, He spake by a parable." It was down by the seaside as we are told in the 13th chapter of Matthew. "A sower went out to sow his seed." Perhaps even as He talked they could see a sower on one of the hillsides. Jesus drew His illustrations from incidents of everyday life. That is why they live, and that is why they appeal still to human hearts today.

"A sower went out to sow his seed; and as he sowed, some fell by the way side; and it was trodden down, and the fowls of the air devoured it." That is a picture readily understood. A sower going out to sow, scattering precious seed as he goes up and down through the field. A great portion seems to be lost and does not bear fruit. "And it was trodden down, and the fowls of the air devoured it." The people might even see the fowls following the sower. "Some fell upon a rock, and as soon as it was sprung up, it withered away because it lacked moisture." There were many such folk on the Palestine hillsides. "Some fell among thorns." And the thorns sprang up with it, and choked it. "And other fell on good ground, and sprang up, and bare fruit an hundredfold." One little seed produces one hundred seeds! What a wonderful miracle that is! Men talk of the impossibility of miracles, but all around us there are miracles. Everywhere in nature we see wonderful evidences of the power of God. "And when He had said these things, He cried, He that hath ears to hear, let him hear." It is so possible to hear something with the outward ear but never to get it in the heart. That is the way many people listen to sermons. They hear words, but no impression is made upon the heart and conscience. If the Word of God is proclaimed, we need to listen and take it in.

When they were alone, away from the crowd, the disciples put the question to Him as to what the parable meant. They did not understand just what it was that He was telling them. "And His disciples asked Him, saying, What might this parable be? And He said, Unto you it is given to know the mysteries of the kingdom of God: but to others in parables; that seeing they might not see, and hearing they might not understand." Now that seems perhaps a little bit strange. First He tells them that they shall know if they want to know. If you want to know the gospel, you may know it. If you will only come to Him in faith, He will give you understanding. He who comes to Christ with an honest heart shall know. The mysteries of the kingdom of God are sacred secrets which the Lord delights to reveal to honest souls.

This refers to God's ways with men since His Son has been rejected. He is now making known secrets hitherto unrevealed; things kept secret from the foundation of the world. In Matthew's Gospel the term "kingdom of heaven" is used, and there only. It is never mentioned by that name in any other part of the Bible. It is Heaven's rule over the earth, to be manifested openly when our Lord returns, but now only recognized by those who are Spirit-taught. The present phase of the kingdom is the sphere of Christian profession—that which we call Christendom. In this sphere many are unreal; so these will be gathered out of His kingdom when our Lord returns (Matt. 13:41). They will then be devoted to judgment.

Our Lord used parables in order to arouse the attention of men. They would want to know the meaning if they were really interested. But of the great majority He said, "Seeing they do not see, and hearing they do not understand." So the Lord Jesus used this parabolic teaching in order to make clear things that He wanted them to understand and to challenge them. But where there was no exercise of soul the parables would only serve to harden them.

To the disciples He explains all. "The seed is the Word of God." Let us be clear about this. We are to give God's Word, not our own thoughts and imaginations. The seed is the Word and those who are children of God should sow the seed. What about the different classes of hearers? "Those by the way side are they that hear; then cometh the devil, and taketh away the Word out of their hearts, lest they should believe and be saved." They listen casually, pay attention for a few months and then become occupied with other things. "Then cometh the devil, and taketh away the Word out of their hearts, lest they should believe and be saved." You remember Paul's words to the Philippian jailor, "Believe on the Lord Jesus Christ and thou shalt be saved." People say that it is too simple; that it is too easy a way. One cannot be saved just by believing the gospel. But even the devil knows that you can! Notice what it says, "Those by the way side are they which hear; then cometh the devil, and taketh away the Word out of their hearts, lest they should believe and be saved." We are told that "he that believeth on Him hath everlasting life." Do you object to this? Stop and think what has transpired that you might have everlasting life by believing. "For God so loved the world that He gave His only begotten Son, that whosoever believeth in Him should not perish, but have everlasting life." You see you cannot separate the last part from the first part of that verse. God has already given His only Son to settle the sin question. "As Moses lifted up the serpent in the wilderness, even so must the Son of Man be lifted up." The Son of Man had to be lifted up on the cross in order that you might be saved. The devil knows this, and that is why he tries to take the Word away from you. That is why we who are servants of God are so eager to have you trust Christ at once because we know how the devil will bring in other things to try to get you not to believe. "They on the rock are they, which, when they hear, receive the Word with joy; and these have no root, which for a while believe, and in time of temptation fall away." It is not always a good sign when people seem to receive the Word with joy. A dear friend of mine told me of a young woman who was frivolous and careless all during a meeting one evening. When he returned the next night someone came up and said, "You remember that girl who was in the service last evening; well, she has found peace at last." The preacher inquired, "Did she ever find trouble?" The servant of God must present to the people the truth of God so that they may see their need of repentance, then judging themselves in the sight of God, He gives peace when they believe the Word. But when people receive the Word only with joy, it is often like the soil in which seed is sown which is just barely covering the top of the rocks. It is generally an evidence of shallowness when people who have known no real exercise about their sins profess to receive the message of the gospel with gladness. God's way is to wound that He may heal (Deut. 32:39). Men need to see their need in order to appreciate the remedy. It is a great mistake to try to lead souls to make a profession of faith in Christ who have never known what it is to face their sins in the presence of God. This is the root-cause of much of the falling away after so-called "revivals," where many, under emotional stress, or over-persuasion, have made a profession of faith, but with no conscience-exercise or repentance.

"And that which fell among thorns are they, which, when they have heard, go forth, and are choked with cares and riches and pleasures of this life, and bring no fruit to perfection." They have heard and really been quite concerned, but they are so occupied with the cares and pleasures of this life that they bring no fruit to perfection. These are people who have been interested to some extent in the gospel message, but are far more interested in the things of this life such as pleasure-seeking, money-making, and similar things. Many of these objects may be innocent enough in themselves, but if you become so occupied with them that you forget your responsibility to God, you will be sorry all through eternity that you did not put the things of the Lord first.

"But that on the good ground are they, which in an honest and good heart, having heard the Word, keep it and bring forth fruit with patience." An honest and good heart! Does not the Bible say that the heart is deceitful above all things and desperately wicked? What then is meant by a good and honest heart? It means one who knows he is wrong but by the grace of God is going to get right, a person who says, "I know I have been wrong and occupied with the wrong things, but I am going to face these things and acknowledge my sins and confess them to God." When a man takes that stand, then he is honest before God.

When a man condemns himself and says, "I have sinned," then the rest is easy. At last he has reached the place where God can justify him.

The four classes of hearers are found wherever the gospel is preached. Some pay no attention and the devil plucks away the good seed. Some give apparent heed, but there is no realization of their guilty condition before God. They accept the gospel mentally, even gladly, but soon give evidence that there was no conscience-exercise. Others are seriously perturbed and appear to be earnest believers, but the things of this world are soon seen to be far more important in their eyes than spiritual realities. A fourth group face their true condition before God, confess their sinfulness and acknowledge their guilt. Trusting in Christ they enter into peace, a peace that abides, and the fruits of which are seen in the life.

The seed is the same in each instance. It is the attitude of the hearer that is different. Some are utterly careless, others effervescent and easily moved, but vacillating. Others again are in earnest to begin with, but allow other interests to crowd out spiritual things. Then there are those who are seeking to know God and are ready to receive His Word when it is presented to them. These bear fruit to perfection, and so glorify the Father. Fruit-bearing is the proof of spiritual life. If there be no fruit, profession is a mere sham, as the after-experience will soon make manifest.

ADDRESS TWENTY-SEVEN

SHINING FOR GOD

✝ ✝ ✝

"No man, when he hath lighted a candle, covereth it with a vessel, or putteth it under a bed; but setteth it on a candlestick, that they which enter in may see the light. For nothing is secret, that shall not be made manifest; neither any thing hid, that shall not be known and come abroad. Take heed therefore how ye hear; for whosoever hath, to him shall be given; and whosoever hath not, from him shall be taken even that which he seemeth to have. Then came to Him His mother and His brethren, and could not come at Him for the press. And it was told Him by certain which said, Thy mother and Thy brethren stand without, desiring to see Thee. And He answered and said unto them, My mother and My brethren are these which hear the Word of God, and do it"—Luke 8: 16-21.

✝ ✝ ✝

EVERY believer is called on to witness for Christ; he is to let his light shine before men. Our Lord Jesus uses here an illustration of which He was evidently very fond. We get hold of certain illustrations that seem to have weight, and help to clarify the truth which we are giving out, and these illustrations we are apt to use again and again as occasion arises. We all recognize our Lord as the Master-Teacher, and it is interesting to note how wonderfully He illustrated His addresses. Some preachers today are averse to such a method, but they need to remember that in criticizing the method they are, whether consciously or not, criticizing the Lord Himself. Spurgeon has said, "The sermon is the house, the illustrations are the windows that let the light in." Our Lord never told stories just for the sake of stirring up the emotions of His hearers; every such incident was a parable, even though it was actually true in fact. We are told that without a parable spake He not unto them. He had a double purpose of using these parables: in the first place, many of them helped to make clear the truth He was seeking to impart; and in the second place, they were a challenge to His hearers, testing them as to whether or not they had any real interest in the truth. If unconcerned, they would listen to the story and go carelessly on their way, paying no further attention to it; if really exercised, they would inquire as to the meaning He wished to convey. We see this frequently in connection with the apostles who came to Him, asking the meaning of stories or illustrations He used. Most of His illustrations had to do with things that were exceedingly commonplace and well-known. It was thus with that of the candle or lamp-stand, which He used on several occasions. We need to learn that the candle was not such as we know, but the word really means one of those metal or pottery lamps which many of us have often seen in pictures or in museums, the bowl of which is filled with olive oil, and a wick protrudes through the spout. When this wick is lighted the lamp (or candle) is placed upon a lamp-stand, or in some other prominent position, in order to illumine the house. So Jesus says, "No man, when he hath lighted a candle, covereth it with a vessel, or putteth it under a bed; but setteth it on a candlestick, that they which enter in may see the light." This is very suggestive. Elsewhere He speaks of hiding the light under a bushel, which answers to the vessel here. Now the bushel naturally reminds us of business, since it was used to measure food; and many Christians, I fear, have hidden their lights under a bushel; they have allowed their business to so occupy them that they have failed to witness for Christ as they should. You may have sometimes heard the expression, "I never mix my religion with my business." Well, it is a very sad thing if you do not, because you are failing altogether in being the kind of business-man the Lord expects you to be. All Christians are not called upon to take an official place, as ministers or public teachers, but God needs Christian business-men to shine for Him. I am always so thankful when I hear people say of some of my brethren who are engaged in various commercial lines, "I have known Mr. So-and-So for years, and I could trust him anywhere; he carries his Christianity into his business." This is letting one's light shine for God in his daily life. A professed Christian who tries to carry on his business without giving Christ the rightful place in his life is a failure.

Then our Lord suggests the possibility of hiding the light under a bed. Now the bed, of course, speaks of taking one's ease. Have we not known many like that? They are interested in the things of God so long as those things do not interfere with their own comfort. How many forget that Sunday is, in a very definite sense, the Lord's Day, and yet they will stay out late on Saturday night, wear themselves out in business or pleasure, and then lie in bed on Sunday morning until it is too late to gather with the people of God, on the plea that they must have rest for body and mind. Surely, a little forethought would suggest carefully conserving the last hours of the week in order that one might be at his best on the Lord's Day, to use the full time for God in such a way as to bring glory to His name by participating in the worship of His people and in the various activities connected with the gospel testimony. It is so easy to hide one's light under the bed and excuse oneself on the ground of physical weariness. Many might have far more active participation in the things of Christ if it were not for slothfulness. I would to God that we Christians might be as much in earnest about witnessing for Christ as are the devil's embassies in serving him. What a stir there often is when a gospel meeting runs over nine o'clock, and yet worldlings can be out at the theatre, or other ungodly places, until midnight and think nothing of it. It is a shame that Christians are so slack in manifesting devotion to Christ. In studying Chinese years ago, I noticed that one of the Chinese characters for "evil" is made up in this way: the upper part is for that which is secondary, and the lower part is the ideogram for "heart;" the meaning is that when that which is highest is given secondary place, it results in evil. May we not all challenge our hearts as to whether we give Christ the first place and make the things of God our immediate aim; or whether, after all, we think first of our own comfort and put the things of God in a secondary place. Our Lord tells us that "nothing is secret, that shall not be made manifest; neither any thing hid, that shall not be known and come abroad." Elsewhere we are told that some day we must all appear before the judgment-seat of Christ in that solemn day when all the purposes of the heart are manifest. How many of us will look back with grief on our lack of real devotion to Christ when we were in this scene! What we need to do is to live more and more in the light of that day of manifestation.

Next we have a word from the Lord to His followers concerning discipleship: "Take heed therefore how ye hear: for whosoever hath, to him shall be given; and whosoever hath not, from him shall be taken even that which he seemeth to have." There are many indifferent hearers; there are people who listen with the outward ear but do not really hear the message at all. We need to remember the sevenfold challenge in the book of Revelation: "He that hath an ear, let him hear." We should listen to the Word of God as the very message of the Lord Himself to our own souls; to do otherwise is to insult Him who thus speaks to us for our instruction and obedience. On the other hand, we need to be careful about listening to that which is false. In the book of Proverbs we read, "Cease, my son, to hear the instruction that causeth to err from the words of knowledge." If men profess to be servants of Christ and yet deny the great truths of Holy Scripture, God holds us responsible. If we continue to listen to such deniers, we not only waste time by doing this but we dishonor God whose Word is thus rejected.

The Lord Jesus stresses the importance of using aright that which is communicated to us: "Take heed therefore how ye hear: for whosoever hath, to him shall be given; and whosoever hath not, from him shall be taken even that which he seemeth to have." It is a very easy thing to become an utter pauper, spiritually, and yet to be quite unconscious of one's true condition. We have an example of that in the Laodicean church, the members of which said, "I am rich, and increased with goods, and have need of nothing;" but the Lord, you remember, said to them, "Knowest not that thou art wretched, and miserable, and poor, and blind, and naked?" They thought everything was well and that they were rich in every way, when, actually, everything was wrong with them. They were in deepest spiritual poverty, because they were not appropriating the riches of grace which God had put at their disposal. So it is with the one who fails to hear and heed the Word of God, and yet congratulates himself on being in a good spiritual frame of mind.

While our Lord was giving this instruction to His hearers, an incident occurred which emphasized the importance of the very thing He was stressing. Someone came suddenly up and interrupted Him, "Thy mother and Thy brethren stand without, desiring to see Thee." Some people, you know, have no sense of the proper time and place for things, they think nothing of interrupting even the most precious unfolding of divine truth; it is often hard for preachers to bear such interruptions. One is inclined to become impatient, but it was otherwise with our blessed Lord. Instead of stopping to greet His loved ones or reprove the one who came to apprize Him of their presence, He used this as a means of pressing home the truth He had been uttering: "My mother, and My brethren are these which hear the Word of God, and do it." I think I see Him raising His hands and looking out upon that audience as He exclaims, "These are My mother and My brethren." Those who love God's truth belong to Him in a peculiar way, they are His intimate relatives. Are you and I numbered among them? On another occasion He said to His disciples, "Ye are My friends, if ye do whatsoever I command you." How precious to be a friend of His, to be one who delights in His company and who seeks to obey His Word!

It is true we are saved by grace alone. We could not do anything to merit our salvation; no work of ours could avail to blot out even one sin, but He who has saved us is now looking for good works in us. He said, "Let your light so shine before men, that they may see your good works, and glorify your Father which is in heaven." We who have believed in God are responsible to be careful to maintain good works. This is the test of discipleship. It is in this way that we shine for Christ, letting the world realize how much He means to us. Perhaps I am speaking to some today who have never yet trusted the Lord Jesus Christ; if so, I plead with you, take heed how ye hear! The Word says, "Hear, and your soul shall live." I remember a lady who said to me years ago, "I went to church all my life but I never heard a sermon till I was fifty-eight years of age." I inquired whether she had been physically deaf. "Oh, no;" she replied; "I sat in church, took part in the singing and listened to the sermons, but I never really heard one in my own soul until one day, for the first time, I realized the message was for me. When the preacher talked of sinners, I used to wonder what wicked people were in the church-building; when he talked of saints, I couldn't imagine who might be there good enough to be so designated. But I'll never forget the time when I realized that I was a lost sinner and needed a Saviour. Then my heart was opened, and I listened earnestly in order to find out how I might be saved, and as the gospel was proclaimed I received it in faith, and ever since I have known the Lord for myself." Jesus said, "Verily, verily, I say unto you, He that heareth My word, and believeth on Him that sent Me, hath everlasting life, and shall not come into condemnation; but is passed from death unto life." Have you heard Him in the gospel message? As Christians we need to have our ears attentive to His Word day after day that we may learn His will for us, and so manifest our discipleship as we walk in obedience to His truth.

"While I live will I praise the Lord: I will sing praises unto my God while I have any being" (Ps. 146:2).

Address Twenty-eight

LORD OF THE WINDS AND WAVES

** * **

"Now it came to pass on a certain day, that He went into a ship with His disciples: and He said unto them, Let us go over unto the other side of the lake. And they launched forth. But as they sailed He fell asleep: and there came down a storm of wind on the lake; and they were filled with water, and were in jeopardy. And they came to Him, and awoke Him, saying, Master, master, we perish. Then He arose, and rebuked the wind and the raging of the water: and they ceased, and there was a calm. And He said unto them, Where is your faith? And they being afraid wondered, saying one to another, What manner of man is this! for He commandeth even the winds and the water, and they obey Him"—Luke 8: 22-25.

** * **

BEFORE our Lord went away He said to His disciples, "Verily, verily, I say unto you, he that believeth on Me, the works that I do shall he do also; and greater works than these shall he do; because I go unto My Father." Many have understood from those words that we as Christians would be able to do greater miracles than He did. If that were what He meant, then the centuries since have proved that His words have failed. So far as the things of nature are concerned there have never been any miracles so great as those which He performed when He was here on earth.

Very frequently God has come in, in grace and healed sick ones, and in answer to the prayers of faith, has often wrought most blessedly, but we have never known of anything like that which is recorded here.

The greatest miracle that our Lord performed in regard to the natural world was this one, when He rose up in that boat and commanded the winds to cease and the waves to be still. He manifested His power as Lord of all creation in a way that no one else has ever surpassed or duplicated. His greatest miracle in regard to the human body was the raising of Lazarus. The little child, the daughter of Jairus, had barely closed her eyes when Jesus came and woke her; the son of the widow of Nain had but lately died and his body was being carried to the tomb; but Lazarus had been dead four days and corruption had already begun, when our Lord came to that sepulchre, and in response to His command, Lazarus came forth alive. That was the greatest miracle Jesus ever performed so far as the human body was concerned.

No one else has ever stilled the waves as Jesus did; no one else has ever raised to life one who had been dead four days. Certainly, then, our Lord did not mean that we were to perform miracles like He did, or greater than He did while He was on this earth. It must, therefore, I take it, be in the realm of the spiritual that works are to be wrought which are greater than those our Saviour accomplished when here on earth. No one who came to Him for physical healing was turned away. He opened the eyes of the blind; unstopped the ears of the deaf; loosed the tongue of the dumb; cleansed the lepers; made the lame man to leap as the hart; provided bread in the wilderness for thousands of people; and, in many other ways manifested His mighty power, witnessing to His Messianic claims. But the amazing thing is, that after all His wondrous works and claims, so few received Him in faith and confessed Him as Messiah and trusted Him as Saviour. After those three and one-half wonderful years of His ministry, we read, only a few hundred gave evidence of personal faith in Him. When He rose from the dead there were some five hundred brethren at the last who gathered about Him, and saw for themselves that He was alive again. Where were all the rest who had heard Him preach, and seen His miracles as He went through Judaea, Galilee, Samaria, and Perea, preaching, teaching, and healing the sick? Doubtless here and there, there were individuals who had trusted Him and were not found with that throng at the last, but comparatively few in Israel had owned His claims and definitely committed themselves to Him, by receiving Him as their Redeemer. But think of what has taken place since: On Pentecost three thousand received the message and were baptized in His name; a few days later, we are told, the number of those that believed became about five thousand; then, as the months and years went on, vast numbers of Jews, and later of Gentiles, accepted the testimony of the gospel and were saved through His matchless grace. All down through the centuries since, millions have come to know Him. Within three centuries after the Twelve first went forth to preach, the idolatry of the Roman Empire was practically destroyed. I do not mean that people everywhere had become Christians, but that Christianity had become the dominant religion, and paganism had almost disappeared throughout the land surrounding the Mediterranean. Some lives since have been a marvelous demonstration of the truth of our Lord's words: "Greater things than these shall ye do, because I go to the Father."

Let us then consider with some degree of care this wonderful account of our Lord's authority over nature. While an actual fact, it is also a beautiful parable, a lovely picture, and brings before us the power of our Saviour to give deliverance under the most difficult and pressing circumstances.

We have first of all a definite, divine purpose here in ver. 22. Our Lord was not acting haphazardly. "Now it came to pass on a certain day, that He went into a ship with His disciples: and He said unto them, Let us go over unto the other side of the lake. And they launched forth." Notice the words, "Let us go over." He knew what He was about to do; His plans were made, and He was going to the other side of the lake to minister there, and taking His disciples with Him. How suggestive this is! We do not know what dangers and difficulties we have to face and what hidden rocks and shoals are ahead of us as we go through life, but we do know our Saviour, and we may be sure He will carry out His purpose and will see us safely over to the other side.

In the words of the closing verses of that wonderful eighth chapter of the Epistle to the Romans, every believer can say, "For I am persuaded, that neither death, nor life, nor angels, nor principalities, nor powers, nor things present, nor things to come, nor height, nor depth, nor any other creature, shall be able to separate us from the love of God, which is in Christ Jesus our Lord."

His love will never be satisfied until all His own are at home with the Lord Himself in the glory. Every Christian should be able, therefore, to say, "I know whom I have believed and am persuaded that He is able to keep that which I have committed unto Him against that day." It is a great thing to rest on the promises of God, and to know that He who has begun a good work in us will perform it until the day of Christ.

He has already gone to the Father's house, and yet He abides with us in the power of the Holy Spirit. He is going to take us through all the perplexing circumstances of the voyage of life until we are landed safely on the other side.

I remember the early years of my Christian experience when I knew that the Lord was with me for the moment, but did not know that He was to be with me forever. I would dread what might happen which would separate me, perhaps, forever from the love of God. I felt somewhat like that Irishman who had been converted, and one day the awful thought came to him, "Suppose I fall into sin and I lose it all!" He felt it would be better never to have been converted at all. One day in church the preacher read, "If ye then be risen with Christ, seek those things which are above, where

Christ sitteth on the right hand of God, for ye are dead, and your life is hid with Christ in God." Pat forgot for a moment where he was, and shouted, "Glory to God! Whoever heard of a man drowning with his head that high above water!" So we can praise Him for every evidence of His love and care, knowing He will see us through to the end.

Notice, in the next place, our Lord's quiet serenity. He was in perfect peace in the midst of the storm. That which caused such distress to His disciples and filled them with terror, did not in the slightest degree disturb His heart. He knew that Satan, the prince of the power of the air, had raised that storm in order to seek to destroy Him before He could go to the cross and accomplish the work of redemption, but there was no possibility of the enemy's plans being carried out. We are told that "as they sailed He fell asleep: and there came down a storm of wind on the lake; and they were filled with water, and were in jeopardy." The angry wind and fierce gale seemed as though they would wreck the little boat, and yet, there lay the blessed Lord, sound asleep. Mark tells us He was asleep on a pillow. I wonder if some kind, loving woman, who had been blessed through His ministry, had not made that pillow for Him and given it to Him. At any rate, there He lay undisturbed; no anxiety, no fear whatever, because He knew that all nature was subject to Him, and as Man here on earth, He rested implicitly in the consciousness of subjection to the Father's will. Oh, that you and I might enter into the same peace and rest that characterized Him! We may if we take heed to the words: "Be careful for nothing; but in everything by prayer and supplication with thanksgiving let your requests be made known unto God. And the peace of God, which passeth all understanding, shall keep your hearts and minds through Christ Jesus."

ADDRESS TWENTY-NINE

CHRIST TRIUMPHS OVER DEMONS

✝ ✝ ✝

"And they arrived at the country of the Gadarenes, which is over against Galilee. And when He went forth to land, there met Him out of the city a certain man, which had devils long time, and ware no clothes, neither abode in any house, but in the tombs. When he saw Jesus, he cried out, and fell down before Him, and with a loud voice said, What have I to do with Thee, Jesus, Thou Son of God most high? I beseech Thee, torment me not. (For He had commanded the unclean spirit to come out of the man. For oftentimes it had caught him; and he was kept bound with chains and in fetters; and he brake the bands, and was driven of the devil into the wilderness.) And Jesus asked him, saying, What is thy name? And he said, Legion: because many devils were entered into him. And they besought Him that He would not command them to go out into the deep. And there was there an herd of many swine feeding on the mountain: and they besought Him that He would suffer them to enter into them. And He suffered them. Then went the devils out of the man, and entered into the swine: and the herd ran violently down a steep place into the lake, and were choked. When they that fed them saw what was done, they fled, and went and told it in the city and in the country. Then they went out to see what was done; and came to Jesus, and found the man, out of whom the devils were departed, sitting at the feet of Jesus, clothed, and in his right mind: and they were afraid. They also which saw it told them by what means he that was possessed of the devils was healed. Then the whole multitude of the country of the Gadarenes round about besought Him to depart from them; for they were taken with great fear: and He went up into the ship, and returned back again. Now the man out of whom the devils were departed besought Him that he might be with Him: but Jesus sent him away, saying, Return to thine own house, and shew how great things God hath done unto thee. And he went his way, and published throughout the whole city how great things Jesus had done unto him. And it came to pass, that, when Jesus was returned, the people gladly received Him: for they were all waiting for Him"—Luke 8: 26-40.

THIS is one of the many passages which bring our blessed Lord before us as absolute Victor over satanic power. Many people today refuse to accept the Bible teaching as to the personality of Satan and his hosts. Many think of the devil as simply the personification of evil, but the Word of God shows us clearly that he who is now the devil was at one time a pure spirit, a holy angel, attendant on the throne of God, but who fell through pride. Jesus says of him: "He abode not in the truth." It is evident that many other angels were involved in his rebellion and are now in league with him in his opposition to God and Christ. There is only one devil, but there are many demons. When, therefore, the plural form "devils" is used in the New Testament records, it should always be understood as referring to demons, for it is a translation of the Greek word which means just that, rather than devils.

In our Lord's earthly ministry He frequently met with people who were under demoniacal possession. We might not be able to understand fully what was involved in this terrible power over men and women, but we know that our Lord was always victorious over it.

Here we learn that when Jesus had arrived at the country of the Gadarenes, which is over against Galilee, a man met Him whose dwelling was in the tombs, who was possessed with, not one, but many demons. Gadara itself was a rather forbidding country, outside the land of Canaan proper, and inhabited by a mixed population. Many of the people were renegade Jews who engaged in customs that were repellent to the more orthodox, some even raising and selling swine. It is evident that the power of Satan was more manifest among these people than in the Land itself. Note the dreadful condition of this possessed creature. Luke tells us he "had devils (or demons) long time, and ware no clothes, neither abode in any house, but in the tombs." He is a picture of fallen man under absolute satanic control. Again and again his friends had tried to restrain him from the power that had imprisoned and bound him, but by superhuman power he snapped his shackles asunder and fled from the ordinary dwelling-places of men and found a refuge for himself among the dead in the tombs.

It is a terrible thing when Satan gets such control of a man that he is no longer amenable to respectability, or even decent restraint; when evil habits so dominate and control that one is outside the pale of ordinary law-abiding circumstances. Yet how many are thus subject to sin and Satan.

We do not know in what way the demons fully gained control of this poor man, but it is evident that sometime or other in his early life, he had opened the door to them; perhaps, by persistence in sins that the law of God condemned, and as a result he was a slave to these evil spirits and had lost the power to control himself.

His friends could do nothing with him. If his parents were living, their hearts must have been broken as they saw him in this hopeless condition. But the day at last came when he was brought into contact with our blessed Lord Himself, and then everything was changed. Jesus was the only One who could help him, and He was there for that very purpose. It is evident that the demons within him recognized the Lord at once, for we are told that when this man saw Jesus, "he cried out, and fell down before Him, and with a loud voice said, What have I to do with Thee, Jesus, Thou Son of God most high? I beseech Thee, torment me not." The demon was speaking through human lips. This unholy, fallen spirit knew exactly who Jesus was; he recognized in Jesus, the Son of God who shall yet sit on the throne of judgment, and already he feared the hour had come when he was to be cast into the lake of fire. The demons all believed that Jesus was the Christ, it was only unrepentant men who questioned this; Satan himself knew that Jesus was the Son of God, the only Saviour. The only persons in the universe who dare to deny that Jesus is the Son of God are Christless men and women who are yet the objects of His favor. But while demons acknowledge that Jesus is the Son of God, they are not entitled to find in Him a Saviour for themselves. The demon in this man recognized Christ as the Judge, and pleaded for an extension of time ere his doom would be consummated. Jesus did not really answer his question, but put another question to this vile spirit: "What is thy name?" He demanded. And the answer came, "Legion;" because we are told, many demons were entered into him. A

Roman legion was ordinarily made up of six thousand men. Perhaps we need not take the legion here literally, but at any rate it indicates that a vast number of demons had entered into this man. He himself was unable to reply personally because he was so completely under their control.

It would seem that these demons, who are disembodied spirits, yearn to come into possession of the bodies of men in order that they may stir them up into unlofty and dreadful passion, which will cause them to insult the God who created them. When the Lord Jesus commanded the legion to leave the body of the man, they begged to be able to take possession of the bodies of a herd of swine which was feeding nearby. The Lord gave consent. Expelled from the man they "entered into the swine: and (note the amazing result) the herd ran violently down a steep place into the lake, and were choked." How amazing is sinful man's ability for evil! Two thousand hogs could not hold the demons that had possessed one man.

Instead of this remarkable evidence of the Lord's power over Satan's kingdom making an impression for good upon the hearts of those who beheld what was done, we are told that "they fled, and went and told it in the city and in the country." They related to their fellow-countrymen the story of the loss of the swine, as well as the deliverance of the demoniac. So troubled were these people by the financial setback involved that after they had come out to see what was done, we are told they "came to Jesus, and found the man, out of whom the devils were departed, sitting at the feet of Jesus, clothed, and in his right mind: and they were afraid." What then? Did they fall at His feet confessing their own sins and seeking deliverance through Him? Not at all! It was the very opposite. They besought Jesus to leave their country. Sorrowfully, we may be sure, He acceded to their request. Luke says, "Then the whole multitude of the country of the Gadarenes round about besought Him to depart from them; for they were taken with great fear: and He went up into the ship, and returned back again." Jesus never remains with people who do not want Him. Men are permitted to choose in such circumstances whether they will receive Him or not. But though He left these Gadarenes at that particular time, we can be thankful to the Lord that the day did come when He returned to the same country and found a wonderful welcome. It was brought about in this way: The delivered man was so happy over the great change that had come to him that he pleaded with the Lord Jesus that he might be with Him. This man would have joined the company of the apostles and gone with the Saviour from place to place. Evidently his heart was so filled with love and gratitude because of his miraculous deliverance that he wanted to remain as near his Redeemer as he could; but Jesus had something else in mind for him. Instead of taking him away with Him, He said to the man, "Return to thine own house, and show how great things God hath done unto thee." He who had been a raving maniac a short while before was now so reasonable that the people listened to him with amazement. He became an evangelist, and went throughout all that region telling the throngs of what Jesus had done for him; from village to village his story was carried. And so, we learn that later on when Jesus went back to that district, known as Decapolis, the multitudes thronged to meet Him and their entire attitude was changed. They did not want Him before; they were too occupied with the loss of their swine and with other evil things which kept them from opening their hearts to Him, but now they were glad to see Him. They brought out their sick in great numbers, and in loving-kindness He healed them all.

Such was the result of the faithful testimony of one man set free from Satan's power by Christ the Lord.

ADDRESS THIRTY

CHRIST TRIUMPHS OVER SICKNESS AND DEATH

✝ ✝ ✝

"And behold, there came a man named Jairus, and he was a ruler of the synagogue: and he fell down at Jesus' feet, and besought Him that He would come into his house: for he had one only daughter, about twelve years of age, and she lay a dying. But as He went the people thronged Him. And a woman having an issue of blood twelve years, which had spent all her living upon physicians, neither could be healed of any, came behind Him, and touched the border of His garment: and immediately her issue of blood stanched. And Jesus said, Who touched Me? When all denied, Peter and they that were with him said, Master, the multitude throng Thee and press Thee, and sayest Thou, Who touched Me? And Jesus said, Somebody hath touched Me: for I perceive that virtue is gone out of Me. And when the woman saw that she was not hid, she came trembling, and falling down before Him, she declared unto Him before all the people for what cause she had touched Him, and how she was healed immediately. And He said unto her, Daughter, be of good comfort: thy faith hath made thee whole; go in peace. While He yet spake, there cometh one from the ruler of the synagogue's house, saying to him, Thy daughter is dead; trouble not the Master. But when Jesus heart it, He answered him, saying, Fear not: believe only, and she shall be made whole. And when He came into the house, He suffered no man to go in, save Peter, and James, and John, and the father and the mother of the maiden. And all wept, and bewailed her: but He said, Weep not; she is not dead, but sleepeth. And they laughed Him to scorn, knowing that she was dead. And He put them all out, and took her by the hand, and called, saying, Maid, arise. And her spirit came again, and she arose straightway: and He commanded to give her meat. And her parents were astonished: but He charged them that they should tell no man what was done"—Luke 8: 41-56.

✝ ✝ ✝

THERE are two incidents in this passage of Scripture which are closely connected. Jairus was the ruler of the synagogue, that synagogue which had been built for the Jews by a Roman centurion, whose ruins have been recently discovered, and are still to be seen. The ruler, with a sad heart, came and fell down at Jesus' feet. He had only one daughter, about twelve years of age. I imagine every parent of a sick daughter can share his feeling. This daughter was the light of her father's eyes and the joy of his soul. It seemed as though no power on earth could save her. But Jairus believed that Jesus had power and could heal his daughter, therefore he sought Him out, and in an attitude of supplication, pleaded with Him to come to his house and heal his daughter. The Saviour immediately started to go with him. On the way, as the crowd thronged Him, a woman who was suffering from a constitutional illness, having heard that Jesus was in the way, said in her heart, "Perhaps He could do something for me." So she endeavored to reach Him.

It is a remarkable fact that Luke the physician should write that this woman had spent all her living upon physicians. Many of the physicians were of an honorable character, but they could not heal her. Luke recognized the case and the futility of it. She had suffered from the use of all kinds of medicines and drugs of those days which were used in her type of disease; she "had suffered many things of many physicians," Mark records, but found no relief; rather, she became steadily worse.

When she learned that Jesus was in the city, she recalled the many instances in which He was reported to have healed people suffering from all kinds of illnesses. Faith sprang up in her soul, and she determined to contact Him. He is the Great Physician. No one came to Him for healing on earth and was rejected. His power is just the same now: Jesus Christ the same yesterday, today, and forever. He who of old could speak the word and even death would flee before Him, is still Lord over sickness and death. On the other hand, it is well to remember that there is no promise in Scripture that He will always deliver those today who come to Him suffering from physical ailments. If this were true, no Christian need ever be sick. Sometimes, instead of healing, He does something better, as in the case of Paul, who sought deliverance from the thorn in the flesh which was causing him so much physical anguish. The Lord said, as it were, I will not free you from suffering, Paul, but I will give you grace to bear it. Some day He will come in glory and we will be delivered from all the effects of sin, sickness, and suffering of every description. That will be the day of the redemption of the body, when these bodies of our humiliation will be made like unto His body of glory. But even now we are at liberty to come to Him and ask Him to heal us, and to pray one for another that we may be healed; but always in subjection to His holy will. It was in this spirit that Jairus came to Him, and in the same way this poor woman sought to get in touch with Him.

Evidently she shrank from coming out in the open and telling her story, knowing that all those people were looking on; but she said within herself, "If I can only touch the hem of His garment I shall be healed." Every orthodox Jew wore a blue border on his garment in accordance with the instructions given in the law of Moses, which indicated that he belonged to the God of heaven. This blue border, undoubtedly, was seen upon the garment of our blessed Lord, who was subjected to the law of God in all things. And so, this poor, sick woman, pressing her way through the crowd and reaching out her trembling hand, touched that blue border; and in a moment she felt in her body that she was free of her disease. Filled with thankfulness to God, she would doubtless have returned to her own home to fall down before Him in prayer and give Him glory for what He had done for her through the Lord Jesus Christ, but our Saviour did not permit her to go away privately. Jesus turned about and asked, "Who touched Me?" All denied, and we are told "Peter and they that were with him said, Master, the multitude throng Thee and press Thee, and sayest Thou, Who touched Me?" It was as though they would reprove Him because of His apparently unreasonable question. With so many people crowding about Him, He must have been touched by numbers of them; but He drew a very definite distinction between the thronging, and touching Him in faith. He replied, "Somebody hath touched Me: for I perceive that virtue is gone out of Me." Notice that whenever the blessed Lord healed anyone, He entered with them into their troubles and pains. That is what Isaiah meant when he said, "Himself took our infirmities and bare our sicknesses." It was not on the cross that He did this but in His life here on earth, as He went about doing good and healing all who came to Him. It cost Him something to deliver people from their sicknesses; He took the burdens, as it were, the suffering, and the grief upon Himself; and so, literally, He gave of Himself in order that they might be healed.

We are told that when the woman saw she was not hid, "she came trembling, and falling down before Him, she declared unto Him before all the people for what cause she had touched Him, and how she was healed immediately." It was a wonderful testimony to His power and compassion, and no doubt, brought a great blessing to this woman's own soul when she made her open confession. It always brings blessing when one confesses the goodness of the Lord; that is why we are told in Romans: "That if thou shalt confess with thy mouth the Lord Jesus, and shalt believe in thine heart that God hath raised Him from the dead, thou shalt be saved. For with the heart man believeth unto righteousness; and with the mouth confession is made unto salvation."

In this instance the Lord Jesus, having heard the healed woman's grateful acknowledgment, said to her tenderly, "Daughter, be of good comfort: thy faith hath made thee whole; go in peace." What blessed assurance these words must have given her, added to the thrill that had gone through her body when she had touched the garment of Jesus. She knew her healing was complete and she was never again to suffer what she had in the past, for she had contacted the Great Healer Himself. Her case is a beautiful illustration of how men and women today, afflicted with the incurable disease of sin, may find deliverance when they reach out their hands in faith and touch the blessed Lord Himself. Reformation will not give this deliverance, neither will joining the church, nor participation in sacramental observances; but Jesus Himself received in faith gives immediate salvation. We cannot see Him now with the visible eye, but He is close beside us nevertheless, near enough for us to reach Him in faith. For that which is seen is not faith: faith consists in taking Him at His word, even though our mortal eyes do not behold Him. He stands beside every sickbed; He is present in every prison-cell; He walks through the mart of commerce; He passes up and down the aisles of every school-room; He is close at hand in every home; and He says, as it were, to every troubled soul: "Just reach out the hand of faith and trust Me; I will make you whole." Think of His words uttered so long ago to a weary, restless world, "Come unto Me, all ye that labor and are heavy laden, and I will give you rest."

If these words come to any who have not yet contacted Him, I plead with you, even now, look up in faith into His blessed face and trust Him for yourself, and hear Him say, "Be of good comfort: thy faith hath made thee whole; go in peace."

But now we turn to consider the second incident in the passage we have before us. We read that while the Lord was on His way to the house of Jairus, one came from that home, saying, "Thy daughter is dead; trouble not the Master." In other words, it was a sad message. It is now too late for Jesus to do anything—if He had gotten there before He might have helped, but now the little one is dead and nothing more can be done. But they were to learn that it is never too late for Jesus; it is never too late for Him to hear the prayer of faith. Jairus had come to Him with earnest purpose of heart, counting on Him to heal his little girl. It looked as though all hope was gone, but he was soon to realize that not only has Jesus power to deliver from sickness, but He is Himself the resurrection and the life. He spoke words of quiet assurance to give rest to that anxious father, "Fear not: believe only, and she shall be made whole." I wish I could so stress those four words, "Fear not: believe only," with such power that any beholding them might feel their force and look up in faith to Jesus. It is so easy to become concerned about the perplexing things of life and the sorrows that we have, that we lose sight of the blessed Saviour and forget that we have to do with One who is omnipotent. If Jesus cannot help in every time of trouble, He is not the Saviour whose coming the prophets of old had predicted; but, He has demonstrated over and over again His power to give deliverance to all who believe His Word.

If these words come to anyone who is suffering because of bereavement, or of a broken home, or on account of wayward children, or severe sickness, or great sorrow, let me plead with you to look up to Him who says, "Fear not: believe only," and be assured that He will undertake for you. You wrong your own soul if you do not bring your griefs to Him.

It is well to remember that nothing takes our blessed Lord by surprise. When He started for the house of Jairus, He knew exactly all that was going to take place. He knew the little girl would die before He reached the home, but He was going there to restore that child to her parents. So when He came to the place of mourning death fled away, as it will when Jesus comes again to call His own to be with Himself, when death will be swallowed up in victory.

Entering the house, the Lord Jesus took with Him Peter, James, and John into the room where the body of the little girl lay. Hired mourners had already been brought in, and in their oriental fashion, they were wailing and weeping and making a great deal of noise and confusion; but the Lord Jesus bade them leave, saying, "Weep not; she is not dead, but sleepeth." Unwillingly they left the room, laughing Him to scorn, we are told, knowing in their hearts that she was dead. They did not understand that all live unto Him; that even though the body may be dead He recognizes the spirit as alive, and He saw in the cold form of that little girl, just a sleeping child soon to be awakened. To Him death was only that. When Lazarus died, you remember, the Lord Jesus said to His disciples, Lazarus sleepeth; but I go, that I may awake him out of sleep." The disciples did not understand and they said, "Lord, if he sleep, he shall do well."

Then Jesus said plainly, "Lazarus is dead." And so He said of the little girl, "She is not dead, but sleepeth." When all had left the room save the parents and the three chosen disciples, the Saviour took that little girl's hand in His and said, "Maid, arise." Or, it might be, "Little girl, wake up." Instantly, the flush of life came back into those hitherto pale, cold cheeks; the warmth of blood circulating anew went through the entire body, for "her spirit came again, and she arose straightway: and He commanded to give her meat." What a moment of joy it must have been to the parents as they clasped their darling in their arms again alive and fully recovered from her disease.

While all this took place literally just as it is written here, it is also a wonderful picture which depicts the way in which those who are dead in trespasses and sins are brought into life through Christ. When a boy or girl puts his trust in the Lord Jesus, immediately he receives divine life; or, whether it be an adult, after years in which it has been demonstrated that the person is dead in trespasses and sins, when Jesus speaks and he hears the Saviour's Word, he is quickened into newness of life.

But the young convert needs food in order to be strengthened and built up; and so, just as the Lord Jesus commanded that something to eat be given the little one, so today young Christians need the sincere milk of the Word that they may grow thereby.

As we think of the joy of Jairus and his wife when their little one was restored to them, we may well look forward with eager expectation to the wondrous moment when millions of parents are going to rejoice when the tombs give up their dead, and their dear ones, who have been taken from them here on earth, shall be given back to them in that glorious day of Christ's triumph. All who have died in Christ will be in that resurrected company, and we may be assured that loved ones will seek each other out and will know even as they have been known.

"When I shall meet with those that I have loved,
Grasped in my eager arms the long-removed,
And know how faithful Thou to me hast proved,
I shall be satisfied."

How sweet the words of Jesus, "I am the Resurrection and the Life: he that believeth in Me, though he were dead, yet shall he live; and whosoever liveth and believeth in Me shall never die!"

Just one added thought, and it is this: There are experiences so sacred between the soul and the Lord that others could not comprehend, and might thoroughly misunderstand if we said much about them. The Lord Jesus charged these astonished parents that they should tell no man what was done. It was to be something between Him and themselves; it was altogether too sacred to be talked about, unless, indeed, as commanded of the Lord. And so, there are precious things revealed to the soul in communion with Christ that are not meant for the outside world. His gospel we are to give to everyone, but there are somethings too precious to pass on to those who have no knowledge of Christ.

ADDRESS THIRTY-ONE

THE MISSION OF THE TWELVE

✝ ✝ ✝

"Then He called His twelve disciples together, and gave them power and authority over all devils, and to cure diseases. And He sent them to preach the kingdom of God, and to heal the sick. And He said unto them, Take nothing for your journey, neither staves, nor scrip, neither bread, neither money; neither have two coats apiece. And whatsoever house ye enter into, there abide, and thence depart. And whosoever will not receive you, when you go out of that city, shake off the very dust from your feet for a testimony against them. And they departed, and went through the towns, preaching the gospel, and healing everywhere. Now Herod the tetrarch heard of all that was done by Him: and he was perplexed, because that it was said of some, that John was risen from the dead; and of some, that Elias had appeared; and of others, that one of the old prophets was risen again. And Herod said, John have I beheaded: but who is this, of whom I hear such things? And he desired to see Him. And the apostles, when they were returned, told Him all that they had done. And He took them, and went aside privately into a desert place belonging to the city called Bethsaida. And the people, when they knew it, followed Him: and He received them, and spake unto them of the Kingdom of God, and healed them that had need of healing. And when the day began to wear away, then came the twelve, and said unto Him, Send the multitude away, that they may go into the towns and country round about, and lodge, and get victuals: for we are here in a desert place. But He said unto them, Give ye them to eat. And they said, We have no more but five loaves and two fishes; except we should go and buy meat for all this people. For they were about five thousand men. And He said to His disciples, Make them sit down by fifties in a company. And they did so, and made them all sit down. Then He took the five loaves and the two fishes, and looking up to heaven, He blessed them, and brake, and gave to the disciples to set before the multitude. And they did eat, and were all filled: and there was taken up of fragments that remained to them twelve baskets"—Luke 9: 1-17.

✝ ✝ ✝

WE have four sections to consider in these seventeen verses: First, the mission of the twelve; secondly, Herod's reaction to the ministry of our Lord Jesus; thirdly, the return of the twelve; and lastly, the feeding of the multitude. All are so closely linked that we will consider them together.

It is important to notice the difference in the commissions which the Lord gave while He was still here on earth, and that which He gave after He had been raised from the dead. He came as the promised King of Israel, the Anointed One of Jehovah. He presented Himself to the people of Israel in that way: "Repent ye, for the kingdom of heaven is at hand." He was there ready to set up the kingdom if they were ready for it. But the people who had waited for the Messiah for so long were not prepared to receive Him. They rejected Him, but He did not reject them. He called seventy disciples to Him and sent them out. Later He called the twelve disciples together and gave them power and authority over all demons, and to cure all diseases. They had no such power in themselves, He gave it to them—the power that belonged to Him. The disciples were to announce that God was calling on all men to recognize the rightful King, and they were to authenticate their message by healing the sick. Notice now the instruction Jesus gave to them: "Take nothing for your journey, neither staves, nor scrip, neither bread, neither money; neither have two coats apiece. And whatsoever house ye enter into, there abide, and thence depart. And whosoever will not receive you, when ye go out of that city, shake off the very dust from your feet for a testimony against them." You see there was a special reason why He instructed His disciples in this way: They were going to the lost sheep of the house of Israel. He had come as the Shepherd of Israel. They were to announce His coming and to call on all to open their hearts to Him. It was seemly that they should be cared for and fed by those to whom they went. We who preach the gospel today would be on very wrong ground indeed if we went forth without money to pay our expenses or without an extra suit of clothes, counting on gifts from our hearers, because we have no right to expect the world to support us and minister to us. In Third John we read of the disciples who went forth "taking nothing of the Gentiles." Paul refused to take anything from the Gentile world, and turned aside and went to tent-making, when necessary, to supply his needs. He would not be a debtor to the world. You see, it was not to the "world," in the sense that we use the word today, that the twelve were sent on this occasion. They went out to the nation of Israel—those who were expectantly looking for the Messiah. The disciples would be received if the hearts of these people were right with God, and they would provide for the disciples. So the Lord commanded the twelve not to take extra clothing, but to go and proclaim the kingdom of heaven at hand. So they went forth. Where they were received, one can imagine the blessed fellowship that they had when they told about Jesus and His birth of a virgin mother, and how He was ready now to establish the kingdom if the nation was prepared to receive Him. On the other hand, if the disciples were not welcomed but told to leave, then they were to "shake off the very dust from their feet for a testimony against them." They were to depart and go on to other towns and preach the kingdom. Everywhere they went they authenticated their message by healing the sick. This is very different to the testimony of servants of God today, who act more on the great commission which is given at the end of each of the Synoptic Gospels.

In the second section of our chapter we have Herod's reaction to the word that came to his ears. He had rejected and beheaded John the Baptist. Here we have him disturbed. "Now Herod the tetrarch heard of all that was done by Him: and he was perplexed, because that it was said of some, that John was risen from the dead; and of some, that Elias had appeared; and of others, that one of the old prophets was risen again." But while our Lord Himself identified John the Baptist with Elias, yet Herod was terrified as he thought of that mighty prophet who had wrought such signs and wonders in the day of Ahab, and wondered if he had come back to earth. "And Herod said, John have I beheaded: but who is this, of whom I hear such things? And he desired to see Him." He did not send for Him nor invite Him to come. He had sent for John the Baptist again and again, and as long as John dealt with kingdom subjects, all was well, but when he pointed directly to Herod's consort, Herodias, whom he had stolen from his brother, Herod became indignant and put John in prison, and Herodias herself had him put to death. Herod never sent for Jesus nor saw Him until our Lord was about to be crucified: Pilate sent Him to Herod. Though Herod had the opportunity to listen to one greater than all the prophets in the past, as our Lord designated John the Baptist, he went out directly into a lost eternity to face forever his sin. What a warning this is to those who persist in sin and turn from Jesus!

We read in verse 10, "And the apostles, when they were returned, told Him all that they had done." They came back happy and told Him what had resulted from their mission. In many places they had evidently been treated wonderfully. Given authority over all diseases, they had delivered many from sickness and demon power. And so they came back triumphantly. "And He took them, and went aside privately into a desert place belonging to the city called Bethsaida." In the Gospel of Mark, we have something added which is most interesting: He turned to them and said, "Come ye yourselves apart, . . . and rest awhile." The Lord Jesus saw that His servants were somewhat overwrought and needed quiet rest. It would be well, I think, if we today would heed His word and come apart and rest for a while. I fancy that there are many of His servants who are working far beyond their strength and take little time to rest at the feet of Jesus. That is why so many are losing their health, having nervous breakdowns, and other frailties. If we would listen to Him and spend more time in His presence, it would be much better for us. It is sometimes said that it is better to burn out than to rust out. That is true, but it is still better to work and then rest, as He commanded. David the Psalmist said, "He maketh me to lie down." The Lord's sheep do not seem to have that much sense! They need to "come apart and rest a while." Sheep will do that very thing.

The place where this incident occurred was not the Bethsaida on the west shore of the lake; this was Bethsaida on the eastern side, and this is where they went to enjoy a little time of rest.

In the last section we read, "The people, when they knew it, followed Him: and He received them, and spake unto them of the kingdom of God, and healed them that had need of healing." In another Gospel we are told that "He could not be hid," for word got out that Jesus was there, and when the people heard it, though the Saviour had taken the twelve away for a little rest, they followed Him, eager to see the works that He performed and to listen to the message that He had to bring. "And He received them, and spake unto them of the kingdom of God, and healed them that had need of healing."

He spoke unto them of the kingdom of God! Of course it involved the evident setting up of a literal kingdom here on the earth, but in order to be fit for that kingdom there must be regeneration. "Except a man be born again, he cannot see the kingdom of God." We may be sure that He not only spoke of this to Nicodemus, that He also stressed that very thing to all. So He proclaimed the message of the kingdom of God, and He healed them that had need of healing. "And when the day began to wear away, then came the twelve, and said unto Him, Send the multitude away, that they may go into the towns and country round about, and lodge, and get victuals: for we are here in a desert place." Evidently the people had been so stirred that they had not thought about their own need; neither had they made provision for food, nor lodgment for the night. Many of them were far from home and night was coming on. This is like many people today—far from home, and hungry. I wonder if I am addressing any like that today, far from home and away from God, and hungry, and the night is coming on. Thank God, the blessed Lord Himself makes provision for you. The disciples did not understand, for they said to Him, "Send the multitude away, that they may go into the towns and country round about, and lodge, and get victuals: for we are here in a desert place. But He said unto them, Give ye them to eat." His command, "Give ye them to eat," is a word for everyone who has partaken of the Bread of Life. We are responsible to pass it on to others. That is the reason we are preaching the gospel and calling men and women to listen to the Word of God. We realize that men are dying in their sins and that they are hungry. Our blessed Lord has provided for daily need, and He has sent us out to tell the multitude. "Give ye them to eat," is what Jesus said to them. "And they said, We have no more but five loves and two fishes; except we should go and buy meat for all this people." We are told in another Gospel that the disciples had figured it all out and told the Master that it would take a whole year's wages to provide for all these people. The word translated "penny" is denarius: a day's wages for a working-man. The disciples said, "Why, Master, it would take two hundred denarii in order to provide food for all this multitude, and there is nothing here but five loaves and two fishes." Where did they get the loaves and fishes? Andrew had been scouting around and found a boy with five loaves and two fishes. No doubt it was the lad's own lunch. Possibly his mother had packed it for him when he left to go after Jesus. He had been so absorbed that he had not thought of his lunch and so he gave it to Andrew. It was a small offering, but in the hands of the Saviour it could meet the needs of all those people. What do you have in your hand that you might give to the Lord which He might bless for others? I read of a missionary offering, and the money was coming in so slowly that a dear little crippled girl gave all that she had to give: she handed her little crutch to the usher to give to the pastor for Jesus, and said, "Sell it, and use the money for missions." The speaker held it up and told the story, and asked, "Who will buy little Mary's crutch?" Hundreds of dollars came in, and then they gave the crutch back to the little girl. So often a little gift may be multiplied when it is given to the Lord. "They were about five thousand men. And He said to the disciples, Make them sit down by fifties in a company." One hundred companies of fifty each!

There they were gathered all about, and the Lord took the five loaves and two fishes and blessed them and began to break, and gave to the disciples to set before the multitude. I can imagine the first folks eagerly reaching for the food, and the people behind saying, "Oh my! there will not be enough for us." But when Jesus sets the table, there is always plenty. "And they did eat, and were all filled: and there was taken up of fragments that remained to them twelve baskets." How many basketfuls were there? Twelve! And I can imagine each of the twelve disciples carrying a basket away. You never give anything to the Lord but that He gives more to you.

Now our Lord took all this and gave it a spiritual application. He explained that the real Bread that satisfies the soul is not natural bread, for man does not live by bread alone. The Bread of God is He who came down from heaven to give life to the world. He is calling men and women today to receive Him who gave Himself for them. "He came unto His own, and His own received Him not. But as many as received Him, to them gave He power to become the sons of God, even to them that believe on His name."

ADDRESS THIRTY-TWO

PETER'S CONFESSION AND TRUE DISCIPLESHIP

"And it came to pass, as He was alone praying, His disciples were with Him: and He asked them, saying, Whom say the people that I am? They answering said, John the Baptist; but some say, Elias; and others say, that one of the old prophets is risen again. He said unto them, But whom say ye that I am? Peter answering said, The Christ of God. And He straitly charged them, and commanded them to tell no man that thing; saying, The Son of Man must suffer many things, and be rejected of the elders and chief priests and scribes, and be slain, and be raised the third day. And He said to them all, If any man will come after Me, let him deny himself, and take up his cross daily, and follow Me. For whosoever will save his life shall lose it: but whosoever will lose his life for My sake, the same shall save it. For what is a man advantaged, if he gain the whole world, and lose himself, or be cast away? For whosoever shall be ashamed of Me and of my words, of him shall the Son of Man be ashamed, when He shall come in His own glory, and in His Father's, and of the holy angels"—Luke 9: 18-26.

WE have two sections to the portion we are now to consider. The first is Peter's confession, and then the price of discipleship. Once more we are reminded of the true humanity of our Lord Jesus which is emphasized in the Gospel of Luke. We notice that each of the Gospels presents Christ in a different aspect: Matthew presents Him as King; Mark as the Servant; John as the Son of God become flesh; and Luke as Man in all perfection. So in this Gospel, again and again we find our Lord in prayer. People have asked to whom the Lord prayed if He was God Himself. He was both God and Man, and as Man He took the place of dependence, and as the Son He enjoyed constant fellowship with His Father. As recorded in this Gospel, He makes no important move without going to God in prayer. He spent whole nights in prayer. On this occasion He was alone praying, and His disciples drew near to Him. He had led them to the far northern border, to the land looking out upon the great Gentile world, conscious of the fact that His own people, Israel, whom He had come to deliver, refused to recognize Him. "He came unto His own, and His own received Him not." It was with the blessing of the Gentile world in view that He asked the disciples, "Whom say the people that I am? They answering said, John the Baptist; but some say, Elias; and others say, that one of the old prophets is risen again." Herod and others said that He was John the Baptist risen from the dead. They did not know of the incident when Jesus came and was baptized by John the Baptist. Others said He was Elias, as prophesied in Malachi 4. They were looking expectantly for the coming of Elias, and did not realize that John had come in his spirit and power. So some of them thought possibly Jesus was he. Others thought that He was one of the old prophets risen again. Jesus said unto them, "But whom say ye that I am? Peter answering said, The Christ of God." After having walked with Him all these months, after having observed His ministry and mighty works, after having listened to the gracious words that proceeded out of His mouth, Peter was assured He was the Christ of God. He spoke for them all.

"The Christ" is synonymous with "the Messiah," and means "the Anointed" — the One promised by the prophets of old. In Matthew's Gospel we read, "Thou art the Christ, the Son of the living God." It was a wonderful confession, because, so far as the record goes, Jesus had never said that this was the truth, but they had deduced it from what they had seen and heard. "And He straitly charged them, and commanded them to tell no man that thing." Why, you would have expected that He should have told them to spread the word around all over, and tell people everywhere just who He was! But it is too late for that. His ministry has been rejected. The hearts of the majority of the people are set upon their own way. They are not prepared to receive His testimony. Israel will receive Him as the Christ of God when He returns the second time. In the meantime they must reap the sad results of their unbelief. That was why He commanded the disciples not to say anything about it then, for He was going down to Jerusalem to die. He had to be who He is in order to do what He did. Many tell us He was the most wonderful prophet and teacher that the world has ever known; they say He knew more of God and manifested more divinity in humanity than anyone else has ever done, but yet they stop short of what Peter in this confession says, "Thou art the Christ of God." Nothing less than that will ever satisfy the Father. He called upon the angels to worship Him. He said, "Let all the angels of God worship Him." In heaven, every tongue confesses Him as the Christ of God. Jesus is God the Son, who came in grace into this world and assumed our humanity in order that He might go to the cross and give His life a ransom on our behalf. He is the Jehovah of the Old Testament. "If thou shalt confess with thy mouth the Lord Jesus, and shalt believe in thine heart that God hath raised Him from the dead, thou shalt be saved." Every blessing for time and eternity is linked up with that confession of the Deity of our Lord Jesus Christ.

In Luke's account of this confession, nothing is said of what is recorded in Matthew as to the special blessing the Lord bestowed on Peter. He passes that over and immediately proceeds with the test of discipleship. Jesus tells them, "The Son of Man must suffer many things, and be rejected of the elders and chief priests and scribes, and be slain, and be raised the third day." He was as truly Man as He was God; God and Man in one blessed and adorable Person. Nothing took Him by surprise; He knew all that was before Him. When He came from glory down to the manger in Bethlehem, He knew what was going to take place. He came to die. He said, "The Son of Man came not to be ministered unto but to minister, and to give His life a ransom for many," in order that He might be the sacrifice for sinners. As a result of this sacrifice our sins are forever put away. He knew that He was to die and that on the third day He was to be raised again. Now in view of all this—the revelation of His Person and the revelation of the work He was to perform—He speaks to

His disciples, as He does to us. He said to them, "If any man will come after Me, let him deny himself, and take up his cross daily, and follow Me." Let us be clear as to that of which He was speaking. He is not telling us how we may obtain forgiveness of our sins; we are told that elsewhere. He is not telling us here how we may obtain eternal life; He makes that clear elsewhere: "For God so loved the world, that He gave His only begotten Son, that whosoever believeth in Him should not perish, but have everlasting life." What is it that He is speaking of here? It is the place that His disciples are to take in this world, the place of identification with Him in His rejection—they are to follow Him. But observe: no one was ever saved through *following* Jesus. If you and I could be saved by following Jesus, then salvation would be the result of human efforts. We cannot be saved by imitating our blessed Lord. We are not told that we are saved by taking up our cross. But after we know that our sins are forgiven and that we have eternal life, we are called upon to follow Him. If you profess to have believed in Him and trusted Him as your Saviour, you are called upon to follow in His steps. You are not left to choose your own path. He has marked out the way that you are to go. It is to such that He says, "If any man will come after Me, let him deny himself, and take up his cross daily, and follow Me." What does it mean to deny oneself? What did it mean for Peter to deny our Lord? They came to Peter and said, "You are one of His disciples." Peter said, "I am not!" They said unto him again, "Of a truth this fellow also was with Him: for he is a Galilean. And Peter said, Man, I know not what thou sayest." Challenged a third time, Peter, with an oath, denied that he was one of Jesus' disciples. He refused to own Christ in any way. What does it mean when Jesus said, "If any man will come after Me, let him deny himself, and take up his cross daily and follow Me?" You are to refuse to know yourself in order that He may have His way with you on this earth. I am no longer to seek my own interest, but I am to seek that which will glorify Him. I am to say, "I know not this man, but I do know that Man, and for Him I will gladly surrender everything."

If you had been living when this Gospel was written and you had seen a man bearing a cross as he walked along the road, you would have known that that man was going out to die. That was what it meant. Jesus, when He carried the cross, was going out to die. So to take up my cross and follow Jesus, means to take the place of death to self, and to be prepared to die for Him. The Apostle Paul said, "I die daily." The consistent disciple says, "I am ready to die to all carnal hopes and selfish interests. I am no longer to be dominated by fleshly desires, but I am to live unto God." Tested by words like these, how little most of us know of real discipleship! "If any man will come after Me, let him deny himself, and take up his cross daily, and follow Me." Let him refuse to know himself and take the place of death. "For whosoever will save his life shall lose it; but whosoever will lose his life for My sake, the same shall save it." What does He mean by that? All down through the centuries there have been those who have said that it costs too much to follow Christ and to yield oneself to His allegiance. It means the loss of the good opinion of loved ones, the loss of friends, and fame, and profit; sometimes it means leaving loved ones and friends and going to another country to preach the gospel. Listen, my dear friends, if the Lord is calling you to some particular path, you cannot afford not to hear and follow Him. "For whosoever will save his life shall lose it; but whosoever will lose his life for My sake, the same shall save it."

I have always been thankful for a little incident that might have seemed trivial at the time. It took place after I had been converted, when I was only a lad, at a Saturday-night meeting on the street-corner, in which I was participating. Along came some of my schoolmates, and they were dumbfounded at seeing me in this meeting, and they listened in amazement when I witnessed for Christ. On Monday when I came to school, they greeted me derisively, shouting "Hallelujah." I said, "Praise the Lord." Then they said, "Praise the Lord." I replied, "Amen." Some who were kind to me said, "Harry, what do you mean by turning religious? You are throwing your life away." Why; that is just what I intended to do! And it came to me so clearly, and I am thanking God that He in His grace started me that way. I wouldn't exchange these fifty-three years of service for the Lord Jesus

Christ for any career that the world might offer me.

It may seem that you are losing grand opportunities for advancement if you deny yourself and follow Jesus, but He has said, "Whosoever will save his life shall lose it; but whosoever will lose his life for My sake, the same shall save it." Think of the noble army of martyrs down through the ages. Think of those who have literally given their lives rather than deny the Lord Jesus. How thankful they are today that they counted all things but loss, even life itself, to glorify the Lord Jesus Christ. Don't hesitate, young Christians, to make your decision, to dedicate yourself to the One who gave His life for you. Say from the heart:

"Jesus, I my cross have taken,
All to leave and follow Thee;
Destitute, despised, forsaken,
Thou, from hence, my all shall be!
Perish every fond ambition,
All I've sought, and hoped, and known;
Yet how rich is my condition,
God and heaven are still my own!"

In the verses that follow, the Lord has a message not only for His disciples, but for the world at large. "For what is a man advantaged, if he gain the whole world and lose himself, or be cast away?" What is a man advantaged if he gain all that the world has to offer, if he piles up a lot of wealth, if he be honored and recognized by his country and even by other countries, what advantage if at last he goes out into a lost eternity? What advantage is this? What advantage to gain the whole world if one be lost himself, or be a castaway eternally? Oh, that we might learn to put first things first, and be right with God before everything else. Trust in God first as your Saviour and then own Him as Lord of your life.

Jesus added this challenge to His disciples, "For whosoever shall be ashamed of Me and of My words, of him shall the Son of Man be ashamed, when He shall come in His own glory, and in His Father's, and of the holy angels." Will you notice first the way in which our blessed Lord speaks of His coming to this earth? The order would be very strange indeed if He were anyone else than the One who Peter said He was. He came once before, but He is coming back again. The world has not seen the last of Jesus. When He returns He "shall come in His own glory." What glory is that?—the glory of His Eternal Sonship — and in His Father's, and the holy angels'. If He had been any less than equal with the Father, He would have had to say, "In His Father's glory," then, "in His own glory." But He was not wrong when, in speaking of His return, He put Himself first, then the Father. God the Father, God the Son, and God the Holy Spirit are One. Do you not want Him to own you then? Will you not want to be numbered among those who are His followers? Then listen, "For whosoever shall be ashamed of Me and of My words, of him shall the Son of Man be ashamed, when He shall come in His own glory, and in His Father's, and of the holy angels." If you have not confessed Him as Saviour and Lord, why not do so now?

ADDRESS THIRTY-THREE

THE KINGDOM IN EMBRYO

✓ ✓ ✓

"But I tell you of a truth, there be some standing here, which shall not taste of death, till they see the kingdom of God. And it came to pass about an eight days after these sayings, He took Peter and John and James, and went up into a mountain to pray. And as He prayed, the fashion of His countenance was altered, and His raiment was white and glistering. And, behold, there talked with Him two men, which were Moses and Elias: who appeared in glory and spake of His decease which He should accomplish at Jerusalem. But Peter and they that were with him were heavy with sleep: and when they were awake, they saw His glory and the two men that stood with Him. And it came to pass, as they departed from Him, Peter said unto Jesus, Master, it is good for us to be here: and let us make three tabernacles; one for Thee, and one for Moses, and one for Elias: not knowing what he said. While he thus spake, there came a cloud, and overshadowed them: and they feared as they entered into the cloud. And there came a voice out of the cloud saying, This is My beloved Son: hear Him. And when the voice was past, Jesus was found alone. And they kept it close, and told no man in those days any of those things which they had seen"—Luke 9: 27-36.

✓ ✓ ✓

JESUS is speaking here. He has been putting before the disciples the cost of following Him. He made it clear that to be His follower often costs a great deal. Then to encourage their hearts, He said, "But I tell you of a truth, there be some standing here, which shall not taste of death, till they see the kingdom of God." By the term "the kingdom of God" we are to understand the authority of God as established over this earth, and necessarily, therefore, in the hearts of men and women. In the Old Testament it was predicted that the kingdom of God should be fully manifested in due time. This has not yet taken place. Satan is still the prince of the power of the air and of the god of this age. The world is in its present evil condition because it has rejected God's King; He alone can bring in the age of righteousness.

In Luke 2 we read, "And the angel said unto them, Fear not: for, behold, I bring you good tidings of great joy, which shall be to all people. For unto you is born this day in the city of David a Saviour, which is Christ the Lord." He came to bring peace to the earth, to manifest God's good will toward men. But they rejected the Prince of peace; and so before the Lord Jesus went away He said, "Think not that I am come to send peace on earth: I came not to send peace, but a sword." God has not changed His plans because men were not ready to receive the kingdom; His kingdom is yet to be set up in this world. The Lord Jesus said to His disciples, "But I tell you of a truth, there be some standing here, which shall not taste of death, till they see the kingdom of God." We are told in the next verse how this came to pass: "About an eight day after these sayings, He took Peter and John and James, and went up into a mountain to pray." This was probably Mount Hermon. When the Lord ascended that mountain with the disciples it was that they might have a picture of the kingdom which was to come. We know that, because Peter tells us (2 Peter 1:16),

"For we have not followed cunningly devised fables, when we made known unto you the power and coming of our Lord Jesus Christ, but were eyewitnesses of His majesty. For He received from God the Father honor and glory, when there came such a voice to Him from the excellent glory, This is My beloved Son, in whom I am well pleased. And this voice which came from heaven we heard, when we were with Him in the holy mount." Peter tells us here that what took place on the mount of transfiguration was really a vision of the coming glory, the kingdom of God in minature.

So with this before us, we look somewhat carefully at what is recorded concerning it. When we ponder Luke's account we find our Lord in prayer as on many other occasions. Sometimes people are perplexed about this, and ask, "How could He be God, and yet feel the need of prayer?" They forget that though He was God from all eternity, yet He chose to become Man, and as Man, He was dependent upon the Father. Prayer was to Him the expression of sweetest communion with the Father; it was the acknowledging of His manhood looking up to heaven for the strength to do the Father's will.

"And as He prayed, the fashion of His countenance was altered, and His raiment was white and glistering." We may know something of this in our own lives, for as we pray we are transformed. Oh, how many times we have known people who are sinful, wicked, crude, uncultured, and uncouth, who came to know the Lord and trusted Him as their Saviour; and then as they communed with Him, even while they prayed, the fashion of their countenance was altered! Many people who were once so unruly and dishonorable have made the most devoted witnesses. As Christians, we cannot afford to neglect prayer. One reason many of us make so little progress in our Christian life is that we do not pray enough. We pray in the time of distress, but when all goes well we do not take time to wait on God and have blessed communion with Him. If we would do this, we would become more like Him, and manifest more of His grace and tenderness and compassion for sinners. We would be less likely to criticize and be unkind to other people if we would pray more. We become more like Christ as we spend time in fellowship with Him.

In John's Gospel we read, "The Word was made flesh and tabernacled among us . . . full of grace and truth." The body of our Lord Jesus Christ is there likened to the tabernacle which Moses set up in the wilderness. In the Holiest, God's presence was manifested as the Shekinah shining between the cherubim. In the blessed body of our Lord Jesus Christ was hidden the glory of His deity, for "God was in Christ reconciling the world to Himself." That glory shone forth in the things that He did; it was manifested in His restoring grace to those who had wandered. Here in a very special way it was seen as He communed with God on the mount, "His raiment was white and glistering." The glory from within shone out, and He appeared as we shall yet see Him when He comes the second time in the glory of His Father and His own glory and in the glory of the angels.

"And, behold, there talked with Him two men, which were Moses and Elias." Moses, the lawgiver, was the representative of the saints of the legal dispensation. Elias was the one sent from God to restore the people to God. These two Old Testament characters appeared with Jesus in the mount and talked with Him. Of what did they speak? What was the theme? Oh, the wonder of it! They were speaking with Him of that which will be our theme all through eternity as we recall what He did for us—suffering and dying for us. "Who appeared in glory, and spake of His decease which He should accomplish at Jerusalem." They had come from God in heaven to spend that little time up there on the mount with the Lord Jesus, to talk with Him of what He would do on the cross of Calvary. It must have been a wonder indeed to the angels and to the saints in heaven, when He came from the throne of glory down to the manger in Bethlehem. They must have asked themselves why He did it. They watched His life on earth, and must have listened earnestly to His words when He said, "The Son of Man . . . must be slain and be raised on the third day." These two men were interested in Him, and they were talking about His death so soon to take place. We speak of it yet, and we should. If He had not done this for us, we would long since have been cast into eternal perdition. His death for us is the most important event of which we read in the Word of God. Listen to the redeemed in heaven as they bow before the throne and sing, "Thou art worthy . . . and Thou wast slain, and hast redeemed us to God." That is what they sing up there. That is the theme that thrills their hearts. Oh, my friends, I must pause here and ask: Does it mean anything to you—the death of Christ? Has it ever spoken to your heart? Does it mean anything to you that Christ laid down His life for you? I may be speaking today to many who have scarcely given a thought to the death of Christ on the cross. Have you never reflected over this solemn and glorious thing, and said, "The death He died was *for me;* the agony He suffered was *for me,* that I might enjoy the blessedness of being with Him forever?"

But we turn again to consider this transfiguration scene. Our Lord Jesus intimated that it was a picture of the coming kingdom. The kingdoms of this world will never become the kingdom of our God and His Christ until the Lord returns again to this earth. He is not coming again as He came before. He will not come in lowliness and poverty; He is coming the second time in power and great glory. Then we read that all the earth shall wail because of Him. All shall bow before His feet.

We have a little picture of the glory which will be His when He comes again. Notice again the two men who appear with Him in His glory. How significant it is that it should be these particular two! First, there was Moses, the man who had died 1500 years before, and whose body God had hidden away so that Satan the corrupter could not touch it. We read that God "buried him in a valley in the land of Moab, over against Beth-peor: but no man knoweth of his sepulchre unto this day." Moses appeared in a physical body shining with the same glory as Jesus Christ. That reminds us that when the Lord comes to set up His kingdom, He will bring those who have died in Him. "For if we believe that Jesus died and rose again, even so them also which sleep in Jesus will God bring with Him."

Then consider the other man, Elias—the man who had never died at all, the man who, in his discouragement, prayed that he might die. He cried, "Lord, let me die." The Lord, as it were, said, "No, Elias; I am not going to answer that prayer; I am going to take you to Myself without dying." So Elias was caught up into glory, and centuries later he appears as we read in these verses. He represents another group—that one of which the apostle Paul speaks in 1 Thess. 4:17, "Then we which are alive and remain shall be caught up together with them in the clouds, to meet the Lord in the air: and so shall we ever be with the Lord." Then He will bring in the kingdom, and our Lord will reign. Oh, how this world needs the return of the Lord Jesus Christ. Our hearts join in the prayer, "Even so, come, Lord Jesus!"

This is the picture then of the coming King. "But Peter and they that were with him were heavy with sleep: and when they were awake, they saw His glory, and the two men that stood with Him." Sometimes when the Lord has the most wonderful things to reveal to us, we are not in condition to receive them. The apostles might have heard more of that conversation between the Lord and Moses and Elias, but they went off to sleep. When they awoke they saw His glory and the two men that stood with Him. Then Peter exclaimed, "Master, it is good for us to be here: and let us make three tabernacles; one for Thee, and one for Moses, and one for Elias: not knowing what he said." Poor Peter! He was always speaking out of turn because he felt he had to say something. Sometimes it is better just to look on and say nothing; but Peter, moved by what he had seen and heard, proposed that booths should be erected in honor of the three who were seen in glory — Jesus, Moses, and Elias. "While he thus spake, there came a cloud and overshadowed them: and they feared as they entered into the cloud." They dreaded the next experience, as we often do. But there was nothing to fear. "There came a voice out of the cloud saying, This is My beloved Son: hear Him." God will not have anyone put on the same level with His Son, Jesus Christ. If people would bow before Moses, Moses must go. The same for Elias. Peter never forgot this voice. When he wrote his second epistle just before he died, he was still thinking of it. "And when the voice was past, Jesus was found alone. And they kept it close, and told no man in those days any of those things which they had seen." The reason for that was the leaders and the people had definitely put themselves on record as rejecting the Saviour, and had refused to accept Him as their

Messiah; and this was revealed only to His disciples for their encouragement in the days to come. Now it can all be told.

Jesus takes the highest station, and His people bow before Him and acknowledge Him in praise and adoration. Soon He will return and the kingdom will come in all its splendor, when He shall reign as King of kings and Lord of lords.

ADDRESS THIRTY-FOUR

AT THE FOOT OF THE MOUNT

"And it came to pass, that on the next day, when they were come down from the hill, much people met Him. And, behold, a man of the company cried out, saying, Master, I beseech Thee, look upon my son: for he is mine only child. And, lo, a spirit taketh him, and he suddenly crieth out; and it teareth him that he foameth again, and bruising him hardly departeth from him. And I besought Thy disciples to cast him out; and they could not. And Jesus answering said, O faithless and perverse generation, how long shall I be with you, and suffer you? Bring thy son hither. And as he was yet a coming, the devil threw him down, and tare him. And Jesus rebuked the unclean spirit, and healed the child, and delivered him again to his father. And they were all amazed at the mighty power of God, but while they wondered every one at all things which Jesus did, He said unto His disciples, Let these sayings sink down into your ears: for the Son of Man shall be delivered into the hands of men. But they understood not this saying, and it was hid from them, that they perceived it not: and they feared to ask Him of that saying. Then there arose a reasoning among them, which of them should be greatest. And Jesus, perceiving the thought of their heart, took a child, and set him by Him. And said unto them, Whosoever shall receive this child in My name receiveth Me: and whosoever shall receive Me receiveth Him that sent Me: for he that is least among you all, the same shall be great. And John answered and said, Master, we saw one casting out devils in Thy name: and we forbad him, because he followeth not with us. And Jesus said unto him, Forbid him not: for he that is not against us is for us"—Luke 9: 37-50.

IT would be a wonderful thing if we might always remain on the mountain with Christ. A mountain in Scripture speaks of a place of special and exalted privilege. It was on the mountain that the disciples witnessed the marvelous transfiguration of our blessed Lord. They would have gladly remained there with Him and with the Old Testament worthies who appeared in glory, speaking of His decease which He was to accomplish on Calvary; but the time came when they had to leave that place of blessing and go down to the foot of the mount to rejoin the rest of the apostles, and to meet the multitudes in their sin and need. Many of us have known similar experiences. It has been our happy privilege on various occasions to enter into most wonderful and precious communion with the Lord, far apart from the ordinary cares and responsibilities of daily life. On the mount of blessing we were free to be occupied with Christ alone. How gladly would we have remained there and never again taken an interest in mundane affairs. But this could not be. We may not always be in the enjoyment of mountain-top experiences. We have to descend to the plains to participate in the ordinary affairs of life. The fact is that the mountain-top experiences are intended by God to fit us for our part in ministering to those who do not know our Lord; or to those who know Him, yet have very little understanding of the precious truths He delights to reveal to us.

And so we read, "It came to pass, that on the next day, when they were come down from the hill, much people met Him." In the throng was a poor, troubled father who had with him a demon-possessed son. The father immediately sought out Jesus, pushing his way through the croud and looking up to Him earnestly, he exclamed, "Master, I beseech Thee, look upon my son: for he is mine only child. And, lo, a spirit taketh him, and he suddenly crieth out; and it teareth him that he foameth again, and bruising him hardly departeth from him." Evidently, satanic power had so controlled this poor lad that he was suffering from something very much akin to epilepsy, but back of it all was demon power. We can well understand the anguish of the father's heart. There is something so pathetic and so gripping in those words, "He is mine only child!" How many parents have known somewhat similar circumstances—an only son or daughter under the power of Satan, and apparently no ability on their part or on the part of others to deliver them. But when we go to the Lord we go to the right Person. Our cries are never unheeded by Him; He is never indifferent to our exercises. He may not instantly heal bodily ailments, He may not immediately save from Satan's power, but we can always be sure of a loving and sympathetic hearing; and we may be certain of this: in God's due time the prayer of faith will be answered.

Oftentimes in our distress we go to fellow-believers, seeking help from them, sometimes to be bitterly disappointed. This poor father said, "I besought Thy disciples to cast him out; and they could not." Now we know that the Lord had given His disciples authority over unclean spirits, and on other occasions that power had been manifested in a marvelous way, but in this particular instance they seemed utterly helpless. Why? Well, the Lord Himself makes it clear. He said, "This kind goeth not out but by prayer and fasting." They were confronted with a problem which they could not solve. Undoubtedly one reason was that they had become occupied with ideas of advancement in the coming kingdom, and so they were out of touch with the Lord. They might go through the ordinary motions of laying their hands upon the demon-possessed, commanding the unclean spirit to go out of him; but there were no results because the disciples were out of fellowship with God who has said to His own, "Seekest thou great things for thyself? Seek them not."

It is so easy for Christ's servants to become professional, or semi-professional, to become self-centered and to give way to pride and self-interest. When this is so, prayer will be neglected and the study of the Word will no longer occupy us; and we will have little power when it comes to personal work and seeking to deliver people from the dominion of the devil. In fact, a believer out of touch with God has no power at all; he becomes the laughing-stock of Satan. He may call upon the demon to depart from his victim, but the evil spirit will refuse to do so; and the poor, unhappy demoniac will find no deliverance. If one is to be in the position where God can use him, there must be self-judgment and confession, daily feeding upon the Word, and he must continue instant in prayer. In this case the disciples could do nothing for this poor, distracted father, and so he turns to Jesus for help. The Lord Jesus rebuked the disciples, saying, "O faithless and perverse generation, how long shall I be with you, and suffer you?" Then He said to the father, "Bring thy son hither." As the poor boy was brought into the Lord's presence, we are told that the demon cast him down and he lay writhing upon the ground and foaming at the mouth. It was a pitiful sight, and the compassionate heart of Christ was deeply touched. He said to the father, "How long is it ago since this came unto him?" He did not ask the question because He did not know, but He wanted to draw out that father's heart and lead him to confide fully in the only One who could give him the help that was needed. The father replied that this had come upon his son when he was but a little child, and that at times while under this awful demon power, he had been cast into the fire and badly burned, and at other times he had been thrown into the waters where he was in danger of drowning. The father, after telling of these sad experiences, exclaimed, "If Thou canst do any thing, have compassion on us, and help us;" and at once, we are told, "Jesus rebuked the unclean spirit, and healed the child, and delivered him again to his father." Oh, the joy that must have welled up in that father's heart when he realized that his boy was free and that the demon's power was broken!

Thank God the Saviour has the same power today. No matter how Satan may have afflicted poor lost sinners; no matter how terrible the bondage under which they have lived for years, when they come to Him who died to redeem them, they can be delivered, set free from the chains that have bound them, and He will give them the joy of His salvation.

It is not always His will now in this dispensation of grace to deliver from bodily affliction. God had promised the people of Israel that if they would walk with Him they would be free from sickness. He has not promised this to those who belong to the Body of Christ; but He has promised something even better—namely, grace to endure. Paul found this out. He suffered from a severe physical affliction, and he besought the Lord thrice for deliverance from it. God did not answer in the way His dear servant at first desired, but said to him, as it were, "No, Paul; I am not going to free you from this affliction, but I am going to do something better for you; I am going to give you grace to bear it." Paul exclaimed, "Most gladly therefore will I rather glory in my infirmities, that the power of Christ may rest upon me."

When the people saw how the boy was delivered from the spirit that had controlled him for so long, we read, "They were all amazed at the mighty power of God." While they were looking on with wonder at the mighty works which Jesus did, He took occasion to tell His disciples that the day was drawing near when He Himself would be delivered into the hands of men. Then, indeed, they would need faith to believe that He was truly the Christ of God. He said to them, "Let these sayings sink down into your ears." When the time actually came they forgot His warning, and so they were in great perplexity. Had they only borne in mind what He had told them, they would not have been so troubled when He was delivered into the hands of men to be crucified. He said to them, as it were, "Do not forget what you have seen and heard, for the day is coming when you will need to call these things to mind, when you see Me led out to die, and apparently left alone and forsaken upon a cross of shame. You will be in danger then of thinking that I have been a deceiver, but remember these things when the hour comes that I am taken from you." They did not understand, however, for it was hid from them, we are told, and "they perceived it not: and they feared to ask Him of that saying." Had they been in more intimate communion with Him, they would have doubtless turned to Him and asked for fuller information, and He would have given it gladly. We notice as we go on through these records that there were times when there seemed to be no restraint, and the Lord was able to speak to them freely of what was in His heart; at other times, when He spoke of His death and resurrection, there seemed to be a barrier between Him and them. They were perplexed. The root-cause of their lack of faith and of understanding is seen in the incident that follows. We read, "Then there arose a reasoning among them, which of them should be greatest. And Jesus, perceiving the thought of their heart, took a child, and set him by Him, and said unto them, Whosoever shall receive this child in My name receiveth Me: and whosoever shall receive Me receiveth Him that sent Me: for he that is least among you all, the same shall be great." How this brings out the distrustfulness, worthlessness, the unreliability of the human heart, even in those who really knew and loved their Lord. The disciples were His own. They were surely among the best in Israel, and yet they were remarkably human, and seemed to forget so easily what was expected of them as followers of the meek and lowly Saviour. He has been speaking of His death, and here they are striving among themselves as to who will be greatest. Think of it! These men who had been with Jesus for so long, and had never seen Him do a selfish thing, nor heard Him say a word that would indicate a proud or haughty spirit, and yet they are so unlike their Master that they are actually quareling among themselves as to who will have the highest place in the coming kingdom. What a lesson for all of us as we realize that "As in water face answereth to face, so the heart of man to man." Note the lovely picture which Jesus put before the disciples. He took a little child and set him by Him and said, "Whosoever shall receive this child in My name receiveth Me." The child is the ideal convert: simple, trustful, confiding, ready to receive because of faith in the person who speaks to it. The little one trusted Jesus and was not afraid of Him, and therefore remained at His side in perfect confidence.

Did the disciples get the lesson? Did they understand that it is the spirit of the little child which the Lord desires to see manifested in His own? Do we realize it today? Do we see Jesus, as it were, in every little child? As we look into those innocent little faces, do we behold Him; and do we say in our hearts, "We must do unto this little child as we would do unto Him"? To receive the child in His name is to receive Him, and to receive Him is to receive the Father who sent Him.

The Lord adds, "He that is least among you all, the same shall be great." Advancement, then, in the kingdom of God comes by taking the lowest place.

In the next verses we have the Lord's rebuke of sectarianism. It is quite possible to be intensely jealous of one's ecclesiastical position while actually out of touch with the Lord Himself. John manifested this when he spoke up and said, "Master, we saw one casting out devils in Thy name: and we forbad him, because he followeth not with us." Evidently this man whom they had seen was one who believed in Jesus and in the power of His name, and he undertook to seek to exorcise demons in the name of Jesus, and evidently the demons came out. But this gave no joy to the heart of John or the other disciples. They were indignant that anyone should be using the name of their Master in this way if he did not actually belong to their little company. How much of that spirit we see among Christians who are so obsessed with the idea that they alone constitute the elect of God, that they find no pleasure in the work which others are doing for Christ who do not belong to their particular sect or group. What a rebuke are the words of the Lord, not only to those disciples of old, but to us: "Forbid him not: he that is not against us is for us." Elsewhere Jesus said that "He that is not for us is against us." Both are true. There is no such thing as neutrality in respect to Christ. We are either for Him or against Him. If for Him, we are not against Him; if not against Him, we must be for Him. If we could ever keep this in mind it would prevent a lot of unhappiness among professed Christians. Just because people do not agree with us in every detail does not mean they are necessarily against Christ. Many would die for His name's sake who might not see with us as to some minor point of doctrine or church order. We may say we do not see why the Lord should use certain people when they do not belong to us, but He continues to use them just the same. Precious souls are being won to Christ through many with whom we might not fellowship.

There are indeed many important lessons to be learned at the foot of the mountain. There the difficulties of life are to be faced. We discover that only by prayer and fasting can we have power to deliver others from satanic influences. Only as we live in fellowship with our Lord Jesus Christ and desire nothing for ourselves, will we be able to understand and enjoy the precious truth of God and to maintain a right attitude toward others. We are slow to learn, but may God give to each one of us His grace to bow in contrition at our Saviour's feet and receive the instruction that He is so ready to give.

ADDRESS THIRTY-FIVE

INTOLERANCE REBUKED; FAITHFULNESS ENJOINED

✝ ✝ ✝

"And it came to pass, when the time was come that He should be received up, He steadfastly set His face to go to Jerusalem, and sent messengers before His face: and they went, and entered into a village of the Samaritans, to make ready for Him. And they did not receive Him, because His face was as though He would go to Jerusalem. And when His disciples James and John saw this, they said, Lord, wilt Thou that we command fire to come down from heaven, and consume them, even as Elias did? But He turned, and rebuked them, and said, Ye know not what manner of spirit ye are of. For the Son of Man is not come to destroy men's lives, but to save them. And they went to another village. And it came to pass, that, as they went in the way, a certain man said unto Him, Lord, I will follow Thee whithersoever Thou goest. And Jesus said unto him, Foxes have holes, and birds of the air have nests; but the Son of Man hath not where to lay His head. And He said unto another, Follow Me. But he said, Lord, suffer me first to go and bury my father. Jesus said unto him, Let the dead bury their dead: but go thou and preach the kingdom of God. And another also said, Lord, I will follow Thee; but let me first go bid them farewell, which are at home at my house. And Jesus said unto him, No man, having put his hand to the plough, and looking back, is fit for the kingdom of God"—Luke 9: 51-62.

✝ ✝ ✝

THIS portion readily divides into two sections. In verses 51-56 we have our Lord's solemn and stern rebuke of the spirit of intolerance. Then in verses 57-62 He lays down certain principles of discipleship which we who profess to love Him need to keep in mind.

We are told that "He steadfastly set His face to go to Jerusalem." He left Galilee knowing exactly what awaited Him in Judea. He had been there before. They had tried to put Him to death then, but, we are told, His hour had not yet come. They could not do a thing to harm Him physically until He voluntarily put Himself into their hands. He could say, "No man taketh My life from Me, I lay it down of Myself." But now the hour was drawing nigh when the purpose for which He came to earth should be fulfilled. Jesus had come to give Himself a ransom for all; so with this in view, He steadfastly set His face to go to Jerusalem. Nothing could turn Him aside. When He spoke of the cross on which He was to be crucified, even Peter remonstrated with Him, saying, "Be it far from Thee, Lord: this shall not be unto Thee." But Jesus rebuked him, saying, "Get thee behind Me, Satan: thou art an offence unto Me: for thou savourest not the things that be of God, but those that be of men." Jesus did not allow anyone or anything to turn Him aside from the great purpose He had come to fulfil.

With His face set as a flint to go to Jerusalem, as He passed with His disciples through a part of Samaria, He sent messengers ahead into a near-by village to make preparations for their night's lodging. We know there was intense hatred between the Samaritans and the Jews, neither wishing to have any dealings with the other. These Samaritans were a kind of mongral race of people, partly of Israelitish extraction and partly decended from the mixed races which the king of Assyria had brought into the land after carrying away the ten tribes. These had intermarried with the remaining Israelites, and a mixed sort of worship had developed among them, based to some extent upon the five books of Moses; but the Samaritans refused to accept all other parts of the Old Testament. They had their own temple on Mount Gerizim, and they looked with suspicion and indignation upon the Jews because of their claim of being the chosen people of the Lord. The Jews, on the other hand, returned the compliment by detesting the Samaritans, whom they looked upon as the followers of a pseudo-religion which had no scriptural basis. As the little company journeyed on through Samaria, the people of the village where they had hoped to spend the night refused to receive them because the face of Jesus was set as though He would go to Jerusalem. Realizing that He was not going to settle down among them as their teacher, but was extending His ministry to those whom the Samaritans hated, they in turn vented their spite upon Him by refusing Him entertainment. Had He come specially to them they might have received Him and His message, but for the time being He was interested in another people.

There is nothing, I suppose, that is more characterized by bitterness than religious intolerance. One group of religious people looks with suspicion upon those of another group; and often the closer they are together, the more intense is the ill-feeling between them. This was clearly manifested in the case of the Jews and Samaritans.

James and John were so indignant because of the way their Master was treated on this occasion that they were ready to go to all lengths to take vengeance upon them. They said to Jesus, "Lord, wilt Thou that we command fire to come down from heaven, and consume them, even as Elias did?" We generally think of James and John as being two very gracious and devoted young men; but gracious and devoted men can become exceedingly hard and bitter when it comes to dealing with others in regard to differences. These disciples whom Jesus named "Boanerges," that is, "sons of thunder," here answer to their name, and thought they were manifesting their faithfulness to Christ by seeking to emulate Elijah and to destroy the Samaritans. They appeared to think that if they did call for fire to come down from heaven, God would answer and blot out the city that had refused to harbor Jesus and His followers for the night; and so they would enjoy seeing their religious enemies completely annihilated.

How awful is such a spirit, and yet how frequently has it been manifested down through the centuries! History tells us how Churches have fought Churches, and Christians have contended with other Christians, using bitterest invective of speech and even going so far as to put one another to death. Our hearts are filled with horror as we think of the myriads of the early Christians who were martyred at the command of the pagan emperors of Rome. But the amazing thing is that during the centuries following the destruction of paganism, we find professing Christians arrayed against others who also bore the Christian name; and Mystery Babylon was responsible for the deaths of far more than pagan Rome ever destroyed. Even in Protestantism during the centuries that followed the Reformation, what unholy strife has often existed; and how sadly have believers failed to walk together in holy fellowship! When at last we all stand before the judgment-seat of Christ, there to give an account of the deeds done in the body, how ashamed we will be if we have ever been guilty of manifesting the spirit that characterized James and John when they would have destroyed that Samaritan village because its people did not understand, and therefore did not receive the Saviour as He was journeying on to Jerusalem.

The compassionate heart of Christ spurned the suggestion of the two energetic disciples, and instead of giving them liberty to do as they desired, He rebuked them and said, "Ye know not what manner of spirit ye are of. For the Son of Man is not yet come to destroy men's lives, but to save them." These two disciples must have felt this stern reprimand keenly, and doubtless they learned a lesson through it which they did not soon forget.

Now let us carefully consider for a few minutes the words of our Lord, for they embody a wondrous truth: "The Son of Man is not come to destroy men's lives, but to save them." Elsewhere He said that He "came not to condemn the world, but that the world through Him might be saved." "God," we are told, "was in Christ, reconciling the world unto Himself, not imputing their trespasses unto them." The Lord Jesus was on His way to the cross to bear the judgment due to sinners; therefore He could say to a poor, lost woman, "Neither do I condemn thee; go and sin no more."

It is precious indeed to realize that:

"There's a wideness in God's mercy,
Like the wideness of the sea:
There's a kindness in His justice,
That is more than liberty.
"For the love of God is broader
Than the measure of man's mind.
And the heart of the Eternal
Is most wonderfully kind."

God looks with tender compassion upon men. Even though they have trampled upon His love and rejected His blessed Son, still His heart is going out to them; He is waiting for them to repent, and longing to save them. He is "not willing that any should perish," but that all should turn to Him and live. Oh, the wonder of His grace! To think that some of the worst enemies of the cross of Christ have been arrested by divine power and gloriously converted, and afterwards have become the greatest advocates of the salvation which the Lord Jesus has wrought out on Calvary. We think of Saul of Tarsus persecuting the Church of God, hailing believers to prison and condemning them to death; and yet at last stopped by the risen Christ on the way to Damascus, and his heart completely won for the Saviour whom he had rejected so long.

But there is something more here, I believe, in these words—"The Son of Man is not come to destroy men's lives, but to save them"—which is not involved in the deliverance from judgment. Many people have the idea that becoming a Christian means to lose all the joy of living, and to go on through the rest of one's days in a melancholy, gloomy kind of existence, afraid of this and afraid of that and, therefore, in constant distress of mind. This is but a caricature of real Christianity. When people think of following Christ as involving a life of constant struggle and repression, they fail to understand the blessedness of the new birth. No one enters into life in reality until he knows Christ. The unsaved may talk of "seeing life" but actually they are but courting death. Only the one who has trusted Christ enjoys life at its best. It is in this sense that Jesus speaks when He said He came not to destroy men's lives. He did not come to take away from us all joy and happiness; He did not come to make His followers gloomy recluses, afraid to enjoy the good things that divine providence lavishes upon us. He came to give us to realize that it is only as we know God revealed in Christ that we get the best out of life.

"Heaven above is softer blue;
 Earth beneath is sweeter green:
Something lives in every hue,
 Christless eyes have never seen.
"Birds with sweeter songs o'erflow;
 Flowers with newer beauty shine,
Since I know, as now I know,
 I am His and He is mine."

Thus one of our Christian poets taught us to sing. No one is so prepared to enjoy the good things of this life as the man who knows what it is to be right with God. We are told in John's First Epistle that "He that hath the Son hath life; and he that hath not the Son of God hath not life." And with this divine, eternal life which is given freely to all who believe on the Lord Jesus Christ, there comes the capacity to enjoy all God's gifts and to recognize that they come down from Him, a loving Heavenly Father who is deeply interested in everything that concerns the welfare of His own. When one comes to know Christ, the things that once seemed of value he discerns to be very unimportant; where as things that at one time he shrank from he now learns to appreciate t the fullest possible way.

In the next section we have our Lord once more laying down principles of discipleship which are applicable throughout the entire period until He returns again in power and glory. We read, "It came to pass, that, as they went in the way, a certain man said unto Him, Lord, I will follow Thee withersoever Thou goest." Here was a man who was evidently attracted by the grace of Christ. He came to Jesus apparently of his own accord, and declared his readiness to be identified with Him, but the Lord Jesus immediately tested him by saying, "Foxes have holes, and birds of the air have nests; but the Son of Man hath not where to lay His head." It is as though He would say to this professed disciple, "If you follow Me you must not expect earthly gain; I do not promise an easy time down here; I do not guarantee temporal comforts. I have no home Myself—I, who came from heaven—I am walking through this scene as a stranger and I have no certain dwelling-place, nor have I earthly riches to bestow upon My disciples; so if you are going to follow Me, it means a life of self-denial, of self-abnegation all the way.

Does this nullify what we have been noticing in connection with the previous verses? Not at all! For there is no happier life in this world than the life into which one enters when he takes his place in fellowship with Christ and goes through this scene as a stranger and a pilgrim.

Conditions of discipleship have not changed, they are still the same as of old. To follow Christ does not insure one a life of comfort and ease. Savonarola well said, "A Christian life consists in doing good and suffering evil." The more faithful we are to Christ the more we may have to suffer from the world, but we can go through this in fellowship with our rejected Lord, and find a joy in sharing His rejection that the soul can never find in the enjoyment of the world's favor. In this instance we do not know whether the man went on with the Lord or whether he turned disappointedly away.

To another Jesus said, "Follow Me," and the one addressed replied, "Lord, suffer me first to go and bury my father." But Jesus, as it were, said, "You must not put anything first. My claims are paramount to every other." This man said, as it were, "Yes, Lord; I love You, and I will be ready to follow You some day; but I have an aged father, and I cannot leave him until he passes away and I bury him; and when that takes place I will be prepared to follow you." The Lord answered, "Let the dead bury their dead: but go thou and preach the kingdom of God." In otherwords, it is as if He had said, "If My message has touched your heart and soul; if I have won your trust and confidence; if you feel a divine call to represent Me in Israel, do not wait until family circumstances change. Begin immediately to tell others what God has done for you and what He can do for them."

I am afraid sometimes many of us have answered the Lord the way this man did. We have allowed the claims of kindred to come between us and the work of Christ; but it must be Christ first, then everything else will follow in its right place.

A third man came up and said, "Lord, I will follow Thee; but . . . " Stop there for just a moment. This little word of three letters has robbed many of their souls and hindered them from giving their lives to Christ. Is it hindering you? What is the "but" you have in mind? "I will follow Thee; but"—I cannot give up this, or that, or something else. Is that it? "I will follow Thee; but"—I cannot yield wholly to Thee on some particular point. What is the "but" that is hindering you? This man said, "Lord, I will follow Thee; but"—I must return and settle things up with the folks at home; I am not ready to follow You yet; I must go and talk it over with them first. He had to learn that the claims of Christ were paramount to every other. Jesus said to him, "No man, having put his hand to the plough, and looking back, is fit for the kingdom of God." Oh, that we might all realize this more and more, and that Christ might ever have the preeminent place in our hearts and lives!

Address Thirty-six

THE MISSION OF THE SEVENTY

"After these things the Lord appointed other seventy also, and sent them two and two before His face into every city and place, whither He Himself would come. Therefore said He unto them, The harvest truly is great, but the labourers are few: pray ye therefore the Lord of the harvest, that He would send forth labourers into His harvest. Go your ways: behold, I send you forth as lambs among wolves. Carry neither purse, nor scrip, nor shoes: and salute no man by the way. And into whatsoever house ye enter, first say, Peace be to this house. And if the son of peace be there, your peace shall rest upon it: if not, it shall turn to you again. And in the same house remain, eating and drinking such things as they give: for the labourer is worthy of his hire. Go not from house to house. And into whatsoever city ye enter, and they receive you, eat such things as are set before you: and heal the sick that are therein, and say unto them, The kingdom of God is come nigh unto you. But into whatsoever city ye enter, and they receive you not, go your ways out into the streets of the same, and say, Even the very dust of your city, which cleaveth on us, we do wipe off against you: notwithstanding be ye sure of this, that the kingdom of God is come nigh unto you. But I say unto you, that it shall be more tolerable in that day for Sodom, than for that city. Woe unto thee, Chorazin! woe unto thee, Bethsaida! for if the mighty works had been done in Tyre and Sidon, which have been done in you, they had a great while ago repented, sitting in sackcloth and ashes. But it shall be more tolerable for Tyre and Sidon at the judgment, than for you. And thou, Capernaum, which art exalted to heaven, shalt be thrust down to hell. He that heareth you heareth Me; and he that despiseth you despiseth Me; and he that despiseth Me despiseth Him that sent Me. And the seventy returned again with joy, saying, Lord, even the devils are subject unto us through Thy name. And He said unto them, I beheld Satan as lightning fall from heaven. Behold, I give unto you power to tread on serpents and scorpions, and over all the power of the enemy: and nothing shall by any means hurt you. Nothwithstanding in this rejoice not, that the spirits are subject unto you; but rather rejoice, because your names are written in heaven"—Luke 10: 1-20.

WE should recognize the fact that in this entire passage we have to do with a former dispensation, and we cannot carry everything in that dispensation over into the present age of grace. There are, nevertheless, important lessons here from which we may draw help and instruction as we seek today to do the will of God.

We have already seen how the Lord commissioned the twelve apostles and sent them out to the cities of Galilee. Now we read that He appointed seventy others. These did not have the official standing that the twelve had. Their commission was for a limited time only, the period during which they would be going from city to city ere His final rejection by the people of Galilee. He sent them out two and two, because He recognized how much they needed fellowship with each other. The preacher in the book of Ecclesiastes tells us that two are better than one, for if one should fall the other can lift up his fellow; and so it seems to be according to divine order, generally, that Christ's servants should labor two or more together. One alone might make many blunders and be discouraged, whereas two could confer together and each be cheered and encouraged by the other.

As the Lord contemplated the multitudes who were as sheep without a shepherd, and to whom He desired His disciples to go with the message of the kingdom, He impressed upon them the need by saying, "The harvest truly is great, but the laborers are few." He bade them pray the Lord of the harvest that He would thrust forth laborers into His harvest. On another occasion, when He sat at Jacob's well, after having revealed Himself to that poor, needy woman who had come to draw water, He turned to His disciples and said, "Say not ye, There are yet four months, and then cometh harvest? Behold, I say unto you, Lift up your eyes, and look on the fields; for they are white already to harvest." That great harvest-field was constituted of the multitude who did not as yet know Him as Saviour, Messiah, and Lord. It is still true, though we live in a different dispensation, that there are vast multitudes, not only in our own land but in all the regions beyond, who need Christ and who are waiting for the messengers of the Lord to go to them with the precious truth of the gospel. We may therefore apply His words to the present time as well as to the past. He still bids us to pray that laborers may be sent out to reap the harvest that is waiting to be garnered.

In verses 3-7 we have the direct commission given to the seventy. The Lord Jesus said, "Go your ways: behold, I send you forth as lambs among wolves." They were to go in simple dependence upon Him, trusting in the power of God to sustain them, and not retaliating in any way if they were ill-treated. Neither were they to make provision for a long journey, for their mission would be ended within a very short time; therefore He added, "Carry neither purse, nor scrip, nor shoes: and salute no man by the way." It would be folly to take these words out of their connection and make them obligatory upon servants of Christ today. The seventy were sent to the people of Israel; they were Israelites themselves. The nation was waiting for the manifestation of the kingdom, and these disciples were to go forth and proclaim the near approach of that kingdom. They had a right to expect entertainment and consideration from those to whom they carried their message. Because of the shortness of the time they were to hasten on their way, and were not to stop for the customary, lengthy, Oriental salutations. They did not need a large sum of money, extra shoes, nor clothing, because the circumstances in which they were found did not demand such provision. In this we may see how different were the circumstances in which they were placed from those in which the average missionary of the cross is found today.

The seventy had a right to expect to be received by their Jewish brethren as they went to them to declare the presence of the King among them. The Lord said to them, "And into whatsoever house ye enter, first say, Peace be to this house. And if the son of peace be there, your peace shall rest upon it: if not, it shall turn to you again." They went forth to proclaim the coming of the Prince of peace, and their salutation was in accordance with this. If the owner of the house was indeed a son of peace, he would gladly welcome His messengers. In that case they were to abide in this house during the time they preached in that particular city or village. If, however, the son of peace did not dwell there, that is, if there was no one in that home who was ready to recognize the mission of the Lord Jesus and to welcome His messengers accordingly, their peace would return to them, and the owner of the house would have lost his opportunity. Alas!

When Christ came to the house of Israel the son of peace was not there, and so we read that, "He came unto His own, and His own received Him not."

These messengers were not out on a pleasure tour, and so they were warned against anything that would look like selfishness or the pursuit of personal enjoyment. They were to remain in the house where they were received, eating and drinking such things as were given to them, recognizing the fact that the laborer is worthy of his hire. They were laborers in Jehovah's great harvest-field; it was for his people to receive and provide for them. They were not to go gadding about from house to house, seeking better entertainment. They had a perfect right to expect the people to receive them as the King's representatives, and therefore they need not feel ashamed to accept whatever entertainment was given them; but they must not give way to indulgence.

During this present age of grace, servants of Christ have no right or reason to expect the world to receive them into their homes or to provide for them in any way; and so this scripture, in the fullest sense, could not be applied to the present day. We read in the Third Epistle of John of traveling brethren, evidently ministers of the Word, who went forth for the name's sake of the Lord Jesus, taking nothing of the Gentiles. The apostle Paul refused to seek his support in the way of taking gifts from the heathen world. He would far rather labor with his hands in order to properly provide for himself and those with him. Conditions were different while our Lord was on earth and ministering to the lost sheep of the house of Israel. His representatives were not trying to impose upon the people when they accepted the accommodations offered. They recognized that it was in this way the people responded to the message of the kingdom, and so whenever a home was opened to them they were to enter into it and gratefully accept the provision offered. It was the duty of the disciples to emphasize the grace of the King. The Lord gave them special power to work miracles in His name. Their message was ever the same: "The kingdom of God is come nigh unto you."

The Old Testament prophets had spoken of this coming kingdom. They had told of One who was to reign in righteousness, and for centuries Israel had been waiting for His manifestation. Now the King was in their midst, and there were few who recognized Him. One can imagine these couriers going from place to place ministering to the needs of the people, and declaring, "The kingdom of God is come nigh unto you," as the folk gathered together. "The Messiah has already appeared and calls upon you to receive Him. The kingdom of God is about to be established in your midst." The great majority spurned the message and refused the claims of the Lord Jesus Christ and would not have Him reign over them. They knew not the time of their visitation, and so they lost their opportunity. Because of not entering into the blessedness of the kingdom, the time came when the Lord, as it were, shook the dust off His feet as a testimony against them, and said to them, "The kingdom of God is taken from you and shall be given to a nation bringing forth the fruits thereof." And for the time being Israel has been set to one side, and there has been brought in an altogether new dispensation. During all this period those who know and love the Saviour are called to represent Him in the world. This is the time when God is taking out from among the Gentiles a people for His name. He is proclaiming peace by Jesus Christ, and though bloody warfare has marked all the centuries since Christ returned to heaven, those who have trusted Him have found lasting peace, even in the midst of trouble. They have proven the truth of the word, "Thou wilt keep him in perfect peace whose mind is stayed on Thee: because he trusteth in Thee." The kingdom is still in the future. The Lord has gone into the far country to receive for Himself a kingdom and to return. Until the day of His Second Advent, His servants are to be busy calling on men to be reconciled to God.

Our scripture deals with a very important time in Israel's history. It was a time of crisis. Everything depended on the attitude of the people toward our Lord Jesus. Would they receive Him? If not, they must remain in their sins, and they would never enter the kingdom for which they had been waiting. There were comparatively few who opened their hearts and homes to the messengers and their message, but to them came blessing. As for the rest, they were left in their sins. The very dust of their cities was a witness against them. Nevertheless the fact remained that the kingdom of God had come nigh unto them.

In the next few verses we hear the Lord pronouncing the judgments that were to come upon the cities in which He had done the most of His mighty works, which had the best opportunities to know Him, and yet had refused Him. Of all such, He says, "I say unto you, that it shall be more tolerable in that day for Sodom, than for that city." From where He was standing He could probably see the cities of Chorazin and Bethsaida; and as He looked upon them, He said, "Woe unto thee, Chorazin! woe unto thee, Bethsaida! for if the mighty works had been done in Tyre and Sidon, which have been done in you, they had a great while ago repented, sitting in sackcloth and ashes." These cities, cities which had been blessed by the personal presence of the Lord, and whose people had seen His face, heard the wonderful words which proceeded out of His mouth, and beheld His mighty acts; yet had turned coldly away and even scornfully refused to acknowledge Him as King and Lord. Today Chorazin is merely a ruin, and until recently it could not be positively identified. I remember when traveling in Galilee I noticed some ruins off to one side as we drove down toward Samaria, and turning to my guide, I said, "I see the ruins of a city over there; do you know what city it was?" He was an Arab. He said to me, "That is the city that is called Chorazin in your Bible." That is all that is left of it, because its people failed to receive the King when He came among them in lowly grace. Bethsaida still remains, but it is a poor, little fishing village on the shores of the Sea of Galilee. I was told it is almost impossible to find a Christian there.

Capernaum was called our Lord's own city, for there He made His home when in Galilee after leaving Nazareth. Surely the people there, who had every opportunity to become well acquainted with Him, would receive Him. But, no! He sadly exclaimed, "And thou, Capernaum, which art exalted to heaven, shalt be thrust down to hell." It was in Capernaum that the Lord had delivered some of His greatest discourses. The Sermon on the Mount was probably preached on the tableland just back of the city. It was there that He found Matthew the publican, and called him away from the tax-collector's office to become one of His apostles. It was there that He restored Peter's wife's mother to health when she was sick of a fever; and there He raised the daughter of Jairus, and healed the poor woman who said, "If I may but touch His garment, I shall be whole." Many other wonders had been done in that city, and yet its people rejected Him; and so, though exalted to heaven in privilege, it was to be thrust down to hell, that is, to hades, the unseen world. So completely was this prophecy fulfilled that for over 1500 years no one knew positively the site of the city of Capernaum. It is only within our own times that it has been uncovered. During those long centuries it was covered over with the sands of the desert, and travelers passing by saw only a low mound. But during the time of the First World War, a group of German monks, interned in their monastery on the side of that hill, began to dig in the ground, and little by little they uncovered the ruins of Capernaum. It is just as true of cities as it is of individuals: judgement comes if they spurn the mercy offered to them. It is a terrible thing to trifle with spiritual realities. "Be not deceived; God is not mocked: for whatsoever a man soweth, that shall he also reap." These words are as true of cities and nations as of individuals.

To refuse to accept the testimony of one who comes bearing the message of Christ is the same as refusing Him. Jesus said, "He that heareth you heareth Me; and he that despiseth you despiseth Me; and he that despiseth Me despiseth Him that sent Me." We should realize that listening to one of God's servants as he reads the Word of God is the same thing as listening to our blessed Lord Himself. What responsibility this puts upon us to take heed how and what we hear!

In verses 17-20 we read of the return of the seventy after they had fulfilled their mission. They evidently had experienced a wonderful time in spite of the indifference of many to them and to their message, for they returned to the Lord with joy, saying, "Lord, even the devils are subject unto us through Thy name." He saw that they were too much taken up with their own accomplishments—and there is always the danger of those who preach the Word to take too much credit to themselves for any results that follow—but as these disciples talked of the subjection of the demons, Jesus looked forward in spirit to the hour when Satan will be finally cast out of the heavens, and He exclaimed, "I beheld Satan as lightning fall from heaven." Then He added, "Behold, I give unto you power to tread on serpents and scorpions, and over all the power of the enemy: and nothing shall by any means hurt you." That He meant this to be taken literally is evident from what we read in the book of Acts, when the apostle Paul was cast on the island of Melita. He and his companions had made a fire in order to warm themselves, and a serpent came out of the fire and fastened upon Paul's hand. He thrust the venomous beast into the fire and was unhurt, due to the preserving power of God over His own when they are actually in His will. This of course is very different from deliberately handling poisonous snakes as some fanatics have done in our day in order to demonstrate their faith.

There is something far more blessed, however, than working miracles. That is the knowledge that one is right with God! The Lord Jesus told these exuberant disciples not to rejoice simply because demons were subject to them, but rejoice rather because their names were written in heaven. This is true of all who have trusted Christ for themselves. All such have their names written in the Lamb's Book of Life, and these names will never be erased, but will remain for all eternity.

ADDRESS THIRTY-SEVEN

THE MYSTERY OF THE INCARNATION

✝ ✝ ✝

"In that hour Jesus rejoiced in spirit, and said, I thank Thee, O Father, Lord of heaven and earth, that Thou hast hid these things from the wise and prudent, and hast revealed them unto babes: even so, Father; for so it seemed good in Thy sight. All things are delivered to Me of My Father: and no man knoweth who the Son is, but the Father; and who the Father is, but the Son, and he to whom the Son will reveal Him. And He turned Him unto His disciples, and said privately, Blessed are the eyes which see the things that ye see: for I tell you, that many prophets and kings have desired to see those things which ye see, and have not seen them; and to hear those things which ye hear, and have not heard them"—Luke 10: 21-24.

✝ ✝ ✝

IT is noticeable that immediately after announcing the coming doom of the cities where most of His mighty works had been wrought, our blessed Lord is said to have rejoiced in spirit. Had He been dependent upon human conditions and worldly circumstances for His joy, as we so often are, He might well have been cast down and depressed when He realized how few there were who seemed to have any heart at all for His message, and who were ready to receive Him as the Messiah. But instead of being discouraged by man's coldness and indifference, He manifested the truth of the Word most preciously. With glad heart He looked up to the Father with whom He had unbroken communion, and said, "I thank Thee, O Father, Lord of heaven and earth, that Thou hast hid these things from the wise and prudent, and hast revealed them unto babes: even so, Father; for so it seemed good in Thy sight." He was content to know that the purpose of God was being carried out in spite of man's rejection and enmity. Those who, by their fellows, were numbered among the wise and prudent, had failed to recognize the Messiah when He came in lowly grace, although they professed to be waiting for Him. The Lord's appearance was not at all what they expected. They were looking for a great and mighty King; they were looking for One who would drive the Romans from the land of Palestine, re-gather Israel and set up His kingdom immediately, sitting on David's throne. Instead, there walked among them a Man content to live in apparent poverty, with no certain dwelling-place, going about proclaiming the love of God for poor sinners and declaring that He had come to give His life a ransom for many! This was not at all the kind of Messiah these wise and prudent ones expected. And so their eyes were blinded, and their ears were closed against Him. The precious things He declared seemed foolishness to them. On the other hand, there were those in Israel who, as compared with the wise and prudent, were but babes in knowledge and intelligence. But to these simple ones the Son was revealed, and they learned to trust Him and saw in Him the promised One for whom their people had waited so long. This was all in accordance with God's purpose of grace; and the Lord Jesus fully acquiesced in His Father's will in this as in every other respect.

In the next verse, which is also found in Matthew's Gospel, we have brought before us in a very striking way, the mystery of the Incarnation. Jesus said, "All things are delivered to Me of My Father: and no man knoweth who the Son is, but the Father; and who the Father is, but the Son, and he to whom the Son will reveal Him." What a rebuke are these words to those theologians who insist upon trying to explain in every detail the union of the human and the divine in Christ. It is quite proper that we should dwell upon what Scripture has declared, but when we attempt to go beyond Scripture, we are almost certain to fall into error; for it is just as true today as it was when Jesus first spoke the words, that, "No man knoweth who the Son is, but the Father." The union of the human with the divine, the two natures in one Person, is beyond our comprehension. We know from Scripture that our blessed Lord was God the Son from all eternity, one Person of the ineffable Trinity. We know that He came from the glory that He had with the Father before the world was, and stooped in grace to be born into the world of a Jewish mother. Scripture insists upon the fact that this mother was a virgin. He had no human father, and therefore we may say that He was the Son of God in two senses: He was the Eternal Son, one with the Father before all worlds, and He was the Son of God as Man when born on earth. But in Him we see deity and humanity united in one blessed, adorable Person. To explain this is impossible. Faith receives it because it is revealed in the Word of God.

Observe the difference between the statement He first makes concerning Himself and the second statement as to the Father. He tells us that no man knoweth who the Father is but the Son. However He immediately adds, "And he to whom the Son will reveal Him." Our Lord Himself came to reveal the Father, who, apart from the Son and His revelation, never could have been known. The creation, of course, bears witness to His eternal power and Godhead, as we are taught in the first chapter of Romans, but it was Christ Himself who made known the Father's name.

This was one of the things hitherto kept secret which the Lord Jesus declared. In Deut. 29:29, we read "The secret things belong unto the Lord our God: but those things which are revealed belong to us and to our children for ever, that we may do all the words of this law." Isaiah writes, "For since the beginning of the world men have not heard, nor perceived by the ear, neither hath the eye seen, O God, beside Thee, what He hath prepared for him that waiteth for Him." This is the passage that the Apostle quotes from the Septuagint in 1 Cor. 2:9. But he immediately adds, "But God hath revealed them unto us by His Spirit: for the Spirit searcheth all things, yea, the deep things of God." Many marvelous truths were hidden in olden times which, since the Advent of our blessed

Lord, have been made known to His own. Some of these things He Himself revealed while on earth; others were opened up by the Spirit after Christ ascended to heaven. It is in view of these new unfoldings of divine truths which He came to give, that the Lord Jesus turned to His disciples and said to them privately, that is, He was not speaking to the world as such, but only to His own: "Blessed are the eyes which see the things that ye see: for I tell you, that many prophets and kings have desired to see those things which ye see, and have not seen them; and to hear those things which ye hear, and have not heard them."

It is a precious privilege indeed to be taken into God's confidence and permitted to share His secrets. We know how friends on earth delight to share with one another certain secret things which they do not make known to strangers; and so our Lord Jesus looked upon His disciples as His intimate friends, and He delighted to open up to them precious things concerning the divine Fatherhood, the wondrous provision God had made for the salvation of the lost, and the preservation of His own.

It is our privilege today to enter into and enjoy these hitherto secret things, now revealed to faith. We do not need visions or new revelations in order to understand and appropriate them. We discover them as we study the Word of God in prayerful dependence upon the Holy Spirit who inspired the writing of it.

I remember well when I was a young Salvation Army officer, I went home at one time on furlough.

My mother and my stepfather lived in southern California on an olive and fig ranch, at a place then called Monte Vista, now known as Sunland. I met a most interesting servant of Christ whose name was Andrew Fraser. He was often called the "Irish Epaphras." He was suffering from tuberculosis, and had come all the way from Ireland, hoping to find relief from this dreadful disease; but he was so far gone that it was not many months before he went home to heaven. My stepfather had pitched a tent out in the orchard, and he was staying there when I was taken to see him. My mother introduced me. I spent one of the most precious hours of my life, listening to the kindly advice and opening up of the Word of God from the lips of this dear dying man, as he turned from scripture to scripture and brought out precious truths that I had never seen. I finally asked him, "Mr. Fraser, where did you learn all this? Can you suggest some book or books that I could read which would make these things plain to me? He replied, "My dear young brother, I learned these things on my knees on the mud floor of a little thatched cottage in the north of Ireland as I waited on God over His Word. You may read many books and often find nice and helpful things in them, but you will never learn the truth of God in the same way or in the same fulness as you can learn it on your knees over an open Bible." As I left I felt I had been in the presence of the Lord, for I had listened to one who was taught of God.

What we all need is to take the place of babes, to whom God may reveal His secrets. He delights to fill the hungry with good things, but the rich He sends empty away. If we come to Him self-emptied and wait on Him to feed us, we shall find, by faithful perusal of the Holy Scripture in dependence upon the Spirit, that wonderful things will be made known to us that otherwise we would never see. Time spent over the Word in a prayerful attitude will produce rich dividends in the way of leading us on into the knowledge of Christ and His truth.

ADDRESS THIRTY-EIGHT

SELF-RIGHTEOUSNESS EXPOSED

✓ ✓ ✓

"And, behold, a certain lawyer stood up, and tempted Him, saying, Master, what shall I do to inherit eternal life? He said unto him, What is written in the law? how readest thou? And he answering said, Thou shalt love the Lord thy God with all thy heart, and with all thy soul, and with all thy strength, and with all thy mind; and thy neighbor as thyself. And He said unto him, Thou hast answered right: this do, and thou shalt live. But he, willing to justify himself, said unto Jesus, And who is my neighbor? And Jesus answering said, A certain man went down from Jerusalem to Jericho, and fell among thieves, which stripped him of his raiment, and wounded him, and departed, leaving him half dead. And by chance there came down a certain priest that way: and when he saw him, he passed by on the other side. And likewise a Levite, when he was at the place, came and looked on him, and passed by on the other side. But a certain Samaritan, as he journeyed, came where he was: and when he saw him, he had compassion on him, and went to him, and bound up his wounds, pouring in oil and wine, and set him on his own beast, and brought him to an inn, and took care of him. And on the morrow when he departed, he took out two pence, and gave them to the host, and said unto him, Take care of him; and whatsoever thou spendest more, when I come again, I will repay thee. Which now of these three, thinkest thou, was neighbor unto him that fell among the thieves? And he said, He that showed mercy on him. Then said Jesus unto him, Go, and do thou likewise"—Luke 10: 25-37.

✓ ✓ ✓

THIS to my mind is one of the most misunderstood passages in the Gospel records. It is related only by Luke, and he tells it for a very definite purpose. People generally think of the parable of the Good Samaritan as simply setting forth a lesson in charity and concern for those who are less fortunate than we. Recently one said to the present writer, "I do not need an atonement for my sins. The religion of the Good Samaritan is good enough for me." He was basing his hopes for eternity upon doing good to his fellow-men, forgetting that on this ground all are under condemnation, for no man, save our blessed Lord, ever truly loved his neighbor as himself. To face the implication of this story honestly is to realize the utter impossibility of obtaining eternal life by doing. We can only be saved by what Christ has done. It is when we realize that we are helpless, like the man dying on the Jericho road, that we are ready to submit to the gospel and receive the salvation the Lord Jesus came to make possible.

While we should recognize the fact that the Lord was seeking to awaken the lawyer's conscience as to his responsibility to his neighbor, yet it is evident that there was something far more than that in His mind. During the early ministry of our Lord, He made clear to His followers the principles that should guide them as they looked forward to the setting up of His kingdom. It was in order to show a lawyer his need of a Saviour that He related the parable of the Good Samaritan. What we have before us is the story of a man who was trying to maintain his own righteousness and did not recognize his lost condition. We are told, "Behold, a certain lawyer stood up, and tempted Him, saying, Master, what shall I do to inherit eternal life?" The lawyer who asked this question was not a sincere inquirer. He was endeavoring to draw Jesus into a controversy as to the Law of

Moses, which declared that he who obeyed its precepts should live, and he who violated them should be accursed.

By the term "lawyer" is meant one who was an exponent of the law of Moses: that is, one who was well versed in the Old Testament Scriptures, particularly the Pentateuch, and who was therefore looked upon as an authority by the people generally. I suppose we would be right in saying that he would answer very much to an accredited doctor of divinity in our day. He should have known, therefore, that no man could ever obtain eternal life by keeping the law of Moses, because no man had ever yet been found who had fully obeyed its holy precepts.

Jesus answered him by asking, "What is written in the law? How readest thou?" Jesus never attempted to argue with one who was unreal. He, in this instance, put the lawyer on the defense, as it were, leaving it to him to answer his own question as far as he thought he could. In this way the lawyer would expose his own attitude toward both God and his neighbor. This was exactly what took place. The law was given to show up the corruption of the human heart, to give sin the specific character of trangression, and to make manifest the utter helplessness of any natural man to obtain salvation by human merit, and to convict of their folly all who, being ignorant of God's righteousness, are going about to establish their own righteousness. The question comes with terrific force: "What is written in the law? How readest thou?"

If conscience be in activity the law must fill the soul with terror as one realizes his utter inability to reach the high standard it sets forth. Apparently the lawyer had no such exercise, for he unhesitatingly replied, "Thou shalt love the Lord thy God with all thy heart, and with all thy soul, and with all thy strength, and with all thy mind; and thy neighbor as thyself." In so replying, the lawyer epitomized the two tables of the law, according to Deuteronomy 6: 5 and Leviticus 19: 18. It was a sad commentary on the state of his soul that he could recite these words so glibly and yet evince no sense of his own lost condition. Who has always lived up to these commands? Yet failure in one point puts man in an utterly hopeless state so far as satisfying the law's demands is concerned. The Lord Jesus calmly replied, "Thou hast answered right: this do, and thou shalt live." It was a sharp thrust with the two-edged sword of the Word of God, but it made little impression on the smug, self-righteous heart of this lawyer. Yet it was but insisting on that which the law demanded, and because of which it became the ministration of death (2 Cor. 3:7) to all who were under it. Had there been any true conscience-exercise, the lawyer would have confessed that he had violated the law already and he would have inquired if there was any way by which he might be delivered from its curse. Instead of this, he attempted to justify himself by asking, "Who is my neighbor?" It was a telltale question! It showed up the true state of this man's heart. Think of one who hoped to gain eternal life by his doings, who could be so indifferent to the needs of suffering humanity all about him that he had not yet discovered the neighbor needing his love and care! And yet he might better have asked, "Who is my God?" For if one does not love his brother, whom he has seen, he can have no real love for the God he has not seen (1 John 4:20). It was in reply to this question that the Lord related what is commonly called the parable of the Good Samaritan. Undoubtedly it was a story of fact, for we need to remember that our Lord Jesus Christ was Himself the Way, the Truth, and the Life. It is unthinkable that He would make up an illustration which had no factual foundation, even in order to press home a definite line of truth, unless He made it clear that He was doing this, as on some occasions when He said, "Hear a parable." In this case He speaks very definitely of a certain man who went down from Jerusalem to Jericho and fell among thieves who wounded him and robbed him, stripping him of his garments and leaving him half-dead by the wayside. In this man we may see pictured unfortunate victims of sin and violence of every type, whose lives have been wrecked and ruined by adverse circumstances, and whose plight should excite the pity and give the urge to help, of every kindly-disposed person. But in telling this story it is evident that Jesus had more than this in mind. The stricken man on the Jericho road is a vivid picture of all men in their natural state, who have been robbed of their comparative innocence and purity and now are helpless and defiled, unable to regain their former state, needing one who can save them from their sin and the consequences thereof.

We next read that by chance (or, rather, coincidence) there came down a certain priest, who looked upon the man and then passed by. He represented the spiritual side of the legal covenant. He saw the afflicted man, but evidently feared to defile himself by touching one so near to death and polluted with his blood (Lev. 21:1). So "he passed by on the other side." Next a Levite came. He seemed to be more interested in the poor, wounded victim of the thieves, for we are told that he "came and looked on him," but again we read that he "passed by on the other side." He represented the manward aspect of the law, but he did not consider it part of his duty to assist one in so deplorable a condition. How possible it is to be intensely religious, devoted to some church or society, and yet have no real exercise of heart for those who are in trouble and distress, or who are perishing in their sins. The Levite was presumably a servant of God, dedicated to ministering in Israel, but in his self-conplacency he ignored the need of the poor, dying wretch, lying on the Jericho road. God grant that all who profess to be servants of the Lord Jesus Christ may ever remember that we have a great responsibility, not only to preach the gospel, but, as much as lieth in us, to do good unto all men.

Finally help came from a most unexpected source. The Jews had no dealings with the Samaritans. A certain Samaritan, as he journeyed, saw the man in his wretched condition and had compassion on him. This was almost the last man in the world from whom the poor, wounded Jew had any right to expect mercy. But the Samaritan's heart was filled with sympathy for the helpless sufferer. When the Jews sought to express their contempt for Jesus, they called Him a Samaritan (John 8:48). It is easy to see in the one who succored the dying traveler, a picture of our blessed Lord Himself, who came to us when we were in our sin and need, and manifested His boundless grace toward us.

The Samaritan bound up the wounds of this poor man, pouring in oil and wine, and set him on his own beast, and brought him to an inn. Using the best remedies he knew, the Samaritan proved himself a real neighbor to the afflicted one. He did not leave him by the roadside, but took him to an inn where he might have proper care. It is an interesting fact that halfway between Jericho and Jerusalem, there remains to this day an inn which is commonly known as that of the Good Samaritan, where travelers may rest on their way up the long incline from the Jordan valley to the city of the Great King.

Nor did the Samaritan's interest in his patient cease when he had brought him to the inn, but ere he left to go on his own journey, we are told that "he took out two pence," that is, two denarii—Roman coins about the size of our twenty-five cent piece, but with the purchasing power, in those days, of many times that amount. He gave the money to the innkeeper and bade him, "Take care of him," promising to meet all further charges on his return. Note his exact words—"When I come again, I will repay thee." How suggestive this promise is! Does it not remind us of the fact that our blessed Lord, who has gone back to heaven, is coming again, and when He returns He will repay for everything that has been done for Him.

One can imagine the object of the Samaritan's bounty growing stronger day by day. As his strength increased, we may think of him as going to the entrance of the inn and looking up the road expectantly. If someone inquired for what or whom he was looking, I think he might have replied, "My friend, the one who was such a good neighbor to me in my need; the one to whom I owe my life. He said, 'I will come again.' I am waiting for his return. I want to fall at his feet and express my gratitude for what he has done for me."

To the lawyer the Lord Jesus put the question, "Which now of these three, thinkest thou, was neighbor unto him that fell among thieves?" It was indeed a searching inquiry, designed to manifest the selfishness of the lawyer's heart and cause him to realize that he was the man on the Jericho road needing Someone who could deliver him from the plight into which his sin had plunged him. But alas! He had no such realization of his need. He replied, "He that showed mercy on him." No thoughtful man could have answered otherwise, and so the lawyer convicted himself out of his own mouth. Jesus simply enjoined him, "Go, and do thou likewise." He left the lawyer then to his own thoughts. Had he been an upright inquirer, he would have acknowledged that so far as obtaining eternal life by law-keeping was concerned, his case was hopeless, for he had violated it already and was under its curse. If he had maintained a right attitude toward God, he would never have been indifferent as to his neighbors. There was no evidence of conviction, for otherwise he would have exclaimed, "I am that man on the Jericho road—I am the one who needs mercy." And then Jesus would not have pointed him to the Levite or the priest for help, but would have said, "I am come to seek and to save that which was lost; I can heal your soul and undertake for you. I have come to give eternal life to all who put their trust in Me."

Legal religion can do nothing for a man already fallen and defiled. The priest and the Levite represented the two tables of the Law, Godward and manward, but once broken, they become a ministry of death and condemnation. Jesus Himself bore that condemnation and died in our place, the Just for the unjust, that He might bring us to God. Thus He has manifested Himself as able to meet every need and to save for eternity all who put their trust in Him.

ADDRESS THIRTY-NINE

SERVICE AND COMMUNION

✓ ✓ ✓

"Now it came to pass, as they went, that He entered into a certain village: and a certain woman named Martha received Him into her house. And she had a sister called Mary, which also sat at Jesus' feet, and heard His word. But Martha was cumbered about much serving, and came to Him, and said, Lord, dost Thou not care that my sister hath left me to serve alone? bid her therefore that she help me. And Jesus answered and said unto her, Martha, Martha, thou art careful and troubled about many things: but one thing is needful: and Mary hath chosen that good part, which shall not be taken away from her"—Luke 10: 38-42.

✓ ✓ ✓

THE certain village into which Jesus entered was, as we know from other scriptures, Bethany, where Martha and Mary lived. Their house seems ever to have been open to the Lord. He had a peculiar love for these two devoted sisters and their brother Lazarus. How blessed is the home where Christ is always welcome, and where loving hearts delight to entertain so wondrous a Guest!

Martha was evidently the elder of the two sisters, for we read, "A certain woman named Martha received Him into her house." She seems to have been recognized as the owner of the house. Attempts have been made to identify Mary, the younger sister, with Mary Magdalene, or with the otherwise unnamed woman of the Seventh of Luke, but there does not seem to be any valid reason for this. There is nothing to indicate that Mary had ever been an unchaste woman or one who had been demon-possessed. In the three definite instances where she appears in Scripture, that is, here and in John 11 and 12, we see her as a contemplative worshiper, to whose heart the blessed Lord was unspeakably precious. There is not the least intimation that she had ever been a woman of bad character, although like everyone else, she was a sinner who needed to be saved by grace divine.

In verse 39 we read that, "She (Martha) had a sister called Mary, which also sat at Jesus' feet, and heard His word." Mary delighted to take the seat of a learner. She revelled in the truth Christ came to reveal, and found her chief joy in sitting at His feet. To some she would seem to be dreamy and impractical, but Jesus appreciated her deep interest in His message and her love for Him. This is most precious. It may well speak to our hearts. Nothing is more important for the child of God than to spend time at the feet of Jesus, pondering over His Word. It is in this way that we grow in grace and in the knowledge of Christ. So Mary becomes an example to us all. You may say that she should have been helping Martha with the dinner. Ah, but the Lord would rather have her sitting at His feet. You remember when He sat at Jacob's well and the disciples had gone for food. Then there came the Samaritan woman to whom He ministered the Word, which became, in truth, the water of life to her thirsty soul. What joy it was to Him to minister to her deep need and to unfold the riches of God's grace to her in such a way that she forgot her waterpot for love of Him and went back to the city to evangelize its men! When the disciples came back they expected to find Him so hungry that He would be ready at once to eat of the food they had brought, but He seemed utterly indifferent to it. They asked concerning Him, "Hath any man brought Him ought to eat? Jesus said unto them, "My meat is to do the will of Him that sent Me, and to finish His work." It was satisfying to Him to have met and saved a poor sinner. And it should be meat for us to sit at His feet and learn from Him. Then we can go forth and feed others.

But Martha did not understand, and so she said to Him, "Lord, dost Thou not care that my sister hath left me to serve alone? Bid her therefore that she help me." We are told Martha was "cumbered about much serving." It is so easy to become burdened with our daily responsibilities and neglect to spend time at the feet of Jesus. "And Jesus answered and said unto her, Martha, Martha, thou art careful and troubled about many things." I think there must have been real sympathy when He repeated her name and referred to her worry and anxiety that He should have a well-cooked and tasty meal. He did not blame her for serving, but that was a small thing compared to sitting at His feet. "Mary," He declared, "hath chosen that good part, which shall not be taken away from her." This was the one thing needful, or one thing whereof there is need. It was not personal salvation to which He referred, or which drew Mary to

His feet. The one prime necessity is to be subject to Christ in all things. This was what characterized Mary, and this He would have her continue to enjoy. In other words, Mary delighted in communion with Him, and thus she was pleasing to His great loving heart. He longs for the fellowship of His people.

"Low at Thy feet, Lord Jesus;
 This is the place for me;
There I have learned sweet lessons,
 Truth that has set me free.

"Free from myself, Lord Jesus,
 Free from the ways of men;
Chains of thought that once bound me
 Never will bind again.

"None but Thyself, Lord Jesus,
 Conquered this wayward will;
But for Thy grace, my Saviour,
 I should be wayward still."

I am ashamed to say that in a very busy life, I have not spent nearly as much time at His feet as I should, but every hour spent there has meant far more than time spent in any other way.

I remember hearing of a dear father who had lost his wife. She had left him one daughter, and he loved to have her with him; but being a busy man they could have only their evenings together. He would come home from work, and after dinner they would spend several hours together, and one or the other would read; then she would play and sing for him. He found his greatest solace in the company of his darling child. It was getting along towards the end of the year, and the daughter said to him one evening, "You will excuse me tonight, father; I have something I should do in my room." The next night it was the same thing, and the next, and the next, much to his disappointment. But he had to get used to it, and he did not like to ask her what she was doing that she had to leave him alone. Finally it was Christmas morning, and she came into his room and called, "Merry Christmas, Dad!" She handed him a pair of crocheted slippers which she had made for him. He said after he had thanked her, "I would much rather have had you with me all those lonely evenings than to have these slippers, beautiful and comfortable as they are." I think our Lord says that to us. We are trying to please Him by much serving, but I am afraid He will say to many of us, "You have spent so many hours in service when I would rather have had you at My feet. You were not there when I wanted to share many secrets with you." May we learn more and more the blessedness of communion with Him!

ADDRESS FORTY

TEACHING ON PRAYER

✝ ✝ ✝

"And it came to pass, that, as He was praying in a certain place, when He ceased, one of His disciples said unto Him, Lord, teach us to pray as John also taught his disciples. And He said unto them, When ye pray, say, Our Father which art in heaven, Hallowed be Thy name. Thy kingdom come. Thy will be done, as in heaven, so in earth. Give us day by day our daily bread. And forgive us our sins; for we also forgive every one that is indebted to us. And lead us not into temptation; but deliver us from evil. And He said unto them, Which of you shall have a friend, and shall go unto him at midnight, and say unto him, Friend, lend me three loaves; for a friend of mine in his journey is come to me, and I have nothing to set before him? And he from within shall answer and say, Trouble me not: the door is now shut, and my children are with me in bed; I cannot rise and give thee. I say unto you, Though he will not rise and give him, because he is his friend, yet because of his importunity he will rise and give him as many as he needeth. And I say unto you, Ask, and it shall be given you; seek, and ye shall find; knock, and it shall be opened unto you. For every one that asketh receiveth; and he that seeketh findeth; and to him that knocketh it shall be opened. If a son shall ask bread of any of you that is a father, will he give him a stone? or if he ask a fish, will he for a fish give him a serpent? Or if he shall ask an egg, will he offer him a scorpion? If ye then, being evil, know how to give good gifts unto your children: how much more shall your heavenly Father give the Holy Spirit to them that ask Him?"—Luke 11: 1-13.

✝ ✝ ✝

IN this passage we have our blessed Lord instructing His disciples as to the privilege of prayer. He had been stressing the lesson of how important it is to sit at His feet, and now His disciples came to Him as He was speaking to His Father. They asked Him to teach them to pray as John the Baptist had taught his disciples. The disciples' plea, "Lord, teach us to pray," implied not only the need of instruction as to the proper language to use in prayer, but it also suggests the need of compelling power to move us to prayer.

Prayer is the normal expression of divine life, just as breathing is of natural life. Of every newborn soul it can be said, as of Saul of Tarsus, "Behold, he prayeth" (Acts 9:11). But there are certain important spiritual laws in connection with prayer which are learned only in fellowship with our blessed Lord. He was Himself a Man of prayer in the days of His humiliation here on earth, and He is still the great Intercessor at the Father's right hand.

In response He gave them the outline of what is commonly called "the Lord's Prayer." Strictly speaking, of course, it was not the Lord's prayer, because He did not pray it. Our blessed Lord could not say the prayer as expressing His own needs and desires, because He was the absolutely sinless One. He, therefore, could not pray, "Forgive us our sins." His disciples were still sinful men as we are, and so they needed to come to the Father for forgiveness. It would rather be designated "the disciples' prayer." It was never intended, apparently, to be used in a formal way, for there is no mention of such use anywhere in the Book of Acts, or in any of the epistles which give us Church practice as well as doctrine. But it is a model upon which all our prayers may well be formed. Used in this way, it fulfils the purpose for which it was given. We need to remember that it was part of our Saviour's instruction to His own disciples. No one else is entitled to come to God in this way. When He is known as Father we are invited to bring our petitions to Him, assured that He delights to answer. If He seems to be indifferent, as in the case of the friend who did not attend immediately to the request of his neighbor, it is only to test our faith and perseverance. Truth is seldom found in extremes. There are some who insist that the so-called "Lord's Prayer" is intended for use on all occasions as a set form, and that the mere repetition of its beautiful phrases has an almost magical effect. Others are averse to using it at all and consider its petitions unsuited for the present dispensation of grace, and applicable only to the days when Christ was on earth and in the tribulation period yet to come. But surely there is no expression in it that the most enlightened Christian may not use on occasion, and as a whole it is of the greatest value in guiding our thoughts when we approach our Father in prayer.

But in Matthew's Gospel, we find it as given for private prayer. Here it perhaps has a wider application. The words are not always the same in both Gospels. There are slight variations showing us that we do not have to say the same expressions each time when we come to God in prayer. Someone has said that it is "the prayer that teaches to pray."

Prayer, with Jesus, was the expression of communion with the Father, from whom, as Man, He drew His strength day by day. His example moved the disciples to cry, "Lord, teach us to pray!" John the Baptist had instructed his followers along prayer lines. They desired Jesus to teach them how to draw nigh unto God. Notice the example given. They were to say, "Our Father which art in heaven." First of all, Jesus emphasizes the Father's name, which He came to declare (John 17:26). It is only those who are born of God who have the right thus to address Him. In true prayer we must know the Father and come to Him with adoring hearts, desiring that His will be done. When unsaved sinners use the prayer that Jesus gave as a religious form, they are appropriating what is not theirs. It is only the one who can say in faith that God is his Father, who has the right to use such words. This is a recognition of the blessed relationship between the saved and the God who saved them. God should be approached with reverence. The prayer begins with worship: "Hallowed be Thy name." It would be well for us if we had His glory and majesty impressed on us. We should bow in adoration before we express a petition of our own.

"Thy kingdom come. Thy will be done, as in heaven, so in earth." Faith looks forward to that time when the Lord shall come the second time and deliver His own from all the distracting conditions that now prevail. In that day all evil shall be put down and men "shall beat their swords into plowshares, and their spears into pruninghooks: nation shall not lift up sword against nation, neither shall they learn war any more." Then indeed the will of God will be done on earth as it is now done in heaven. All real blessing for mankind is bound up in the doing of His will. Some people act as though doing the will of God would take all the joy out of life, but it is just the opposite.

Next we have the matter of our temporal provision. "Give us day by day our daily bread." We are instructed to come to the Father about our daily needs. He has promised to supply our every need as we walk in obedience to His Word (Matt. 6:33). We are told elsewhere that we are to be anxious for nothing, but in everything, by prayer and supplication with thanksgiving, to make our desires known. Though He knows all about our desires already, He is delighted to have us bring all to Him from day to day.

"And forgive us our sins; for we also forgive every one that is indebted to us. And lead us not into temptation; but deliver us from evil." It is not the sinner who is in view, but the failing believer. If we will not forgive, we cannot be forgiven (Mark 11:26). This is an unalterable principle in God's government of His family. When a believer has sinned and seeks restoration, he is forgiven as he forgives. This is not the same thing as the justification of a sinner, which is by faith alone. But having been ourselves forgiven, we are to forgive those who offend us, "even as God for Christ's sake hath forgiven us" (Eph. 4:32). We are told, "Even as Christ forgave you, so also do ye" (Col. 3:13). If we do not obey His Word, we will knock in vain at the door of restoration when we ourselves have failed. When we confess our sins, we dare not harbor ill-will even to those who have wronged us most. The poor sinner finds forgiveness when he trusts the Lord Jesus as his own Saviour. "Through His name whosoever believeth in Him shall receive remission of sins." But what we have here is the Father's forgiveness when His own children fail, and if we forgive not our brethren then the Father will not grant us restorative forgiveness.

Next we have the acknowledgment of recognized weakness: "And lead us not into temptation; but deliver us from evil." As if to say, "My Father, I am so weak myself, grant that I might not be put in a place of temptation which I could not stand and overcome." That is, recognizing our weakness, we pray not to be exposed to a test too great for us.

Following this, our Lord gave His disciples a parable in order that they might be encouraged in importunate prayer. Sometimes we come to God in the attitude of prayer, but there is no real exercise of soul, and so He waits until there is greater concern before He answers. Our Lord illustrates it like this: "And He said unto them, Which of you shall have a friend, and shall go unto him at midnight, and say unto him, Friend, lend me three loaves." The friend here pictures God who is the Friend of all, and would have us repair to Him in every trying circumstance and in every hour of need. He speaks of intercession on behalf of another. He pictures a man who has lost his way, coming to a friend of his and seeking refreshment and shelter. But the other finds himself out of needed provision, so he says, "I am sorry, but I do not have enough to help you. I have a friend who will, I am sure, be able to supply the need." So off to his friend he goes at midnight, and rouses him up and pleads for bread to meet the need of his visitor. He says, "Friend, lend me three loaves; for a friend of mine in his journey (or, literally, out of his way) is come to me, and I have nothing to set before him." It is intercession concerning the needs of another. In full confidence the householder seeks the help of his friend, assured that he will not be denied.

But the householder is not willing to disturb his whole family at that hour of the night. He pleads to be left alone, for he has retired, and his children also are all in bed. Such might well be the answer even of the most faithful friend disturbed at the midnight hour. This is used only as an illustration of what, to our poor finite minds, might seem to be the attitude of God when we do not receive immediately the answer to our prayer. No request of ours can ever be a trouble to Him. His delays are not denials, but are meant to test our faith.

In this story the suppliant continues to knock. He refuses to be denied. He will not take "no" for an answer. Finally one can imagine his friend saying to his wife, "We shall have no sleep tonight unless I attend to his plea." So he goes to the pantry and gets the bread, and gives it to his persistent neighbor. We are taught to continue instant in prayer (Rom. 12: 12) until the answer comes. We are not to be discouraged because God does not respond to our call at the first moment when we go to Him in regard to some particular matter.

Jesus applies the story by stressing three words in regard to prayer — *"Ask . . . Seek . . . Knock."* It is for our own soul's good that we become earnest in our supplications, pouring out our hearts in unremitting intercession, literally storming the gate of the storehouse of blessing until the answer comes. God will never deny the prayer of faith. "Ask," "Seek," "Knock," are degrees of importunity. As we continue to besiege the throne of grace we shall be moved to heart-searching and to self-judgment, that thus we may pray according to the will of God.

"Every one that asketh receiveth." The promise is very broad. It does not ignore instruction given elsewhere in regard to prayer, but it speaks of that which is normal: the believing soul going to God in unselfish intercession, counting on Him to meet every need. He can be depended upon to honor His Word and to give according to His infinite wisdom. Prayer is not trying to make God willing to bless. It is taking that place before Him where He can bless consistently with His own holy nature.

"If a son shall ask bread of any of you that is a father, will he give him a stone? Or if he ask a fish, will he for a fish give him a serpent? Or if he shall ask an egg, will he offer him a scorpion?" Just as no loving, earthly parent would disappoint his child by giving what is worthless or harmful instead of the good sought, neither will God (though He reserves the right to give according to His wisdom rather than according to our asking) ever give what will, in the long run, be a disappointment to us. If He substitutes something else for what we ask, we can be sure it will be better than that for which we have pleaded. The egg would sustain life; the scorpion would destroy it. No loving parent would thus deceive his child.

"How much more shall your heavenly Father give the Holy Spirit to them that ask Him?" This is the supreme gift for those who have trusted the Son. The Holy Spirit is the abiding Guest in the heart of all believers. His power will be made manifest in their lives as they are yielded to God, who is the Source of all blessing.

Prayer is the expression of dependence and confidence. Because we are weak in ourselves we turn for help to One who is almighty. Knowing His love as our heavenly Father, we trust Him, and so come into His presence with holy boldness to make known our requests. In answer to prayer He has chosen to give certain blessings which we will never receive if we do not pray, in order that He might draw our hearts out into communion with Himself and give us positive proof that we have to do with a living God. Our very needs furnish Him with the opportunity to display His tender love and compassion for us, and to manifest Himself as a personal God who delights to hear our cries and rejoices in coming to our relief.

It is a very blessed privilege to know God in such intimacy that we can go to Him on behalf of others. "This honor have all His saints" (Ps. 149:9). We do not pray aright if we are not subject to the will of God.

Only as we are walking in the Spirit can we pray in the Holy Spirit. This is characteristic of prevailing prayer in the new dispensation.

Address Forty-one

MISUNDERSTANDING JESUS

✝ ✝ ✝

"And He was casting out a devil, and it was dumb. And it came to pass, when the devil was gone out, the dumb spake; and the people wondered. But some of them said, He casteth out devils through Beelzebub the chief of the devils. And others, tempting Him, sought of Him a sign from heaven. But He, knowing their thoughts, said unto them, Every kingdom divided against itself is brought to desolation; and a house divided against a house falleth. If Satan also be divided against himself, how shall his kingdom stand? because ye say that I cast out devils through Beelzebub. And if I by Beelzebub cast out devils, by whom do your sons cast them out? therefore shall they be your judges. But if I with the finger of God cast out devils, no doubt the kingdom of God is come upon you. When a strong man armed keepeth his palace, his goods are in peace: but when a stronger than he shall come upon him, and overcome him, he taketh from him all his armour wherein he trusted, and divideth his spoils. He that is not with Me is against Me: and he that gathereth not with Me scattereth. When the unclean spirit is gone out of a man, he walketh through dry places, seeking rest; and finding none, he saith, I will return unto my house whence I came out. And when he cometh, he findeth it swept and garnished. Then goeth he, and taketh to him seven other spirits more wicked than himself; and they enter in, and dwell there: and the last state of that man is worse than the first. And it came to pass, as He spake these things, a certain woman of the company lifted up her voice, and said unto Him, Blessed is the womb that bare Thee, and the paps which Thou hast sucked. But He said, Yea rather, blessed are they that hear the word of God, and keep it"—Luke 11: 14-28.

✝ ✝ ✝

THERE are five sections to this portion of Scripture. First, in verses 14-16, we have the Lord casting out demons, the wonder of the people and evil thoughts running through the minds of His enemies—certain of the Pharisees who were looking on. Second, in verses 17-20 our Lord is talking with the Pharisees. Third, in verses 21-23, the parable of the stronger one who takes away the armour of the strong. In verses 24-26 we have the parable of the unclean spirit cast out, and the empty house. Then in verses 27 and 28 we have our Lord's words to the woman who had ascribed special honor and glory to the mother of Jesus. He refused anything of the kind, because it is not the will of God that we should put the mother in the place of the Son.

In the first part, then, we find the Lord Jesus, as usual, ministering mercy and grace to needy souls; and among others, there was one who was demon-possessed. The demon had such control of the man that he was unable to speak. But when the Lord cast out the evil spirit the man spoke freely, and the people wondered. But while they marveled at what was done, they did not recognize the fact that a great prophet had arisen among them, nor that One stood in their midst to show them the way to God. So they found fault with Him. They were continually misunderstanding Him, mainly because they did not desire to know the truth. How many people there are in our own day who will find fault with the Bible, with Christianity, with the Lord Jesus Christ, but who never make any effort to discover the truth. They seldom look into the pages of the Bible; they do not seem to want to find out what God has to say. They do not attend meetings where they might hear the Word preached, or observe what is taking place; and yet they are insistent on finding fault with the teachings of the Book they never open. I think one of the best ways to silence people like that is to challenge them to search the Bible for themselves and find the truth.

Often we hear something like this: "I hear the preacher teaches so and so," or "The Bible teaches so and so." We should ask them, "Do you ever read the Bible?" You will find that they do not know the Scriptures with which they are finding fault. And so it was when our Lord was here. They had no desire to understand Him; they had no thought of taking His messages seriously. They had made up their minds that He could not be the Messiah, and so everything He did and said they misinterpreted. Even when He manifested His mighty power by casting out demons, some said, "He casteth out demons in the name of Beelzebub, the chief of the demons." It was as much as to say that the demons are subject to a leader, which of course is absolutely true. They called that leader "Beelzebub," which is another name for Satan. The name of one of the Phoenician gods was Beelzebub, which means "the lord of flies." Such pagan nations had gods over everything. These Jews were really saying that the Lord Jesus was able to cast out demons because He was in league with the prince of the demons, and that the prince of the demons gave Him authority, and that the demons obeyed. There was no proof of this. They had never investigated. They never so much as talked it over with Him. They never looked into the matter, but they just jumped at that conclusion. And so men jump at conclusions today. Jesus has always been misunderstood. These people were hypocrites. They were trying to cover up their sins with a cloak of pretended righteousness, and when Jesus exposed their hypocrisy they hated Him for it.

You remember the story of the African chieftainess in the days of Robert Moffat. He had notice one day that he was to be visited by this chieftainess, and so he dressed up in his best clothes in order to meet her. She came attired in barbaric splendor. As she talked with him she happened to see a mirror hanging from a tree outside his cabin door. She had never seen anything like it before. She went up to examine it, and what she saw startled her. She beheld the ugliest face she had ever seen. She looked on the other side but saw nothing. Then she asked for an explanation. Whose was that awful face she saw in the glass? He explained that it was her own face. When at last she was convinced it was true, she demanded the mirror. He did not want to part with it; he needed it to shave, to trim and comb his hair. But she was insistent and offered to buy it from him, giving in trade elephant-tusks, or something else of value. He thought it would be better to be on good terms with her and so he sold it to her. And when she received it she took one last look at herself in it and dashed it to pieces on the ground, declaring that it would never tell on her again. That suggests why these hypocrites were always finding fault with our Lord. We read in John's Gospel that the True Light gives light to, or, literally, casts light upon every man that cometh into the world. Their wickedness was manifested in the light of His purity and holiness, and so they charged Him with being in league with the prince of the demons. They tempted Him by asking for a sign from heaven: "If You are what You claim to be, then do what Elijah did — command fire to come down from heaven." But our Lord never performed any miracle to gratify curiosity, but only to meet the needs of poor, suffering humanity. So He told them, "Every kingdom divided against itself is brought to desolation; and a house divided against a house falleth. If Satan also be divided against himself, how shall his kingdom stand?" If what they insisted upon was true, then Satan was trying to destroy his own kingdom. The Lord Jesus said, "You say I cast out demons in the name of Beelzebub; what about your own sons? Here are Peter, James, and John and the other apostles, who also cast out demons. You say I cast them out by the power of the devil, then you are saying this of your own sons."

"When a strong man armed keepeth his palace, his goods are in peace: but when a stronger than he shall come upon him, and overcome him, he taketh from him all his armour wherein he trusted, and divideth his spoils. He that is not with Me is against Me: and he that gathereth not with Me scattereth." It is easy to see who the strong man is, even Satan himself, who has held mankind in bondage for centuries, yes, thousands of years; but when Jesus came into the world He bound the strong man. When Satan came to tempt Jesus in the wilderness our Lord met him every time with the Holy Scripture. He broke the power of Satan in the lives of people who had been his poor slaves. Now it becomes us to take sides with Him against Satan. "He that is not with Me is against Me: and he that gathereth not with Me scattereth." You know what Jesus has done for you: He has delivered you from the power of sin. You know He has broken the chains of habit that bound you; but do you fully yield to Him? Have you taken your place in association with Him, owning Him before the world not only as your Saviour but as your Lord?

Next comes the parable of the unclean spirit to show the danger of professing outward allegiance to Him and having nothing in the heart. "When the unclean spirit is gone out of a man, he walketh through dry places, seeking rest: and finding none, he saith, I will return unto my house whence I came out. And when he cometh, he findeth it swept and garnished. Then goeth he, and taketh to him seven other spirits more wicked than himself; and they enter in, and dwell there: and the last state of that man is worse than the first." Jesus likens the body and soul of a man to a house in which the evil spirit has dwelt. After the demon has been driven out, the house is empty, for the Spirit of God does not come into the man who has not accepted Christ. He pictures the demon as one going out into the wilderness seeking an abode, wandering through desolate places and finding no home. At last he says, "I will return to my house from whence I came." When he returns he finds it swept and garnished. There is no one living in it. There may be no evil habits in the life, but Christ has not found lodgment in that heart; so the evil spirit says, "I will take me seven other evil spirits, and we will take up our abode in him." Thus the last state of that man becomes worse than the first.

This has a special application to Israel. The unclean spirit of idolatry had been cast out of Israel, as a result of the Babylonian captivity. God sent them into Babylon to cure them of idolatry. Whatever else they failed in, they were never again an idolatrous nation. All down through the centuries since, Israel has maintained its confession, "The Lord our God is One." The house was empty, swept and garnished when God sent His blessed Son to bring salvation to all who would trust Him. He was not received, so the religion of Israel has remained in the same empty condition ever since. The day is coming when the evil spirit of idolatry will return to the nation, with seven other spirits more evil than itself. In the great tribulation Israel will be given over to worse corruption than they have ever known before, when they accept the antichrist instead of the Christ of God. What a dangerous thing it is when the house has been delivered from evil habits and not given to Christ! Unless He does come in and take possession it is not enough to be freed from certain evil habits. We say, "Nature abhors a vacuum;" and it is just as true in the spiritual realm.

"And it came to pass, as He spake these things, a certain woman of the company lifted up her voice, and said unto Him, Blessed is the womb that bare Thee, and the paps which Thou hast sucked. But He said, Yea rather, blessed are they that hear the word of God, and keep it." This woman's cry meant, "Blessed be Your mother;" and Jesus immediately answered, "Blessed, rather, are they that hear the Word of God and keep it." All down through the centuries there has been a tendency to put the mother in the place of the Saviour, to make Mary the mediator, giving her the place that belongs alone to Christ. "There is one Mediator between God and men, the Man Christ Jesus." Our Lord would not for a moment have us adore His mother, blessed as she is; but He pronounces a special blessing on those who honor and obey the Word of God. May we take His messages to heart and walk in subjection to the Holy Scriptures, not substituting human tradition for His revealed will.

ADDRESS FORTY-TWO

RESPONSIBILITY ACCORDING TO LIGHT

ł ł ł

"And when the people were gathered thick together, He began to say, This is an evil generation: they seek a sign; and there shall no sign be given it, but the sign of Jonas the prophet. For as Jonas was a sign unto the Ninevites, so shall also the Son of Man be to this generation. The queen of the south shall rise up in the judgment with the men of this generation, and condemn them: for she came from the utmost parts of the earth to hear the wisdom of Solomon; and, behold, a greater than Solomon is here. The men of Nineve shall rise up in the judgment with this generation, and shall condemn it: for they repented at the preaching of Jonas, and, behold, a greater than Jonas is here. No man, when he hath lighted a candle, putteth it in a secret place, neither under a bushel, but on a candlestick, that they which come in may see the light. The light of the body is the eye, therefore when thine eye is single, thy whole body also is full of light; but when thine eye is evil, thy body also is full of darkness. Take heed therefore that the light which is in thee be not darkness. If thy whole body therefore be full of light, having no part dark, the whole shall be full of light, as when the bright shining of a candle doth give thee light"—Luke 11: 29-36.

ł ł ł

WE are taught throughout the Word of God that our responsibility depends upon the light that God graciously gives us. The other day a young soldier wrote me from far-off New Guinea. He said, "I never in my life realized the true condition of the heathen until I got down here in New Guinea." He told me that he had gone out among the raw heathen who had never heard of Christ or known anything about the gospel. He said it is awfully hard to believe that these men are going to be lost because of their ignorance. "I can't understand it. Have you anything that would help to cast light on this problem?" he asked. One can turn only to the Word of God for light; there is none to be found anywhere else. In the book of Job (34:23) we read definitely that God will not lay upon any man more than is right. In the day of judgment He will deal righteously. We are taught that, "To him that knoweth to do good, and doeth it not, to him it is sin." In the first chapter of the Epistle to the Romans we read that paganism is not a step upward in the evolution of religion as many try to make it appear, but it is a definite declension. It is a degradation; it is a condition into which men have fallen, because of having turned away from the light which they once had. Man did not begin as a pagan, reaching up out of the darkness and seeking after God. He began with a full, clear revelation of God. In the beginning all men had the truth of the one living God. But many do not like to face that knowledge today; they do not like to realize that they have to do with God and that He is infinitely holy and righteous. This was so in the past ages when men turned away from the truth because they did not like to retain the knowledge of God.

In that first chapter of Romans we get the expressions, "God gave them up" and "God gave them over," four times. Why? Because they gave *Him* up; they turned away from *Him*. They refused to walk in the light He had given them, and so He gave them up to darkness. But even today, although men are in darkness, everyone has a conscience. Every man knows something of right and wrong.

His own conscience tells him he should love his fellowmen; that he should be pure, and kind, and true. But instead of that, men turn away from God and become impure, unkind, and untruthful; and all the time their consciences are convicting them of wrongdoing. In the day of judgment God is going to deal with men according to the light they have had and the light they have rejected. He will not cast the heathen into hell-fire simply because they never knew and believed in the Lord Jesus Christ when nobody carried the message to them; but the heathen are lost because of their own sin, because of their own wickedness, the vileness of which they are guilty. Thank God, "the Son of Man is come to seek and to save that which was lost." That is where our responsibility comes in. We are to go to them and tell them how they may be saved. But let us suppose there is a heathen man living in darkness who wants to know the right way, who wants to be right before God; then I dare to say and believe that God will make Himself responsible to give him light enough to be saved. We may be sure that God will never allow a man to be lost who desires to be saved; He will give him light in some way or another.

But we at home need to be concerned about ourselves. We who have heard the gospel and have had the knowledge of Christ, we who know what our responsibility is, who have heard it all through the years, yet have done nothing about it! When our Lord Jesus was here on earth, those to whom the revelation of the Old Testament had been given came to Him wanting to see a sign from Him. They had a sign. They had the Bible. They should have known who Jesus was; they should have known when the Messiah was to come, and where He was to be born, and what kind of personality He would be. Though professing to believe the Bible, they did not search the Scriptures to find out whether or not Christ was the Son of God. They said, rather, "We would see a sign from heaven," a sign to gratify their curiosity.

I can remember when I was a lad, deeply concerned about my own soul, I read in my Bible of angels appearing to men, and I went to my room, closed the door and said, "O God, if You will only send an angel to me to reveal things to me I will be saved." But no angel appeared, and I am glad of it now. Instead of sending an angel He sent me back to His Word, and not long after, through the Word, I was saved. Just as these Jews came to Jesus seeking a sign, so many in our generation seek a sign. It is the evidence of our unbelief and unwillingness to rest on His simple promise. Jesus said, "There shall no sign be given it, but the sign of Jonas the prophet, for as Jonas was three days and three nights in the belly of the sea-monster, so shall the Son of Man be three days and three nights in the heart of the earth." In other words, the sign that was to be given was that of our Lord's resurrection from the dead. Alas, many people still come seeking for a sign, refusing to believe in the risen Saviour in the face of the evidence of the empty tomb. He said that the Queen of the South, that is, of Sheba, who came to hear the famous Solomon concerning the name of the Lord, "shall rise up in the day of judgment with the men of this generation, and condemn them: for she came from the utmost parts of the earth to hear the wisdom of Solomon; and behold, a greater than Solomon is here." Sheba's queen dwelt a long way from Jerusalem, but she had a hungry heart, and she was anxious to know the truth of God. She had heard that there was a great king in Jerusalem to whom great wisdom had been given, and who knew the true God and would be able to answer her questions and solve her problems. So she, at great cost to herself, came to Jerusalem, and when she met Solomon and communed with him, she was so stirred that she said, "The half hath not been told me." The Lord Jesus said in the day of judgment Sheba's queen will rise up against the men and women who have had every opportunity to know God, to know the truth, to know Christ, and yet they do not avail themselves of their privileges. In the day of judgment, if you who are living in a Christian land, go on as you are, you who have heard the gospel read and expounded from babyhood and yet have never opened your heart to Jesus Christ—if you go into eternity like that, how terrible it will be when you see standing beside the Son of God, the Queen of Sheba who gave so much to hear the truth. She will point her finger at you and say, "If only I had lived when you lived and had your opportunities how gladly would I have availed myself of them." It is a terrible mistake to sin against the light that God gives us.

Then our Lord Jesus said to the self-righteous Jews, that in the day of judgment, "The men of Nineve shall rise up in the judgment with this generation, and shall condemn it: for they repented at the preaching of Jonas, and behold, a greater than Jonas is here." Many men reject the story of Jonas, and some who even stand at the sacred desk in our churches would cast out this story as false; but our Lord Jesus, God manifested in the flesh, said that as Jonas was three days and three nights in the belly of the sea-monster, He would be three days and three nights in the heart of the earth. Thus He has placed His seal of authority upon that little Old Testament book which has been rejected and ridiculed by agnostics throughout the centuries. Jesus knew Jonas, and Jesus knew the men of Nineveh, and it is recorded that the men of Nineveh repented. Think of facing the men of Nineveh and having them look at you and say, "You had so many privileges and opportunities and yet you spurned them. We believed the first message from God that we ever heard. We believed the first time a prophet came to proclaim the divine truth, and God had mercy on us and saved us; but you have heard the Word expounded over and over again, and you turned away because of your love for the world. You were more concerned about gratifying your natural desires on earth than about obtaining a holy home in heaven." The men of Nineveh shall rise up in the judgment with this generation and condemn it, for they repented, and you have repented not. God grant that you may repent today and say to Him, "I have heard the Word so many times. I have had so much light; yet I have gone far from it; I have walked in darkness. Now I come confessing my sins and trusting Thy Son."

When we receive light then we are responsible to pass it on to others. Our Saviour gave the parable of the lighted candle, "No man, when he hath lighted a candle, putteth it in a secret place, neither under a bushel, but on a candlestick, that they which come in may see the light." If I have received light from heaven I am not to hide my light under a bed or a bushel or in a secret place. I am not to allow anything in my domestic life or in my business to hinder me from shining for God. Wherever I am and whatever my circumstances, I am responsible to pass on to others the light which He has given to me. Let us face this very seriously, my Christian brethren and sisters. Are we allowing anything in our behavior which is dimming the light? How about our next-door neighbors? Do they believe in our Christian profession, or is our light so hidden that they cannot see it, and do not even know that we are Christians?

I once knew a man who was going away for the summer to cut timber, and expected to be back in the fall. I said to him, "You will find yourself among the ungodly, and may the Lord help you to stand firm in your testimony." He said he would be all right. He came back after three months. I said, "I am glad to see you. How did you get along this summer; did you find any other Christians there?" He said, "I was the only one, but I did not have any difficulty with the unsaved men. As a matter-of-fact, I managed to keep it so quiet that no one ever found out that I was a Christian." That is hiding your light, and that is the very thing the Lord tells us we are not to do. If I know Christ as my Saviour, instead of keeping quiet about it I am to speak for Him, speaking not only with my lips but with my life as well. If lips and life do not agree, the testimony will not amount to much.

The Saviour uses another beautiful illustration: "The light of the body is the eye." Therefore when my eye is single ("single" really means "sound"), that is, when it is healthy, the whole body is full of light. My feet do not have any eyes, but my feet know where to go if I have sound eyes; my hands do not have eyes, but my hands know how to perform aright if I have sound eyes. If I have sound eyes my whole body is full of light. On the other hand, if my eye is evil, that is, if the eye is diseased, then the whole body is full of darkness. When my eye is diseased I cannot see where to go, and I do not know how to use my hands; I need someone to direct me all the time. As Christians we are to have a single, or sound, eye. We will keep our eyes fixed on Christ when the eye is sound.

"When my eyes are fixed on Jesus
I lose sight of all beside;
So enchained my spirit's vision,
Gazing at the Crucified."

When I am occupied with Him I have no difficulty finding my way through this world and doing that which He would have me do, but I need to be careful lest something come to spoil my eyesight. It is so easy to fall into habits that lead to moral darkness, or take up with things that will darken the spiritual eyesight. Give attention to God's Word; cultivate the desire to read the Word of God. Nothing will kill the desire to read the Word of God so much as the habit of reading the trashy literature that prevails in so many places today. You cannot get spiritual light in this manner. People say, "I read my Bible, but I do not get much out of it." The reason is that the eye is not sound; it has become dull, partially blinded and occupied with things that are opposed to the truth of God and the Holy Spirit who dwells within you. If, on the other hand, your eye be sound then your whole body will be sound, having no part darkness. So our blessed Lord stresses firmly the importance of walking in the light that He gives. Think of the responsibility of those who have already come to God in Christ, to pass that light on to others, and to so live before God that they will always have clear vision themselves to do what the Lord would have them do. If you have not received the light of life, if you have never trusted Christ as your Saviour, oh, I warn you, be careful! All men by nature are in darkness, but there is something worse than that. When you refuse the light that is offered you the darkness becomes far more serious than that darkness in which you were born. We read, "Men love darkness rather than light because their deeds are evil." That is wilful darkness. If men persist in going on in darkness, turning their backs to the light, the day may come when God will give them up to judicial darkness. In Jeremiah 13:16 we read, "Give glory unto the Lord your God before He cause darkness, and before your feet stumble upon the dark mountains, and while ye look for light, He turn it into the shadow of death, and make it gross darkness." If you persist in loving darkness rather than light God may some day say, "If you want the darkness you may have it," and you will enter into the darkness forever. That is the doom of those who have refused the light—eternal darkness!

ADDRESS FORTY-THREE

SEARCHING TABLE-TALKS

✓ ✓ ✓

"And as He spake, a certain Pharisee besought Him to dine with him: and He went in, and sat down to meat. And when the Pharisee saw it, he marvelled that He had not first washed before dinner. And the Lord said unto him, Now do ye Pharisees make clean the outside of the cup and the platter; but your inward part is full of ravening and wickedness. Ye fools, did not He that made that which is without make that which is within also? But rather give alms of such things as ye have; and, behold, all things are clean unto you. But woe unto you, Pharisees! for ye tithe mint and rue and all manner of herbs, and pass over judgment and the love of God: these ought ye to have done, and not to leave the other undone. Woe unto you, Pharisees! for ye love the uppermost seats in the synagogues, and greetings in the markets. Woe unto you, scribes and Pharisees, hypocrites! for ye are as graves which appear not, and the men that walk over them are not aware of them. Then answered one of the lawyers, and said unto Him, Master, thus saying Thou reproachest us also. And He said, Woe unto you also, ye lawyers! for ye lade men with burdens grievous to be borne, and ye yourselves touch not the burdens with one of your fingers. Woe unto you! for ye build the sepulchres of the prophets, and your fathers killed them. Truly ye bear witness that ye allow the deeds of your fathers: for they indeed killed them, and ye build their sepulchres. Therefore also said the Wisdom of God, I will send them prophets and apostles, and some of them they shall slay and persecute: that the blood of all the prophets, which was shed from the foundation of the world, may be required of this generation; from the blood of Abel unto the blood of Zacharias which perished between the altar and the temple: verily I say unto you, It shall be required of this generation. Woe unto you, lawyers! for ye have taken away the key of knowledge: ye entered not in yourselves, and them that were entering in ye hindered. And as He said these things unto them, the scribes and the Pharisees began to urge Him vehemently, and to provoke Him to speak of many things: laying wait for Him, and seeking to catch something out of His mouth, that they might accuse Him"—Luke 11: 37-54.

✓ ✓ ✓

WE have noticed before in our attempt to expound this Gospel that Luke frequently tells of the Saviour's being invited out to dinner and his participation at the table with various groups of people. We have mentioned that there is no place nor circumstance which draws a man out and shows what he really is more than the dinner-table, when surrounded either by friends with whom he may have fellowship, or in the midst of enemies who are ready to find fault with him. A great part of the Gospel of Luke is made up of the table talk of our Lord. We have already considered some instances, and here we have another. On every such occasion His words are most faithful. Our Lord Jesus was always honest with people; He never flattered them; He never pretended to be what He was not; He never endorsed anything which was wrong; nevertheless He was never rude nor offensive, but faithful and true in all circumstances.

Here we read that a certain Pharisee invited Jesus to dine with him, and "He went in, and sat down to meat." There were other Pharisees present, and the host noticed that when Jesus was ready to recline at the table He did not go through a ceremony that was customary among them—He did not "baptize" before eating. This did not refer simply to the washing of the hands but to an elaborate cleansing in order that one might be fit to partake of the meal. This was of a religious nature, and they thought when this ceremony was finished they were clean before God. So the Pharisees marveled that Jesus had not "baptized" before eating. The Lord said unto them, "Now do ye Pharisees make clean the outside of the cup and the platter; but your inward part is full of ravening and wickedness. Ye fools, did not He that made that which is without make that which is within also?" In these words our Lord Jesus Christ insisted that though these religious zealots laid great stress upon the externals of piety, they neglected the internal realities that should have meant so much more to them. Many professed Christians make the same mistake today. They lay far more stress on outward ceremonies than on the inward life. There are those, for instance, who imagine that the ordinance of baptism cleanses them from sin, and that they are regenerated thereby.

The Lord saw into the very hearts of men, and He told them it was not enough to observe legal ordinances. If He were here today He would rebuke, just as strongly as He rebuked these Pharisees, those who imagine that being a Christian depends on church-membership and ritual-services, rather than the cleansing of the soul before God. Our Lord told these Pharisees that they were very careful about cleaning the outside of the cup, but they did not clean the inside. They did not seem to understand that He who made the outside made also the inside. They cleansed the body with water, but the heart was full of ravening and wickedness. What God wants above everything else is a clean heart.

Our Lord was not ignoring the importance of the cleansing of the body, but that alone is not enough: the heart must be purified by faith. "Blessed are the pure in heart: for they shall see God." "But rather give alms of such things as ye have; and, behold, all things are clean unto you." That is, when the love of God fills the heart so that one will be concerned about the needs of others, then only will these outward observances have any real value. How we need to take that to heart today! We receive blessing after blessing from God, and how seldom do we remember that we are to communicate to others of the good things which God has given to us. You can test the measure of a man's spirituality, not by a pious look on his face, nor by his words, but very largely by his use of the means which God has entrusted to him. He who is constantly gathering up for himself, in utter indifference to the poor and needy about him, gives evidence that the love of God does not dwell in him.

Our Lord pronounced three woes upon the Pharisees. First because of the way they emphasized tithing of minor things while neglecting the more important things of life: "But woe unto you, Pharisees! for ye tithe mint and rue and all manner of herbs, and pass over judgment and the love of God: these ought ye to have done, and not to leave the other undone." They might go into the garden or out on the hillside or down by the seaside and gather these herbs. Then they always put away one-tenth of them for God, and thought when they had done this, when they had tithed these little things, that God must be pleased wtih them. But Jesus pointed out that while they were careful about tithing, there were other great matters of justice and the love of God which should have come first. It was perfectly right to apply the rule of tithing even to the smallest things, even though of little value, but the most important thing was a godly walk—to walk in justice and righteousness before God and man, and to manifest the love of God in the life. The trouble with many religionists is that they have never known the reality of the new birth. Jesus said to Nicodemus, "Ye must be born again," and, "Except a man be born again he cannot see the kingdom of God." Outward observances will never make up for this lack of inner life.

The second woe was pronounced because of the devotion of the Pharisees to the uppermost seats in the synagogue: "Woe unto you, Pharisees! for ye love the uppermost seats in the synagogues, and greetings in the markets." They were fond of outward show. They enjoyed having people look up to them when they entered the synagogue, which answers to the church today. Some men like the head usher to approach them and say, "Come here; we have a special seat for you." And everybody says, "He must be somebody; who is he?" "Oh," someone explains, "he is Dr. So-and-So, one of the great religious leaders." And this dignitary sits complacently enjoying the admiration of the company while pretending to worship God. In reality he is but seeking satisfaction from the recognition given him. Such conduct is abhorrent to God who knoweth the proud afar off.

The third woe dealt with hidden uncleanness: "Woe unto you, scribes and Pharisees, hypocrites! for ye are as graves which appear not, and the men that walk over them are not aware of them." We need to understand something of what was written in the Law in order to get the full force of these words. According to the Law of Moses, an Israelite was defiled if he walked over a grave or came in contact with the bones of a dead body. He had to go through a process of cleansing before he could again take his place with the worshippers in the house of the Lord. These Pharisees, who should have been examples of holiness, who should have been the ones to whom others might come for help and guidance, were corrupt themselves and misleading, by their unhallowed influence and hypocritical lives, those who trusted them. They were utterly false. To associate with them was like coming in contact with dead men's bones and becoming defiled, though they did not realize it. These were the scorching words of our Lord, and the worst of the matter was that they were absolutely true and every Pharisee at that table realized that they were true, though they may have gnashed their teeth with indignation when they heard Jesus say these things.

There were lawyers present, that is, men whose business it was to expound the law of Moses, men who had given themselves to years of study in the sacred Scriptures. When questions came up as to the interpretation of passages, these men were supposed to be able to give the final word. One of them, evidently stirred to the depths of his soul, said, "Master, thus saying Thou insultest us also." The word "insultest" is a better translation than "reproachest": "You insult us in talking like this."

His own conscience condemned him, for he knew what the Lord had said of the Pharisees was just as true of him and his fellow-lawyers. Jesus did not retract His words for one moment. He was not trying to insult anyone. He was absolutely faithful. He would not cover up their sins; He brought them into the light, that they might be judged in the presence of God.

Jesus pronounced three woes upon the lawyers as He had upon the Pharisees. The first was because they laded men with burdens grievous to be borne, and they themselves touched not the burdens with one of their fingers. These lawyers not only expounded the Law of Moses but they had also added to that Law many human traditions. Jesus said, "You have made the Law of God of none effect by your traditions." They could explain to the people all these different commandments and rules and regulations, but Jesus declared that while they made these things clear to other people they themselves did not obey them. They were not genuine but insincere. Jesus emphasized the importance of obedience to God. They urged upon the common people obedience to the law and the traditions they had added to it but they did not obey many of the commandments themselves. In other words, they were saying, "Do as I say, but not as I do."

In the second place, the Lord reproved and pronounced a woe upon the lawyers for absolute hypocrisy. They made a great deal of the sacred shrines. Jesus said, "Woe unto you! for ye build the sepulchres of the prophets, and your fathers killed them.

Truly ye bear witness that ye allow the deeds of your fathers: for they indeed killed them, and ye build their sepulchres. Therefore also said the Wisdom of God, I will send them prophets and apostles, and some of them they shall slay and persecute." This is the only place in the New Testament where the Wisdom of God is personified. In the book of Proverbs we have this personification. In chapter 8 Wisdom warns men of the danger of insincerity and sinful folly. Here in the New Testament the Wisdom of God speaks, telling men of the doom that comes upon those who have not heeded the revelation God has given, though they profess to honor those through whom it came. The Wisdom of God said, "I will send them prophets and apostles, and some of them they shall slay and persecute, that the blood of all the prophets which was shed from the foundation of the world, may be required of this generation: from the blood of Abel unto the blood of Zacharias." Whether this refers to Zechariah, the author of the book which bears his name (who, according to the Jewish Targum, was slain in the sanctuary), or to that earlier Zechariah whose death is recorded in 2 Chron. 24:20, 21, is a moot question. But the important thing to see is that God held unbelieving Israel accountable for all the blood that had been shed because of faithfulness to Him. The same spirit of rejection of the Word and opposition to the messengers of God was seen in that generation. As we know, terrible judgments soon followed.

The third woe is found in ver. 52, "Woe unto you, lawyers! for ye have taken away the key of knowledge: ye entered not in yourselves, and them that were entering in ye hindered." The key was looked upon as the symbol of knowledge. The doctors of learning in Israel wore a key just as some of our college graduates, for instance, who have specially excelled in Greek, wear the *Phi Beta Kappa* key. Jesus referred to that when He said to Peter, "I give to you the keys of the kingdom of heaven." To these lawyers He said, as it were, "You have the key of knowledge; you are supposed to know, and you are recognized as men familiar with the Scriptures. Why do you not give to others the Scriptures in their simplicity? You have taken them away from the people and are keeping them for yourselves; yet you do not heed them, and the people are left in ignorance." It is a solemn warning against the misuse of the Scriptures. If God has entrusted one with the knowledge of the Word, he is responsible to give out that Word clearly and helpfully so that others may share the blessing.

With these sayings our Lord's table talk on this occasion came to a close. As He said these things unto them, the scribes and Pharisees began to question Him, trying to catch something out of His mouth whereby they might accuse Him. They desired to find some evidence showing that His teaching was contrary to the law of Moses; but they had no concern about getting right with God themselves.

ADDRESS FORTY-FOUR

THE SIN THAT NEVER CAN BE FORGIVEN

"In the mean time, when there were gathered together an innumerable multitude of people, insomuch that they trode one upon another, He began to say unto His disciples first of all, Beware ye of the leaven of the Pharisees, which is hypocrisy. For there is nothing covered, that shall not be revealed; neither hid, that shall not be known. Therefore whatsoever ye have spoken in darkness shall be heard in the light; and that which ye have spoken in the ear in closets shall be proclaimed upon the housetops. And I say unto you My friends, Be not afraid of them that kill the body, and after that have no more that they can do. But I will forewarn you whom ye shall fear: Fear Him, which after He hath killed hath power to cast into hell; yea, I say unto you, Fear Him. Are not five sparrows sold for two farthings, and not one of them is forgotten before God? But even the very hairs of your head are all numbered. Fear not therefore: ye are of more value than many sparrows. Also I say unto you, Whosoever shall confess Me before men, him shall the Son of Man also confess before the angels of God: but he that denieth Me before men shall be denied before the angels of God. And whosoever shall speak a word against the Son of Man, it shall be forgiven him: but unto him that blasphemeth against the Holy Ghost it shall not be forgiven. And when they bring you unto the synagogues, and unto magistrates, and powers, take ye no thought how or what thing ye shall answer, or what ye shall say: for the Holy Ghost shall teach you in the same hour what ye ought to say"—Luke 12: 1-12.

FOLLOWING the pronouncement of the woes upon the Pharisees and lawyers, we find, in the present chapter, Jesus looking forward to a day when He would be no longer here on earth, but His disciples would be here, and they would be the objects of bitter persecution by those who rejected their Lord and spurned the testimony which He gave. In verses 1-3 He warns against unreality. That is something to which we are all prone. It is so easy to pretend to be more than we are. We may appear to be more devoted than we are and assume a profession of piety to which we have not actually attained. So we may well take these words of our Lord to heart. We are told that an innumerable multitude of people were gathered together. The common people loved to hear the Lord Jesus. Actually it was they who sought Him rather than the religious leaders. We are told elsewhere that "the common people heard Him gladly." But it is one thing to hear Him; it is quite another thing to receive His words into the heart and turn to God in repentance. How many there were in this great group who truly received Christ as Saviour, recognizing their own sinful state and their need of a Deliverer, we have no way of knowing; doubtless many did. But the great majority were simply interested in hearing His message and seeing His works of power. There were so many, we are told, that they trode one upon another; and He began to say to His disciples, "Beware ye of the leaven of the Pharisees, which is hypocrisy." In the Old Testament the Jews were forbidden to have leaven in their homes at Passover time. Leaven is a type or symbol of evil. Throughout all Scripture this holds good. In the Gospels we have the Lord referring to leaven in three different ways. Here He warns His disciples to beware of the leaven of the Pharisees, and we are told definitely that it is hypocrisy. Elsewhere He warns His disciples to beware of the leaven of the Sadducees—that is materialism, or false doctrine. The Sadducees did not believe in the resurrection of the dead, neither in angels nor in spirits.

In another place He warns His disciples against the leaven of Herod, which is worldliness, political corruption: the failure to give God His rightful place in the government of the land. The Herodians courted the favor of the Romans and in order to obtain that favor they were untrue to the revelation which God had given them.

Leaven then is always a type of wickedness, a symbol of evil. Some think of the parable of the leaven, and say, "Surely the leaven hidden in the meal is not a symbol of evil. Is this not the gospel that is gradually converting the whole world?" But, surely the "three measures of meal" is not a picture of the world. It is the meal-offering, a type of the true and perfect humanity of our Lord Jesus Christ. The fact that the woman hid the leaven in the three measures of meal indicates that she was doing something which she knew to be wrong. There was to be no leaven at all in the meal-offering. The parable is not a picture of the gospel working among men, but it is error working where truth has been made known, and giving men wrong ideas concerning the Person and work of our Lord Jesus. Leaven is always evil, never good, and so the disciples were to beware of it in any form. How we need this admonition today! As Christians we are to put away the leaven of malice and wickedness. Our lives should be as open books. We should be able to say with the saintly Fletcher of Madeley, "I would that a mirror might be placed over my heart that men might be enabled to look in and see how true it beats toward God." Would that this were so of everyone of us, because "there is nothing covered, that shall not be revealed." We may think we are hiding something; we may think we are covering up something by making bold professions, but all is coming out some day and will be fully exposed. It is better to judge every evil way now, rather than wait and have it manifested at the judgment-seat of Christ. We are told that every man's work shall be manifested of what sort it is. Jesus says, "Whatsoever ye have spoken in darkness shall be heard in the light; and that which ye have spoken in the ear in closets shall be proclaimed upon the housetops." If we would keep that in mind I think it would stop a great deal of gossip. If we realized that everything we whisper about another person, every unkind criticism and evil story which we spread abroad concerning others will at last be made known to them and to everyone else, would it not have a tendency to make us very much more careful as to the use of our tongues? It is all coming out some day for, "Every idle word that men shall speak they shall give account thereof in the day of judgment."

In the second part of this discourse we have an exhortation for the comfort of the disciples because of what they will have to suffer. Soon He, the Master, after having been rejected and crucified, will rise from the dead and be received back into the glory. His people are to be left in the world to tell others of His grace. He said, "I say unto you My friends." There is something very precious about this expression—"My friends!" He owns as His friends all who love Him and evidence their love by obedience to His Word. "My friends!" How much is involved in that term! When the Lord addresses His own as "My friends" it is because He has a deep personal interest in everyone of them, and there should be a ready response on our part as we claim Him as our "Friend that sticketh closer than a brother."

In the fifteenth chapter of John our Lord says, "I call you not servants, for the servant knoweth not what his lord doeth; but I have called you friends; for all things that I have heard of My Father I have made known unto you." The master is not expected to open his heart to a servant and reveal all his secrets to him. But our Lord loves to do that very thing to those whom He calls "My friends." Three times in Scripture Abraham is honored by being called "the friend of God," for when He was about to bring judgment upon Sodom, God said, "Shall I hide from Abraham that which I am about to do?" In His grace He condescended to "commune with Abraham" as to His purpose. To me it is really thrilling to think that I, who was once a poor sinner on my way to eternal judgment but now saved through infinite grace, am able to look up into the face of the Lord Jesus and say, "Thou art my Friend."

He said unto them, "My friends, be not afraid of them that kill the body, and after that have no more that they can do. But I will forewarn you whom ye shall fear: Fear Him, which after He hath killed hath power to cast into hell; yea, I say unto you.

Fear Him." After the body is killed the spirit lives on, either in happiness or in misery. Materialists may refuse to believe this, but our Lord definitely affirms it. The soul cannot be destroyed when the body is killed. Matthew reports our Lord as saying, "Fear not them which kill the body and after that are not able to kill the soul, but rather fear Him which is able to destroy both soul and body in hell." The word "destroy" is used in the sense of *lost*, elsewhere in the parables—to be lost in hell. Though men might kill the body they cannot touch the soul. When the body dies the soul of the believer departs from the body and is immediately present with the Lord. Who then would fear death with that glorious prospect in view? On the other hand, if one is not right with God he may well fear Him who, after the death of the body, has power to cast the soul into hell. "Yea," says Jesus, "I say unto you, Fear Him." There are men today who do not believe in a judgment-day, men who do not believe in hell and punishment after death. But all the arguments that they may bring against these truths cannot take them out of the Word of God. The Scriptures declare that, "It is appointed unto men once to die, and after this the judgment." Our Lord had more to say about judgment after death than any other New Testament preacher.

In the next section of His address the Lord comforts His disciples concerning the experiences through which they may be called upon to pass while they live here on earth: "Are not five sparrows sold for two farthings, and not one of them is forgotten before God? But even the very hairs of your head are all numbered. Fear not therefore: ye are of more value than many sparrows." Sparrows were very worthless. People trapped them, took them home and dressed them, and sold them on the market at two for a farthing, five for two farthings. They were bought by the poorest people who could afford no better food. Speaking of the five sparrows, Dr. James S. Brookes used to say, "I think that must be how I got saved: four others were converted, and I was just thrown in for good measure." Jesus says not one of these sparrows are forgotten before God. "Even the very hairs of your head are all numbered. Fear not therefore: ye are of more value than many sparrows." Somebody has said God goes to every sparrow's funeral! Jesus said not one falls to the ground without the Father's knowledge. How much more is He interested in you who trust the Father and believe in His Son!

In verses 8 and 9 He speaks of confessing or denying Him, and this is a very serious thing. "Also I say unto you, Whosoever shall confess Me before men, him shall the Son of Man also confess before the angels of God: but he that denieth Me before men shall be denied before the angels of God." Observe, it is not a question of whether you believe that Christ is the Son of God, but it is a question of whether you have definitely confessed Him. "If thou shalt confess with thy mouth the Lord Jesus, and shalt believe in thine heart that God hath raised Him from the dead, thou shalt be saved. For with the heart man believeth unto righteousness; and with the mouth confession is made unto salvation." There are many people who have heard the gospel story all their lives and possibly do not for a moment question its great truths, but they have received these truths as they accept any other historical facts, and have never trusted their own souls to Christ and confessed Him as their Saviour. Oh, that you might make that confession today! Put yourself on record by saying, "Yes, I confess Jesus Christ the Son of God as my Saviour; I confess that henceforth I take my stand with Him." If you will so confess Him, then He says, "I will confess you before the angels. I will say that you belong to Me, that you are Mine, that I have bought you with My precious blood." But on the other hand, no matter how much you may believe concerning Him, if you refuse to own Him as your Saviour, if you deny Him in this day of His rejection, He will refuse to own you; He will deny you in that day of His manifestation, for, "He that denieth Me before men shall be denied before the angels of God." If you want Him to confess you then, it is incumbent upon you to confess Him now.

In verse 10 we come to the solemn truth which suggested the heading for this section: *The sin that never can be forgiven.* Let us pause here for a moment. The Lord Jesus knew how many had spoken against Him; He knew the wicked things that had been said about Him, but still He declared that all would be forgiven if they would turn to God and put their trust in the One against whom they had sinned. All their sins and iniquities would be blotted out. "But," He added, "unto him that blasphemeth against the Holy Ghost it shall not be forgiven." While He was here on earth He cast out demons by the power of the Holy Spirit, thus attesting His Messiahship. Some attributed this power to Beelzebub—this is the sin against the Holy Ghost. It was because they were determined not to accept His miracles as evidencing the truth of His testimony that they attributed His work to the devil. For that sin Jesus said there was no forgiveness in that age nor in the age to come. To blaspheme against the Holy Ghost in that age was to refuse to accept the Holy Ghost's witness to the Person and work of the Lord Jesus Christ. It is the same today. The one sin that never can be forgiven is the final rejection of the Holy Ghost's testimony to the Lord Jesus. If you reject Christ there is nothing else for you but judgment. All sin—stealing, murder, drunkenness, evil-speaking, maliciousness, hatred—all these were atoned for on Calvary's cross, and the Holy Spirit came from heaven to bear testimony to this. But if men reject this testimony they deliberately sin against the Holy Ghost. There is no forgiveness for them. Oh, I beg of you, if unsaved, do not risk the continued rejection of Christ, lest you come to a place where for the last time the Holy Ghost will strive with you, and for you there shall be no forgiveness.

In the last two verses of this section our Lord tells His disciples that the same Holy Spirit would be the power by which they were to proclaim the gospel in the days to come: "And when they bring you unto the synagogues, and unto magistrates, and powers, take ye no thought how or what thing ye shall answer, or what ye shall say; for the Holy Ghost shall teach you in the same hour what ye ought to say." We have illustrations of this in the Book of Acts. When the apostle Peter was brought before the Sanhedrin he did not work out a great discourse which he was to deliver the next morning. The Holy Ghost gave him utterance. He stood before those men and preached Christ, and he did it with such power that they knew not how to reply to him. When Saul of Tarsus appeared before kings and governors, and high-priests, and rulers of Israel, it was no worked-up message that he gave; but in the power of the Holy Spirit he made his defence in an unanswerable way. The only real preaching today is preaching in the power of the Holy Spirit. We do not say that ministers of the gospel should not give much time to prayer, study, and to the Word that they may be prepared to give that Word when the time comes, but their dependence must be upon the power of the Holy Spirit of God who alone can make that Word fruitful.

Thus our Lord had shown His disciples where their strength was to be found in the days when they were to go forth in His name to proclaim His message to the world. How wonderfully He has honored that Word down through the centuries! And how we can thank Him that He has been pleased to use it so blessedly in the salvation of men and women everywhere, who have received it in faith and so made Christ Jesus their own Saviour and owned Him as their Lord!

ADDRESS FORTY-FIVE

THE SIN AND DANGER OF COVETOUSNESS

✝ ✝ ✝

"And one of the company said unto Him, Master, speak to my brother, that he divide the inheritance with me. And He said unto him, Man, who made Me a judge or a divider over you? And He said unto them, Take heed, and beware of covetousness: for a man's life consisteth not in the abundance of the things which he possesseth. And He spake a parable unto them, saying, The ground of a certain rich man brought forth plentifully: and he thought within himself, saying, What shall I do, because I have no room where to bestow my fruits? And he said, This will I do: I will pull down my barns, and build greater; and there will I bestow all my fruits and my goods. And I will say to my soul, Soul, thou hast much goods laid up for many years; take thine ease, eat, drink, and be merry. But God said unto him, Thou fool, this night thy soul shall be required of thee: then whose shall those things be, which thou hast provided? So is he that layeth up treasure for himself, and is not rich toward God"—Luke 12: 13-21.

✝ ✝ ✝

THERE is one sin expressly forbidden in the Ten Commandments that few people think of as wicked: namely, "Thou shalt not covet." The apostle Paul tells us in the seventh chapter of the Epistle to the Romans that this was the only commandment that convicted him of the sinfulness of his nature. Elsewhere he says that so far as the righteousness of the law was concerned he had lived a blameless life. He had never bowed the knee to an idol; he had never taken the name of God in vain, nor had he dishonored his parents. He had not lied, stolen, murdered, nor been guilty of adultery. He had not committed any of the sins forbidden in the first nine commandments, but when it came to the tenth he had to plead guilty. The commandment said, "Thou shalt not covet." He found that it actually stirred within his heart unlawful desires, and he realized he was a sinner because of this. Within himself he found all manner of covetousness. He was unable to control his thoughts and desires, and so he knew he was a transgressor of the law. How few people think of covetousness as an actual sin. What is covetousness? It is a desire to grasp that which God has withheld from us though He may have given it to others. We ought to be content with such things as we have, but we grasp after other things which God has not seen fit to bestow upon us; thus we are guilty of the sin of covetousness. It is one of the most subtle of sins. People may put on a show of piety and religiousness and yet be guilty of this sin. Our Lord Jesus Christ reproved men for this sin of covetousness in no uncertain terms.

We have in this instance, the story of a man who came to Jesus and said, "Master, speak to my brother, that he divide the inheritance with me." Now there does not seem to be anything wrong about that. Evidently the father had died and the inheritance had been left in charge of this man's brother. Perhaps one son was living at home and the other at a distant place, and the son at home concluded the possessions were his. Both brothers may have known Jesus and had great confidence in His justice; so the one said to Him, "Speak to my brother about this matter." But Jesus did not come into the world to regulate things of that character. He did "not come to condemn the world, but that the world through Him might be saved." He said, "Take heed, and beware of covetousness: for a man's life consisteth not in the abundance of the things which he possesseth." This very request indicates restlessness, dissatisfaction, a state of the heart reaching out for something which God for the present has withheld. Why not be subject to His will and be content with what He has already given? Beware of covetousness! This is not only love for money, but it is also the attempt to find satisfaction in temporal things. "A man's life consisteth not in the abundance of the things which he possesseth." We go through life accumulating "things," many of them absolutely worthless; but we hoard them. We strive to have a beautiful home, more land, more expensive furniture than other people possess, a nicer set for the table, more elegant apparel, and in many other ways we go on hoarding and accumulating, until at last death comes, and my! what a time our executors have dividing up the rubbish! "A man's life consisteth not in the abundance of things which he possesseth." Yet people act as though the greatest good on earth consists in adding to their possessions. Some may say, "Well, what should be done with the things we do not need?" Elsewhere the Lord Jesus tells us if we want happiness we should distribute our possessions to others instead of hoarding them for ourselves. The happiest man is not the one who possesses the most, but the man who gives the most, the man who shares with others the good things God has intrusted to him. We can get more happiness in dividing a dollar with someone else than by spending it all on ourselves. The rich young ruler went to Jesus and said, "What must I do to inherit eternal life?" The Lord said, "Sell that thou hast, and give to the poor, and thou shalt have treasure in heaven." He did not mean he could earn salvation by giving away money or goods. But it is quite possible to miss salvation by violating the commandment which says, "Thou shalt not covet." No man will ever be saved who is living just for himself. He must come to the place where being convicted of his sin, he confesses and turns from it, and puts his trust in Christ alone for salvation. We all do well to take this warning to ourselves: "Take heed and beware of covetousness." Paul said, "For me to live is Christ." Living for Christ means living for others, and this is life at its best.

The Jews used to say that a child is born into this world with his hand clenched, that is, with his fists clenched, grasping after everything he can obtain. But we die with our hands wide open; we have nothing in them. We cannot take anything with us; we have to go empty-handed. Why hoard things? Why not use them and enjoy them while we live? The Lord related a parable in order to impress this. He told of a certain landowner, a rich man, who thought only of himself and his own comfort, and never realized for a moment that what God had intrusted to him should be used for His glory and for blessing of others. He said, "What shall I do, because I have no room where to bestow my fruits? And he said, This will I do: I will pull down my barns, and build greater; and there will

I bestow all my fruits and my goods." There is nothing in this parable to warn us against making proper provision for the future; there is nothing here to condemn any of you housewives who put up fruit in the summer to use in the winter; there is nothing to condemn putting something away while one is earning wages in order to provide for old age. But this man was thinking only of himself. He said, "I will build greater barns and I will bestow *all* my goods." If he had said, "I shall not need all these goods. There is that poor widow down the lane who lives in that little cabin. . . . How much it would mean to her to have a little fruit and other things. Then there is that poor crippled boy. I shall leave a lot of things on his doorstep. When he wakens in the morning he will not know from whom they came; he will not know they came from a stingy old man like me. I shall have the joy of knowing I have done something really unselfish." So he might have gone down the line from one needy person to another. But he was thinking only of himself. He said, "I will bestow all my fruits and goods in this new barn I am going to build, and say to my soul: Soul, thou hast much goods laid up for many years; take thine ease, eat, drink, and be merry." A selfish, covetous, godless man thinking only of gratifying his own desires, contemplating a life of ease through the years to come instead of seeking to be the blessing to others he might have been! Smug in his own conceit, smug in his covetousness and grasping spirit, he goes to his bed that night, perhaps between beautiful linen sheets and enjoying every luxury. Suddenly in the midst of the night he is wakened, perhaps with a terrible pain, and he cries, "A heart attack! What is going to happen!" Then he seems to hear ringing down through the darkness of the night, "Fool, tonight thy soul shall be required of thee: and then whose will these goods be?" And within a day or two friends are passing by his coffin. They are looking down into his face and saying, "My, how natural he looks!" Then they go on their way, and within a little while the lawyers are squabbling over his estate, and all the things he laid up are being scattered far and wide. That is the end of earth for the covetous man, but it is not the end of his existence. He goes out into eternity to meet the God whom he has ignored, to meet the God who has showered mercy upon him all his life, but who has never received a thought of gratitude. He goes out into eternity to face the Lord Jesus whose claims he had never recognized. He has been so busy laying up treasures for himself on earth that he has made no provision for eternity.

Let me say to you: no man is rich whatever his wealth may be, however vast his lands and estates may be, if he does not know the Lord Jesus Christ. There were those in the church of Laodicea who said, "I am rich, and increased with goods, and have need of nothing." The Lord Jesus said, "Thou art wretched, and miserable, and poor, and blind, and naked." They thought they had everything, but actually they had nothing! They were without Christ. If one is without Christ he is poorer than the poorest. Such a one may pride himself on having a little of this world's goods, but he stands before God an absolute pauper. The Lord says to all such, "I counsel you to buy of Me gold tried in the fire, that thou mayest be rich." That wealth God gives to all who will ask Him. If you do not have Christ you are miserably poor.

After we have trusted Christ we are warned against laying up treasures for ourselves on earth, where moth and rust corrupt, and where thieves break through and steal. Even Christians are in danger of this spirit of covetousness. Happy is he who, instead of laying up treasures on earth, is sending treasure on ahead to be enjoyed in heaven. How do I lay up treasure in heaven? Why, everything I do for others in His name, everything that I give to the needy in His name, is treasure deposited in the bank of heaven. Such deposits draw ten thousand per cent interest; for Christ said, "There is no man that hath left house, or parents, or brethren, or wife, or children, for the kingdom of God's sake, who shall not receive a hundredfold in this life." A hundredfold is ten thousand per cent. But that is only in this life, for He adds, "And in the world to come life everylasting."

One may say, "I do not see that there is much wrong in covetousness. What is there about it that is actually wrong?" You may not see anything very serious about it now, but if it keeps you out of heaven you will find it serious indeed. Untold thousands have been kept out of heaven by this sin of covetousness. It has come between them and the salvation of the soul.

Address Forty-six

LIVING WITHOUT ANXIETY

✝ ✝ ✝

"And He said unto His disciples, Therefore, I say unto you, Take no thought for your life, what ye shall eat; neither for the body, what ye shall put on. The life is more than meat, and the body is more than raiment. Consider the ravens: for they neither sow nor reap; which neither have storehouse nor barn; and God feedeth them: how much more are ye better than the fowls? And which of you with taking thought can add to his stature one cubit? If ye then be not able to do that thing which is least, why take ye thought for the rest? Consider the lilies how they grow: they toil not, they spin not; yet I say unto you, that Solomon in all his glory was not arrayed like one of these. If then God so clothe the grass, which is today in the field, and tomorrow is cast into the oven; how much more will He clothe you, O ye of little faith? And seek not ye what ye shall eat, or what ye shall drink, neither be ye of doubtful mind. For all these things do the nations of the world seek after: and your Father knoweth that ye have need of these things. But rather seek ye the kingdom of God; and all these things shall be added unto you. Fear not, little flock; for it is your Father's good pleasure to give you the kingdom. Sell that ye have, and give alms; provide yourselves bags which wax not old, a treasure in the heavens that faileth not, where no thief approacheth, neither moth corrupteth. For where your treasure is, there will your heart be also"—Luke 12: 22-34.

✝ ✝ ✝

AFTER relating the sad story of the rich fool, who, despite his carefulness and self-interest, lost everything, Jesus turned to His disciples and talked to them of the blessedness of a life free from care and anxiety, a life of dependence on the living God, who is the Father of all who believe His Word.

He said, "Take no thought for your life, what ye shall eat; neither for the body, what ye shall put on. The life is more than meat, and the body is more than raiment." He was not advocating thriftlessness, nor was He inculcating idleness, nor unconcern as to one's future responsibilities. The admonition was that His disciples should avoid anxious thought. It is not becoming for a child of God to worry about food and clothing, and how to meet the various needs that arise from day to day. We have seen the motto: "If you worry, you do not trust; if you trust, you do not worry." It was just this that the Lord sought to impress upon His disciples. Faith can count upon God to meet each need as it arises, provided one is walking in obedience to the Word.

Jesus directed attention to the ravens, which were generally in evidence in Palestine. Unable to either sow or reap they were provided for by their benevolent Creator. It is unthinkable that He should have more concern for the fowls of the air than for His own children.

Besides, what is accomplished by worrying? Can one by anxious thought add to his stature? We grow in height from childhood to maturity as ordered of God. Why not trust Him for the rest?

The lilies of the field, more delicately beautiful than any artistic work of man, are clothed in their lovely garb by God. They neither toil nor spin, yet their's is a radiant beauty such as even Solomon in all his glory never knew. Every flower, every blade of grass, is a witness of the wisdom and power of the Creator, who is our God and Father. We may be sure that He who displays His providential care over all the lower creation, will not fail to undertake for His own as they commit all their affairs to Him.

To make the obtaining of food and drink the great object of our labor is to miss altogether the true goal of life. The nations of the world who know not God may have no higher standards than these; but it should be otherwise with those to whom He has revealed Himself in grace and compassion.

Put first things first. Seek not that which ministers to selfish desire, but rather seek the kingdom of God, which implies the recognition of the divine authority over all our lives, and all else will be added as God sees fit.

Industriousness and faith go hand in hand. It does not signify, however, that one has real faith in God because he gives up temporal employment and declares he is going to trust the Lord to meet his needs. If so busily engaged in the ministry of the Word that one cannot also labor with his hands, even as Paul sometimes did, he is entitled to look to God in confidence that He will meet every need. But ordinarily it is in full accord with the path of faith to remember that God has said, "If any would not work, neither should he eat" (2 Thess. 3:10). And we need to recall the primeval admonition, "In the sweat of thy face shalt thou eat bread" (Gen. 3:19). No one is more able to impress people with the reality and sterling character of a true Christian experience than the laboring man, or the business executive, who, while working to support himself and his family, lives a life of daily dependence on God, looking to Him to provide the employment whereby his temporal responsibilities are met.

There is a difference between faith and presumption. Faith acts on the revealed Word of God. Presumption attempts to harness God to a human program, and the result is inevitable failure. God has promised to answer the prayer of faith; He has never promised to gratify the desires of men who do not act according to His Word.

During the present age the people of God, who know their loving Father's care, are a little flock indeed, exposed to the misunderstanding and even the hatred of a cruel and unfeeling world. But to them the promise is given: "It is your Father's good pleasure to give you the kingdom."

Therefore, one, conscious of his relationship to God and the fact that he is an heir of the kingdom, can well afford to hold everything here with a light hand, knowing that eternal riches have been laid up for him in glory, and while passing as a stranger and pilgrim through a hostile scene, he can count on both divine protection and divine provision.

Instead of hoarding earthly treasure, the follower of the Lord Jesus will find his greatest joy in sharing with others the temporal benefits bestowed upon him. No man can really put this world beneath his feet until he has seen a better world above his head. Knowing he is an heir of the kingdom, knowing he is to share that treasure that faileth not, a treasure which thieves cannot filch nor moths destroy, why should he set his heart upon the poor tawdry things of this world, which, as we read elsewhere, are all to perish with the using.

It is simply a question of where the heart is. If we covet worldly pelf and the fading glory of this earth, it is because our hearts are still in the world. But if we have learned to value the eternal riches and the glories that shall never pass away, it is because our hearts are fixed on that Home from which the Saviour came and to which He has returned. So, in Col. 3, we are enjoined to set our affection (or mind) on things above, where Christ sitteth at the right hand of God. Nothing will ever divorce us from occupation with the passing things of time except the consciousness that our citizenship is in heaven and our portion is there.

This will not lead us to be indifferent to our obligations as temporary residents of this world, nor will it have a tendency to make us indolent or careless as to proper provision for daily life. But it will deliver us from worry and anxiety, and it will give us the quiet confidence which enables us to rest in the Lord as we endeavor to glorify Him in all the responsibilities He puts upon us.

Address Forty-seven

WAITING FOR THE LORD'S RETURN

"Let your loins be girded about, and your lights burning; and ye yourselves like unto men that wait for their lord, when he will return from the wedding; that when he cometh and knocketh, they may open unto him immediately. Blessed are those servants, whom the Lord when he cometh shall find watching: verily I say unto you, that he shall gird himself, and make them to sit down to meat, and will come forth and serve them. And if he shall come in the second watch, or come in the third watch, and find them so, blessed are those servants. And this know, that if the goodman of the house had known what hour the thief would come, he would have watched, and not have suffered his house to be broken through. Be ye therefore ready also: for the Son of Man cometh at an hour when ye think not. Then Peter said unto Him, Lord, speakest Thou this parable unto us, or even to all? And the Lord said, Who then is that faithful and wise steward, whom his lord shall make ruler over his household, to give them their portion of meat in due season? Blessed is that servant, whom his lord when he cometh shall find so doing. Of a truth I say unto you, that he will make him ruler over all that he hath. But and if that servant say in his heart, My lord delayeth his coming; and shall begin to beat the menservants and maidens, and to eat and drink, and to be drunken; the lord of that servant will come in a day when he looketh not for him, and at an hour when he is not aware, and will cut him in sunder, and will appoint him his portion with the unbelievers. And that servant, which knew his lord's will, and prepared not himself, neither did according to his will, shall be beaten with many stripes. But he that knew not, and did commit things worthy of stripes, shall be beaten with few stripes. For unto whomsoever much is given, of him shall be much required: and to whom men have committed much, of him they will ask the more"—Luke 12: 35-48.

OUR Lord's Galilean ministry was drawing rapidly to a close. The time was near when He would go to Jerusalem to die. In view of this and His promised return He urged upon His disciples the importance of loyalty when He should no longer be present with them in person. He was going on to Calvary—there to make an atonement for sin. And in God's due time He will return, not as He came before—by the gate of birth, as a little Babe, as a lowly Man to be despised—but as King of kings and Lord of lords, to whom every knee shall bow. We read in the Revelation, "Behold, He cometh with clouds: and every eye shall see Him, and they also which pierced Him: and all kindreds of the earth shall wail because of Him." It is in view of this great event that He says here, "Let your loins be girded about, and your lights burning." It is the "loins of the mind" of which He speaks (1 Pet. 1:13), and the girdle is the truth of God (Eph. 6:14). In other words, as the flowing garments of the Oriental are held in place by the girdle, so every thought is to be brought into captivity to the obedience of Christ (2 Cor. 10:5). The light of testimony is to be kept shining during the time of our Lord's personal absence. The language is highly figurative. The bridegroom at a wedding ceremony, in the days in which Jesus lived here on earth, would go forth to meet his bride and return with her to his own home. His friends would be properly attired, their loins girded and their lights burning as they went out to meet the bridegroom.

Now we were just as much saved when we were born again as we shall be after we have lived for God for fifty or sixty years. I have known God for fifty years, but I am not *more* saved now than I was fifty years ago. These years have been wonderful and glad years of service for my Saviour, but as far as my own personal salvation is concerned, I was saved the moment I trusted Christ. I was left here to witness for Him, and you are left here to witness for Him, and so our lamps are to be kept burning. It is possible to become so taken up with the theory of the second coming that we lose sight of the One who is coming. We ought to be occupied with Christ Himself. We do not know when He will come, neither the day nor the hour. It might be today; it may be longer than many of us think, but we are to be always "like unto men that wait for their lord." Just as the friends of the Eastern bridegroom waited eagerly for him to bring his bride back to his home where they could rejoice together, so we are to maintain an attitude of expectancy while we wait for the return of our Saviour. "Blessed are those servants whom the Lord when He cometh shall find watching." There is nothing that has such a sanctifying influence on the soul as watching for the Lord's return. We are called to serve in faithfulness now. When Christ returns it will be His delight to minister to those who have endured and suffered for His name's sake during His present session at the Father's right hand (Rev. 6:21). I may be called at any time to meet my Lord; any moment He may come to take me away from this scene—how anxious I should be to see Him! If we are watching and waiting He will make us to sit down together and He will serve us. Is that not wonderful? If we serve Him on earth, He says, He is going to serve us over there. It will be His delight to serve us in the place He has prepared for us.

The Roman watch was three hours long. The night was divided into four watches. If the Lord came in the second watch it would still be dark; if He came in the third watch it would be before the morning dawned. Whenever He comes He will find His servants waiting for Him. Of such He says, "Blessed are those servants."

If a householder knew that a thief was coming at a given time to appropriate his goods, he would be waiting for him. He would not be taken by surprise but would watch and protect his house. Our Lord would have us always on the alert, for we do not know the hour when He will come.

To unwatchful ones the Lord's return will be unexpected and even unwelcome, as that of a thief in the night (Rev. 3:3); but it will be far otherwise to those who are instructed out of the Word and are waiting for God's Son from Heaven (1 Thess. 5:4). "Be ye therefore ready also: for the Son of Man cometh at an hour when ye think not." It is all-important to keep this in mind and not attempt to set dates or pretend to know the exact time when the second advent will take place. Jesus has told us, "It is not for you to know the times or the seasons, which the Father hath put in His own power" (Acts 1:7).

Simon Peter said, "Lord, speakest Thou this parable unto us, or even to all? And the Lord said, Who then is that faithful and wise steward, whom his lord shall make ruler over his household, to give them their portion of meat in due season? Blessed is that servant, whom his lord when he cometh shall find so doing." Peter inquired as to whether the illustration was used for themselves alone or for all Christ's disciples. The answer shows it was intended for all professed believers to the end of the dispensation.

Then the Lord promised that when He comes back He will reward each faithful servant. The true servant of Christ recognizes that whatever truth he has received is a stewardship committed to him to be administered for the good of others, and for which he must some day give account (1 Cor. 4:1, 2). In that day faithfulness will be abundantly rewarded. In verses 43, 44 He pronounces a blessing on the servant whom He will find so doing at His return. There is always the temptation to slothfulness and carelessness when the master is not present, but every employer values that type of service which is as conscientiously performed in his absence as when he is personally supervising it. Such a servant will be promoted to a greater stewardship because of his integrity in a lesser position. The servant who forgets that his master may return most unexpectedly and who behaves tyrannically and unfaithfully because he imagines his faults will never be discovered, is due for a rude awakening. "The lord . . . will come in a day when . . . he is not aware." Remark. that it is not exactly the Lord Jesus Himself who is here in view. Christ is speaking in a parable. It is the lord of the wicked and slothful servant who, upon returning, visits condign punishment upon the one who had so misused his position and betrayed his trust. But the lesson is too obvious to need emphasis or explanation.

The Lord then tells of the judgment that will be meted out in that day. God will not be unrighteous in dealing with anyone. "And that servant, which knew his lord's will, and prepared not himself, neither did according to his will, shall be beaten with many stripes." That which made his conduct so heinous was that he "knew his lord's will, and prepared not himself." The indignant master will mete out the punishment to suit the offence. "But he that knew not, and did commit things worthy of stripes, shall be beaten with few stripes. For unto whomsoever much is given, of him shall be much required: and to whom men have committed much, of him they will ask the more." When one is ignorant of what the master expects he will be dealt with more leniently, although ignorance does not excuse slothfulness. But it is a principle of Scripture that responsibility and privilege go together. Men recognize this in their dealings with one another. So does God Himself, who will deal with each case on its merits.

When God commits any talent, ability, or knowledge of truth to His servants, it is that they may use all for His glory. During our Lord's present session at the Father's right hand, His disciples are called upon to represent and act for Him here on earth. This involves our recognition of service as a sacred trust or stewardship committed to us by Christ Jesus, to be administered for His glory and the blessing of a needy world, and to be rewarded at His personal return. To fail to act in accordance with the revealed will of God will cause us to suffer loss when we are called to give an account of our stewardship at the judgment-seat of Christ, where all our works will be tested by the fire of God's holiness (1 Cor. 3:13-15).

In studying our Lord's parables we need to bear in mind the fact that each one was given to emphasize some important line of truth. It is often a mistake to try to fit every part of such an illustration into a theological, or eschatological mould. In the parable of the master and his servants we must not confuse the earthly lord with our divine Lord. The one is used only as an illustration in so far as his character and behavior may coincide with those of Christ.

There are two aspects of Christ's second advent, though it was no part of our Lord's purpose in this particular discourse to distinguish between the rapture and the appearing, two stages of His coming again which are developed clearly in the Epistles. It is the fact that He who was going away will return again that is emphasized, and the responsibility of His people is viewed in the light of this great fact. It is the will of God that all our lives should be lived in view of the near return of His Son from Heaven. Are we, like the Thessalonians, serving and waiting with that glorious event as the lodestar of our souls? (1 Thess. 1:9, 10). Scripture insists on the imminency of Christ's second coming. If we are to put a millennium between us and that blessed fulfilment of His promise, how, then, can we watch and wait for His return? It is a poor thing to talk of "holding the second coming" if the second coming does not hold us, and mould us, too.

Address Forty-eight

THE OFFENCE OF THE CROSS

✝ ✝ ✝

"I am come to send fire on the earth; and what will I, if it be already kindled? But I have a baptism to be baptized with, and how am I straitened till it be accomplished! Suppose ye that I am come to give peace on earth? I tell you, Nay; but rather division: for from henceforth there shall be five in one house divided, three against two, and two against three. The father shall be divided against the son, and the son against the father; the mother against the daughter, and the daughter against the mother; the mother-in-law against her daughter-in-law, and the daughter-in-law against her mother-in-law. And He said also to the people, When ye see a cloud rise out of the west, straightway ye say, There cometh a shower; and so it is. And when ye see the south wind blow, ye say, There will be heat; and it cometh to pass. Ye hypocrites, ye can discern the face of the sky and of the earth; but how is it that ye do not discern this time? Yea, and why even of yourselves judge ye not what is right? When thou goest with thine adversary to the magistrate, as thou art in the way, give diligence that thou mayest be delivered from him; lest he hale thee to the judge, and the judge deliver thee to the officer, and the officer cast thee into prison. I tell thee, thou shalt not depart thence, till thou hast paid the very last mite" —Luke 12: 49-59.

✝ ✝ ✝

IN the previous verses we noticed that our Saviour is coming again, thus indicating that He was leaving the world for the time being. He left by the way of the Mount of Olives, the cross, and the tomb. He was going away because of the attitude toward Him of His own people, Israel, and of the world in general: "He came unto His own, and His own received Him not." In Hosea 5: 15 we read, "I will go and return to My place, till they acknowledge their offence, and seek My face: in their affliction they will seek Me early." When He came in humiliation the angels announced His birth, proclaiming, "Glory be to God in the highest, and on earth peace, good will toward men." But men refused to acknowledge Him. He was rejected and crucified. In addressing the people of Israel Peter said, "And now, brethren, I wot that through ignorance ye did it, as did also your rulers." The people of Israel did not recognize in the lowly Saviour, the promised King of the prophetic Scriptures.

In His absence His gospel is to be proclaimed everywhere. When men receive that gospel and come out definitely for the Lord, they, like Him, will be rejected by the world. Christ said in His great High Priestly prayer, "They are not of the world, even as I am not of the world." It means something to be a Christian; it means something to be identified with the One whom the world has rejected. And so as the world hated and rejected Him we need not be surprised if it hates and rejects us—these are the consequences of the cross. Sometime ago when a vote was taken on the best-loved song sung over the radio, "The Old Rugged Cross" was found to be the most popular in the thousands of answers which poured into the offices of one of our leading newspapers. But I am sure there are a vast number of people who sing of "The Old Rugged Cross," who do not sense the meaning of the cross. Singing of the cross moves their hearts; but they have never yet trusted the One who died upon that cross, nor taken their places in identification with Him in His rejection.

In the opening verses of the present section our Lord refers to this rejection and to that which was to be accomplished on the cross. He said, "I am come to send fire on the earth, and what will I, if it be already kindled?" The symbol of fire speaks of God acting in judgment against sin. Jesus came not to condemn men but to save them; yet the world put itself in the place of condemnation by rejecting Him. God's test is, "What is your attitude toward My Son?" or, "What think ye of Christ?" If men receive Him, if they trust Him, if they take their places with Him, then they enter into peace and blessedness; but if they spurn Him, then they expose themselves to the wrath and judgment of God.

Jesus said, "But I have a baptism to be baptized with, and how am I straitened till it be accomplished!" He was referring to that baptism of divine judgment which He was to undergo on the cross. We noticed in connection with John's baptism that it was unto repentance. When people confessed their sins he led them into the waters of baptism. Baptism did not cleanse them from sin but signified repentance. The people went down into the waters of baptism, confessing that they were sinners and that they deserved to die. Jesus took His place with these sinners in this baptism, as pledging Himself to settle for their sins, though He was the sinless One. It was as though He were endorsing the notes which all these debtors were giving to God. When one endorses a note the day eventually comes when it falls due. If the debtor cannot pay, then the endorser must do it. Jesus had endorsed the notes for all these people. Now three-and-one-half years had passed and the fulness of time had come when the notes must be paid, when everything must be settled; and He saw the cross before Him where He was to meet every claim God had against sinners. He said, "I have a baptism to be baptized with, and how am I straitened till it be accomplished!" His own soul was moved deeply as He looked forward to that cross and to the judgment against sin which He was to endure there.

That cross was to divide the world. The Lord Jesus said, "Suppose ye that I am come to give peace on earth? I tell you, Nay; but rather division." Did He not come to give peace? Peace was offered through Him. If men had received Him they would have had peace, but they spurned Him. For nearly two thousand years war and confusion have prevailed instead of the peace promised by the prophets of old through Messiah's advent. Peace will not come until He returns. In the meantime there will be strife and distress: "For from henceforth there shall be five in one house divided, three against two, and two against three. The father shall be divided against the son, and the son against the father; the mother against the daughter, and the daughter against the mother; the mother-in-law against her daughter-in-law, and the daughter-in-law against her mother-in-law." Thus it has been ever since He left this scene. Families and nations have been broken up and divided, all because of their attitude toward the Lord Jesus. Many of us know something of that. Those of you who were born into families where the gospel was not known and loved, and yet through the grace of God you were reached and saved, know something of the bitter opposition of those intimately related to you. It has cost many of you a great deal of suffering for the Lord's sake. Other members of your family called you a fanatic and a fool because you trusted the Saviour. But it is for you to go on trusting Him and to be faithful to Him because of the grace that has saved you. He has pardoned you, and by that very fact you may be sure that He is interested in all your family. Ask Him to bring the others to Himself. But until that takes place do not become discouraged. Before you were saved you did not understand why Christians could give up gladly everything for Christ's sake, and so you need not expect to be understood now by those who are still in their sins.

Let me warn you who are already Christians: Do not play fast and loose with the world which crucified your Lord. I always feel sad when earnest young people inquire if there is any harm in this or in that. It is better to ask, "Will it honor my Lord?" "Will it make me more Christ-like?" "Will it make me more spiritual?" You may do freely that which will have a tendency to create in your soul a greater appreciation of Christ.

He is coming back again one of these days! He went away as the rejected One; He is coming back as the glorified One. When He came the first time the people could not discern the signs of the times, and there is danger lest we should be just as ignorant in regard to His second coming. He said: "When ye see a cloud rise out of the west, straightway ye say, There cometh a shower; and so it is. And when ye see the south wind blow, ye say, There will be heat; and it cometh to pass." They had the Scriptures of the prophets in their hands, and yet they could not see the signs which were being fulfilled all about them. We have the Bible today, and there are many things being fulfilled which tell us of the near return of our Lord; but how few there are who realize this! "Yea, and why even of yourselves judge ye not what is right?" The standard is the Word of God. Study the Scriptures and you will learn from them the path you should take as you pass through this world. "When thou goest with thine adversary to the magistrate, as thou art in the way, give diligence that thou mayest be delivered from him; lest he hale thee to the judge, and the judge deliver thee to the officer, and the officer cast thee into prison. I tell thee, thou shalt not depart thence, till thou hast paid the very last mite." In other words, try to settle this matter out of court. Do not wait until the day of manifestation, whether you think of the judgment of the Christless at the Great White Throne, or whether you think of the day when the Lord shall descend from heaven and His own shall appear before Him. Do not leave matters to be straightened out till that day. It is better to face everything in this life and so obtain the certainty of divine forgiveness now. It will be too late to put things right in eternity. No man by any effort of his own, by any merit that he might accumulate, can ever meet the demands of Divine justice. But Christ has paid for all who will trust in Him! Justified by faith before God we are responsible to so behave toward our brethren here on earth that we shall keep a conscience void of offence toward God and man.

ADDRESS FORTY-NINE

A CALL TO NATIONAL AND INDIVIDUAL REPENTANCE

“There were present at that season some that told Him of the Galileans, whose blood Pilate had mingled with their sacrifices. And Jesus answering said unto them, Suppose ye that these Galileans were sinners above all the Galileans, because they suffered such things? I tell you, Nay; but, except ye repent, ye shall all likewise perish. Or those eighteen, upon whom the tower in Siloam fell, and slew them, think ye that they were sinners above all men that dwelt in Jerusalem? I tell you, Nay: but, except ye repent, ye shall all likewise perish. He spake also this parable; A certain man had a fig tree planted in his vineyard; and he came and sought fruit thereon, and found none. Then said he unto the dresser of his vineyard, Behold, these three years I come seeking fruit on this fig tree, and find none: cut it down; why cumbereth it the ground? And he answering said unto him, Lord, let it alone this year also, till I shall dig about it, and dung it: and if it bear fruit, well: and if not, then after that thou shalt cut it down”—Luke 13: 1-9.

THERE are two sections in this portion which is now before us. The first five verses contain a solemn warning, based on two events which had taken place recently in Palestine. Then in verses 6 to 9 we have a parable emphasizing the same truth which our Lord stresses in the first part.

The Lord was ministering in the city of Capernaum which He called His own city—the city to which He had transferred His residence, and to which He seems to have taken His mother after leaving Nazareth. As the people listened to Him, some came to tell Him of terrible things which had occurred just a few days before in Jerusalem. There had been an uprising among certain zealots from Galilee. The Roman Governor, Pilate, had commanded a squad of soldiers to put an end to this rebellion, and a number had been killed in the very courts of the Temple. Naturally the Galileans were greatly distresesd and disturbed. They wondered why God had allowed this wholesale destruction of their own kinsfolk. The people thought that He saw some wickedness in them greater than in ordinary folk; otherwise He would not have allowed them to be slain in this way. Jesus declared that this was not necessarily true. The Galileans had not been killed because they were guilty of greater wickedness than that of ordinary men. Then He solemnly warned all His hearers, saying, "I tell you, Nay: but, except ye repent, ye shall all likewise perish." In other words, He warns them that the judgment of God is hanging over all unrepentant men; the judgment will fall eventually upon all who have never been cleansed from their sins. These are solemn words indeed! They ought to be taken to our hearts in day like this when there is such widespread individual and national departure from God.* It is easy for us, as a people and as a nation, to sit down in our complacency and self-sufficiency and imagine that in the sight of God we are far superior to some of the nations which are suffering so terribly in this present world conflict. But above the sound of battles, above the roaring of the

---

* These addresses were given during the Second World War.

bombs, above the agony of the cries of the wounded and dying, we may hear the words of our Lord Jesus Christ: "I tell you, Nay: but, except ye repent, ye shall all likewise perish."

The incident brought before us in these first three verses was one of violence, but the next was an accidental occurrence. Jesus speaks of "those eighteen upon whom the tower in Siloam fell." Evidently a faulty tower had collapsed, jarred perhaps by an earthquake, and a number of men had been killed. There was a tendency to say, "Well, they must have been great sinners to have been exposed to such a death as that; otherwise a good God, a gracious, kind Creator, would have protected them from that accident." But that does not follow, because accidents come to good and evil alike. The righteous as well as the unrighteous suffer from them—from pestilence, conflagrations, hurricanes, and natural disturbances of various kinds. So again Jesus rebuked the people for supposing that those who had died were sinners above others. He said again, "I tell you, Nay: but, except ye repent, ye shall all likewise perish."

The call to repentance is one of the missing links in the preaching of modern times. Some of our brethren are almost afraid to speak of repentance, lest people think of it as something meritorious. Repentance is not a work of merit: repentance is an acknowledgment that one has no merit, that in himself he is just an undeserving sinner exposed to the judgment of God. God "commandeth all men everywhere to repent." Repentance is not to be confounded with mere penitence. Penitence is sorrow for sin, but we are told, "Godly sorrow worketh repentance to salvation not to be repented of." It is not mere sorrow because one has done wrong. I may grieve in my heart to think of the wrong I have done, of the injury I have caused another, and yet I may not really be repentant toward God. Repentance is not to be confounded with what some call "penance." Penance is an effort to atone for something which one has done by suffering voluntarily; but no physical suffering or self-denial can ever make up for the wrong we have done to God and to man. Repentance is not to be confounded with reformation. Some people have the idea that repentance is trying to break off from their sins and live righteously. There may be reformation apart from repentance, but there never can be true repentance apart from reformation, because if I really repent I shall certainly seek to reform. The word "repent" means a change of mind; it is not merely a change of viewpoint. It is not like a change which one might make, for instance, from one political party to another: a man might be a Democrat today and a Republican tomorrow, or *vice versa*—that is not repentance! Repentance is a change of mind which results in a complete change of attitude. When a man, who has been living in sin and utter indifference to God, confesses his sin and judges his wickedness and earnestly seeks to be delivered from it, when he is determined to walk, not in his old ways or live as he formerly lived, but turns to the God he had spurned and puts his trust in the Saviour He has provided—this is genuine repentance! We read of *"Repentance toward God, and faith toward our Lord Jesus Christ."* The repentant man now finds in Christ not only a Saviour from all his sin and guilt, but also One who gives him a new life in order that he may walk henceforth in a new way. He will live no longer in bondage to the things which dominated and controlled him in the past.

How men need to heed the call to repentance! The apostle Paul, from the very first day of his ministry, stressed that all men should repent and turn to God. Men of the world need to repent of their sins; and Christians need to repent of their coldness and indifference. In the letters to the churches in the book of the Revelation, seven times over the Spirit of God says, "He that hath an ear, let him hear what the Spirit saith unto the churches." Seven times in these letters the call is given to professing .Christians to repent and get right with God!

What need there is for national repentance! Our Lord Jesus called the children of Israel to repent, but they refused to hear His voice. He said, "O Jerusalem, Jerusalem, which killest the prophets, and stonest them that are sent unto thee; how often would I have gathered thy children together, as a hen doth gather her brood under her wings, and ye would not!" Because, as a nation, they refused to repent they were given up to judgment. Oh, how loudly this demand should ring through the land today, calling upon us as a people to repent of the sins of corruption and wickedness, covetousness and violence that characterize us! How we have misused God's mercies and forgotten our responsibility to honor Him! Thank God, no matter how far down a man or a nation may go, there is still hope in Christ; but if there be no repentance there can be only judgment at last.

Next we have a parable which shows how Israel failed to honor God and how patient He had been: "He spake also this parable; A certain man had a fig tree planted in his vineyard; and he came and sought fruit thereon, and found none. Then said he unto the dresser of his vineyard, Behold, these three years I come seeking fruit on this fig tree, and find none: cut it down; why cumbereth it the ground? And he answering said unto him, Lord, let it alone this year also, till I shall dig about it, and dung it: And if it bear fruit, well: and if not, then after that thou shalt cut it down." The fig tree planted in the vineyard was the Jewish nation in the land of Palestine, and the Dresser was the Lord. For three years Jesus had been ministering to Israel: He had gone about calling men to repentance and preaching the kingdom of God, but there were few who had ears to hear and hearts to understand. So God's patience was exhausted; and He said, "Cut it down; why cumbereth it the ground?" But the Dresser of the vineyard interceded, saying, "Lord, let it alone this year also, till I shall dig about it, and dung it: and if it bear fruit, well: and if not, then after that thou shalt cut it down." And so the fourth year of ministry began, during which time

Jesus continued to proclaim the truth and call men to repentance. But in the midst of the year the Jews rose up against Him and the Roman soldiers led Him to Calvary and crucified Him. There was no national repentance, and as a result the fig tree was cut down: the people of Israel were scattered throughout the world, even as we see them to this day. What a lesson to learn! God has borne with us as a people, not for three years but for a century and a-half, and we are drifting farther and farther from Him. The sentence may soon go forth: "Cut it down; why cumbereth it the ground?" Other nations have lost their heritage; other nations have been destroyed because of their godlessness. Why should we be spared? But still the Holy Spirit is working; still the message of God is going forth. Oh, that we may have ears to hear and hearts that will respond, that individually and as a people there may be sincere repentance, that we may turn to God and thus avert the threatened doom!

ADDRESS FIFTY

MAKING CROOKED PEOPLE STRAIGHT

"And He was teaching in one of the synagogues on the sabbath. And, behold, there was a woman which had a spirit of infirmity eighteen years, and was bowed together, and could in no wise lift up herself. And when Jesus saw her, He called her to Him, and said unto her, Woman, thou art loosed from thine infirmity. And He laid His hands on her: and immediately she was made straight, and glorified God. And the ruler of the synagogue answered with indignation, because that Jesus had healed on the sabbath day, and said unto the people, There are six days in which men ought to work: in them therefore come and be healed, and not on the sabbath day. The Lord then answered him, and said Thou hypocrite, doth not each one of you on the sabbath loose his ox or his ass from the stall and lead him away to watering? And ought not this woman, being a daughter of Abraham, whom Satan hath bound, lo, these eighteen years, be loosed from this bond on the sabbath day? And when He had said these things, all His adversaries were ashamed: and all the people rejoiced for all the glorious things that were done by Him"—Luke 13: 10-17.

AS we go over this account we are reminded that all through the three and one-half wonderful years of our Lord's ministry, as He went about doing good and healing all oppressed of the devil, He found Himself in conflict with a certain group of legal formalists in Israel who put far more value upon outward observances, sacred ceremonies and religious rites than upon the human soul. And yet the soul of man is more to God than all such rites and ceremonies. Our Lord Jesus never lost an opportunity to rebuke this type of hypocrisy. He calls it that very definitely.

Many people go along the line of least resistance, because they do not want to bow their heart before God and really get right with Him. They place the emphasis upon outward things—attending church, ordinances, such as baptism or the Lord's Supper, or elaborate ritualistic services. They stress these things rather than the recognition of the Lordship of Christ and the salvation of men.

There are some spiritual lessons set forth here which the Lord would have us learn. He was teaching in one of the synagogues in Capernaum on the Sabbath. It might have been, possibly, the very synagogue which has been uncovered within our own times from the dust of nearly two millenniums. While teaching there one Sabbath day He observed before Him a poor woman to whom His sympathy immediately went out. He knew she "had a spirit of infirmity eighteen years, and was bowed together, and could in no wise lift up herself." It might have been arthritis or some type of spinal trouble which bowed her down. She had doubtless gone to physicians and sought help and failed to obtain it. But as the Lord looked upon her, His heart went out to her in compassion and He called her to Him, and said unto her, "Woman, thou art loosed from thine infirmity." There is no form of suffering which we endure but that the Lord looks upon us in compassion, ready to give needed grace, and sometimes He heals us if that is His highest will for us; if it is not His will to heal us He will give needed grace to sustain the spirit in the midst of trials, so that we can learn to glory in tribulation and to rejoice even in our infirmities. Jesus looked upon this poor woman with compassion, and called her to Him. He does the same with us. He looks upon us; He has compassion upon us, and He calls us and bids us come to Him and bring to Him all our ailments, our difficulties, our perplexities, assuring us that He is ready to undertake for us in His own marvelous way.

The woman left her place and came forward. The eyes of all in the synagogue were fastened upon her. I imagine she was a rather humble-looking person; her poor, bent body witnessed to her suffering. But oh, how all was changed as she came to the front! The Lord laid His hands upon her—those hands which were so often lifted up in blessing; those hands which were laid upon the eyes of the blind, and they were opened; those hands which were laid upon lepers, and the leprosy was cleansed; those hands which were so soon to be pierced with the nails on the cross—He laid those hands upon this poor woman, and she felt the thrill of a new life coursing through her entire body; and she who had been crooked was made straight in a moment. And we are told she glorified God. She realized that He who had wrought this miracle upon her must be God's Servant, for she recognized the fact that the healing was from the Lord. How far she entered into the truth of the Saviour's Deity, I cannot say; but she recognized at least that the power of God had wrought this miracle. We might expect that there would have been great rejoicing on the part of all who were present, that a paean of praise would have risen from the throng who had witnessed this manifestation of the love and power of God. But though this was true of some, there were those who looked upon it all with jealous eyes and with bitter envy in their hearts. Even the ruler of the synagogue was indignant. To him it was a profane interruption of a sacred service. He did not speak to Jesus face-to-face but turned to the people and said, "There are six days in which men ought to work: in them therefore come and be healed, and not on the sabbath day." But God finds more glory in delivering people from their suffering, physical and spiritual, than in any formal religious service. Our Lord Jesus Christ said, "Thou hypocrite." That word "hypocrite" is really the Greek word for an actor, and literally means "second face." Greek actors did not appear on the stage showing their own faces but put on masks, and so the word "second face" was given to an actor. It is applied here by our Lord to one who is not real—Thou hypocrite, thou two-faced one! Jesus thus exposed the unreality of this man, who was one thing before men and quite another before God. He was altogether different in his home, and possibly altogether different in his business and in his relations with other persons than he was as ruler of the synagogue. There are many such hypocrites still: men, and women too, who can be very pious when they are in church but very impious when driving a hard bargain through the week; or who make everyone miserable in the home because of a violent temper and a hard and cruel manner in dealing with the family. Bunyan pictures one like this: "A saint abroad and devil at home." Two faces: one face for the public, another face for other relations. There are many who resent a preacher's speaking like this. They do not like to have sin called "sin"; they do not want anything that will disturb them in what they call their "religious exercises." Our Lord knew this man, and He exposed the corruption of his heart as He exclaimed "Thou hypocrite, doth not each one of you on the sabbath loose his ox or his ass from the stall, and lead him away to watering? And ought not this woman, being a daughter of Abraham, whom Satan hath bound, lo, these eighteen years, be loosed from this bond on the sabbath day?" When they attended to their animals on the Sabbath it was all right; but when He healed a poor, suffering woman and delivered her from an infirmity of eighteen years' standing, they looked upon that with indignation. Yet this woman was a daughter of Abraham whom Satan had bound: that is, she was one who believed in God as Abraham did; she was a true daughter of the covenant. She was not merely a Jewess by natural birth, not merely one who sprang from the line of Abraham, but she was a woman of faith, in spite of the affliction wherewith Satan had bound her. She believed God; she had faith in Him. We read that, "They which be of faith are blessed with faithful Abraham." She was a woman of faith and now her faith was rewarded. She was healed of her infirmity, and some who should have rejoiced only complained!

Notice how definitely Jesus traces her infirmity back to Satan himself. Sickness never comes directly from God. God is infinitely pure; there is no corruption in Him. All the sickness, all the infirmity that anyone has to endure is the direct or indirect result of sin. Do not misunderstand me. I do not mean one's own personal sins are responsible for his infirmities. It would be cruel to take the stand which was taken by Job's friends, that calamity comes to one only because of personal sin. But no one would ever have been ill if sin had not come into the world by Adam's fall. There are times when in a very special way Satan undertakes to inflict punishment upon God's people, but he can do that only as God gives permission. This is clearly illustrated when Satan went before God, and God said, "Hast thou considered My servant Job, that there is none like him in the earth?" Satan replied, "Thou hast given him everything a man could desire, and that is the reason he fears Thee, but take it away from him and then Thou wilt see that he will curse Thee to Thy face." God gave Satan permission to test Job in this manner, and Satan went forth and took everything away from him: his sons, daughters, and all his possessions. The only thing he left Job was a wife with a bad temper; all else was gone. But Job looked up to God and said, "The Lord gave, and the Lord hath taken away; blessed be the Name of the Lord." Satan went before God again, and God said, "Hast thou considered My servant Job, that there is none like him in the earth, a perfect and an upright man, one that feareth God, and escheweth evil? and still he holdeth fast his integrity, although thou movedst Me against him, to destroy him without cause." Satan said, "Skin for skin, yea, all that a man hath will he give for his life. But put forth Thine hand now, and touch his bone and his flesh, and he will curse Thee to Thy face. And the Lord said unto Satan, Behold, he is in thine hand; but save his life. So went Satan forth from the presence of the Lord, and smote Job with sore boils from the sole of his foot unto his crown. And he took him a potsherd to scrape himself withal; and he sat down among the ashes." Some physicians consider that this was a form of elephantiasis, a lothsome disease with excruciating agony. His wife said, "Why not curse God and die?" But Job said, "We receive good at the hand of God, and shall we not also receive evil?" God demonstrated to the devil that Job's love was for Himself alone. In similar ways Satan is permitted to try God's people still. He is permitted to put illness upon us; but the Lord will turn it all into blessing if only we learn to receive it as from His own hand and recognize no second causes.

In this case, notice again the way the Lord puts it: "Ought not this woman . . . whom Satan hath bound, lo, these eighteen years, be loosed from this bond?" Do you see what He had done? He had made a crooked woman straight! Of course her ailment was physical; but I think there is a spiritual lesson here for us. All through the centuries since, that is what the gospel has been doing—it has been making crooked people straight. Sin makes us crooked. We have "all gone out of the way." "All have sinned, and come short of the glory of God." "There is not a just man upon the earth, that doeth good, and sinneth not." As God looks down upon us He discerns the crookedness in all of us; but when we come to Christ He can straighten us out. The lives of some people are more crooked than others. Some people can cover their crookedness from the eyes of their fellows, but it is useless to try to hide their crookedness from God. There are many who have never come to the place where they have confessed their crookedness, acknowledged their sinfulness, and faced their true condition before God. He desires to do something for them; He wants to straighten them out, but they refuse to come to Him, for they do not realize their need of His grace.

One of the most crooked persons I ever knew was a man who was crooked in his business. All who patronized him found that he cheated them. But when he came to Christ it was not long before people were saying, "You know Mr. So-and-So is a different man: he is straight in all his dealings." Many people have been morally crooked, licentious, and given to vile habits; but they have come to Jesus and trusted Him, and He has made them upright. We cannot do this for ourselves. Only the Lord can straighten us. If you are morally crooked, and you have tried to straighten yourself and have not been able to do so, I plead with you: come to Jesus; look to Him; confess your failure and your sin to Him, and you will find that He is able to make you straight. He does not merely improve the old life; He gives a new life. When you receive this new life you will learn to hate the things you once loved and to love the things you once hated.

Coming back to our story—a picture of what Jesus can do for all crooked people who come to Him—we are told that, "When He had said these things, all His adversaries were ashamed: and all the people rejoiced for all the glorious things that were done by Him." Evidently there were many besides the rulers who were opposed, many critical Jews who were angry, because of the healing of this poor woman on the Sabbath. But they were ashamed; they did not dare say anything more. And all the people, that is, the common people—the people who loved to hear the words of Jesus and to see His works of power—"rejoiced for all the glorious things that were done by Him." Thank God, He is still doing glorious things! He is still straightening up crooked people; He is still delivering folk from their infirmities. If you, to whom this message comes, have not known in your own life God's wonderful work of grace, He bids you come to Him just as you are, and He will make you straight.

Address Fifty-one

TWO ASPECTS OF THE KINGDOM OF GOD

✓ ✓ ✓

"Then said He, Unto what is the kingdom of God like? and whereunto shall I resemble it? It is like a grain of mustard seed, which a man took, and cast into his garden; and it grew, and waxed a great tree; and the fowls of the air lodged in the branches of it. And again He said, Whereunto shall I liken the kingdom of God? It is like leaven, which a woman took and hid in three measures of meal, till the whole was leavened"—Luke 13: 18-21.

✓ ✓ ✓

WE are told in the beginning of this and the other Synoptic Gospels that John the Baptist came preaching repentance because the kingdom of God was at hand. The Lord Jesus took up the message as He began His ministry. For centuries, ever since the dispersion and partial return to the land, the Jews had looked for the King who was to deliver them from Gentile domination and set up the dominion of righteousness on the earth. Now the King was among them, and they knew Him not. The same prophets who told of the kingdom also predicted the rejection of the King at His first coming; and foretold a second and glorious advent when He should return in power and regal splendor, at which time the years of their mourning would be ended, and Israel would enter into fulness of blessing.

But what of the period lying between these two advents? Will the kingdom remain utterly in abeyance; or will it take some other form unpredicted by the prophets of old? These questions are answered, at least in part, in the two parables now before us. Here they are called parables of "the kingdom of God." They are found also in Matthew's Gospel (chap. 13), but there the term "kingdom of heaven" is used, an expression peculiar to that Evangelist. This is really synonymous with what we commonly call Christendom. There is a large part of the world where Christ is acknowledged outwardly as the earth's rightful King, at least. There may or may not be heart-subjection to Him; but men professedly own allegiance to Him, as indicated by the very letters "A. D."—"In the year of our Lord," which we use in dating all our correspondence and other documents. "Christendom" really means "Christ's Kingdom." This is what our Lord referred to when He spoke of the mystery of the kingdom of God. It is the kingdom in mystery-form while the King Himself is absent in the heavens.

There are two different aspects of this kingdom brought before us in the two parables given here. Matthew gives both, as mentioned above, in a series with five other parables in the thirteenth chapter of his Gospel, where we have a remarkable outline of the whole history and the moral principles that were to characterize the kingdom of heaven while the King remains away. "Unto what is the kingdom of God like? and whereunto shall I resemble it? It is like a grain of mustard seed, which a man took, and cast into his garden; and it grew, and waxed a great tree; and the fowls of the air lodged in the branches of it." Elsewhere we are told that the mustard seed is the smallest of all seeds. This does not mean that it is the smallest of all seeds in the vegetable world but the smallest in the herb gardens. And yet that little seed produces the greatest tree of all the herbs. It grows very rapidly and soon overshadows everything around it. Now this is the picture the Lord gave of the outward development of the kingdom of God. Have you ever stopped to think this through? When our Lord first ascended to heaven there were eleven men defiinitely committed to Him, recognized as His apostles, to bear His message to the world. There were some few hundreds of others throughout Judaea, Galilee and Samaria, who acknowledged His claims. That small beginning was like the mustard seed, the nucleus of the kingdom. These eleven were commissioned to go everywhere preaching the kingdom of God, and telling of the Saviour who had died to put away the sin of mankind and who had ascended to heaven, and is coming again to judge the world. You know how rapidly the kingdom expanded. Within a very short time after the ascension of the Lord Jesus we come to Pentecost, and on that day three thousand souls openly confessed their allegiance to Him. Then within a short time after the healing of the lame man at the temple gate, the number became five thousand; and as the days went on more and more throughout all Jerusalem and Judaea came out for Christ. The gospel reached Samaria, and many hundreds of Samaritans believed, and so it went on to the Gentile world. The remarkable fact is that though the gospel had to contend with idolatry of the worst kind, within three hundred years paganism in the Roman empire had been practically conquered, and Christianity superseded it. Early Christian writers about that time taunted the enemies of Christianity with words something like these: "Your temples are deserted. Christians are found everywhere throughout the Empire." So the Word went on and on until today there are untold millions of people in the world who profess allegiance to the Lord Jesus Christ. But our Lord said the tree grew until it "waxed a great tree; and the fowls of the air lodged in the branches of it." If we turn back to the eighth chapter of this Gospel we find the parable of the sower who went out to sow his seed, "And as he sowed, some fell by the way side; and it was trodden down, and the fowls of the air devoured it." When our Lord gives the interpretation of that parable in the eleventh and twelfth verses, He says, "The Seed is the Word of God. Those by the way side are they that hear; then cometh the devil, and taketh away the Word out of their hearts, lest they should believe and be saved." In this our Lord shows that the fowls of the air represent evil emissaries, agents of Satan, who are seeking to destroy that which is of God, and to keep the good seed of the kingdom from bearing fruit in the hearts of those who hear. Is it not a remarkable thing then that only a short time afterward He likens the kingdom of heaven to a mustard tree, with branches spreading abroad in a remarkable way, but in which the fowls of the air actually find lodgment? But does not that agree with the history of Christendom? The way in which nation after nation has been brought out of the darkness of paganism to a knowledge of our blessed Saviour has been truly miraculous; but oh, what unspeakable evils have been hidden in the professing Church of the living God! When we think of the many emissaries of the devil who have found shelter inside the great Christian organizations, who are filled with bitter hatred for the gospel, and endeavor to turn people away from the truth, one might well be appalled and disheartened if the Lord had not foretold all this.

The next parable is that of the leaven, "which a woman took and hid in three measures of meal, till the whole was leavened." Let me suggest a word of caution here: Do not say that the kingdom itself is like leaven. That is what many people believe. They have the idea that leaven is a symbol of the kingdom, and just as a housewife puts yeast in dough, so the gospel has been committed to Christ's servants to be carried to the end of the world; and it will go on working and working until everybody will be converted, and this whole universe will be brought to the feet of our Lord Jesus Christ. Now that would be a wonderful thing if it were true, but many scriptures show that it is not so. Our Lord Jesus put the question: "When the Son of Man cometh, shall He find faith on the earth?" He told of ever-increasing apostasy as the end draws near. He said, "As it was in the days of Noah so shall the coming of the Son of Man be." The whole world was not converted in Noah's day; neither will the whole world be converted before our Lord comes again.

In an earlier section of this exposition we have discussed the meaning of leaven and seen that throughout Scripture it represents always that which is evil, either in practice or in doctrine. We are warned in both 1 Cor. 5: 6 and in Gal. 5: 9, that "a little leaven leaveneth the whole lump." Leaven is ever and always evil. In the light of this fact, what do we really see here? The Lord was telling what was going to take place after He went away. He showed how the kingdom was going to spread throughout the world. He knew that millions would profess faith in His name, and to them His truth was to be committed. It was to be kept inviolate, unleavened. But He foresaw the efforts that false professors would make to turn His disciples away from the truth and to bring in the leaven of evil teaching. Like Jezebel of old, the woman here works surreptitiously to pervert the truth. Thus she, the false church, hides the leaven in the food of the children of God. In Revelation (Chap. 17) we have that evil woman, Babylon the Great, riding the beast and dominating the affairs of this world, professing to be the Lamb's wife, but branded by God Himself as a false harlot and the persecutor of the saints. This, I believe, is the woman we have pictured here, coming from the outside into Christianity, professing to teach the truth which God revealed to His people. Think of the widespread perversion of the truth. For instance, Christ told His disciples to go into all the world and baptize believers from among all nations. Soon this simple ordinance was said to produce the new birth, and it was taught that only by baptism could we be assured of salvation. Jesus instituted the precious ordinance of the Lord's Supper, to be observed in memory of Him till He comes again. It was not long before people were taught that the bread and wine were transubstantiated into the very body and blood of Christ and offered as a sacrifice for the sins of the living and the dead. That which was intended to be a beautiful testimony to the finished work of Christ was made to mean the very opposite. There are literally thousands of people who are taught to go to Mary instead of to Christ, to pray to Mary and to the apostles and other saints who came after them, as though the saints in heaven could hear. Nowhere are we told that the saints can hear our prayers. God, revealed in Christ, is the only One who knows our hearts, and who can hear the cry of our lips. "There is one Mediator between God and man, the Man Christ Jesus." A picture came to me this past week, sent by someone, I suppose, who desired to enlighten me. It represented two ladders leading to heaven. At the top of one was what was meant to be a picture of Christ, and at the top of the other was a picture of Mary, His mother. At the bottom of Mary's ladder was a group of priests and nuns urging people to climb up to her for salvation. All such received a glad welcome. Those who insisted on taking the other ladder met, at the top, a scowling Christ, cold, severe and merciless. The picture showed some people climbing up that ladder, and after getting halfway up they tumbled off. But Mary was pictured as the blessed one with a kindly face, looking down in compassion upon the people as they climbed to heaven. They were making it through Mary when they could not make it through Christ! There you have an illustration of what I mean by the insertion of the leaven of error in the meal. Think of the Blessed Lord who said, "Come unto Me, all ye that labor and are heavy laden, and I will give you rest." Is He cold and unconcerned? And is it His mother, Mary, who is tender and loving and ready to help sinners? What a travesty on the gospel! As our Lord looked forward He said, all this "is like leaven, which a woman took and hid in three measures of meal, till the whole was leavened." Oh, how thankful we can be that we can come right back and test everything by this Book, and rejoice today that we know Christ as the One who came down from His glory to accomplish the work that saves, and to give assurance of eternal life to all who trust Him!

ADDRESS FIFTY-TWO

A GREAT CRISIS

✝ ✝ ✝

"And He went through the cities and villages, teaching, and journeying toward Jerusalem. Then said one unto Him, Lord, are there few that be saved? And He said unto them, Strive to enter in at the strait gate: for many, I say unto you, will seek to enter in, and shall not be able. When once the master of the house is risen up, and hath shut to the door, and ye begin to stand without, and to knock at the door, saying, Lord, Lord, open unto us; and He shall answer and say unto you, I know you not whence ye are: then shall ye begin to say, We have eaten and drunk in Thy presence, and Thou hast taught in our streets. But He shall say, I tell you, I know you not whence ye are; depart from Me, all ye workers of iniquity. There shall be weeping and gnashing of teeth, when ye shall see Abraham, and Isaac, and Jacob, and all the prophets, in the kingdom of God, and you yourselves thrust out. And they shall come from the east, and from the west, and from the north, and from the south, and shall sit down in the kingdom of God. And, behold, there are last which shall be first, and there are first which shall be last. The same day there came certain of the Pharisees, saying unto Him, Get Thee out, and depart hence: for Herod will kill Thee. And He said unto them, Go ye, and tell that fox, Behold, I cast out devils, and I do cures to-day and to-morrow, and the third day I shall be perfected. Nevertheless I must walk to-day, and to-morrow, and the day following: for it cannot be that a prophet perish out of Jerusalem. O Jerusalem, Jerusalem, which killest the prophets, and stonest them that are sent unto thee; how often would I have gathered thy children together, as a hen doth gather her brood under her wings, and ye would not! Behold, your house is left unto you desolate: and verily I say unto you, Ye shall not see Me, until the time come when ye shall say, Blessed is He that cometh in the name of the Lord"—Luke 13: 22-35.

✝ ✝ ✝

THIS portion of Luke's Gospel brings us to a great crisis in the history of Israel. For three years our blessed Lord had presented Himself to the people as the promised King, the One who the Old Testament prophets had predicted would come in the fulness of time to reign here on the earth; but He had met with ever-increasing opposition. The leaders rejected Him from the very first. They would not recognize Him nor His credentials. They positively refused to see in Him the promised Messiah. For three years they had closed their hearts to Him, and the time had come when Israel, for the present, must be set to one side, and soon the call of God would go out to the Gentile world.

Jesus left Galilee and traveled slowly down the eastern side of the Sea of Galilee and the Jordan River, through Decapolis and Perea, in order to reach Jerusalem in time for the Passover—the last Passover which He was to eat with His disciples. On the very day of the feast He was to die as the true Paschal Lamb. As they journeyed through the villages and talked together, one turned to Him and asked, "Lord, are there few that be saved?" This is a question that arises in many hearts. Will there be comparatively few in heaven, or will there be many? Now the Lord does not exactly answer this question here. There are several passages of Scripture which I think answer it very clearly. We know that all children who die in infancy will be saved, because our Lord Jesus definitely declared, "It is not the will of your Father which is in heaven, that one of these little ones should perish." This, in itself, gives us some idea of the vast multitude of the redeemed. But of those who have grown to years of maturity, there have been far more who have spurned the Word of

God than who have received it. None will be saved who reject the light which God gives them. All such are condemned justly. But on this occasion, our Lord, instead of answering the question, stressed the importance of being tremendously in earnest in view of the coming day. He said unto them, "Strive to enter in at the strait gate: for many, I say unto you, will seek to enter in, and shall not be able." It is not that we are to be saved by our own efforts, for by these we would never be saved at all; but we must be in earnest when the door to life stands open, and we are invited to enter in; we must be sure that we heed the gracious invitation and do not pass carelessly by, lest we find at last that we have lost our opportunity.

Jesus adds, "When once the master of the house is risen up, and hath shut to the door, and ye begin to stand without, and to knock at the door, saying, Lord, Lord, open unto us; and he shall answer and say unto you, I know you not whence ye are." We may well take these warning words to our hearts today for they are intended for us as truly as for the people of Israel of old. The door into the kingdom of God still stands open, but it is a narrow door. None can pass through that door with their sins upon them. But as Christ Himself is the Door, we may find in Him deliverance from our sins, and thus enter into the way of life. The narrow way is that of subjection to Christ; a way that involves denial of self and recognition of our responsibility to live for Him whose grace alone can save us.

I plead with you to give heed to the words of our Lord, "Strive to enter in at the strait gate." Do not let anything keep you from making sure of your eternal salvation. But be like the man in Bunyan's *Pilgrim's Progress,* who, when he heard of the impending destruction of the city in which he lived and learned that life was to be found only through entering the wicket gate, refused to be turned aside by any of his own townspeople, and putting his fingers in his ears, ran from them crying, "Life! Life! Eternal Life!" and so made his way toward the shining light pointed out to him by Evangelist.

Jesus warns of the danger of unreality as He continues His discourse: "Then shall ye begin to say, We have eaten and drunk in thy presence, and thou hast taught in our streets." Or, as many might put it, "We have attended church; we have sung gospel hymns; we have listened to sermons; we have given money to help in missionary endeavors." But these things cannot save. So He adds, "But he shall say, I tell you, I know you not whence ye are; depart from me, all ye workers of iniquity." You will remember in the tenth chapter of John's Gospel, our Lord says: "My sheep hear My voice, and I know them, and they follow Me: and I give unto them eternal life; and they shall never perish, neither shall any man pluck them out of My hand. My Father, which gave them Me, is greater than all; and no man is able to pluck them out of My Father's hand." Now observe the contrast. His own sheep are those who entered by the strait gate and took the narrow way. They are all those who believed the gospel. He says of these, "I know them." Notice the difference as to those mentioned here to whom "He shall say, I tell you, I know you not whence ye are; depart from Me, all ye workers of iniquity." There are none to whom He will say, "I used to know you but I do not know you anymore; I knew you once, but you have forfeited the right of all recognition." He says to all who are lost: "I *never* knew you!" Not one soul will be found knocking on the outside of that closed door who was once saved and then forfeited salvation; but there will be thousands, I am afraid, perhaps myriads, who thought they were Christians, and their friends on earth thought they were, and yet the Lord will say to them in that day, "I never knew you!" They have never been really born of God.

The Lord was speaking particularly to those of Israel who had heard His message, who had been told He was the promised Messiah and King; yet the great majority had refused to believe in Him. He says, "There shall be weeping and gnashing of teeth, when ye shall see Abraham, and Isaac, and Jacob, and all the prophets, in the kingdom of God, and you yourselves thrust out." Notice the evidence of full recognition of those who had entered into the other world—they will know Abraham, Isaac, and Jacob, and the prophets. They will behold them even though they are on the other side of the great gulf; they will see beyond into the heavenly aspect of the kingdom, the fathers of Israel, and the prophets whose Scriptures they had professed to cherish; but they, themselves, who had failed to recognize the Redeemer when He came to deliver them, will be shut out in the darkness. Oh, be warned lest the day come for you when you shall see in yonder glory, father, mother, friends, and dear ones who knew and loved Christ; yet you, yourself, be shut out because you did not receive the Saviour. Receive Him now if you have never received Him before, even as these words ring in your ears. You need His blood to wash away your sins. Receive Him now in faith. The moment you do so He receives you, and you pass through the strait gate. Israel had that opportunity but they lost it. They forfeited their privileges; therefore, the day drew near when they would be cast out and others would take their place. "And they shall come from the east, and from the west, and from the north, and from the south, and shall sit down in the kingdom of God." There are millions from the Gentile world who have come in to appropriate and enjoy that which Israel despised. So we are told, "And, behold, there are last which shall be first, and there are first which shall be last." Israel was first in God's plan for blessing and now she is last.

"The same day there came certain of the Pharisees, saying unto Him, Get Thee out, and depart hence: for Herod will kill Thee." They pretended to be interested in saving the life of our Lord, but they did not understand that no one could take it until He Himself laid it down. Knowing all that was before Him and perceiving their deceitful attitude, "He said unto them, Go ye, and tell that fox,

Behold, I cast out devils, and I do cures to-day and to-morrow, and the third day I shall be perfected." That is, perfected as to salvation. We read in the second chapter of Hebrews that He who was ever perfect as to His character; was made perfect as the Captain of our salvation by His death on the cross.

He had set His face to go to Jerusalem and finish His testimony there, where He was to lay down His life for our redemption. As He thought of that city —the city that was privileged above every other city on earth but which knew not the time of its visitation—He cried, "O Jerusalem, Jerusalem, which killest the prophets, and stonest them that are sent unto thee; how often would I have gathered thy children together, as a hen doth gather her brood under her wings, and ye would not!" In these words He tells us the yearning that is in the heart of God, not only for Jerusalem and for the people of Israel, but for all men everywhere who turn carelessly and indifferently away from His message.

"From heaven His eye is downward bent,
Still glancing to and fro
Where'er in this wide wilderness,
There roams a child of woe.

"And as the rebel chooses wrath,
God wails his hapless lot,
Deep-breathing from His heart of love,
I would, but ye would not!"

If unsaved, I plead with you, do not hurt the heart of God by continuing to reject His Son. He loved you enough to give Christ to die for you. You could not insult Him more than by spurning that Gift, and saying, "I am not interested in Christ." On the other hand, there is nothing you could do which would gladden the heart of God more than to say, "I receive Thy Son; I trust Him now as my Saviour; I own Him as my Lord." It is written, "That if thou shalt confess with thy mouth the Lord Jesus, and shalt believe in thine heart that God hath raised Him from the dead, thou shalt be saved."

We have next the Lord's words directed to those who had spurned His testimony. With Israel it was final rejection. They did not realize that they had crossed the dead-line. The Lord said, "Behold, your house is left unto you desolate: and verily I say unto you, Ye shall not see Me, until the time come when ye shall say, Blessed is He that cometh in the name of the Lord." The crisis had been reached in God's dealing with Israel for that age. From that time on, as one may see by reading any of the Gospels, there was no attempt made to win the whole nation of Israel. They have closed the door upon themselves. So God gave them up to hardness of heart. Not until the Lord returns will the nation come to repentance. Ever since He said, "Your house is left desolate," Israel has been set aside and is no longer in the place of a favored people. On the other hand He offers deliverance to every individual Israelite who will turn to Him and trust Him. There is no difference, for "all have sinned, and come short of the glory of God." "There is no difference between Jew and Greek: for the same Lord over all is rich unto all who call upon Him." In the book of Acts we see the Lord through Peter, pleading with the people of Israel to save themselves from that unrighteous generation by acknowledging the Saviour whom the nation, as such, has repudiated. But the day of Israel's regeneration as a whole is deferred until the once-rejected Jesus is manifested in glory, and they look upon Him whom they pierced and bow in repentance at His feet.

ADDRESS FIFTY-THREE

THE PARABLE OF THE GREAT SUPPER

* * *

"And it came to pass, as He went into the house of one of the chief Pharisees to eat bread on the sabbath day, that they watched Him. And, behold, there was a certain man before Him which had the dropsy. And Jesus answering spake unto the lawyers and Pharisees, saying, Is it lawful to heal on the sabbath day? And they held their peace. And He took him, and healed him, and let him go; and answered them, saying, Which of you shall have an ass or an ox fallen into a pit, and will not straightway pull him out on the sabbath day? And they could not answer Him again to these things. And He put forth a parable to those which were bidden, when He marked how they chose out the chief rooms; saying unto them, When thou art bidden of any man to a wedding, sit not down in the highest room; lest a more honorable man than thou be bidden of him; and he that bade thee and him come and say to thee, Give this man place; and thou begin with shame to take the lowest room. But when thou art bidden, go and sit down in the lowest room; that when he that bade thee cometh, he may say unto thee, Friend, go up higher: then shalt thou have worship in the presence of them that sit at meat with thee. For whosoever exalteth himself shall be abased; and he that humbleth himself shall be exalted. Then said He also to him that bade Him, When thou makest a dinner or a supper, call not thy friends, nor thy rich neighbors; lest they also bid thee again, and a recompence be made thee. But when thou makest a feast, call the poor, the maimed, the lame, the blind: and thou shalt be blessed; for they cannot recompense thee: for thou shalt be recompensed at the resurrection of the just. And when one of them that sat at meat with Him heard these things, he said unto Him, Blessed is he that shall eat bread in the kingdom of God. Then said He unto him, A certain man made a great supper, and bade many: and sent his servant at supper time to say to them that were bidden, Come; for all things are now ready. And they all with one consent began to make excuse. The first said unto him, I have bought a piece of ground, and I must needs go and see it: I pray thee have me excused. And another said, I have bought five yoke of oxen, and I go to prove them: I pray thee have me excused. And another said, I have married a wife, and therefore I cannot come. So that servant came, and showed his lord these things. Then the master of the house being angry said to his servant, Go out quickly into the streets and lanes of the city, and bring in hither the poor, and the maimed, and the halt, and the blind. And the servant said, Lord, it is done as thou hast commanded, and yet there is room. And the lord said unto the servant, Go out into the highways and hedges, and compel them to come in, that my house may be filled. For I say unto you, That none of those men which were bidden shall taste of my supper"—Luke 14: 1-24.

ONCE more we find our Lord invited out to dinner. In this instance, one of the chief Pharisees is His host. Whether he asked Jesus to dine with him and some of his friends because of a genuine interest in Him and His message, or whether he simply did it out of curiosity, or in order to criticize His words and behavior, we are not told. In any case, Jesus accepted the invitation, and as usual He was soon the real Host rather than just a special guest. Wherever He went men had to recognize His superiority, although He was ever meek and lowly in heart. There was something so compelling about His words and His bearing that even His enemies had to acknowledge the authority with which He taught.

The other guests on this particular occasion consisted of a number of lawyers and Pharisees who were watching Jesus intently, eager to find something against Him. The opportunity soon came, for there was a poor, distressed man present on that Sabbath day, who was afflicted with the dropsy. To him the Lord's heart went out in pity and compassion. Evidently the sick man was hopeful that the

Lord would do something for him, and he was not disappointed, for Jesus turned to the other guests and asked, "Is it lawful to heal on the Sabbath day?" He knew their prejudices, and how they had found fault with Him on many previous occasions for freeing people from their diseases on the Sabbath. They were far more concerned about outward ceremonies than about the needs of a man, but when the Lord spoke directly to them, they did not commit themselves audibly. When they did not answer Him, Jesus, we are told, "took the man and healed him and let him go." The Lord knew what was in their hearts; so turning to them He asked: "Which of you shall have an ass or an ox fallen into a pit, and will not straightway pull him out on the sabbath day?" They would consider it quite proper and right to deliver one of their beasts from a calamity even on the Sabbath, but they would have him ignore the needs of troubled and distressed humanity. They could not answer Him as to these things.

As there was no response on the part of the baffled lawyers and Pharisees, Jesus next addressed Himself to the guests as a whole. He observed how each one sought to obtain the best places at the table. We read, "And He put forth a parable to those which were bidden, when He marked how they chose out the chief rooms; saying unto them, When thou art bidden of any man to a wedding, sit not down in the highest room; lest a more honorable man than thou be bidden of him; and he that bade thee and him come and say to thee, Give this man place; and thou begin with shame to take the lowest room. But when thou art bidden, go and sit down in the lowest room; that when he that bade thee cometh, he may say unto thee, Friend, go up higher: then shalt thou have worship in the presence of them that sit at meat with thee. For whosoever exalteth himself shall be abased; and he that humbleth himself shall be exalted." He was suggesting merely that others should do as He had done. He who was entitled to the highest place of all came from the Father's house down to this earth. Here He took the lowest place; but in God's due time He was given the highest place where today He sits on the right hand of the Father. It is He who teaches us these lessons of humility, and what a rebuke they are to our pride! We are always looking for recognition, and we feel hurt if we do not have it; but our Lord was ever ready to take the lowest place. Surely this should put us to shame.

Next we find that the Lord not only instructed the guests, but also as He was looking about He saw the kind of persons who were present. He addressed His host and, indirectly, all the guests: "Then said He also to him that bade Him, When thou makest a dinner or a supper, call not thy friends, nor thy brethren, neither thy kinsmen, nor thy rich neighbors; lest they also bid thee again, and a recompense be made thee." Is not that one of the reasons we select certain guests? When we give a dinner, most of us go over the list and determine who are likely to return the compliment by inviting us to their homes when they put on a similar affair. This is the accepted procedure in the world, but it should not be practised by those who profess to follow Christ. He said, "When thou makest a feast, call the poor, the maimed, the lame, the blind: and thou shalt be blessed; for they cannot recompense thee: for thou shalt be recompensed at the resurrection of the just." This is the first resurrection—the resurrection of life when all who have died in the Lord will rise and appear before the judgment-seat, there to be rewarded according to the deeds done in the body.

It is evident that the instruction given by Jesus at that table so impressed one man that he was carried away with a holy enthusiasm which led him to exclaim, "Blessed is he that shall eat bread in the kingdom of God!" That is, if the kingdom of God is the sphere where all seek the lowest place, and where the poor and disfigured are assured of a glad welcome, it must be indeed a great privilege to participate in such a wondrous fellowship.

In reply Jesus related the parable of the Great Supper to show that there are few comparatively who are willing to avail themselves of the invitation to eat bread in the kingdom of God. He told of a certain man who made a great feast, and at supper time he sent his servant to call the invited guests. But "all with one consent began to make excuse." This is the way men treat the gospel invitation. The natural man has no desire for the things of God. The privilege of a place at the great supper of salvation means nothing to him. For him the feast is spread in vain. It is only when God's

Spirit works in the heart and conscience of a man that he is ready to enter and sit down at the gospel feast. When in love God spread the feast for Israel, they would not go in. It is just as true of many Gentiles today. I do not know of anything else in which men are in such agreement. They are not in agreement on political questions or on religious questions, but they do not want Christ, and do not want to submit their lives to the Saviour whom God has provided until they are convicted by the Holy Spirit of their lost, needy state.

"And they all with one consent began to make excuse. The first said unto him, I have bought a piece of ground, and I must needs go and see it: I pray thee have me excused. And another said, I have bought five yoke of oxen, and I go to prove them: I pray thee have me excused." Trivial excuses indeed and utterly foolish. At last came a man who felt that he had an absolutely unshakable alibi. He said, "I have married a wife, and therefore I cannot come." How many men allow the wife to come between the Lord and them, and how many wives allow the husband to come between the Lord and them. "So that servant came, and showed his lord these things. Then the master of the house being angry"—Stop there! Does God become angry with men? Scripture tells us, "God is angry with the wicked every day." When one deliberately spurns His Son, His heart is filled with holy indignation. God loves His Son and He desires to see men honor the Son even as they honor the Father.

Rejecting in his anger those who spurned his feast, the master bade his servant, "Go out quickly into the streets and lanes of the city, and bring in hither the poor, and the maimed, and the halt, and the blind. And the servant said, Lord, it is done as thou hast commanded, and yet there is room." So, following the setting aside of Israel, the gospel invitation has gone out widely, but the house is not filled yet. "And the lord said unto the servant, Go out into the highways and hedges, and compel them to come in, that my house may be filled. For I say unto you, That none of those men which were bidden shall taste of my supper." It is dispensational. The message first came to the Jews, and they refused it, and then it was carried to the Gentiles. The apostle Paul says, "They will hear it," but not all of them. Throughout the centuries there have been millions who have accepted the invitation, but the house is not filled yet. There is still room for more, and the invitation is extended to all who are sin-sick and sad. The master sent his servant to "compel them to come in." The Servant here is the Holy Spirit. It is He alone who can compel men to come to Christ. In Matthew's account of the marriage feast it is the servants who gave the invitation. They can only bid men come; they cannot compel. But here it is the Servant, not servants. He compels by convicting men of sin and impressing upon them their need of a Saviour.

"Why was I made to hear Thy voice
And enter whilst there's room,
When thousands make a wretched choice
And rather starve than come?

" 'Twas the same love that spread the feast
That gently forced me in;
Else had I still refused to taste
And perished in my sin."

ADDRESS FIFTY-FOUR

COUNTING THE COST

"And there went great multitudes with Him: and He turned, and said unto them, If any man come to Me, and hate not his father, and mother, and wife, and children, and brethren, and sisters, yea, and his own life also, he cannot be My disciple. And whosoever doth not bear his cross, and come after Me, cannot be My disciple. For which of you, intending to build a tower, sitteth not down first, and counteth the cost, whether he have sufficient to finish it? Lest haply, after he hath laid the foundation, and is not able to finish it, all that behold it begin to mock him, saying, This man began to build, and was not able to finish. Or what king, going to make war against another king, sitteth not down first, and consulteth whether he be able with ten thousand to meet him that cometh against him with twenty thousand? Or else, while the other is yet a great way off, he sendeth an ambassage, and desireth conditions of peace. So likewise, whosoever he be of you that forsaketh not all that he hath, he cannot be My disciple. Salt is good: but if the salt have lost his savour, wherewith shall it be seasoned? It is neither fit for the land, nor yet for the dunghill; but men cast it out. He that hath ears to hear, let him hear"—Luke 14: 25-35.

THE last verses of this chapter constitute a challenge to everyone of us. They were intended to be such to our Lord's listeners when He was here on earth, and they have continued to speak powerfully through all the centuries He has been in the glory. "He that hath ears to hear, let him hear!" In this entire passage the Lord Jesus is dealing with the responsibility of discipleship. He is not telling how poor, lost sinners may be saved, nor is He speaking of the cost of that salvation. God's salvation is without money, but we pay bitterly if we do not accept it. Have you counted the cost if your soul should be lost? After having heard the gospel, after listening to the message of Christ, if you turn away from it, expecting some day to accept Him, and you live and die having neglected this great salvation, you will find you have done so at a terrible price. I remember hearing that great man of God, Dr. Walter B. Hinson, a number of years ago, preach on the text: "What shall it profit a man, if he gain the whole world, and lose his own soul?" Before he discussed the text itself he turned it roundabout and said, "Think first of this: what shall it profit a man though he lose the whole world and lose his own soul in the bargain?" It is at awful cost that men go out into a lost eternity. Some people seem to think that they are doing God a favor by trusting His Son and following Him; but it is quite the other way. God is offering to you eternal favor in saving you from an endless judgment, and if you refuse His mercy you do so at your own great loss.

In the verses we have read, there is no question raised of salvation but rather of discipleship. Our Lord's words here are addressed to those who have already trusted Him, to those who believe Him to be the Son of God, the Messiah of Israel and Saviour of sinners. Those who have put their faith in Him are now called upon to be His disciples. And discipleship costs! We cannot serve our Lord Jesus Christ as we should without tremendous cost to ourselves. So when great multitudes were gathering about Him, "He turned and said unto them,

If any man come to Me, and hate not his father, and mother, and wife, and children, and brethren, and sisters, yea, and his own life also, he cannot be My disciple. And whosoever doth not bear his cross, and come after Me, cannot be My disciple." This is a hard saying, but we need to remember that sometimes the Lord uses very strong expressions in a different way from that in which we use them. For instance, in the Old Testament, in the book of Malachi, we find the words, "Jacob have I loved, and Esau have I hated." Now God did not really hate anyone in the sense we use the word sometimes. "God so loved the world, that He gave His only begotten Son, that whosoever believeth in Him should not perish, but have everlasting life." "God commendeth His love toward us in that while we were yet sinners, Christ died for us." "Herein is love, not that we loved God, but that He loved us, and sent His Son to be the propitiation for our sins." So we may be sure that God loved the children of Esau just as He loved the children of Jacob; but when He said, "Jacob have I loved, and Esau have I hated," He was referring to special privileges here on earth. God had given certain privileges to the children of Jacob which had been denied the children of Esau. He had given the people of Israel a holy Law and a special care that were not given to any other nation, and He gave them teachers such as no other people had ever had; He gave them a land flowing with milk and honey, and made them the people of His own peculiar concern. The children of Esau dwelt in the wilderness, a dry, barren and thirsty land. They had very few privileges such as the people of Israel enjoyed. But this does not mean that God was not interested in the children of Esau. We may be sure His grace went out to every individual Edomite who repented of his sin and idolatry. So here our Lord says, "If any man come to Me, and hate not his father, and mother, and wife, and children, and brethren, and sisters, yea, and his own life also, he cannot be My disciple." This does not mean that we are to have ill will toward our loved ones; it does not mean that we are to bear malice toward them. But our consideration for Christ, our love for Him who died for us is to be so great that, in comparison to our interest in our dearest on earth, if they oppose what is right, our attitude will seem almost as hatred. I have seen very definite examples of this. I remember a dear, young Jewish girl who came to the Lord Jesus Christ and was saved. When she was to be baptized her Jewish mother, who loved her tenderly, said in a paroxysm of anger, "Oh, my daughter, do you hate your mother so much that you would go down to that church and be baptized?" The daughter insisted that she loved her mother, but that she loved Christ more. Her mother said, "You do not love me, or you would never be baptized. You hate me; that is why you are being baptized." The daughter knew that faithfulness demanded that she turn away from her dear mother as though she hated her, although it was almost more than she could endure. This illustrates what our Lord meant. Nothing must come between you and faithfulness to Christ; you must be true to Him whatever it means. So discipleship does cost. Many people have had to leave their homes for Christ's sake, and their names have been cast down as evil, because they loved Him supremely. Many of us belong to Christian families and have been brought up in homes where loved ones were interested in our salvation; nevertheless, the challenge comes to us just the same. If anyone, no matter how dear, would come between Christ and us we are to hate that person in comparison with our love for Him.

"Yea, and his own life also." Elsewhere we read, "He that loveth his life shall lose it; and he that hateth his life in this world shall keep it unto eternal life." There are many people who have to give up splendid prospects on earth in order to put Christ's interests first. He who refuses to do this will lose his life, while the one who counts all things as dross for Christ's sake will keep it unto life eternal. Many young men and women are facing this question. Is Christ to have the preeminent place in your heart? Are you so yielded to Him that you are prepared to let Him have His way in your life? You know Christ and you have the message the world needs. Will you give up worldly interests and go forth at His call to proclaim the gospel to those who are sitting in darkness? Do you think of your pleasant prospects and how well you are getting on in the world, and are you so intent on making money that you have turned away from the call of God? I know everyone is not called to relinquish all secular employment in order to give full time to Christian service, but it means much to be yielded to God for whatever plan He has for you. How terrible it is in the end for one, for instance, who has been called to be a missionary, but who remains at home, and as the years go on he perhaps makes a good home and accumulates a comfortable fortune, but misses entirely the path the Lord had for him. How blessed the reward in that day for one who renounces all this and goes out in faith, trusting the Lord, to a distant land, among people who are often very disagreeable, but who need someone to tell them of Jesus. Those who, for Christ's sake and the gospel's sake, have hated their own lives, what a reward will be theirs at the judgment-seat of Christ!

There is something here for everyone of us to consider thoughtfully. The Lord adds, "Whosoever doth not bear his cross, and come after Me, cannot be My disciple." Just what does "whosoever" mean? The Scottish laddie's answer is a true one: "You, me, or any ither body." It is not a question of bearing Christ's cross. You and I cannot bear His cross, though we may glory in it. The apostle Paul said, "But God forbid that I should glory, save in the cross of our Lord Jesus Christ, by whom the world is crucified unto me, and I unto the world." My substitute died in my stead. His death is my death, and I am dead to all to which He died as a Man. I am one with Him whom the world has rejected. That is what it means to enter into the truth of His cross. Here the Lord Jesus Christ speaks of the disciple carrying his own cross. If you had been in Palestine and seen a man going along a road carrying a cross, you would have known that he was going out to die. Our blessed Lord went forth bearing His cross to Calvary. During the centuries of Roman dominion those who died upon the cross were under the ban of the Government, and everyone was expected to carry his own cross to the place of execution. So what the Lord Jesus meant when He said, "Whosoever does not bear his cross, and come after Me, cannot be My disciple," was that, unless one is willing to go even to death for Christ's sake, he is not a true disciple. I repeat: it is not a question of salvation; it is a question of devotion to Christ in discipleship. The path of discipleship may lead to death, and of course this is not something to enter into thoughtlessly and carelessly. Many people fail to realize the seriousness of this matter of discipleship. It is not for one emotionally aroused to say, "I am ready to be a missionary or a preacher." One needs to weigh the question thoughtfully and seriously to realize the truth of the oft-repeated verse:

"Only one life, 'twill soon be past;
Only what's done for Christ will last."

What shall I do with this life? Shall I live for myself, or shall I live for Christ? Count the cost! The Lord Jesus used the illustration of the builder and the tower, "For which of you, intending to build a tower, sitteth not down first, and counteth the cost, whether he have sufficient to finish it? Lest haply, after he hath laid the foundation, and is not able to finish it, all that behold it begin to mock him, saying, This man began to build, and was not able to finish." We have heard of men attempting to build a great mansion or tower without counting the cost. They have started the building and have found themselves financially embarrassed, and so they could not continue. Such buildings have been pointed out to me—unfinished structures—because someone started to build and could not finish. So when you are called to devote your lives to God it is well to count the cost, and ask yourselves the question, "am I ready to face all that is involved in discipleship and loyalty to my Lord Jesus Christ?"

The second illustration is somewhat similar: "Or what king, going to make war against another king, sitteth not down first, and consulteth whether he be able with ten thousand to meet him that cometh against him with twenty thousand? Or else, while the other is yet a great way off, he sendeth an ambassage, and desireth conditions of peace." Those who began the Second World War, those who were responsible for it, felt that the democratic nations were decayed, that they would never be able to rise up against the Fascist powers, and that before these nations could even begin a defence the Fascist powers would have dominion of the world. So they started a conflict which they were not able to bring to a successful conclusion. In the great spiritual warfare with the evil hosts in heavenly places, how you and I need to consider whether we are ready to yield ourselves wholly to the control of our blessed Lord through the Holy Spirit, that we may be able to fight the good fight of faith. The apostle Paul was one who counted the cost. He faced everything; and having looked all the gains and losses in the face, he said, "But what things were gain to me, those I counted loss for Christ. Yea doubtless, and I count all things but loss for the excellency of the knowledge of Christ Jesus my Lord: for whom I have suffered the loss of all things, and do count them but dung, that I may win Christ." God grant that we may be motivated by the same spirit of devotion! "So likewise, whosoever he be of you that forsaketh not all that he hath, he cannot be My disciple." Do not misunderstand that. It does not mean that if you have a home you are to give it away; it does not mean that if God has intrusted you with wealth you have to toss it to the wind; it does not mean that if you have friends you must spurn them: but it does mean that you must hold everything you have as subject to God Himself. David Livingstone expressed it, I think, when he wrote in his diary, "I am determined not to look upon anything that I possess except as in relation to the kingdom of God." That is what it means to hold everything for Him.

There is a solemn warning in the last two verses. They suggest the possibility of a disciple, who was at one time a bright witness for the Lord, becoming useless and worthless to God and to man in so far as being a testimony to the world is concerned. "Salt is good: but if the salt have lost his savour, wherewith shall it be seasoned? It is neither fit for the land, nor yet for the dunghill; but men cast it out. He that hath ears to hear, let him hear." Salt *is* good. It preserves from corruption, and the people of God in this world are the preserving salt. Jesus said, "Ye are the salt of the earth." But if salt has lost its savour it is no good. Salt, when exposed to certain chemical influences, loses its saltiness, and it is worthless. It does not fulfil the purpose for which it was intended. It is possible for the Christian to become so careless and so contaminated by the principles of the world that he fails to fulfil the purpose for which God made him.

If God's only thought were to save our souls for heaven He could have taken us away five minutes after our conversion. I can never be any more fit for heaven than I was five minutes after I was saved. The dying robber on the cross was railing against our Lord, until suddenly he discerned the Person of the Son of God in that One on the central cross, and his heart went out to Him in repentance, and he confessed Him as the sinless One. He prayed, "Lord, remember me when Thou comest into Thy kingdom." Jesus said, "Today shalt thou be with Me in paradise." We might have gone home the moment He saved us if that were His only purpose; but He has saved us that we may serve Him here, that we may witness for Him, and be His disciples. Oh, God grant that we may never become salt that has lost its savour!

"He that hath ears to hear, let him hear!" Have you counted the cost? Jesus did, and He endured the cross of shame. Shall we shrink from the privileges extended to us? Are we more concerned about our prospects here below than we are about hearing the "Well done, thou good and faithful servant" from His lips when we stand at the judgment-seat of Christ?

ADDRESS FIFTY-FIVE

LOST ONES FOUND

"Then drew near unto Him all the publicans and sinners for to hear Him. And the Pharisees and scribes murmured, saying, This Man receiveth sinners, and eateth with them. And He spake this parable unto them, saying, What man of you, having an hundred sheep, if he lose one of them, doth not leave the ninety and nine in the wilderness, and go after that which is lost, until he find it? And when he hath found it, he layeth it on his shoulders, rejoicing. And when he cometh home, he calleth together his friends and neighbours, saying unto them, Rejoice with me; for I have found my sheep which was lost. I say unto you, that likewise joy shall be in heaven over one sinner that repenteth, more than over ninety and nine just persons, which need no repentance"—Luke 15: 1-7.

ALL through the years of our Lord's gracious ministry here on earth there were those of legalistic mind who failed to understand His interest in lost, sinful men and women. They fancied they were not lost; they professed to be among the righteous. They were punctilious about obeying the commandments of the law, not only that which was divinely given, but also many other commandments which had been added. So many had been added that the Lord Jesus Christ Himself said, "Ye have made the commandments of God of none effect by your tradition." They were even more particular about keeping the traditions of the elders than they were about obeying the commandments of God. They trusted in their own righteousness, and they did not realize how far short they came.

Our Lord Jesus Christ was always interested in sinners. He came down from the glory of His Father's house to save sinners. These legalists could not understand it. We are told here that a great company of publicans and sinners drew near to Jesus but the self-righteous and haughty scribes and Pharisees looked on with contempt, for they could not comprehend why Jesus did not withdraw Himself from these wretched and wicked people, and why He did not rather seek out such respectable individuals as they thought themselves to be. They murmured among themselves, saying, "This Man receiveth sinners, and eateth with them." They did not know they were declaring a wonderful truth when they said that. Jesus does receive sinners, and He takes them into fellowship and communion with Himself. Thank God, this has been true all through the centuries since. Is it not wonderful grace that He receives all who will come, and He delivers them from their sins?

"Sing it o'er and o'er again;
Christ receiveth sinful men."

If these words come before any who have been in doubt as to whether or not the Lord Jesus Christ will accept you, oh, let me tell you, "This is a faithful saying, and worthy of all acceptation, that Christ Jesus came into the world to save sinners!" He is interested in you; He is interested in me. I came as a sinner, and He did not turn me away. He received me and saved me, and He will do the same for you if you will come to Him.

In answer to the murmuring of the scribes and Pharisees, the Lord Jesus related the threefold parable which we have in this chapter. We need not think of three separate parables. It is the story of the grace of God pictured in three ways. The first part deals with a lost sheep in which the shepherd was interested. The second deals with a lost coin, and shows the woman's interest as she shed the light into the corners and swept the house in order that she might find it. The last part has to do with a lost son whom the father gladly welcomed home when he returned confessing his sin and failure and was ready to accept his father's forgiveness.

Jesus said, "What man of you, having an hundred sheep, if he lose one of them, doth not leave the ninety and nine in the wilderness, and go after that which is lost, until he find it?" You are all familiar with this story as it is portrayed in that beautiful old gospel hymn which Ira D. Sankey made so popular, and which we all love. You remember what it says,

"There were ninety and nine that safely lay
In the shelter of the fold."

But this is not what Jesus said. He said, "Doth he not leave the ninety and nine in the wilderness"—not "safe in the fold" but "in the wilderness"—"and go after that which is lost until he find it?" The ninety and nine were like the legalists who imagined they were righteous. They did not consider that they were lost, and so they did not think they needed to be sought and found. The lost sheep is the poor sinner who knew he was lost, who knew he needed a Saviour. The Shepherd leaves the ninety and nine in the wilderness, in their self-complacency, and goes out for that which is lost, and He does not give up until He finds it.

Years ago I was staying with friends who had a great sheep ranch, and one evening we were awaiting supper until the husband came home. We expected him to arrive about six o'clock, but he was late. When he came into the house he said to his wife, "My dear, I shall have to drink a cup of coffee and eat only a snack tonight, for as I came from the station I heard the bleating of a lost lamb, and I must hurry and find it before the coyotes or rattlesnakes get it." I asked if I might go with him, and he consented. I was amazed to see that man's interest in one lost lamb. He and a friend had more than five thousand sheep, and literally thousands of lambs; and yet that one lost lamb had such a place in his heart that he could not resist going out in the night to find it. I said, as we went along a narrow trail, "You have so many sheep and lambs, I wonder why you are so much concerned about one." He said, "I would not be able to sleep tonight for thinking about that little lamb out in the wilderness, and perhaps torn into pieces by the coyotes or bitten by a rattler." He called out as we went along the trail, "Bah-h-h, bah-h-h, bah-h-h, bah." He listened eagerly for an answer. At last we heard, from far down in the canyon among the thick brush, a little voice crying, "Baa . . . baa . . . baa." My friend answered with a loud "Bah-h-h, bah-h-h, bah-h-h, bah." He said, "There it is. You stay here; I'll go down and get it." And down he went, holding on to his flashlight; and when he got to the bottom he shouted back, "I have it; it is all right!" We went home rejoicing together. I thought what a perfect picture of our Lord Jesus Christ searching for poor lost sinners! He knew men had wandered from God, and needed finding, and so He came from heaven down into this dark world, and He went about seeking those who were lost. Here we read that "When he had found it he laid it on his shoulders rejoicing." He did not find it to leave it and let it make its way home as best it could. Just as in the case of that little lamb of which I spoke, the shepherd did not put it down until it was back in the fold. "He put it on his shoulders." So our Lord does not save us, and then tell us to follow and keep up with Him if we can. He carries us home rejoicing. "I say unto you, that likewise joy shall be in heaven over one sinner that repenteth, more than over ninety and nine just persons, which need no repentance." Whatever else our friends in heaven may know or may not know in regard to what is going on here on earth, there is one thing they do know: they always know when the Good Shepherd finds a lost sheep, for He gathers them about Him and says: "Rejoice with Me; for I have found My sheep which was lost."

In the second part of the parable the Lord presents the matter in a different way, in order to illustrate our utter helplessness and the need of divine enablement.

"Either what woman having ten pieces of silver, if she lose one piece, doth not light a candle, and sweep the house, and seek diligently till she find it? And when she hath found it, she calleth her friends and her neighbours together, saying, Rejoice with me; for I have found the piece which I had lost"—vers. 8-10.

This is a beautiful picture. One of ten pieces of silver is lost. These pieces of silver were joined together in a chain and given by the husband to seal the marriage ceremony. They were worn across the wife's forehead and valued as a wedding-ring is among us. If one coin should be lost it was thought to indicate the wife's unfaithfulness to the husband. Naturally, when one of the coins had disappeared the woman would say, "What will my husband say if he should come home and find I have lost one of these pieces?" In her trouble and distress she lighted a candle and swept the floor carefully, and finally she found the coin which perhaps had rolled into a corner. She went to the door and called her neighbors, saying, "Oh, you will be glad to hear that I have found my coin which was lost!" Then carefully she put it back into the place where it belonged. It was necessary that she be active in order to discover the coin. It could not find its way back to her. In this we see the activity of the Spirit of God working through His people. We have our part in seeking for the lost. It is the light of the Word that reveals their true condition and enables us to find them. The Lord Jesus said, "Likewise, I say unto you, there is joy in the presence of the angels of God over one sinner that repenteth." "Joy in the presence of the angels." Notice He does not say what some people seem to think He says. He does not say, "There is joy among the angels," although I am sure they do rejoice; but that is not what He says; He says, "In the *presence* of the angels." Who then are in the presence of the angels? All the redeemed who are absent from the body and present with the Lord—they are in the presence of the angels. Our Lord Jesus says to them, "Rejoice with Me; for I have found that which was lost." In heaven, where they know so well the worth of a soul, all rejoice when one is saved.

"And He said, A certain man had two sons: And the younger of them said to his father, Father, give me the portion of goods that falleth to me. And he divided unto them his living. And not many days after the younger son gathered all together, and took his journey into a far country, and there wasted his substance with riotous living. And when he had spent all, there arose a mighty famine in that land; and he began to be in want. And he went and joined himself to a citizen of that country; and he sent him into his fields to feed swine. And he would fain have filled his belly with the husks that the swine did eat: and no man gave unto him. And when he came to himself, he said, How many hired servants of my father's have bread enough and to spare, and I perish with hunger! I will arise and go to my father, and will say unto him, Father, I have sinned against heaven, and before thee, and am no more worthy to be called thy son: make me as one of thy hired servants. And he arose, and came to his father. But when he was yet a great way off, his father saw him, and had compassion, and ran, and fell on his neck, and kissed him. And the son said unto him, Father, I have sinned against heaven, and in thy sight, and am no more worthy to be called thy son. But the father said to his servants, Bring forth the best robe, and put it on him; and put a ring on his hand, and shoes on his feet: and bring hither the fatted calf, and kill it; and let us eat, and be merry: for this my son was dead, and is alive again; he was lost, and is found. And they began to be merry. Now his elder son was in the field: and as he came and drew nigh to the house, he heard music and dancing. And he called one of the servants, and asked what these things meant. And he said unto him, Thy brother is come; and thy father hath killed the fatted calf, because he hath received him safe and sound. And he was angry, and would not go in: therefore came his father out and intreated him. And he answering

said to his father, Lo, these many years do I serve thee, neither transgressed I at any time thy commandment: and yet thou never gavest me a kid, that I might make merry with my friends: but as soon as this thy son was come, which hath devoured thy living with harlots, thou hast killed for him the fatted calf. And he said unto him, Son, thou art ever with me, and all that I have is thine. It was meet that we should make merry, and be glad: for this thy brother was dead, and is alive again; and was lost, and is found"—vers. 11-32.

In this third part we have perhaps the tenderest story that our Lord Jesus ever related while here on earth. It is a story which we all know well, and yet it never seems to lose its sweetness and preciousness. In the first part one sheep was lost; next, one coin was lost; and now, a son is lost! There were two sons, and one was lost. These two sons are typical of all mankind. Here we think of God as the Father of spirits, the Creator of all men. While the Word of God gives no support of the modern theory of the universal fatherhood of God and universal brotherhood of man; nevertheless in chapter three of this gospel we find that in tracing the genealogy of our Lord Jesus back to Adam, we are told that Adam was the son of God. In this sense God is the Father of all mankind.

"And the younger of them said to his father, Father, give me the portion of goods that falleth to me. And he divided unto them his living." Without being content to await the time when the father would die, the younger son asked for his part of the estate at once in order that he might enjoy it beforehand. The father yielded to him and counted out to him that which was to be his. And not many days after the younger son gathered all together, and took his journey into a far country, and there wasted his substance with riotous living." There he could live as he liked, in independence of his father's will. So he had "his fling" as we say, until all was gone. "And when he had spent all, there arose a mighty famine in that land; and he began to be in want." I am sure that every repentant soul can say, "I too have wandered away from God, and I too have squandered the good things which He has bestowed upon me. I have lived in the far country, and I know all that is involved in these experiences." It is not a question of the amount of sin one commits that makes him a prodigal. This young man was just as truly a sinner against his father's love the moment he crossed the threshold of the door as he was in the far country. He did not want to be subject to his father; he desired to get away where he could live as he pleased. The father did not follow him. He did not insist that the son return, but allowed him to go and learn some lessons which he never could learn in any other way.

The day came when he had spent everything and found himself in dire distress. The friends he had made—where were they? They were his friends only as long as he had money. When at last everything was gone, when his fortune was spent, these fair-weather friends were not to be found; they left him in his deep need, and no one gave unto him. In his distress, in order to keep from starvation, he was obliged to do something which to a Jew of ordinary good breeding or conscience would be most revolting. "And he went and joined himself to a citizen of that country; and he sent him into his fields to feed swine." It was there among these unclean beasts, himself unclean, that he began to realize his folly and ingratitude. He could not feed upon the swine's food; he would have done so if he could. But he was a man created in the image of God who had put in him something which only God could satisfy. It is absolutely impossible for us who were created for eternity, ever to find anything in the things of this world to satisfy our souls. The day came when this young man was in such distress that he did not know where to turn. It was then that "he came to himself." That is a significant expression! Sin is a terrible thing; it is an insanity. This young man had been suffering from a mental abberation. Now he regained his right mind. He began to realize for the first time the fool he had been in turning away from the father's house, in trying to find satisfaction in the far country. Have you ever come to that place? Am I addressing anyone who has tried for years to find satisfaction in the things of this world and has never been able to do it? Oh, that you might come to yourself and face conditions as they really are, and turn to the God from whom you have wandered for so long!

This young man came to himself; he began to think. If you can get people to think then something will happen. The devil is doing his best to keep people from thinking. Some people wonder why we as Christians object to worldly amusements. They think we are very narrow and bigotted because we disapprove of them. Well, we know they are designed of Satan to keep men and women from facing the realities of life and recognizing their true condition before God. He wants to keep people from thinking, to forget they are lost sinners going on to destruction. When men begin to think they are well on the way to salvation. This young man came to that place. He said practically, "What a fool I have been, leaving my father's house and my home." "How many hired servants of my father have bread enough and to spare, and I perish with hunger! I will arise and go to my father, and will say unto him, Father, I have sinned against heaven, and before thee, and am no more worthy to be called thy son: make me as one of thy hired servants." Oh, if any who read these lines are unsaved, would God you might come to the same decision, that you might say with the same purpose of heart, "I will arise; I will go to my Father. I will go back to God, and I will tell Him I have sinned!" The Scriptures say, "He looked upon men, and if any say, I have sinned, and perverted that which was right, and it profited me not; He will deliver his soul from going down to the pit, and his life shall see the light." "If we confess our sins, He is faithful and just to forgive us our sins, and to cleanse us from all unrighteousness." That young man, feeling his unworthiness, had determined in his heart all he was going to say. He was going to tell his father he was unworthy to be called a son, and ask him to make him as one of his hired servants. But you will note when he reached his father he had to leave out a lot of that. The father did not wait to hear it. "He arose and came to his father." I have seen many pictures of the prodigal son being welcomed by the father, but I have not seen one which seems to be fully in accord with the story. I have seen pictures of the father standing in the doorway gorgeously robed and reaching out his arms to the son, but that is not what Jesus tells us. He said, "But when he was yet a great way off, his father saw him, and had compassion, and ran, and fell on his neck, and kissed him." He did not wait for the boy to get to the doorstep; he did not wait for him to reach the house, but he saw him coming down the road, and he said, "There is my boy! I have been waiting for him all these months!" What an affecting scene as Jesus pictures it. It is the picture of God the Father. When the sinner returns to Him, He is there to meet and welcome him. The poor boy began to speak out, "I have sinned against heaven, and in thy sight, and am no more worthy to be called thy son . . ." That is as far as he got; he did not say any more. He did not ask to become as one of the hired servants. The father had servants enough. It was a son he was welcoming home. He cried out in his joy, "Bring forth the best robe and put it on him"—for us that robe is Christ's perfection. "Put a ring on his hand"—the ring tells of undying affection. "And shoes on his feet"—slaves went barefooted, but sons wore shoes. "And bring hither the fatted calf, and kill it; and let us eat, and be merry: for this my son was dead, and is alive again; he was lost, and is found. And they began to be merry." And that merriment has never ended. Oh, in that home, of course, the time came when the feast was finished. But when the Father wins a poor sinner to Himself and says, "This My son was lost and is found," and they enter into communion together, the merriment which begins goes on for all eternity.

But now there is an added and a jarring note. His elder brother was in the field. He is just a Pharisee, who would not dare say he was saved but did not imagine he was lost. In his heart there is no more real love for the father than there had been in the heart of the younger boy. "Now his elder son was in the field: and as he came and drew nigh to the house, he heard music and dancing. And he called one of the servants, and asked what these things meant. And he said unto him, Thy brother is come; and thy father hath killed the fatted calf, because he hath received him safe and sound." Now this brother, instead of rejoicing and saying, "Oh, let me meet him; let me have part in that merriment," "was angry, and would not go in: therefore came his father out and intreated him." He was like those scribes and Pharisees who said, "This Man receiveth sinners, and eateth with them." He considered that his father was degrading himself in treating this prodigal boy like that; one who had misbehaved as he had done! He was angry and would not go in. His father came and intreated him, but he said, "Lo, these many years do I serve thee, neither transgressed I at any time thy commandment: and yet thou never gavest me a kid, that I might make merry with my friends. But as soon as this thy son was come, which hath devoured thy living with harlots, thou hast killed for him the fatted calf." It was just the same spirit that had led the younger son to leave the house and go into the far country. This son remained at home and was more respectful, but he was no better than the younger. He actually upbraided the father for his kindness. He does not say, "My brother, for whom I have prayed so long," not "my brother," but "your son." The father said to him, "Son, thou art ever with me, and all that I have is thine." It was for him to appropriate and enjoy it all if he desired. The father reminds the elder brother of that which he had overlooked: "It was meet that we should make merry, and be glad: for this thy brother was dead, and is alive again; and was lost, and is found." The legalist can never understand the grace of God. It is utterly foreign to him.

God grant we may not fail to understand and appreciate the grace of God, as this poor disgruntled elder brother did!

Address Fifty-six

THE UNJUST STEWARD

⸝ ⸝ ⸝

"And He said also unto His disciples, There was a certain rich man, which had a steward; and the same was accused unto him that he had wasted his goods. And he called him, and said unto him, How is it that I hear this of thee? Give an account of thy stewardship; for thou mayest be no longer steward. Then the steward said within himself, What shall I do? for my lord taketh away from me the stewardship: I cannot dig; to beg I am ashamed. I am resolved what to do, that, when I am put out of the stewardship, they may receive me into their houses. So he called every one of his lord's debtors unto him, and said unto the first, How much owest thou unto my lord? And he said, An hundred measures of oil. And he said unto him, Take thy bill, and sit down quickly, and write fifty. Then said he to another, And how much owest thou? And he said, An hundred measures of wheat. And he said unto him, Take thy bill, and write fourscore. And the lord commended the unjust steward, because he had done wisely: for the children of this world are in their generation wiser than the children of light. And I say unto you, Make to yourselves friends of the mammon of unrighteousness; that, when ye fail, they may receive you into everlasting habitations. He that is faithful in that which is least is faithful also in much: and he that is unjust in the least is unjust also in much. If therefore ye have not been faithful in the unrighteous mammon, who will commit to your trust the true riches? And if ye have not been faithful in that which is another man's, who shall give you that which is your own? No servant can serve two masters: for either he will hate the one, and love the other; or else he will hold to the one, and despise the other. Ye cannot serve God and mammon. And the Pharisees also, who were covetous, heard all these things: and they derided Him. And He said unto them, Ye are they which justify yourselves before men; but God knoweth your hearts: for that which is highly esteemed among men is abomination in the sight of God. The law and the prophets were until John: since that time the kingdom of God is preached, and every man presseth into it. And it is easier for heaven and earth to pass, than one tittle of the law to fail. Whosoever putteth away his wife, and marrieth another, committeth adultery: and whosoever marrieth her that is put away from her husband committeth adultery"—Luke 16: 1-18.

IT is with the first part of this passage that I desire to deal particularly at this time. The parable of the unjust steward is one which has been misunderstood frequently. In these occidental countries we have a different conception of a steward than in oriental lands. Then too, we read that the lord commended the unjust steward. Many people are perplexed about this, because they have failed to notice that "lord" begins with a small letter instead of a capital. It was not our Lord who commended him but the master of the unjust steward. In an eastern home a steward is overseer of the affairs of the whole household, and the master turns over to him a certain amount of money with which to buy the necessities for the comfort of the family. If the steward is able to purchase these things at a price lower than the ordinary market value, then that is money in his pocket. A wise steward is a very valuable personage in an oriental home, and nobody begrudges him the perquisites he earns. If this be kept in mind we shall understand better what our Lord meant here. "And He said also unto His disciples, There was a certain rich man, which had a steward; and the same was accused unto him that he had wasted his goods." Just as it was possible throught thrift, carefulness, and economy to save money for his master and also gain a substantial profit for himself, so it was possible for an unfaithful steward to waste what was entrusted to him by reckless buying, or keeping dishonest accounts. Such was evidently the case in this instance.

"And he called him, and said unto him, How is it that I hear this of thee? Give an account of thy stewardship; for thou mayest be no longer steward. Then the steward said within himself, What shall I do? for my lord taketh away from me the stewardship: I cannot dig, to beg I am ashamed." We can imagine him saying, "I am going to lose my job, and I cannot work hard." After thinking the matter over, he says, "I know what I'll do; I'll call in my master's debtors and see what I can do with them." So he summoned the first one and asked, "How much do you owe my lord?" He replied, "One hundred measures of oil." "Well," said the steward, "just cut that in half. Change the bill to fifty." By remitting this part of the indebtedness, actually the steward cut out that which would come to himself. Then he said to another, "How much do you owe?" He said, "One hundred measures of wheat." He told this one to deduct twenty measures. When this came to the ears of the master of the steward, "The lord commended the unjust steward, because he had done wisely: for the children of this world are in their generation wiser than the children of light." You see the master of the house could readily understand the wisdom of this procedure, and he said, "After all, he has acted very wisely. He has made good friends for himself by cutting off his own profits." These friends would be ready to welcome and assist him in his hour of need. The Lord Jesus makes the application that the children of this world are wiser in their generation than the children of light. How many of God's children are very much more concerned about present gains than they are about future blessings. The Lord makes this definite application: "And I say unto you, Make to yourselves friends of the mammon of unrighteousness; that, when ye fail, they may receive you into everlasting habitations. He that is faithful in that which is least is faithful also in much: and he that is unjust in the least is unjust also in much. If therefore ye have not been faithful in the unrighteous mammon, who will commit to your trust the true riches?" He speaks of making friends by the right use of wealth. The word "mammon" really means "riches." Actually it was originally the name of a Canaanite god of wealth, and the word had been carried over into the language of the Israelites as a synonym for riches or treasure. So the Lord Jesus says, as it were, "If God entrusts riches to you, you can make friends therewith," even though He calls them "the riches of unrighteousness." If man had not fallen he would have lived a pure, innocent life here on earth, receiving everything at God's good hand instead of having to toil and labor for the means of sustenance. There would have been no occasion for money as a medium of exchange. The fact that one happens to have a few dollars in his pocket is, in itself, a witness that sin is in the world; so mammon, riches, is the mammon of unrighteousness. Someone might ask, If it is true that money came into the world only because of sin, why should we not endeavor to get along without it? Under present conditions that is impossible. We cannot get along without it in a world like this. But if God has given us wealth we should use it to His glory in spreading His gospel, and in relieving distressed and suffering humanity. In this way we make friends by the mammon of unrighteousness; and when we come down to death and leave this world behind, those friends we have made through the right use of the mammon of unrighteousness will receive us joyfully into the everlasting habitations. To illustrate: Suppose the Lord Jesus has entrusted an amount of money to you, and you say, "God has given me this money. I am going to give a certain portion of it to help send the gospel to heathen lands." And you contribute regularly to some missionary, and because of your support that missionary is enabled to go forth and present the gospel to lost souls. Here on earth you may never see those who have been won through that missionary's efforts; but by-and-by, when you leave this scene and go home to heaven; you will find there those who will greet you with gladness as they say, "It was your money that enabled the teacher to come to me and to lead me out of the darkness of heathenism into the light of the gospel of Christ. We have been waiting here to welcome you into these everlasting habitations and to tell you how grateful we are to you for the interest which you took in us!" You can apply the principle in a thousand ways. You may use some of your money to help a poor, needy brother or sister, or to assist some underprivileged children. Your kindness and goodness to them may never be fully appreciated or recognized here on earth, but the day will come, if they are in Christ, when they will meet you in yonder land and express their gratitude to you for the way in which you used the mammon of unrighteousness.

Our Lord here is impressing upon us the stewardship of money. He says, "He that is faithful in that which is least is faithful also in much." Money in God's sight is a very little thing; in the sight of man it is most important. In the book of Ecclesiastes we read, "Money answereth all things." Someone has said, "Money is a universal provider for everything but happiness." We have heard of the father who said to his son, "My son, make money. Make it honestly if you can, but make money." Some people have the idea that there is nothing more important. But our blessed Lord speaks of it as a very little thing; and He says, "He that is faithful in his use of money will be faithful also in greater things." Have you noticed that a man's use of his money is often the acid test of his character? A man who loves money will be unkind and evil in many other ways. The love of money is not exactly *the* root of all evil, but it is *a* root of all evil. The definite article in the Authorized Version is somewhat misleading here. Covetousness is like a hardy root on which all kinds of evil plants may be grafted. If a man loves money inordinately he exposes himself to every other kind of iniquity.

"If ye have not been faithful in that which is another man's, who shall give you that which is your own?" One may ask, In what way shall I know whether or not I am faithful in regard to unrighteous mammon? When we turn to the First Epistle to the Corinthians (1 Cor. 16:2) we read, "Upon the first day of the week let every one of you lay by him in store, as God hath prospered him." That is a rule which every Christian should observe. If we fail to do so we lose in many ways. Then one may ask, How much should be used for myself, and how much should be set aside for God and for others? If you had been a Jew under the law you would have been required to give ten per cent. As a Christian under grace you surely do not want to give less than a Jew gave under the law. One ought to give more if he can, and in so doing he is faithful in that which is least, and will also be faithful in that which is much.

"No servant can serve two masters: for either he will hate the one, and love the other; or else he will hold to the one, and despise the other. Ye cannot serve God and mammon." You cannot be a lover of God and a lover of money at the same time. If you are afraid that perhaps the love of money is getting a grip upon you just try giving away some of it, and if you feel more cheerful and happy than before, then love of money has not gotten hold of you. But if you find that it it hurts to give, then you may well be fearful lest covetousness is getting a grip on your soul. The world admires the man who does well for himself; the world admires him who becomes wealthy and can live in a beautiful mansion. But God estimates true greatness in an altogether different way. God's heart goes out in loving appreciation to the man who lives for the benefit of others and uses that which is entrusted to him in the light of eternity.

"The law and the prophets were until John: since that time the kingdom of God is preached, and every man presseth into it. And it is easier for heaven and earth to pass, than one tittle of the law to fail." The ministry of John the Baptist ushered in a new era. The old dispensation was drawing to a close, soon to be ended at the cross. Meantime the kingdom of God was proclaimed, and men were invited to enter through the door of repentance and faith. Many tried to press in who were not, in reality, children of the kingdom. Only by new birth, as our Lord explained to Nicodemus (John 3:3), can one actually enter that kingdom. No word which God has spoken can fail in fulfilment, however man might react to the kingdom proclamation. All the demands of the law must be met either by those who come under its condemnation, or by Him who came in grace to bear its curse for others. God's Word was to be carried out even to the crucifying of His own blessed Son when He took the sinner's place.

The last verse of this section is of tremendous importance in these days when people look so leniently upon the violation of their marriage vows. "Whosoever putteth away his wife, and marrieth another, committeth adultery." If those words could be blazoned across the sky they might bring conviction to thousands who are living in that sin which is here condemned. It is true that on one occasion Jesus made an exception, which leaves the innocent party, where one has been divorced because of immorality, free to marry another. But the Word of God denounces any who treat lightly this sacred relationship. Marriage is for life, not to last only as long as people seem to take pleasure in each other. The tie once formed can be dissolved only by death or by grave sin.

Address Fifty-seven

BEYOND THE VEIL

✓ ✓ ✓

"There was a certain rich man, which was clothed in purple and fine linen, and fared sumptuously every day: and there was a certain beggar named Lazarus, which was laid at his gate, full of sores, and desiring to be fed with the crumbs which fell from the rich man's table: moreover the dogs came and licked his sores. And it came to pass, that the beggar died, and was carried by the angels into Abraham's bosom: the rich man also died, and was buried: and in hell he lift up his eyes, being in torments, and seeth Abraham afar off, and Lazarus in his bosom. And he cried and said, Father Abraham, have mercy on me, and send Lazarus, that he may dip the tip of his finger in water, and cool my tongue; for I am tormented in this flame. But Abraham said, Son, remember that thou in thy lifetime receivest thy good things, and likewise Lazarus evil things: but now he is comforted, and thou art tormented. And beside all this, between us and you there is a great gulf fixed: so that they which would pass from hence to you cannot; neither can they pass to us, that would come from thence. Then he said, I pray thee therefore, father, that thou wouldest send him to my father's house: for I have five brethren; that he may testify unto them, lest they also come into this place of torment. Abraham saith unto him, They have Moses and the prophets; let them hear them. And he said, Nay, father Abraham: but if one went unto them from the dead, they will repent. And he said unto him, If they hear not Moses and the prophets, neither will they be persuaded, though one rose from the dead"—Luke 16: 19-31.

✓ ✓ ✓

BEFORE considering this solemn story concerning which there has been so much controversy, particularly in recent years because of the revolt against the doctrine of eternal punishment, let me suggest two considerations which it is well to keep in mind. First, He who related this incident was the tenderest, gentlest, most gracious Man who ever trod this earth. Certainly He never would have attempted to portray human suffering beyond the grave unless He knew and wished to impress upon His hearers the awfulness of living and dying without God. If there were any possibility that men might live in their sins and yet find peace and blessing in another world, He would have made it known. The impression left upon everyone of His hearers who listened thoughtfully to what He had to say must have been the same as that which is stressed in the Epistle to the Hebrews (10:31): "It is a fearful thing to fall into the hands of the living God." The second consideration I would present is this: We have no reason whatever to look upon this story as an imaginary incident which had no foundation in fact. The question has been often raised as to whether it is a parable or not. If by parable we are thinking of a fictitious tale to illustrate some moral or spiritual lesson, I believe we are right in saying that it is not a parable. On the other hand, if we think of any incident used to illustrate truth as parabolic, then it is perfectly right to speak of the parable of the rich man and Lazarus.

In what is probably the earliest book of the Bible, that of Job, the question is raised (14:10), "Man dieth, and wasteth away: yea, man giveth up the ghost, and where is he?" Apart from divine revelation there can be no satisfactory answer to this inquiry. The human mind cannot pierce the veil and tell us whether or not there be personal consciousness in other worlds than this; but in the incident here recorded He who had come from the Father's house into this world of sin in order to redeem mankind, draws aside, as it were, the heavy curtain that hides the unseen realms from view and shows us plainly what takes place after death for both the righteous and the unrighteous.

Once more, as on other occasions recorded in this Gospel, Jesus uses the expression, "There was a certain rich man." Was there, or was there not? He definitely declared that there was. He did not introduce the story by saying, "Hear a parable," as on some other occasions; neither did He say, "The kingdom is as if there were a certain rich man and a poor beggar," or some similar language. But in the clearest, most definite way He declared, "There was a certain rich man." If any of His hearers had inquired the name of the man and of the town in which he lived, dare we doubt our Lord's ability to have answered both questions definitely? He knew this man; He knew how he had lived; He knew what took place after he died. We do not know his name and never shall know it until he stands before the great white throne. Ordinarily we call him Dives, but Dives is not a name; it is simply the Latin equivalent of the Greek for "rich man." Yet this unnamed man stands out on the pages of Holy Scripture as a distinct personality, the representative of many others who live for self and ignore the two great commandments which inculcate love to God and love to man. He was "clothed in purple and fine linen, and fared sumptuously every day." He enjoyed the best that earth could give and had no interest in the things of eternity.

Next we are told that "there was a certain beggar named Lazarus, which was laid at his gate, full of sores, and desiring to be fed with the crumbs which fell from the rich man's table: moreover the dogs came and licked his sores." This poor beggar is mentioned by name because the Good Shepherd "calleth His own sheep by name." In spite of his wretched circumstances, Lazarus (which means "God is my help") was a man of faith, a true son of Abraham. Had conditions been right in Israel no son of Abraham would have been found in such a plight, but Lazarus was suffering because he was part of a nation that had drifted far from God and had forfeited all right to claim His temporal mercies, mercies which were promised to the nation if obedient to the divine law. Apparently the rich man felt no concern whatever for this poor beggar who was daily brought to his gate by friends or relatives with the hope that Lazarus might receive sufficient alms to nourish him and prolong his life. He seems to have been passed by with contemptuous indifference. The dogs showed more concern for him than his own kind who thought only of gratifying their selfish desires.

But at last a great change came. The beggar died and was carried by the angels into Abraham's bosom. Possibly Dives and his associates did not even hear of the death of this man. We have no record of a funeral service. The poor, wretched, starved body was thrown, perhaps into the continual fires burning in the valley of Hinnom, or left to be devoured by hyenas or jackals; or if there were someone who was sufficiently interested to give it a burial it must have been of the simplest possible character. And yet as we look beyond the veil, enabled to do so by our Lord's words, we see a convoy of angels waiting to conduct the spirit of this erstwhile poverty-stricken wretch into the bosom of Abraham, the father of the faithful. It is distinctly a New Testament revelation that when believers die now they depart to be with Christ which is far better; but before the cross the highest hope of the godly Hebrew was to be welcomed by Abraham, with whom the covenant had been made, into an abode of bliss. We should not make the mistake of thinking of Abraham's bosom as the name of a locality in Hades. The locality was paradise. Abraham's bosom was the bosom of Abraham. In other words, Abraham, a living person, even though his body was long since dead, welcomed to that abode of happiness this child of faith when he moved out of his afflicted body.

We are not told how soon after the death of Lazarus the rich man also died, but it could not have been very long. We read that he "was buried." That, in itself, is significant. Undoubtedly he had a great funeral service with many hired mourners and every possible honor paid to the lifeless clay that had once housed his selfish spirit, but while the funeral service was being held on earth, he himself, the real man, was in hell enduring the torments of the damned.

I know that many today will object to this. Some will cry out, "Stop a moment. The word translated *hell* there does not refer to the final abode of the lost which is really Gehenna," and we grant that. They insist that Hades does not convey any thought of judgment to come. But let us read the passage again and use the Greek word and see how it sounds. "The rich man also died, and was buried: and in *Hades* he lift up his eyes, being in torments." Observe that "torments" was not done away with by changing the word from English to Greek. Others insist that Hades, after all, does not mean the "world of the lost"; it simply means "the grave," and should be so translated. While we do not for a moment accept this view, let us read it that way and see if it helps us to escape the apparent teaching of the story: "The rich man also died, and was buried: And in *the grave* he lift up his eyes, being in torments." Notice that the torment is still there even though we have changed the word so drastically. Was the man buried alive that he suffered torments in the grave? No; we are told he died, and after he died, in another world than this, he suffered torments.

Next we learn two remarkable things: First, that spirits out of the body are perfectly conscious and able to converse one with another. Second, that there is recognition in the unseen world. There is recognition of the redeemed in paradise by the lost who are in hell, even though between the two there is a great gulf fixed.

As we pursue the story we see that the separation which takes place in the hour of death remains for all eternity. Dives looked up in his torment and saw Lazarus in Abraham's bosom. That lost man looked into paradise and there he beheld what he had missed. He saw what would have been his if only he had given God His rightful place in his life: he saw the one who had lived as a neglected beggar at his gate, now enjoying a bliss which he himself would never know. In his distress he began to pray. Think of that—a praying man in hell! But the trouble is he began to pray on the wrong side of the tomb. While on earth he felt no need of prayer; he lived his own self-centered life in utter indifference to the claims of God and man. But in eternity he began to pray when prayer was useless. He did not ask for much at first, simply a drop of cold water on the tip of the beggar's finger, but even that was denied him. He used the language of the physical although it was spiritual thirst—a thirst which he never would have known if he had availed himself of the offer to drink of the living water while he was on earth. Now it was too late. Abraham, to whom the prayer was addressed, replied, "Son, remember that thou in thy lifetime receivedst thy good things, and likewise Lazarus evil things: but now he is comforted, and thou art tormented." Son, remember! What a terrible thing memory will be for the unsaved: to remember throughout all eternity every sin committed and unrepented of, and therefore unforgiven; to remember every opportunity to get right with God which had been carelessly passed by; to remember every gospel message one has ever heard and yet refused to believe. Memory will be indeed as the worm that dieth not, tormenting the soul forever.

Abraham's words show that one might have on earth everything the heart could desire and have nothing for eternity. On the other hand, one might seem to have nothing on earth to minister to his need and comfort, and yet have everything for the world to come.

Then the words that follow tell us of the impossibility of any change throughout the ages to come. "And beside all this, between us and you there is a great gulf fixed: so that they which would pass from hence to you cannot; neither can they pass to us, that would come from thence." A great gulf fixed! The separation of the saved and the lost is final when one has passed through the gate of death into worlds unseen. Here is the death-blow to universalism. Naturally we would like to believe that there is some way by which those who have died without repenting of their iniquities, might be cleansed from their sins, even after ages of suffering, and enjoy the beatific vision, but the gulf is impassable. The saved can never lose their blessing and fall into perdition; the lost can never attain to blessing and enjoy salvation.

Hopeless of any alleviation of his own misery, the rich man suddenly became missionary-minded. Pitifully he pleaded for his five brothers still on earth and begged that Lazarus might be sent to them from the dead to warn them, so that they might not come to that same place of torment. We have heard unsaved people flippantly exclaim at times, "Well, if I am lost I shall have plenty of company in hell." We have no suggestion here of anything like that. This man does not desire company; he does not want his most intimate relatives to be there. It gives us some conception of the awful loneliness of hell. Even if one should be conscious of the nearness of those whom he had known on earth it would only add to his wretchedness.

Think of the family to which this man belonged: there were six brothers, one was in hell and five were on the way! Yet for all of them Christ had come to die. They need not have been lost if they had been ready to receive the message of grace.

This second prayer, like the former, had to go unanswered. Abraham replied, "They have Moses and the prophets; let them hear them." That is to say, they have God's Word; they have their Bibles; let them read the Word; let them heed what they find therein, and they will never know the meaning of a lost eternity. But if they refuse the Word then not even a man coming back from the dead could persuade them to repentance. Dives reasons otherwise. He exclaimed, "Nay, father Abraham: but if one went unto them from the dead, they will repent." The answer comes back sternly in the negative, "If they hear not Moses and the prophets, neither will they be persuaded, though one rose from the dead." The man who refuses to heed the clear, definite instruction of the Holy Scriptures would never believe though one came to him asserting that he had been on the other side of the tomb and had returned to warn him to flee from the wrath to come.

Surely no thoughtful person can read this story seriously without realizing that our Lord Jesus meant us to understand that if we die in our sins, if we go out of this world loving the things which God hates and hating the things which God loves, we must be separated from Him forever.

But now another consideration ere we close this message. If this story be only a parable, as some tell us, what is it meant to teach? The answer given by materialists of different groups who deny the consciousness of man after death and refuse the doctrine of eternal retribution for sin, is ordinarily something like this: The rich man, we are told, pictures the Jewish people who in centuries gone by enjoyed all the blessings of God and kept them selfishly to themselves; the poor man, despite his Jewish name, represents the Gentiles who were strangers to the covenants of promise but lay, as it were, outside the door of the favored Jew. A new dispensation is represented by their death. Now it is the Gentile who is in the place of privilege, even in Abraham's bosom, having become an heir to the promises to which before he had no claim. The Jew is the outcast now, and has been suffering all down through the centuries because of the sins of his fathers. At first this seems plausible enough, but now let us go a step further. This outcast Jew and this highly privileged Gentile—are they separated by a gulf that cannot be passed? Is it true that the Jew cannot come from his present place of suffering into the privileges of Christianity? Is it also true that the favored Gentile cannot refuse the grace of God in Christ and go over, if he will, to the place in which the Jew himself is found? Surely not. No such gulf has ever been fixed on earth. Any Jew may accept Christ and enter into all the blessedness of gospel light and privilege; and any Gentile who refuses the grace of God passes over to the place in which the unsaved Jew is found under the judgment of God.

The only legitimate deduction therefore is that our Lord related this incident to bring clearly before us the importance of being right with God in this world in order that we might enjoy His favor in the world to come.

ADDRESS FIFTY-EIGHT

SUBJECTION TO CHRIST

ꝛ ꝛ ꝛ

"Then said He unto the disciples, It is impossible but that offences will come: but woe unto him, through whom they come! It were better for him that a millstone were hanged about his neck, and he cast into the sea, than that he should offend one of these little ones. Take heed to yourselves: if thy brother trespass against thee, rebuke him; and if he repent, forgive him. And if he trespass against thee seven times in a day, and seven times in a day turn again to thee, saying, I repent; thou shalt forgive him. And the apostles said unto the Lord, Increase our faith. And the Lord said, If ye had faith as a grain of mustard seed, ye might say unto this sycamine tree, Be thou plucked up by the root, and be thou planted in the sea; and it should obey you. But which of you, having a servant plowing or feeding cattle, will say unto him by and by, when he is come from the field, Go and sit down to meat? And will not rather say unto him, Make ready wherewith I may sup, and gird thyself, and serve me, till I have eaten and drunken; and afterward thou shalt eat and drink? Doth he thank that servant because he did the things that were commanded him? I trow not. So likewise ye, when ye shall have done all those things which are commanded you, say, We are unprofitable servants: we have done that which was our duty to do"—Luke 17: 1-10.

ꝛ ꝛ ꝛ

OUR blessed Lord has given us a great deal of practical instruction in the four Gospels. This is something we shall never get beyond as long as we are down here in this world. Everything that is spiritual in any part of the Bible is for us. There are certain things, we know, that have a special dispensational application; but all the great moral and spiritual truths apply at all times. As Christians we ought to come back again and again to the teaching given by Jesus in the Gospels that we may learn of Him how to walk and to please God as we pass on through this scene.

He speaks here of four different subjects. First He gives us a solemn warning concerning stumbling-blocks. We read that Jesus said "unto the disciples, It is impossible but that offences will come: but woe unto him, through whom they come!" The word translated *offences* really means *stumbling-block*. From time to time there will come occasions of stumbling. Some will forget their responsibilities and allow themselves to be guilty of things that will prove to be stumbling-blocks to others. They will offend or scandalize their weaker brethren, but we are not to excuse these things in ourselves or in others. We may find it easy to say, "I did not mean any harm." But we are responsible to so walk that others following our example may not go astray into the path of sin through our bad example. We shall have to answer for it if we offend in this way. Jesus said, "It were better for him that a millstone were hanged about his neck, and he cast into the sea, than that he should offend one of these little ones." One might be terrified almost at these words. They should cause us to "walk circumspectly, not as fools, but as wise, redeeming the time, because the days are evil." One might say, "I live my own life, and I do not care what people think. I live according to my own judgment." But that is not the spirit of Christ, and it is not the spirit that should characterize those who profess to be His disciples. There may be many things which we think are all right, but we are to consider our weaker brother. The apostle Paul dealt with this at great length in his Epistles. In Romans 14: 21 he said, "It is good neither to eat flesh, nor to drink wine, nor any thing whereby thy brother stumbleth, or is offended, or is made weak. Hast thou faith? have it to thyself before God." Do not parade your liberty before another who is likely to be influenced wrongly by your behavior.

In the second instance our Lord speaks of the forgiveness of injuries, real or fanciful. In verses three and four He says, "Take heed to yourselves: If thy brother trespass against thee, rebuke him; and if he repent, forgive him. And if he trespass against thee seven times in a day, and seven times in a day turn again to thee, saying, I repent; thou shalt forgive him." Let us stop here for a moment. "If thy brother trespass against thee, rebuke him." That is, if you feel your brother has said something or done something to injure you, do not talk about it to other people; do not seek some sympathetic person and pour your troubles into his ear, lest in a little while he spread it all through the church. There is an old saying:

> "If you are wise you'll advertise;
> And here are all the points essential:
> First, tell your business to a friend;
> Then say, 'It's strictly confidential.'"

So if somebody has offended you, do not tell it to anyone else. Go to him who has done the wrong and rebuke him for it. "And if he repent, forgive him." Go straight to the one who has offended you; tell him exactly what he has said or what he has done that is grieving you. That takes real manhood. Sometimes it is so much easier to go round muttering and talking to other people about offences instead of going to the one who has done the wrong and telling him what is on your mind. We are great for avoiding our own responsibility. We would rather pass it on to someone else. We would rather bring a charge before the church. But Jesus plainly tells us we are never to bring a matter like that to the church until we have first gone to the person himself. Go to your brother and rebuke him, and if he says, "I am sorry; I did not mean it that way," or "I am sorry, forgive me," then you will be able to straighten the matter out at once, and you are not to say anything about it again; that should be the end of it. If we would act on these words more fully how many hurt feelings would be saved; how many church strifes would be avoided! You say, "Well, I talked to him about it, and he said he repented, and I forgave him; but he did the same thing again. What am I to do now?" The Lord says, "And if he trespass against thee seven times in a day, and seven times in a day turn again to thee, saying, I repent; thou shalt forgive him." This is enough to make almost anybody lose confidence in a man: he says, "I repent," and then he does it again and again. I cannot believe in a person like that, you say. Never mind that; you do not have to believe in him if you will only forgive him. If he trespasses seven times in a day and says, "I repent," then you are to forgive him. Remember on another occasion (Matt. 18:21, 22) Peter said, "Lord, how oft shall my brother sin against me, and I forgive him? till seven times? Jesus saith unto him, I say not unto thee, Until seven times: but, until seventy times seven." I am afraid none of us have ever had to forgive that many times. Of course, we are not called upon to proclaim forgiveness until the other person professes to repent. I do not have to run after someone, calling, "I forgive you! I forgive you!" He is likely to say, "I do not want you to forgive me; I do not need your forgiveness." But we are to maintain always an attitude of mercy and to love him until at last he breaks down and says he repents. Then we are to forgive as freely as God forgives us.

The third lesson we have here is that of the power of faith. When Jesus told these things to His disciples, they looked at Him, as much as to say, "You are setting up a standard so high we cannot attain to it." They exclaimed, "Lord, increase our faith. And the Lord said, If ye had faith as a grain of mustard seed, ye might say unto this sycamine tree, Be thou plucked up by the root, and be thou planted in the sea; and it should obey you." Do not misunderstand that. He did not mean that we are to go about demonstrating our power over nature. Faith, you know, is believing God, and faith leads one to act in accordance with His revealed will. Now if God reveals to you that you should pray that some sycamine tree be plucked up and cast into the sea, He will give faith for it; but that is not the customary thing. What the Lord is teaching is that if you have real faith you will be able to triumph in spite of all outward circumstances. You have heard of the Irishman who said, "I learned to trust

God, and He has done such wonderful things for me that if He tells me to jump through a stone wall I'll jump, and I know He will make a way through." But do not jump if God has not told you to do it! Faith leads us to act in accordance with the Word of God, and when we do God can be depended upon to see us through.

In the fourth instance, the Lord says some things to keep us from over-estimating our own devotedness, or the value of our own service. He uses a very simple illustration: He speaks of a farm-hand working in the field, plowing, or feeding the cattle, and doing other duties, then coming back to the house where it is his business to help prepare the meal and to wait upon the owner of the farm. He says in a case like that, after you have done your plowing, carried food to the cattle and finished a number of other duties that are yours and you come to the house, you do not expect the owner to say to you, "Sit down here while I prepare the meal, and I shall be glad to wait on you." No; you are not looking for that. You are a hired hand, a servant, and you are appointed to do certain things for which the owner pays you. You do not feel that any special commendation is due to you for doing that for which you are being paid. The arrangements were made when you came to work on the farm, and so you do not expect any special consideration. You do not say, "I have given my time, and I think I deserve a great deal more attention." So the Lord warns His disciples not to allow themselves to be carried away with the idea that because of their service they deserve special commendation. We are bought with His precious blood, and our work is to serve with gladness. We are but imperfect workmen at best. He says, "When ye shall have done all those things which are commanded you, say, We are unprofitable servants: we have done that which was our duty to do." It is our duty to continue in the service of our Lord Jesus Christ. We leave it to Him to appraise our work. He will take note of all service for Himself, and everything that has been done out of love for Him will be rewarded, even to a cup of cold water given in His name.

Address Fifty-nine

WHERE ARE THE NINE?

✝ ✝ ✝

"And it came to pass, as He went to Jerusalem, that He passed through the midst of Samaria and Galilee. And as He entered into a certain village, there met Him ten men that were lepers, which stood afar off: and they lifted up their voices, and said, Jesus, Master, have mercy on us. And when He saw them, He said unto them, Go show yourselves unto the priests. And it came to pass, that, as they went, they were cleansed. And one of them, when he saw that he was healed, turned back, and with a loud voice glorified God, and fell down on his face at His feet, giving Him thanks: and he was a Samaritan. And Jesus answering said, Were there not ten cleansed? but where are the nine? There are not found that returned to give glory to God, save this stranger. And He said unto him, Arise, go thy way: thy faith hath made thee whole"—Luke 17: 11-19.

✝ ✝ ✝

THIS is one of the incidents of our Lord's life recorded only in this Gospel. There are quite a few parables which Luke alone gives us, and there are several of His miracles of which no other Evangelist tells us. This is an outstanding instance. Jesus had left the upper parts of Galilee and was now on His way to Jerusalem for the last time. On two other occasions He had gone there to keep the feast of the Passover, and on one occasion to keep a winter feast. Soon He was to partake of the Passover with His disciples for the last time, and then to die as the One of whom every Passover lamb was but a type. He started out from the western shore of the Sea of Galilee, passing through the province of Galilee into Samaria, and thence over the Jordan and down through Perea until He came to the Jordan ford, opposite the city of Jericho, and so on to Jerusalem.

"And He entered into a certain village." We do not know its name but it was evidently near the border of Galilee and Samaria. As He drew near the village, "There met him ten men that were lepers, which stood afar off." In keeping with the law of Moses when a man was found to be a leper he had to leave his home and friends and dwell apart from them in the wilderness. When anyone came near him he had to cry, "Unclean! unclean!" There is a previous instance of a leper who came to the feet of our Lord and besought Him to heal him, and the Lord touched him and the leper was cleansed immediately. But these ten, having respect to the law, felt that they did not dare draw near; so they stood afar off and cried, "Jesus, Master, have mercy on us." That reminds me of a certain class of sinners—men who feel their sins so keenly that they do not have the assurance that they are free to draw near to Christ. But the fact is, Christ invites sinners of every kind to draw near to Him. He has ever a welcome for them, no matter how defiled they may be. But these men were under the law and acted in accordance with it when they called to Him from a distance. They were tremendously in earnest. The great trouble with many today is that while they acknowledge their need of a Saviour and admit they are sinners, yet actually they are not in earnest about finding salvation. If you speak to them and press upon them the importance of coming to Christ, they say, "I know I should be a Christian, and some day I intend to trust Christ." But they do not come to the point of settling the matter now.

Hell is filled with people who expected to come some day to Jesus for salvation. I do not suppose there is a lost soul in the pit below who ever intended to be there; everyone thought that some time things would be changed, and they would feel more like closing with the gospel invitation. They hoped, like Felix, for a more convenient day. But a more convenient season never came, and they, unsaved, unforgiven, uncleansed, passed out of time into eternity. Oh, if you are still out of Christ, I plead that, like these ten unclean lepers, you will be in earnest about the question of your deliverance. The lepers were so anxious to be healed, so desirous to be cleansed, that though they did not feel they dared to come near to Jesus, they lifted up their voices and cried from afar, "Jesus, Master, have mercy on us." No one ever cried to Him like that to be refused; no one ever came to Him for salvation to be turned down. You need not be afraid to come. It is written (Romans 10: 13), "Whosoever shall call upon the name of the Lord shall be saved."

"And when He saw them, He said unto them, Go show yourselves unto the priests." Now I fancy that was a disappointment to these men. They had heard that the Lord Jesus healed immediately other people of all kinds of diseases. He had cleansed many lepers by a word or a touch. He had said to one, "I will; be thou clean," and the leper was cleansed. But the Lord does not deal with everyone in the same way. In response to the plea of these lepers He tells them to go show themselves to the priest. In the book of Leviticus (Chapter 14) we read that when a man was healed of leprosy he was to go and show himself to the priest, and then the priest was to offer certain sacrifices for him in order that he might be officially cleansed and restored to his place in the congregation of the Lord. So the Saviour said to these men, "Go show yourselves unto the priests," implying that ere they reached the priest they would be cleansed. There would be no use to show themselves to the priest if they were still leprous, for in that condition there was nothing he could do for them. Possibly everyone of them, with the exception of the Samaritan, had been to the priest long ago, and he had proclaimed them lepers and told them they would have to live apart in a desert place. They might have hesitated and said, "Well, Master, look at these hands; look at these blotches upon our faces; we are covered with leprosy. Why should we go to the priest?" But they did not hesitate. They knew what His words implied: they would be cleansed. And so they turned to go as He had commanded. They were acting in obedience to the Word of our Lord, and cleansing came. It is just as true today when men and women act upon the Word, our Lord delivers them. I think I can see these men as they went along the road trying to cheer one another as best they could. Their faces must have been horrible to look upon, their bodies in a terrible state; but on they go to Jerusalem. Suddenly one of the men turns to another and says, "Oh, you are healed!" The other exclaims, "I thought I felt some change taking place. Have all those blotches disappeared from my face? Why, you have none on your face!" All begin to look at each other and find that each of them has been healed, and they recognize that the healing had been wrought by the Lord. How they must have rejoiced!

Jesus had said, "Go show yourselves unto the priests." Why did He want them to do this? Because it would be a testimony to the priests. For fifteen hundred years after the law was written we never read of one solitary Israelite who had been cleansed. Miriam, Moses' sister who became leprous, was healed; and many years later Naaman the Syrian also was healed, but he was not an Israelite, and naturally he was not required to obey the law about going to the priests. Otherwise we never read in all the Old Testament records of one leper being cleansed during fifteen hundred years, and the priests must have wondered why that fourteenth chapter of Leviticus was in the Bible. They would naturally say, "I have read that chapter over and over but have never had to apply it." But when Jesus came things were different. One leper after another was sent to the temple at Jerusalem to be pronounced clean, and when he appeared before the priests he was found to be healed of his leprosy. What a witness this was to those priests in Israel. They saw so many testimonies to the power of the Lord Jesus Christ that it ought to have been easy for them to believe that He was the Son of God. So in keeping with the law these lepers journeyed on toward the temple.

But there was something even higher than that. We find that one of the lepers, who was a Samaritan, when he saw that he was healed of this awful disease, and the terrible ulcers were gone from his flesh, turned about and hastened to the feet of Jesus. He felt there was no use for him to go on to the priests. He went back to the One who healed him, "and with a loud voice glorified God and fell down on his face at His feet, giving Him thanks." At whose feet? Notice what it says: "With a loud voice glorified *God*, and fell down on his face at *His* feet." When you have a pronoun like that you must have a noun as a precedent of it. The noun that precedes *His* is *God*. He realized that God was there in the person of Jesus of Nazareth, and so he glorified God and fell down at the feet of God manifested in flesh, to worship and adore Him. He realized that only God could cleanse a leper, and that Jesus was worthy of worship and adoration. This man, who might have been considered the very worst of the whole company, manifested more spiritual insight than the rest, who were Israelites. The Jews ordinarily despised the Samaritans. We are told in the fourth chapter of John that the Jews have no dealings with the Samaritans. But Jesus healed this poor leprous Samaritan. His heart was filled with praise and thanksgiving for the blessing he had received. It is true that the more God does for a person the more grateful he is likely to be. People are sometimes amazed when they hear the testimonies of men and women who have been saved in missions, who have been outcasts and have been delivered from gross sin, and now their hearts are filled with such praise and thanksgiving that are far above that of those who have been Christians for years and lived lives of respectability. The more sin there is in the life to be forgiven the more a person realizes how wonderfully God has dealt with him. When this cleansed leper fell down at the feet of Jesus and worshipped Him, did Jesus resent it? Did He say, "Oh, no; do not worship Me; worship God. I am only a Man?" No; Jesus gladly accepted the worship, for He was the Eternal Son who came from God, and He was going back to God. But He asked a question which indicated disappointment or a grieved spirit: He "answering said, Were there not ten cleansed? but where are the nine? There are not found that returned to give glory to God, save this stranger." Well, Jesus had told them to go to the priests, but this man felt there was something that must come first: he must go back to the One who had healed him and tell Him how grateful he was for his cleansing. If there had been the same gratitude in the hearts of the others they, too, would have fallen down at the feet of Jesus, then gone on to the temple to show themselves to the priests as a testimony. They did the thing Christ had bidden them, but this Samaritan had recognized there was a higher responsibility, and he returned to worship and praise the Lord ere he went on to the priests in the temple. Is there not a lesson in this for us? There is so little real worship on the part of Christian people today. Even when believers come together so often it is not to worship God. Do we realize God is seeking worshippers? I am afraid too many have the idea that God is seeking workers, but there is something that must come before work, and that is worship. To be in the presence of God with a heart filled with adoration means more to Him than to busy ourselves in His service. We shall not serve any less acceptably or earnestly because we worship first, rather than if we gave all our time to service. The Lord Jesus is still saying, "Where are the nine?" He appreciates those who come into His presence with worshipful hearts, but He misses those who have been saved by His grace and do not return to give Him glory.

Then He turned to this man and gave him the assurance that perhaps the others did not receive. It is one thing to be cleansed, to have forgiveness, to have salvation; it is another thing to have the full assurance based on the Word of God. And so Jesus turned to this Samaritan and said, "Arise, go thy way: thy faith hath made thee whole." I take that expression as an indication of far more than the assurance that he was physically whole. I take it the Lord was telling this man that he was not only healed of his disease, but also that he was spiritually cleansed because of the faith which he manifested. I can see him rejoicing as he returns to his own home which he had left so long ago when afflicted with this dreadful disease. I can see his friends retreating as they see him coming, and calling out to him, "Don't come near us; you are unclean!" But he answers, "You do not need to be afraid, for I am healed, and He who cleansed me made me perfectly whole." That is what Jesus is still doing for those who trust Him fully; they find themselves cleansed completely from sin. Then it should be our delight to come into the presence of God to worship Him and adore Him for His matchless grace. How little time we usually take in telling the Lord how grateful we are for what He has done for us. This is so important. Take that little prayer our Lord taught His disciples: Have you noticed that about two-thirds of it is taken up with worship and only one-third with petitions? Oh, may the Lord teach us more and more the blessedness of worship, of coming into His presence to praise and adore Him, and then may we go forward to serve in newness of spirit!

ADDRESS SIXTY

CHRIST'S SECOND ADVENT

✝ ✝ ✝

"And when He was demanded of the Pharisees, when the kingdom of God should come, He answered them and said, The kingdom of God cometh not with observation: neither shall they say, Lo here! or, lo there! for, behold, the kingdom of God is within you. And He said unto the disciples, The days will come, when ye shall desire to see one of the days of the Son of Man, and ye shall not see it. And they shall say to you, See here; or, see there: go not after them, nor follow them. For as the lightning, that lighteneth out of the one part under heaven, shineth unto the other part under heaven; so shall also the Son of Man be in His day. But first must He suffer many things, and be rejected of this generation. And as it was in the days of Noe, so shall it be also in the days of the Son of Man. They did eat, they drank, they married wives, they were given in marriage, until the day that Noe entered into the ark, and the flood came, and destroyed them all. Likewise also as it was in the days of Lot; they did eat, they drank, they bought, they sold, they planted, they builded; but the same day that Lot went out of Sodom it rained fire and brimstone from heaven, and destroyed them all. Even thus shall it be in the day when the Son of Man is revealed. In that day, he which shall be upon the housetop, and his stuff in the house, let him not come down to take it away: and he that is in the field, let him likewise not return back. Remember Lot's wife. Whosoever shall seek to save his life shall lose it; and whosoever shall lose his life shall preserve it. I tell you, in that night there shall be two men in one bed; the one shall be taken, and the other shall be left. Two women shall be grinding together; the one shall be taken, and the other left. Two men shall be in the field; the one shall be taken, and the other left. And they answered and said unto Him, Where, Lord? And He said unto them, Wheresoever the body is, thither will the eagles be gathered together"—Luke 17: 20-37.

✝ ✝ ✝

THERE are several distinct sections to this portion of scripture. In verses 20 and 21 we have the question of the Pharisees concerning the kingdom of God, and our Lord's answer. Remember, Jesus had been ministering in the land of Palestine for three and one-half wonderful years, and He had given evidence after evidence of His Messiahship. On more than one occasion the Father's voice had proclaimed from heaven, "This is My beloved Son, in whom I am well pleased;" John the Baptist bore witness of Him before He came and after; His own works testified to His true character, to His Deity, in that He was the Son of God as well as the Son of Man. But these blind Pharisees did not see the truth concerning Jesus. We say sometimes that there are none so blind as those who will not see. These Pharisees were like that. They would not recognize His authority; and therefore nothing that He did, no witness that the Father bore of Him, nothing John the Baptist had said, could convince them. They were determined to refuse His claims. Now they came and put the question to Him: "When will the kingdom of God come?" It was as much as to say, You have been preaching about the kingdom of God; when will this kingdom actually appear? He answered, "The kingdom of God cometh not with observation." That is, it will not come with outward show. They were looking for the Son of David to appear among them, to raise up an army and deliver them from the Roman yoke and proclaim Himself King over all the world. But Jesus did not have any such program in mind. He came to sow the good seed of the kingdom, and so He said the kingdom would not come with an outward show. He declared, "The kingdom of God is within you." There is a question among competent Christian scholars as to the exact meaning of this expression. If we take it just as it is translated here—that the kingdom of God is within us—then it means that the kingdom of God has to do with the acknowledgement of the Lord's authority in our own lives, sanctifying the Lord God in our own hearts, recognizing Him as the righteous Sovereign. On the other hand, there are many who believe that this expression should have been translated, "the kingdom of God is among you." That is, the kingdom was already present in embryo. Frankly, I rather think that is the real meaning of the Lord's words. These Pharisees asked when the kingdom would be set up, and Jesus said the kingdom is here now, and you have not eyes to see. The kingdom of God is among you. The King Himself is here, attended by the members of His cabinet. In the regeneration, the golden age to which men have always been looking forward, He says, as recorded in Matthew 19:28, "Ye also shall sit upon twelve thrones, judging the twelve tribes of Israel." The twelve apostles, in that sense, were His cabinet, the official members of His kingdom. So the kingdom of God was in their midst and they knew it not.

After the Pharisees had left He turned to His disciples and gave them a word of warning. He was going away as He had told them several times before, but they had not understood. In His absence they would be exposed to many dangers and to false leaders. So Jesus said to them, "The days will come, when ye shall desire to see one of the days of the Son of Man, and ye shall not see it." It is as though He said, You will be longing for the Son of Man and you will not see Me, I will be absent from you, away in the heavens. "And they shall say to you, See here; or, see there: go not after them, nor follow them." Time after time through the centuries since Jesus went back to the glory, men have appeared who have given out that they had come to fulfil the promises of God, each claiming to be the Christ. But those who bear in mind the Saviour's warning are not deceived by these charlatans. When Jesus returns again it will not be in weakness but in power. He will not come into this world a second time through the gate of birth, but will be revealed from heaven in power and great glory. "For as the lightning, that lighteneth out of the one part under heaven, shineth unto the other part under heaven; so shall also the Son of Man be in His day." "The Lord Jesus shall be revealed from heaven with His mighty angels, in flaming fire taking vengeance on them that know not God." His advent will be altogether different from that in which He came in lowly grace to give His life for the salvation of a lost world.

But the Lord reminded His disciples that first He must suffer many things and be rejected of that generation, even as it came to pass. He is the rejected One still, even though throughout Christendom people profess to revere His Name; but the great majority have never yet opened their hearts to Him and owned Him as their Redeemer and King.

"Our Lord is now rejected;
And by the world disowned,
By the many still neglected,
And by the few enthroned;

But soon He'll come in glory,
The hour is drawing nigh,
For the crowning day is coming
By-and-by."

Some have an idea that He will not come again until the whole world is converted, until His gospel has permeated the nations, and all have acknowledged His righteous rule; but that is not what Jesus taught; it is not what He told His disciples. He said, "And as it was in the days of Noe, so shall it be also in the days of the Son of Man." The whole world was not converted in the days of Noah. "They did eat, they drank, they married wives, they were given in marriage, until the day that Noe entered into the ark, and the flood came, and destroyed them all." Corruption and violence filled the earth in those days. There were a few families where God was known, but they finally dwindled down to one—Noah and his household. When the Lord comes the second time He will not find the whole world waiting to receive Him, but sin will be rampant as in the days of Noah. Observe that the antediluvians were interested in the ordinary things that occupy the minds of men and women. They did not believe the message of Noah, but lived in utter indifference to God until the day when Noah entered into the ark, and the flood came and destroyed them. So we gather from this passage that the world will go on as it is going now. Men will be occupied with the various affairs of life but indifferent to the claims of Jesus until that hour when He returns. He is coming back in power and glory, and men will realize too late how foolish they have been to reject Him.

The Lord uses another illustration along the same line. He says, "Likewise also as it was in the days of Lot; they did eat, they drank, they bought, they sold, they planted, they builded; but the same day that Lot went out of Sodom it rained fire and brimstone from heaven, and destroyed them all." There is nothing wrong in these things to which He calls attention. There is nothing wrong in eating and drinking, in buying or selling; there is nothing wrong in planting or building. These things are perfectly right in themselves, but it is wrong to be so occupied with them as to forget the things of God and eternity. Jesus did not even mention the terrible sins that characterized the cities of the plain; He speaks only of ordinary things. They were living as though there were no judgment to come, as though there were no God to whom they were responsible. And while they were going on like this the judgment came; it came so suddenly that there was no escape from it. We read, "But the same day that Lot went out of Sodom it rained fire and brimstone from heaven, and destroyed them all." The Lord makes the application: "Even thus shall it be in the day when the Son of Man is revealed." Because that day will be one of terrible confusion here on the earth, He says, "In that day, he which shall be upon the housetop, and his stuff in the house, let him not come down to take it away: and he that is in the field, let him likewise not return back." That is, there will be no use trying to save something out of the wrecked world; it will be too late. It will be useless to attempt a way of escape for men who have rejected the only One in whom they might have found security.

In just three words our Lord next gives a very solemn warning: "Remember Lot's wife." Why should we remember her? Because she was almost saved, and yet she was lost. She was a wife of a godly man; she had even entertained angels in her home; she was in the way to being saved, but she was destroyed at last. Why? Because after she had left Sodom, her heart was still there. She had never taken her true place before God, and when Sodom went down she went down with it. We may well remember Lot's wife. Especially does this warning apply to those who belong in Christian homes, who have had godly parents, who have heard the Word all their lives, and with whom the Spirit of God has striven. They have said in their hearts, "I ought to turn to Christ, I ought to trust Him, but I cannot yield myself to Him now." Remember, oh, remember Lot's wife! Remember, one may be almost saved but lost forever.

" 'Almost' cannot avail;
'Almost' is but to fail!
Sad, sad, that bitter wail—
'Almost—but lost!' "

Our Lord adds, "Whosoever shall seek to save his life shall lose it; and whosoever shall lose his life shall preserve it." That is, he who lives for self, for pleasure, or wealth, for what this earth has to offer, will find at last that he has missed everything really worth-while. Whereas, he who is content, for Christ's sake, to forego what men of the world value will find that he has riches for eternity of inestimable worth. I presume that during the years Lot dwelt in Sodom he had made quite a little fortune. Probably he had a very fine residence. I gather from the Scriptures that he had succeeded in making a name for himself. We read that he "sat in the gate of Sodom," which implies that he was a judge. When the judgment fell, Lot was saved, but only by fire. He got out of Sodom in time, but he lost everything for which he had labored during all those years. He himself was saved, but everything else was lost. There are many who will be in heaven because they have really trusted Christ, but who will find that all their works will be burned up at the judgment-seat of Christ.

Jesus uses next a very striking illustration to show the separations that will take place in the day of His coming. In one part of the world it will be night when that event takes place. So He says: "I tell you, in that night there shall be two men in one bed; the one shall be taken, and the other shall be left." In another part of the world it will be sunrise, and women will be preparing the morning meal. So He tells us, "Two women shall be grinding together; the one shall be taken, and the other left." Elsewhere it will be full day, and He declares, "Two men shall be in the field; the one shall be taken, and other left." How solemn! It speaks of an eternal separation. His coming is certain, but the time is uncertain. It behooves us all to be ready. When He comes judgment will be meted out to all Christ-rejecters.

"Wheresoever the body is, thither will the eagles be gathered together." Dispensationally, the carcass, refers to the putrid mass of false profession centered in Jerusalem in the last days. The eagles are the armies of the nations that will be gathered together against that city. But looked at morally, the lesson is a solemn one for every unsaved person who is found out of Christ in the day of His wrath, who will be exposed to the wrath of God. Like eagles, or really vultures, devouring decaying carcasses, so the judgments of God will fall on all who have spurned His grace.

ADDRESS SIXTY-ONE

IMPORTANT PRAYER

✓ ✓ ✓

"And He spake a parable unto them to this end, that men ought always to pray, and not to faint; saying, There was in a city a judge, which feared not God, neither regarded man: and there was a widow in that city; and she came unto him, saying, Avenge me of mine adversary. And he would not for a while: but afterward he said within himself, Though I fear not God, nor regard man; yet because this widow troubleth me, I will avenge her, lest by her continual coming she weary me. And the Lord said, Hear what the unjust judge saith. And shall not God avenge His own elect, which cry day and night unto Him, though He bear long with them? I tell you that He will avenge them speedily. Nevertheless when the Son of Man cometh, shall He find faith on the earth? And He spake this parable unto certain which trusted in themselves that they were righteous, and despised others: Two men went up into the temple to pray; the one a Pharisee, and the other a publican. The Pharisee stood and prayed thus with himself, God, I thank Thee, that I am not as other men are, extortioners, unjust, adulterers, or even as this publican. I fast twice in the week, I give tithes of all that I possess. And the publican, standing afar off, would not lift up so much as his eyes unto heaven, but smote upon his breast, saying, God be merciful to me a sinner. I tell you, this man went down to his house justified rather than the other: for every one that exalteth himself shall be abased; and he that humbleth himself shall be exalted. And they brought unto Him also infants, that He would touch them: but when His disciples saw it, they rebuked them. But Jesus called them unto Him, and said, Suffer little children to come unto Me, and forbid them not: for of such is the kingdom of God. Verily I say unto you, Whosoever shall not receive the kingdom of God as a little child shall in no wise enter therein"—Luke 18: 1-17.

✓ ✓ ✓

IT is very evident that the first parable has a definite dispensational aspect. God Himself is not an unjust judge but is put in contrast with such an one. The widow does not represent the Church of God, for the Church of God is not a widow. The Church is a virgin espoused to Christ; the marriage feast is to take place after we are caught up to meet the Lord in the air. The woman here undoubtedly represents Israel. She was called the wife of Jehovah, but because of her sins, unbelief, and spiritual adultery, she was separated from her rightful Husband, and abides in the world today as a widow. What suffering she has endured down through the centuries! During all these long years her earnest cries have gone up to heaven, that she might be avenged of her cruel adversaries. It might seem as though God is as indifferent as the unjust judge. He appears to have no regard for the sufferings of Israel, no interest in their sad experiences. "There was in a city a judge, which feared not God, neither regarded man: and there was a widow in that city; and she came unto him, saying, Avenge me of mine adversary." Her crying at first did not affect him; he was not concerned about her case. But afterwards he became tired of her incessant pleading for help, and he said, "Though I fear not God, nor regard man; yet because this widow troubleth me, I will avenge her, lest by her continual coming she weary me." Now the Lord does not tell us that this is the attitude of God, but He explains that it was the attitude of an unjust judge who had no fear of God. How much more will God hear His children, for He is deeply interested in all their trials. He cannot turn a deaf ear to the cry of the afflicted, but in due time He will avenge His own elect. These are the elect of Israel, not of the Church. The cries of God's elect have been going up to Him day and night, and the time is coming when He will answer their cries. Jesus said, "I tell you that He will avenge them speedily.

Nevertheless when the Son of Man cometh, shall He find faith on the earth?" This is a remarkable question. It suggests that instead of the whole world becoming converted, the great bulk of mankind will be found in opposition to God when Christ returns. This is in accordance with what is elsewhere revealed. At the coming again of the Son of Man to set up His kingdom of righteousness, He will avenge Israel of those nations that have persecuted her.

Though this is the dispensational teaching, it is evident from the first verse that the Lord Jesus meant us to get something more out of it for our own soul's blessing, for we read, "And He spake a parable unto them to this end, that men ought always to pray, and not to faint." This is a message for everyone of us. Oftentimes when we cry to God in distress or trouble there seems to be no answer; yet all the time His heart is deeply concerned about us, and we are not to cease to pray; nor, because we do not get the answer immediately, are we to give up in despair. We need to remember that God is working out certain counsels in connection with His great plan that runs through all the ages, which may necessitate that some time must elapse before our prayers are actually answered. We find a very significant illustration of this in the tenth chapter of Daniel. We read the prophet prayed about a certain thing for three full weeks, twenty-one days, and during those three weeks he ate neither bread nor meat, nor drank wine. One can imagine how he must have felt as the hours lengthened into days, the days into weeks, and the weeks went on until three had passed. Then at the end of the twenty-one days, he tells us there appeared to him an angel sent direct from the High Court of heaven. The angel said to him: "From the first day that thou didst set thine heart to understand, and to chasten thyself before thy God, thy words were heard, and I am come for thy words. But the prince of the kingdom of Persia withstood me one-and-twenty days." It is a most remarkable thing—something I would not believe if it were not in my Bible—that God actually heard the prayer of Daniel the first day he began his supplication, and He dispatched an angel to tell him that his prayer was heard, but the angel was twenty-one days fighting his way through the fiends of the upper air to get down to Daniel to bring the answer to him. "The prince of the kingdom of Persia" was not the earthly ruler who sat on the throne of Persia, but an evil angel who sought to control the king's heart and to thwart the plan of God. In the New Testament Satan is called "the prince of the power of the air." We are taught that "we wrestle not against flesh and blood, but against principalities, against powers, against the rulers of the darkness of this world, against spiritual wickedness in high places." So this angel from heaven was twenty-one days in conflict with the evil powers before he could get to Daniel. Then he said, "When I leave you I have to go and face the prince of Grecia." That was another evil spirit seeking to control the heart of the Grecians. This is a marvelous thing, and it gives us an idea of what goes on in the unseen world, and explains in a very large measure why the answers to many of our prayers seem so long delayed. Perhaps we have been praying for mother, for daughter, for husband, or some other loved one who is still unsaved, and we wonder why God has allowed so much time to elapse ere answering our petition, but there is a conflict going on in the unseen world. Do not give up praying. By your importunate intercession you are putting yourself over on the side of God in this conflict, and He will hear His own elect in due time, who cry unto him night and day.

The second parable is designed to impress upon us the true attitude we should take before God when we come to Him in prayer. "And He spake this parable unto certain which trusted in themselves that they were righteous, and despised others." We cannot come to God on the ground of our own righteousness; we have no title to approach Him in that way. All our righteousnesses are as filthy rags in His sight. We can come to God only as confessed sinners, recognizing that all He does for us must be on the ground of grace. These two men had gone to the temple which God had ordained as a house of prayer for all men. One was a Pharisee, a self-righteous man, giving himself credit for exceptional merit. Significantly we read: "He prayed with himself." That is, his prayer never went up to God at all; it went no higher than the ceiling, because he was simply speaking of his own goodness. Yet it was a prayer of thanksgiving. Is it not right to come to God with thanksgiving? We are taught again and again that is the way we should approach God. But notice this man was not thanking God for what grace had done for him; he was thanking God for what he himself had done, and that is the wrong attitude. When I approach God my heart should be filled with thanksgiving because of what He has done for me, recognizing that everything I have comes by divine grace. But this man said, "I thank Thee for my own goodness; I thank Thee I am not as other men are." You, perhaps, would not use the same language, but do you approach God in that attitude? "I thank Thee that I am not as other men are, extortioners, unjust, adulterers." Then the Pharisee looked and saw the publican standing there, and he said, "Or even as this publican. I fast twice in the week, I give tithes of all that I possess." Surely these things are all good, but no man has a right to plead his own goodness as the reason why God should hear his cry. And, actually, most of his prayer was just pretence, claiming a righteousness he did not possess.

The publican stood afar off, conscious of his unworthiness. He "would not lift up so much as his eyes unto heaven, but smote upon his breast, saying, God be merciful to me a sinner." Literally, it might be translated, "God be propitiated to me, the sinner." Calvary's cross was the answer to that prayer when the Lord Jesus became the propitiation for our sins. This man, recognizing he needed propitiation, cried to God for that which he knew he did not deserve, but which must come to him by grace if it was to come at all. And Jesus said, "This man went down to his house justified rather than the other: for every one that exalteth himself shall be abased; and he that humbleth himself shall be exalted."

In which man's company are you found? Do you stand with the Pharisee, trying to make out a case for yourself? or with the publican, acknowledging you are a sinner, and that your only hope is in the propitiation which God has provided?

In the next verses we have a beautiful scene. We have enacted a picture of the right attitude of soul in which God delights. "And they brought unto Him also infants, that He would touch them: but when His disciples saw it, they rebuked them." The disciples felt that the parents were only troubling Jesus, He could not afford to waste His time with children, but the disciples did not know His heart. He is interested in all; and so He rebuked His disciples, and called the parents to Him and said, "Suffer little children to come unto Me, and forbid them not: for of such is the kingdom of God." Children, in simplicity, believe what you tell them of the Lord. These are the ideal members of the kingdom, who simply take Him at His word. "Verily I say unto you, Whosoever shall not receive the kingdom of God as a little child shall in no wise enter therein." That used to trouble me. Though I knew I was saved, yet when I came to that verse and the kindred one in Matthew, I used to wonder if I had qualified in this way: I am not like a child; I am not as innocent as a little child; I have not the same hopeful attitude toward life as little children. How can I, a sinner by practice, ever get back to the comparative purity and goodness of a little child? Then I noticed that "Jesus called a little child unto Him, and set him in the midst of them, and said, Verily I say unto you, Except ye be converted, and become as little children . . . " He called and the child came. That is what He means when He says, "Whosoever shall not receive the kingdom of God as a little child shall in no wise enter therein."

It is when we heed His blessed call and come to Him in unquestioning faith that we enter the kingdom. It is this alone that puts us on praying ground and entitles us to bring all our troubles and perplexities to Him, and He has promised to undertake for us.

ADDRESS SIXTY-TWO

THE GREAT REFUSAL

✝ ✝ ✝

"And a certain ruler asked Him, saying, Good Master, what shall I do to inherit eternal life? And Jesus said unto him, Why callest thou Me good? None is good, save One, that is, God. Thou knowest the commandments, Do not commit adultery, Do not kill, Do not steal, Do not bear false witness, Honour thy father and thy mother. And he said, All these have I kept from my youth up. Now when Jesus heard these things, He said unto him, Yet lackest thou one thing: sell all that thou hast, and distribute unto the poor, and thou shalt have treasure in heaven: and come, follow Me. And when he heard this, he was very sorrowful: for he was very rich. And when Jesus saw that he was very sorrowful, He said, How hardly shall they that have riches enter into the kingdom of God! For it is easier for a camel to go through a needle's eye, than for a rich man to enter into the kingdom of God. And they that heard it said, Who then can be saved? And He said, The things which are impossible with men are possible with God. Then Peter said, Lo, we have left all, and followed Thee. And He said unto them, Verily I say unto you, There is no man that hath left house, or parents, or brethren, or wife, or children, for the kingdom of God's sake, who shall not receive manifold more in this present time, and in the world to come life everlasting"—Luke 18: 18-30.

✝ ✝ ✝

THE Lord Jesus Christ is not only a Saviour from judgment, but He is also the Lord of our life. In our unconverted days we lived for ourselves; we lived in different ways; we chose our own paths, but our one great object was to please self.

"I lived for myself, for myself alone,
For myself and none beside,
Just as if Jesus had never lived,
And as if He had never died."

So our blessed Saviour came into this world to do more than to redeem us from our sins and from the judgment of God. He came to make us His own in a practical sense, that in all our ways down here on earth we might live to His glory. Instead of being self-centered, the child of God should be Christ-centered, able to say with the Apostle Paul, "For me to live is Christ." This comes out very clearly in the passage before us.

First we have the story of the rich young ruler: "And a certain ruler asked Him, saying, Good Master, what shall I do to inherit eternal life?" I do not know exactly what was in the mind of this young man when he used the term "eternal life." It certainly could not mean to him all that it means to us. Our Lord Jesus said, "This is life eternal, that they might know Thee the only true God, and Jesus Christ, whom Thou hast sent." Eternal life is that which gives the ability to enter into and enjoy fellowship with Divine Persons: the Father and the Son by the power of the Holy Spirit. Evidently this young man thought of eternal life as a happy experience and prolongation of human life here on earth, and assurance of happiness after death. He spoke from the standpoint of the law of Moses when he asked, "What shall I do to inherit eternal life?" What must I do in order to be the possessor of this great blessing? Notice the way he addressed the Lord Jesus, "Good Master." He acknowledged the Lord to be a Master, a Teacher, as thousands do today. Jesus said, "Why callest thou Me good? None is good, save One, that is, God." Was He saying, "I am not God, and therefore you should not address Me as Good Master"? No; the Lord was testing this young ruler. No one is intrinsically good but God, and God was manifest in Christ. The question was, did this young man recognize Jesus as such? He did not. Then our Lord said to him, "Thou knowest the commandments, Do not commit adultery, Do not kill, Do not steal, Do not bear false witness, Honor thy father and thy mother." Now the law says that the man who obeys these commands shall live. The Lord Jesus mentioned only the commandments that have to do with the outward life, our relation to our fellow-men; He did not mention those that have to do with our relation to God. It was not what he was before God but what he appeared to be before his fellows that concerned the young man. He looked up complacently and said, "All these have I kept from my youth up." Probably he was honest in saying that; possibly he had never been guilty of violating any of these commandments, but the Lord Jesus saw that he was resting in his own self-righteousness. To keep these commandments as they should be kept means more than simply refraining from overt acts of evil; it means to love our neighbor as we love ourselves, and so the Lord now put this young man to the test by saying, "Yet lackest thou one thing." Your life may be outwardly pure; it may be comparatively clean; in the eyes of your fellow-men you may be a very noble personage, but if you are living for self rather than for God, you are under the condemnation of the law. The Lord Jesus tested this young man in this way, "Yet lackest thou one thing: sell all that thou hast, and distribute unto the poor, and thou shalt have treasure in heaven: and come, follow Me."

Did He mean that the way to obtain eternal life is by giving everything one possesses to the poor? Not at all; but He was testing this young man, who was egotistic and self-satisfied. Certainly there was nothing to be said against his moral character, but his life had been a selfish life; he had vast possessions; he had great riches, and men and women were living in poverty all about him; yet he continued to go on as he was and did not realize that God had entrusted him with this wealth that he might use it for Him. If God entrusts wealth to you, He makes you a steward, and you are to use your riches to the glory of God and to the blessing of mankind. If we fully surrender our lives and our possessions to the Lord Jesus we shall not be concerned about ourselves; we shall be concerned about the needs of others, and our one object will be to glorify the One who has redeemed us. So the test here is, will you let Christ be Lord of your life? We read that when the ruler heard these words he was very sorrowful, for he had great possessions, and he turned away. He did not meet the test which the Lord put to him. He refused the path of subjection to Christ. Many have taken the same course.

It is not wrong to be rich, but it is a terrible thing if riches keep you out of heaven. God giveth us richly all things to enjoy, but it is a catastrophe if one becomes so occupied with earthly treasure that he misses the path of eternal life as this man did.

"And when Jesus saw that he was very sorrowful, He said, How hardly shall they that have riches enter into the kingdom of God!" It is difficult for one who has plenty of this world's goods to realize his need and to come to God as a poor, poverty-stricken sinner. We know this is true practically, for there are very few of the great and wealthy of this world who have turned to Christ and put their lives under His control. Jesus said, "For it is easier for a camel to go through a needle's eye, than for a rich man to enter into the kingdom of God." You know the illustration that has been used so often—I presume it is correct: There is a little gate in one of the larger doors called the "needle's eye"—I saw such gates when I was in Palestine—it was possibly the same in the time of our Lord. If a traveler reaches the city late at night and knocks at the gate, the guard from within will allow him to pass through the needle's eye, but his camel has to kneel down in order to crawl through. The traveler's goods have to be left outside until morning. So Jesus said, "It is easier for a camel to go through a needle's eye, than for a rich man to enter into the kingdom of God." The rich man has to unload; he has to turn over all he has to the authority of the Lord Jesus Christ.

The disciples were amazed when they heard this. They thought, as many think today, that it is poverty that keeps people out of the kingdom of God. If we could only do away with poverty, if we could eliminate the slums of our cities, then we could get people to turn to Christ! But it does not work that way. We read of "the poor of this world who are rich in faith." Riches often prove a real hindrance to the salvation of the soul. The disciples asked, "Who then can be saved?" And our Lord replied, "The things which are impossible with men are possible with God." It is not impossible for the rich to be saved. It is possible for the wealthy to know Christ if they are willing to repent and trust Him and own Him as Lord, which will mean a complete revolution in the way they have lived.

Thank God there are those among the rich who have put their whole lives and riches in subjection to Christ. We have recently lost a man of God of our own city to whom the Lord entrusted ability and riches. He turned all he had over to the Lord. I refer to that merchant-prince, Mr. Henry P. Crowell. And there are other men like him; men whom the Lord can entrust with great wealth because they use it not for themselves but to the glory of God. On the other hand, because we are poor, we must not think that poverty is a title to heaven. Nothing of the kind. The poor and the rich meet together; they all need to be saved in the same way: "For all have sinned, and come short of the glory of God."

Speaking for the apostles, Peter said, "Lo, we have left all, and followed Thee." There was not very much to leave. If I remember correctly, it was a boat and a broken net that Peter left behind, but it meant a lot to him—that fishing business in Capernaum. Jesus said, "Verily, I say unto you, There is no man that hath left house, or parents, or brethren, or wife, or children, for the kingdom of God's sake, who shall not receive manifold more in this present time, and in the world to come life everlasting." Make Christ the Lord of your life; trust Him as your Saviour; yield your all to Him, and you will eventually receive more than you have ever left. God will see that it is made up to you in an abundant measure, for He tells us that He gives an hundredfold to all who yield themselves to Him; and one hundredfold is 10,000 per cent. Most of us are satisfied, in these days, if we can get three or four per cent on our investments. Yet we shrink from making an investment that would yield us 10,000 per cent! We are afraid to submit our lives into the hands of the Lord, but He never fails those who submit to Him. And when we come to the end of the way, how we shall praise Him that we ever heard His voice calling us to trust Him and to acknowledge His authority over our lives. We have eternal life now through faith, but when we reach the heavenly city we shall enter into everlasting life in all its glory.

There will be no one in that day who will look back and say, "I wish I had been more self-centered; I wish I had not been so devoted; I wish I had not yielded so much to Jesus Christ." There will be no one who will speak like that in the coming day; but there will be many of us who will say, "I wish I had been more unselfish; I wish I had been more devoted; I wish I had yielded myself more definitely to the Lord Jesus Christ." God grant that everyone of us may surrender our lives to Him and acknowledge Him in all our ways, that we may walk as He would have us walk as we go through this scene.

ADDRESS SIXTY-THREE

CHRIST'S ANSWER TO FAITH'S PLEA

"Then He took unto Him the twelve, and said unto them, Behold, we go up to Jerusalem, and all things that are written by the prophets concerning the Son of Man shall be accomplished. For He shall be delivered unto the Gentiles, and shall be mocked, and spitefully entreated, and spitted on: and they shall scourge Him, and put Him to death: and the third day He shall rise again. And they understood none of these things: and this saying was hid from them, neither knew they the things which were spoken. And it came to pass, that as He was come nigh unto Jericho, a certain blind man sat by the way side begging: and hearing the multitude pass by, he asked what it meant. And they told him, that Jesus of Nazareth passeth by. And he cried, saying, Jesus, Thou Son of David, have mercy on me. And they which went before rebuked him, that he should hold his peace: but he cried so much the more, Thou Son of David, have mercy on me. And Jesus stood, and commanded him to be brought unto Him: and when he was come near, He asked him, saying, What wilt thou that I shall do unto thee? And he said, Lord, that I may receive my sight. And Jesus said unto him, Receive thy sight: thy faith hath saved thee. And immediately he received his sight, and followed Him, glorifying God: and all the people, when they saw it, gave praise unto God"—Luke 18: 31-43.

THIS portion divides into two parts: verses 31 to 34 stand together, and verses 35 to 43 go together. In the first section we read that Jesus and the disciples turned their faces toward Jerusalem. This was for the last time. Our Saviour had visited Jerusalem on other occasions—though after leaving Nazareth He made His earthly home in Capernaum of Galilee—but now He was going to Jerusalem in order to fulfil the purpose for which He came from the Father's glory into this poor world: He was going to Jerusalem to lay down His life as a sacrifice for sin. He understood perfectly what would happen. People have often spoken as though our Lord was overtaken by surprise, as though He had ventured too much in going to Jerusalem where so many were opposed to Him, and that He might have lived longer and accomplished more if He had been more cautious and remained in Galilee where many were learning to know and love Him, but this is contrary to the Word of God. Such reasoning makes manifest how people misunderstand the mystery of His Person. He came from heaven to give His life a ransom for many, but until the set time appointed of the Father when that great sacrifice was to be made, He could not die. No man could take His life from Him. But when the hour to which all eternity past had been looking forward, and to which all eternity future will ever be looking backward—when that hour came, then He laid down His own life. So with full knowledge of what was before Him, He said to His disciples, "Behold, we go up to Jerusalem, and all things that are written by the prophets concerning the Son of Man shall be accomplished." Notice that everything that had been declared of Him before by inspired men was now about to be fulfilled. All Scripture is "God breathed." There is no word in it that is void of power. And so our Lord told His disciples that everything the prophets had written was about to be fulfilled: that is, everything in connection with His first coming. The Son of Man was going to Jerusalem that He might die for the sin of the world.

Every prophecy that had reference to His first coming was fulfilled literally while He was here on earth, or when He hung upon the cross. Because of that we may be very sure that every scripture that has to do with His second coming—that glorious advent which many feel is to take place very soon—will be fulfilled just as definitely. Patrick Henry said to the Assembly of Virginia, "I have no way of judging the future but by the past." So we too have no way of judging the future but by the past. Judging by the past we see that everything that had to do with the first advent was literally fulfilled; therefore, everything that has been predicted concerning the second advent will be fulfilled in the same way. Many attempt to spiritualize the prophecies and try to apply promises to the Church of God that refer primarily to Israel and to the land of Palestine. All will be fulfilled as written, for so it has been throughout the past centuries.

The Lord Jesus told His disciples that He would be delivered unto the Gentiles, and He was; that He would be mocked, and He was; that He would be spitefully entreated, and He was; that He would be spat upon, and, yes, He was. The holy Son of God, they spat in His lovely face, and they mistreated Him in every way that the satanic influence could suggest; yet He gave His life as a ransom for their sins. He saw it all as though it had already been accomplished, but He went on unflinchingly to accomplish the work of redemption. He looked beyond the cross and told His disciples that on the third day He would rise again. One would suppose that those listening to Him as He spoke these words would have understood exactly what He was talking about; but the disciples were expecting Him to go down to Jerusalem and declare Himself the promised King, overthrowing at once the Roman power, and restoring Israel to the first and pre-eminent place among the nations of the earth. They were so obsessed with these ideas that they could not understand even the plainest words concerning His rejection, His crucifixion, and His coming resurrection. We read that "they understood none of these things: and this saying was hid from them, neither knew they the things which were spoken." It is significant enough that after these words were fulfilled concerning His rejection and death, His enemies remembered what His disciples had forgotten, for we read that they came to Pilate and said, "We remember that that deceiver said, while He was yet alive, after three days I will rise again. Command therefore that the sepulchre be made sure until the third day, lest His disciples come by night, and steal Him away, and say unto the people, He is risen from the dead." And Pilate said, "Ye have a watch: go your way, and make it as sure as ye can." And so they went and made it as sure as they could; but they could not overthrow the purpose of God. When the third day dawned Jesus rose in triumph from the grave. But His disciples had not understood; their minds were blinded. They were so occupied with the idea of His setting up immediately His kingdom and with the restoration of Israel, that they could not comprehend what His words really meant.

In the second section we have the story of blind Bartimæus. In it we see the wonderful way in which God responds to faith. "Without faith it is impossible to please Him: for he that cometh to God must believe that He is, and that He is a rewarder of them that diligently seek Him" (Heb. 11:6). Here we have a beautiful picture, historically exact, but a lovely picture nevertheless, of the reward of faith. On His way to Jerusalem, going down through Perea, on the eastern side of the Jordan, our Lord made His way across the ford, into the land of Judaea. As He was drawing near to the city of Jericho (not the Jericho of Joshua's day; that was destroyed, but another Jericho that had grown up near the site of that ancient city), we are told, "A certain blind man sat by the way side begging." Matthew's Gospel tells us there were two blind men, and that Jesus healed them both. Those who like to find fault with the Bible and try to discredit the truth of its inspiration, point to these two different accounts and say, "Can both be inspired? One writer says there are two blind men, and another says there is only one." But notice that Luke does not say there was only one; he does not say there was no other. Matthew went farther than Luke and said there were two, and he was correct. But Luke fastens our attention on the one man who had the greater faith. There may have been a measure of faith in the other man, but that of Bartimæus was outstanding. There is no contradiction here; it is simply that Matthew gives added information which the Holy Spirit was pleased to withhold when Luke wrote his account. Every incident in the four Gospels where there seem at times to be discrepancies could be easily explained if only we knew more of the facts. God's Word is perfect; it is our understanding that is limited. Here we are told, "And it came to pass, that as He was come nigh unto Jericho, a certain blind man sat by the way side begging: and hearing the multitude pass by, he asked what it meant." What a picture of hopelessness and distress. I suppose this man had been without sight for many years, and there was no one to care for him, and so he earned a precarious living by begging, sitting day by day on the side of the highway leading to Jericho, in order to receive gifts from the passing multitude. Those who have visited Palestine, as some of us have, find it easy to visualize that sight. One will see the same thing today: there are sick people, those who are blind and maimed, sitting along the highway, crying, *"Backsheesh! Backsheesh!"* It seemed to me we heard that word more than any other all the time we were in Palestine. It means "a gift! a gift!" Sometimes there will be thirty or forty crying, *"Backsheesh."* One's heart aches as he gazes upon them and realizes how miserable and wretched many of them are. So there was this blind man, Bartimæus. "And hearing the multitude pass by, he asked what it meant. And they told him, that Jesus of Nazareth passeth by." Oh, what a message that was! "Jesus of Nazareth passeth by!" Jesus, the Friend of sinners; the One whose voice has power; the One who had healed the lepers, and who, on many other occasions, had opened the eyes of the blind. Bartimæus had heard that name. He said in his heart, "He is the One who can do something for me!" Bartimæus felt his need. The trouble with many today is that they do not feel their need; they are contented and self-satisfied just as they are. They have no sense of their true condition before God. Bartimæus felt his need: he had suffered for years. He was in earnest as he cried, saying, "Jesus, Thou Son of David, have mercy on me." He expressed himself intelligently. He recognized the fact that Jesus was truly the promised Messiah of Israel. That is what was involved in using the expression, "Thou Son of David." For many centuries the people had waited for the coming of the promised Son of David, who was to bring everlasting blessing to them, and Bartimæus had heard enough about Jesus to be convinced in his own soul that He was the promised One. That is real faith based on the Word of God. "And they which went before rebuked him, that he should hold his peace: but he cried so much the more, Thou Son of David, have mercy on me." The more they tried to quiet him, the more he cried, "Thou Son of David, have mercy on me." There are some people who think it is a terrible thing when folk become a little effervescent about religion. They do not like emotion in religion, but they get excited about everything else. They go to a ball-game, and yell themselves hoarse as they watch someone chasing after a little globe as though it were the most wonderful thing in the world; but when they go to a gospel meeting and find people who are anxious about their souls, they say, "Oh, there is too much excitement about this!" If one is out of Christ and he becomes excited about his soul, it is something worth getting excited about. Many are like the sluggard in the Book of Proverbs (6:10), who cried, "Yet a little sleep, a little slumber, a little folding of the hands to sleep." A little more sleep and many will awake in hell to sleep no more! It is time to waken and become excited, as this man Bartimæus was. You have a soul to be saved; you have a soul to be lost if it is not saved, and you should be in earnest about your salvation.

Bartimæus would not be put to one side; he must reach Jesus, and so he continued crying. And no one ever cried to Him in vain: "Whosoever shall call upon the name of the Lord shall be saved" (Romans 10:13). You lift up your heart to Him; you cry out, "Jesus, Thou Son of David, have mercy on me!" and He will hear. "And Jesus stood, and commanded him to be brought unto Him: and when he was come near, He asked him, saying, What wilt thou that I shall do unto thee?" This is a question that He is asking today. Do you want something from Him? Be definite about it. If you are unsaved, look up to Him as He asks this question and say, "Lord, I would that Thou wilt save my soul, that Thou wilt give me eternal life, and the assurance that I have peace with God." He is waiting to grant your request. If you are in any trouble or distress, He is ready to give you peace and to hear your supplication. But be sure you ask in faith, "nothing wavering. For he that wavereth is like a wave of the sea driven with the wind and tossed"

(James 1:5). Bartimæus had genuine faith. He had a real need and he wanted that need met. "And he said, Lord, that I may receive my sight." "Receive thy sight: thy faith hath saved thee." That was God's answer to faith's plea. "Thy faith hath saved thee!" The Lord discerned the faith that was in the heart of this man. And so Bartimæus was not only healed, but he was also saved. Christ will do the same for you if you will come to Him as Bartimæus did, in simple faith and put in your plea.

He received the answer, and we read, "And immediately he received his sight, and followed Him, glorifying God: and all the people, when they saw it, gave praise unto God." When we are saved, when we ourselves have received spiritual sight, when we have been delivered, we are interested in Christ; we want to follow Him and to be in His presence; we want to keep company with Him; we enjoy fellowship with Him, and the heart goes out in worship, praise and thanksgiving. So we read that Bartimæus glorified God. He was not like many who receive God's good gifts and never think to lift their hearts to Him in a word of acknowledgement. This man's deliverance was a testimony to the multitude when they saw him giving praise unto God, and thus witnessing for the Lord Jesus. You who have had your eyes opened, you who can say, "One thing I know, that, whereas I was blind, now I see," do you seek to witness for Him that others too may be attracted to Christ and led to trust and praise Him?

ADDRESS SIXTY-FOUR

GRACE: WHAT IT IS AND WHAT IT DOES

"And Jesus entered and passed through Jericho. And, behold, there was a man named Zacchaeus, which was the chief among the publicans, and he was rich. And he sought to see Jesus who He was; and could not for the press, because he was little of stature. And he ran before, and climbed up into a sycomore tree to see Him: for He was to pass that way. And when Jesus came to the place, He looked up, and saw him, and said unto him, Zacchaeus, make haste, and come down; for today I must abide at thy house. And he made haste, and came down, and received Him joyfully. And when they saw it, they all murmured, saying, That He was gone to be guest with a man that is a sinner. And Zacchaeus stood, and said unto the Lord; Behold, Lord, the half of my goods I give to the poor; and if I have taken any thing from any man by false accusation, I restore him fourfold. And Jesus said unto him, This day is salvation come to this house, forsomuch as he also is a son of Abraham. For the Son of Man is come to seek and to save that which was lost"—Luke 19: 1-10.

THIS is another incident preserved for our edification for which we are indebted wholly to Luke, writing under the guidance of the Holy Spirit. We do not read in any other of the four Gospels of this visit to the house of Zacchaeus.

The Lord Jesus was nearing the city of Jericho. As He entered it He would pass the customs house, which was at the entrance-gate on the side nearest to the river. It was there, in all probability, that Zaccheaus had his office, for he was the chief publican. No one admired a publican. Such an one was looked upon as a traitor to his own people. The Jews were looking for the time when the promised Messiah would appear to deliver them from the power of Rome. They detested the Imperial Government and hated to be taxed by it. What made it worse was that the position of tax-collector was sold to the one who offered the most money for it. He who secured the privilege imposed heavy taxes on the people so as to reimburse himself for all he had paid for his position and to obtain a good living besides. If he were a reasonably honest man he could do well, but if he were a rogue or a rascal, he might accumulate vast wealth. Zacchaeus was the chief among the publicans, and he was rich. This tells its own story. We can well understand why the Jews detested him: he had made himself wealthy by oppressing his own people.

This man heard that Jesus was coming to his city. I do not know how much he knew about Jesus, perhaps very little; perhaps he had been told by others that Jesus was the Prophet who was to come into the world and re-establish the kingdom of Israel and bring them back to God. At any rate, he had heard of Jesus and wanted to see Him. There was a crowd gathered about our Lord, and Zacchaeus, being small of stature, could not get sight of the face of Jesus. He ran ahead and climbed into a sycamore tree, or really a wild-fig tree, a very leafy tree. Ensconced in its branches he thought he could see, without himself being seen. This man, Zacchaeus, in one respect at least, is like all of us: he was a "come-shorter." He had come short. The Bible tells us that "All have sinned, and come short of the glory of God." Zacchaeus was a sinner, he was a come-shorter, and he thought he had to do something in order to see Jesus. Many people have that idea. They imagine that they must do something special if they are going to make contact with the Saviour. The Lord Jesus came that way. He stopped and looked up into the leafy tree; He could see the little man up there on that limb. At once He called him by name, "Zacchaeus, make haste, and come down; for today I must abide at thy house." Jesus knew his name. Elsewhere we read, "He calleth His own sheep by name." So evidently the Lord had marked this man out and knew he would respond to His solicitation. We read that Zacchaeus "made haste and came down, and received Him joyfully." No one else in all Jericho had invited Jesus to his home. We read in this Gospel of many people inviting Him to be their guest, and He always accepted; we never read that He refused an invitation. But no one in this village was concerned enough about Jesus to offer Him entertainment; so He invited Himself to the home of the man who was considered by the stricter Jews to be the chief of sinners. In answer to His request we are told that Zacchaeus "made haste, and came down, and received Him joyfully. And when they saw it, they all murmured, saying, That He was gone to be guest with a man that is a sinner." He invited Himself, and Zacchaeus was delighted to have Him enter his house. That little man got out of the tree in much less time than it took him to climb up, we may be sure. We can imagine him exclaiming, "My Lord, come right along; I never dreamed of anything like this." And home they went; and the door was closed. Inside that home something was going on that you and I will never know till we get to heaven. It must have been a wonderful experience for this despised publican. We may be sure that Jesus was faithful to him, that He told Zacchaeus of his need to repent and to get right with God.

Outside the people could not hear what was going on between Jesus and Zacchaeus. It is always that way when the soul and the Lord Jesus get into close contact. Something goes on between Christ and the sinner that no one else can enter into. Friends sometimes only hurt instead of helping; they get in the way. The Lord wants to speak to people alone. So this day, while Jesus sat at Zacchaeus' table, enjoying the food prepared for Him, the great throng outside look at the house and said to one another: "Think of Him, a Prophet forsooth! He says He is the Messiah, but see what He has done; He has gone in with a publican, a man who is a sinner!" Where else could He go? There was not a house in all the world where He would not have to be entertained by a sinner, for "There is not a just man upon earth that doeth good and sinneth not." These Pharisees knew that Zacchaeus was a sinner, but they esteemed themselves as righteous and did not think that they too were sinful and needed a Saviour.

Oftentimes when one tries to speak to people about the Lord—about their need of redemption—they start talking of their own goodness, their charity, the money they give to certain good causes; and they think they do not need to repent. We want to lead them to Christ, but they are trying to make out that they are not sinners and so have no need of a Saviour. If you are not a sinner then there is no salvation for you. If you can prove that you are not a sinner, then I can prove to you that there is no Saviour for you, and you will never go to heaven, because heaven will be filled with redeemed sinners —sinners cleansed by the precious blood of Christ. Only sinners need to be saved; so if you are righteous in yourself then you have no need of Christ. Jesus said He came not to call the righteous but sinners to repentance. These Pharisees did not realize they were sinners. They knew that man inside the house was a sinner, for all publicans were sinners, but not such people as the Pharisees themselves! They were proud of their own self-righteousness. In Isaiah 64:6 we are told that all our righteousnesses are as filthy rags. This does not mean rags made unclean merely by the dirt of the streets, but it refers to garments defiled by that which exudes from within, as from the sores of a leper. No matter how beautiful such clothing might be, no matter how fine the texture, they were all contaminated from the corruption within. You would not thank a person for bringing you a beautiful robe which had belonged to a leprous friend who had died and willed the robe to you. No. You would say, "Take it away; it is filthy. I do not want it; it is contaminated by the uncleanness of leprosy." Well, that is how God looks upon our own righteousness. Our hearts are evil, and yet we draw apart from other people and pride ourselves on being better than they. We say, "Stand by thyself, for I am holier than thou." But the Word says, "There is no difference: for all have sinned, and come short of the glory of God." Some realize their sinfulness; others do not, but God's holy eyes see all to be alike. Zacchaeus was a sinner. Yes, Jesus had gone to be guest with a man who was a sinner. Those who were finding fault with Zacchaeus were also sinners, but they did not realize their need of a Saviour as did Zacchaeus.

By-and-by the doors of the house were flung open. Zacchaeus came out into the light of day again, and by his side was Jesus. The crowd had been wondering what was going on, and Zacchaeus evidently knew what was in the hearts of those Pharisees. He knew how he was hated and detested; he knew how he had been looked down upon. But he had spent an hour or two alone with Jesus, and something had happened to this man which was to change everything. Zacchaeus said, "Behold, Lord, the half of my goods I give to the poor; and if I have taken any thing from any man by false accusation, I restore him fourfold." Expositors are not agreed as to whether Zacchaeus spoke of what had been characteristic in his life, or whether he was declaring his intentions for the future. But his wealth declared him to be dishonest. I take it that he had been brought to know the grace of God in Christ, and this grace had changed his heart and his whole attitude. He said, "From now on everything is going to be different; I am going to divide my wealth with the poor; and then above that, if anyone can come to me and prove that I have taken anything by false accusation, I will give him four times what I took from him wrongfully." "And Jesus said unto him, This day is salvation come to this house." Why? Because of his giving half of his goods to the poor? Oh, no! Because he is restoring fourfold? No. Why, then? "This day is salvation come to this house, forsomuch as he also is a son of Abraham." We are told that they who have faith are blessed with faithful Abraham. This poor sinner, this despised publican, had real faith in the Lord Jesus Christ and recognized Him as the Son of God and his Saviour, and so salvation had come to his house. Grace had saved him and changed his whole attitude.

"For the Son of Man is come to seek and to save that which was lost." This was the very purpose for which He came to earth. He was ever on the lookout for sinners who knew their need and were ready to be saved. It is His gracious mission still. Though seated on the Father's throne He is working by the Holy Spirit in the hearts of His servants as they carry the glad tidings to lost men, telling them of salvation from sin and its judgment through faith in Him who died to redeem them.

Address Sixty-five

WHEN THE KING RETURNS TO REIGN

✝ ✝ ✝

"And as they heard these things, He added and spake a parable, because He was nigh to Jerusalem, and because they thought that the kingdom of God should immediately appear. He said therefore, A certain nobleman went into a far country to receive for himself a kingdom, and to return. And he called his ten servants, and delivered them ten pounds, and said unto them, Occupy till I come. But his citizens hated him, and sent a message after him, saying, We will not have this man to reign over us. And it came to pass, that when he was returned, having received the kingdom, then he commanded these servants to be called unto him, to whom he had given the money, that he might know how much every man had gained by trading. Then came the first, saying, Lord, thy pound hath gained ten pounds. And he said unto him, Well, thou good servant: because thou hast been faithful in a very little, have thou authority over ten cities. And the second came, saying, Lord, thy pound hath gained five pounds. And he said likewise to him, Be thou also over five cities. And another came, saying, Lord, behold, here is thy pound, which I have kept laid up in a napkin: for I feared thee, because thou art an austere man: thou takest up that thou layedst not down, and reapest that thou didst not sow. And he saith unto him, Out of thine own mouth will I judge thee, thou wicked servant. Thou knewest that I was an austere man, taking up that I laid not down, and reaping that I did not sow: wherefore then gavest not thou my money into the bank, that at my coming I might have required mine own with usury? And he said unto them that stood by, Take from him the pound, and give it to him that hath ten pounds. (And they said unto him, Lord, he hath ten pounds.) For I say unto you, That unto every one which hath shall be given; and from him that hath not, even that he hath shall be taken away from him. But those mine enemies, which would not that I should reign over them, bring hither, and slay them before me"—Luke 19: 11-27.

✝ ✝ ✝

OUR blessed Lord had passed through Jericho and was well on His way to Jerusalem. He knew that many were expecting Him to set up immediately the kingdom which had been predicted for so long by the prophets. Many of the Jews looked for Him to enter the royal city and declare Himself Israel's Messiah. They expected Him to put Himself at the head of an army of Jewish zealots and drive out the Romans, take over the throne of His father David and begin His reign on Mount Zion. Some day these Old Testament prophecies will be fulfilled, but the time had not yet come, and it is still in the future. During the present age the kingdom of God cometh not with outward show; the kingdom is now apprehended by faith. It is a spiritual kingdom in the hearts of men and women who are born again, and who own the authority of the Lord Jesus Christ. The gospel is preached in order that men may be saved and reign with Him when He returns.

The Lord Jesus related a parable to make it plain that His kingdom was not to be set up at His first coming but will be manifested when He comes back: that is, at His second advent. This parable was based on an historical incident that had taken place not many years before, and with which the people generally would be familiar. When King Herod died, that is, the Herod who lived when our Lord Jesus Christ was born, and who decreed that all babies in Bethlehem should be put to death, he decreed in his will that Archelaus should succeed him on the throne. But the Jews hated this man and did not want him to reign over them, and so he went over the sea to Rome to confer with Augustus Caesar, and to secure his approval regarding the kingdom. Before going away he entrusted large sums of money to many of his friends and gave instructions as to how this money was to be used in his absence, in order to make other friends who would forward his interests and be ready to acknowledge his claims. But the Jews who hated him sent an embassy after him and said to Caesar, "We do not want this man to reign over us. He is cruel; we hate every member of his house." Archelaus conferred with the Emperor, secured his approval and eventually returned to Jerusalem to be proclaimed king over Judaea. He then sent for the servants to whom he had entrusted the money and inquired as to the use they had made of it, rewarding them according to their faithfulness to his interests. After that he summoned his enemies who had been determined that he should not be recognized as king, and put many of them to death.

All this was fresh in the minds of the people, for it had occurred when Jesus was only a little lad. He based His parable upon that incident, because there was a certain likeness in what took place then and what will take place in connection with His present rejection and future return.

"And as they heard these things, He added and spake a parable, because He was nigh to Jerusalem, and because they thought that the kingdom of God should immediately appear. He said therefore, A certain nobleman went into a far country to receive for himself a kingdom, and to return." "A certain nobleman": the Nobleman is the Man Christ Jesus, and He has gone into a far country. He has gone to the Father's house, not like Archelaus to confer with some earthly ruler, but He has gone to confer with His Father and to remain with Him yonder until the time when He is to take the kingdom. Ere going away the nobleman "called his ten servants, and delivered them ten pounds, and said unto them, Occupy till I come." Our blessed Lord has conferred upon all His servants certain treasure, certain talents, certain abilities, all of which He holds us responsible to use for His glory during His absence. Every Christian has something committed to him which he can use for Christ. Suppose you have the talent of public speaking: you can preach the gospel before great throngs; you can tell of the Saviour who died, and who has been raised again—if you have this talent then you are responsible to proclaim His message. But suppose you say you have no special gift. Well, you can live for Christ in your own home. You can so live for Him before your friends and your neighbors that they will realize the importance of owning His authority over their own lives. Possibly yours is the talent of singing. Then He would have you dedicate your voice to Him, and use that talent He has given you to make Him known to men. I heard of one young lady who had a talent along that line. Her worldly father had spent great sums of money to fit her for the opera platform or stage, but just as she was completing her musical education—if you can ever complete a musical education—she was saved at a special meeting and yielded her life to the Lord. When she returned home, she said, "Father, I cannot go on the opera-stage now: Christ has saved me; I have yielded my life to Him. He has given me my voice, and now I want to use it for Him." Her father was intensely angry; and he finally said to her, "My daughter, I am going to give you one more opportunity. We have planned a great party to welcome you home—your graduation party. Now your friends will be here tonight, and when they come I want you to sing for them some of those operatic songs that you have learned; and if you do not I shall disown you and cast you out." She waited until evening came. Her friends arrived, and she was presented to them. The hour came when she was asked to go to the piano and sing. She breathed a prayer in her heart and went over to the instrument and sat down. After the first introductory note, she began to sing with her beautiful, trained voice:

> "No room for mirth or trifling here,
> For worldly hope or worldly fear,
> If life so soon is gone;
> If now the Judge is at the door,
> And all mankind must stand before
> The inexorable throne."

She sang all four stanzas of that old Wesleyan hymn. After she finished she rose from the piano, expecting her father to dismiss her from the house, but he came forward with tears streaming down his face and said, "My daughter, I too want to know your Saviour." The reward of dedicating her voice to the Lord was the winning of her own father to Christ. We all have talents committed to us which we are to use in His interests during His absence.

Just as in the case of Archelaus, we read of those who hated our Lord and sent a messenger after

Him, saying, "We will not have this Man to reign over us." I do not think I am stretching it by saying that the messenger was no other than Stephen, the first martyr of Christianity, who went into the presence of the Lord to bear witness that they did not want Jesus to reign over them. They stoned Stephen to death because of his message. And he went to be with Christ and to give the decision of the people. That was their attitude then, and it has been their attitude all through the centuries since. They said, "We have no king but Caesar." They refused to own Jesus as their rightful Ruler, and so they abide still in unbelief.

As our Lord looked forward to His second advent, He said, "And it came to pass, that when he was returned, having received the kingdom, then he commanded these servants to be called unto him, to whom he had given the money, that he might know how much every man had gained by trading." Only three are mentioned particularly, as examples. "Then came the first, saying, Lord, thy pound hath gained ten pounds. And he said unto him, Well, thou good servant: because thou hast been faithful in a very little, have thou authority over ten cities." By wise and careful investment the first servant had made an excellent profit on what had been committed to him. His integrity and trustworthiness were recognized by the master, and he was rewarded accordingly. This of course suggests the way Christ's faithful servants will be compensated at His return for all they have accomplished for Him in His absence. If you are faithful even in a little now, you will reign with Him in power then. The measure of our authority in our association with Him when He comes back will be according to the measure of our devotion to Him now.

The second servant came and said, "Lord, thy pound hath gained five pounds. And he said likewise to him, Be thou also over five cities." All have not the same business acumen, nor the same talents and abilities. But this man, too, had acted wisely and with concern for his master's interests. The reward was not so great as in the other case, but it was in proportion to the gain that had resulted from the servant's business activities. You see the place given us is according to the work done. I am afraid there are many of us who are Christians, who know our souls are saved, but who are going to find out when the King returns that we have lost out terribly, because we have done so little self-denying service for Him. We have lived to please ourselves to a great extent. So there will be very little for which He can reward us.

"And another came, saying, Lord, behold, here is thy pound, which I have kept laid up in a napkin." It was an inexcusable fault thus to have failed in the trust committed to him, not realizing that "It is required in stewards, that a man be found faithful" (1 Cor. 4:2). Yet how many Christians are failing in the same way, not using that which God has entrusted to them. Clean, straightforward business methods are as important in the Lord's work as in secular affairs. This man said, as it were, "Master, here is your money. I have not lost it;

but I have not used it, because I was afraid I could not use it satisfactorily. I knew that thou wert a hard man to please." "For I feared thee, because thou art an austere man: thou takest up that thou layest not down, and reapest that thou didst not sow"—"I knew you demanded a lot, and so I did not try to do anything." It shows how little he knew his master. If the servant really believed this, it was all the more reason why he should have been diligent in business, in order that he might have pleased the one who employed him (Rom. 12: 11; Prov. 22:29). Is there anyone who says, "I have only one talent, and I can do so little; I cannot do enough to win His approval, and so I will not do anything at all"? This nobleman turned to the slothful servant and said, "Out of thine own mouth will I judge thee, thou wicked servant. Thou knewest that I was an austere man, taking up that I laid not down, and reaping that I did not sow: wherefore then gavest not thou my money into the bank, that at my coming I might have required mine own with usury?" The servant's excuse was hypocritical. He did not know his master, and he did not want to put himself to any trouble on his behalf. Sternly the master rebuked the slothfulness of his servant, pointing out that if he feared to make any investments, he might, at least, have placed the money where it would have drawn interest and thus not have stood idle. It is a salutary lesson in the right use of capital which God has put in our hands, and the spiritual lesson is even clearer. We shall be held responsible, not alone for overt acts of evil, but also for sins of omission. And so he had all taken from him, and he found himself without reward because of his failure to serve. That which is not used will profit nothing, rather shall we suffer loss. Whereas they who wisely use what they have will be further rewarded.

Actually, I gather, from the fourth chapter of the First Epistle to the Corinthians, that there will be no Christian left without reward, for we read, "Then shall every man have praise of God" (4:5). But I am afraid there will be many of us who will have very little reward because we have done so little real service for our Lord Jesus Christ. "Unto every one which hath shall be given; and from him that hath not, even that he hath shall be taken away." The first half of the verse is clear enough and requires no comment. The latter part may be better understood if we paraphrase slightly, so that it would read: From him who hath not used that which was entrusted to him, even that itself shall be taken. Opportunities neglected are lost forever.

The nobleman then commanded that his enemies be brought before him, "But those mine enemies, which would not that I should reign over them, bring hither, and slay them before me." And in that coming day when Christ returns, those who reject His grace, those who refuse to own Him, those who spurn His love, will have to know His judgment when He is "revealed from heaven with His mighty angels, in flaming fire taking vengeance on them that know not God." Have you bowed your heart before Him? Have you recognized Him as the rightful King? Have you put your trust in Him as Saviour? Do you own Him as Lord of your life? "If thou shalt confess with thy mouth the Lord Jesus, and shalt believe in thine heart that God hath raised Him from the dead, thou shalt be saved. For with the heart man believeth unto righteousness; and with the mouth confession is made unto salvation." If you have never recognized Him as your rightful Lord, do it today. It is not yet too late. The King has not returned, although His coming draws nigh. He will soon be back, and then it will be too late to get right with Him. Why not make this the occasion when you yield your heart and your life to Him and acknowledge Him as earth's rightful Lord and King?

Address Sixty-six

WELCOMING THE KING

✝ ✝ ✝

"And when He had thus spoken, He went before, ascending up to Jerusalem. And it came to pass, when He was come nigh to Bethphage and Bethany, at the mount called the mount of Olives, He sent two of His disciples, saying, Go ye into the village over against you; in the which at your entering ye shall find a colt tied, whereon yet never man sat; loose him, and bring him hither. And if any man ask you, Why do ye loose him? thus shall ye say unto him, Because the Lord hath need of him. And they that were sent went their way, and found even as He had said unto them. And as they were loosing the colt, the owners thereof said unto them, Why loose ye the colt? And they said, The Lord hath need of him. And they brought him to Jesus: and they cast their garments upon the colt, and they set Jesus thereon. And as He went, they spread their clothes in the way. And when He was come nigh, even now at the descent of the mount of Olives, the whole multitude of the disciples began to rejoice and praise God with a loud voice for all the mighty works that they had seen; saying, Blessed be the King that cometh in the name of the Lord: peace in heaven, and glory in the highest. And some of the Pharisees from among the multitude said unto Him, Master, rebuke Thy disciples. And He answered and said unto them, I tell you that, if these should hold their peace, the stones would immediately cry out. And when He was come near, He beheld the city, and wept over it, saying, If thou hadst known, even thou, at least in this thy day, the things which belong unto thy peace! but now they are hid from thine eyes. For the days shall come upon thee, that thine enemies shall cast a trench about thee, and compass thee round, and keep thee in on every side, and shall lay thee even with the ground, and thy children within thee; and they shall not leave in thee one stone upon another; because thou knewest not the time of thy visitation. And He went into the temple, and began to cast out them that sold therein, and them that bought; saying unto them, It is written, My house is the house of prayer: but ye have made it a den of thieves. And He taught daily in the temple. But the chief priests and the scribes and the chief of the people sought to destroy Him, and could not find what they might do: for all the people were very attentive to hear Him"—Luke 19: 28-48.

WE come now to the Lord's last days on earth. Notice in the first part of this passage how careful He was to fulfil everything that was written of Him in the Prophets. In the book of Zechariah (9:9), it was written some five hundred years before, that the King would come riding upon the colt of an ass: "Rejoice greatly, O daughter of Zion; shout, O daughter of Jerusalem: behold, thy King cometh unto thee: He is just, and having salvation; lowly, and riding upon an ass, and upon a colt the foal of an ass."

Nearing Jerusalem, Jesus came to Bethany which is over the slope of the mount of Olives. He said to His disciples, "Go ye into the village over against you; in the which at your entering ye shall find a colt tied, whereon yet never man sat: loose him, and bring him hither." He was the omniscient One, and He knew exactly where the disciples would find the ass. He said to them, "And if any man ask you, Why do ye loose him? thus shall ye say unto him, Because the Lord hath need of him." This colt was only a dumb beast, but it knew its Owner. We read in Isaiah 1:3, "The ox knoweth his owner, and the ass his master's crib: but Israel doth not know, My people doth not consider." The lower creatures act in subjection to the will of the Lord. Man alone of all God's creatures—man, who is made a little lower than the angels, with his remarkable powers and his wonderful intellect—sets himself in opposition to the will of God. Jesus sent His disciples over to get this colt, and we read that it was one "whereon yet never man sat." It was an unbroken colt. You know that, ordinarily, it takes a rider of some dexterity to break in a colt; but here we find this unbroken colt in complete subjection to the will of its Creator. The One who was to ride that colt was the Creator whose power had brought it into existence. "And they that were sent went their way, and found even as He had said unto them. And as they were loosing the colt, the owners thereof said unto them, Why loose ye the colt?" They answered as they had been instructed by the Lord, and the owners gave consent to take him and use him as Jesus desired. "And they brought him to Jesus: and they cast their garments upon the colt, and they set Jesus thereon." So He began His so-called "triumphal entry," and the people hailed Him as their King as they led Him into the city. "And when He was come nigh, even now at the descent of the mount of Olives, the whole multitude of the disciples began to rejoice and praise God with a loud voice for all the mighty works that they had seen; saying, Blessed be the King that cometh in the name of the Lord: peace in heaven, and glory in the highest." Another scripture was fulfilled as the people were doing all this. Long years ago, in the 118th Psalm (ver. 26), it was written that the people should greet their King with the cry, "Blessed be He that cometh in the name of the Lord." And so His disciples and the little children who had heard of the promised King, shouted with joy as He entered His capital, for they thought He was immediately to set up His kingdom. They had to learn that there could be no kingdom for Him before the cross; that He must die for our sins before He could establish His throne in power and glory. So in the next verse of that 118th Psalm (ver. 27) we read, "Bind the sacrifice with cords, even unto the horns of the altar." He was to offer Himself a sacrifice on our behalf ere He could "take His great power and reign."

The religious leaders of the people who professed to be waiting for the Messiah were out of sympathy with all this. They looked on with indignation and turned to the Lord Himself and said, "Master, rebuke Thy disciples." They would have had Him repudiate the extravagant claims, as they considered them, which the disciples were making on His behalf. But Jesus, instead of rebuking them, rebuked the critics and said, "I tell you that, if these should hold their peace, the stones would immediately cry out." Those who welcomed Him with cries of joy acted as the Scriptures predicted. It was foretold by God that they should receive Him in this way. If they had not done so the stones would have cried out to welcome the glorious King.

So He entered the city, but He did not find the populace ready to receive Him. "He came unto His own, and His own received Him not." "His own" in the original text is neuter. First it refers to "His own things." In the second instance, it is personal and refers to "His own people." "He came unto His own *things,* and His own *people* received Him not." Here we behold Him coming to His own city, and His own temple, but His own people—the nation that had been waiting for Him for so long—received Him not. Knowing exactly what their attitude was to be, His great heart was breaking as He looked down over the city and realized all that Israel must suffer in the centuries to come as well as in the near future. He wept over the city. He saw, as no one ese could, all the sin and iniquity of which the people of Jerusalem were guilty. This is one of the three times when He is said to have wept. What a sad sight must any one of our great cities present to the all-seeing eyes of our Lord as He beholds them today! Beneath all the outward splendor of architecture, beautiful parks, schools, and great business houses, His holy eyes discern all the hidden sin, the selfishness, the unbridled lust, the vice and corruption, the hypocrisy and hardness of conscience which call as loudly for judgment now as the evils tolerated in Jerusalem cried to God for destruction so long ago. Jerusalem was the city Jehovah had chosen to place His name there; and and He was rejected. Its men and women preferred to go on in their own godless ways. As He wept over the city He exclaimed, "If thou hadst known, even thou, at least in this thy day, the things which belong unto thy peace! but now they are hid from thine eyes." "If thou hadst known!" But they did not know. That was the trouble with people then, and that is the trouble with people now: they do not know. There is a solemn pathos in His lament. They might have known, but there was no desire to understand, and so they had to suffer for their wilful ignorance. We read that Peter said to the people concerning the crucifixion of our Lord, "Through ignorance ye did it." They did not understand, neither did the princes of this world, "For had they known it, they would not have crucified the Lord of Glory." In the day of judgment we shall not be able to say, "I did not know who Jesus was." We have the Word; we have heard it again and again. The people of Israel did not know, and because they did not know, they fulfilled their own Scriptures in rejecting their Messiah. "If thou hadst known!" It was too late! They had turned their hearts against Him; they had spurned His grace. And now their judgment was on its way. He said, "For the days shall come upon thee, that thine enemies shall cast a trench about thee, and compass thee round, and keep thee in on every side." He foresaw the Roman armies under Titus surrounding the city and cutting off all sources of provision for its trapped populace. Graphically He portrayed what became actual history forty years afterward. It was all fulfilled literally when the Roman legions besieged the city, and at last entered it and destroyed its great buildings as Jesus had predicted. "And shall lay thee even with the ground, and thy children within thee; and they shall not leave in thee one stone upon another; because thou knewest not the time of thy visitation." Think of a statement like that! As the disciples looked upon that vast city with its great and wonderful buildings, and the Lord Jesus dared to say that not one stone should be left upon another! It must have seemed, even to His disciples, as though His words never could be fulfilled literally, yet in due time they were carried out to the letter, for Jerusalem became but a ruined heap. Long before, God had declared, "Therefore shall Zion for your sake be plowed as a field, and Jerusalem shall become heaps" (Micah 3:12). God's Word never fails. All that He has declared must come to pass.

Notice the reason for all this: "Because thou knewest not the time of thy visitation." God Himself had come to them in the Person of His Son, but they realized it not. Unsaved one, this is the time when God is visiting you, and if you refuse Him, some day you must stand before Him in judgment, because you knew not the day of your visitation.

"And He went into the temple, and began to cast out them that sold therein, and them that bought; saying unto them, It is written, My house is the house of prayer: but ye have made it a den of thieves." In that temple everything spoke of Him. He acted as Son over His own house (Heb. 3:6) in casting out those who sought to commercialize that which had been dedicated as a house of prayer for all nations. It was presumably for the accommodation of visitors from distant lands that the money-changers and vendors of doves, and so on, were first given places in the temple courts, but through covetousness they made merchandise of these things and so dishonored God.

From that time He taught the people in that temple until the time came when He was to be offered upon the cross. But the leaders sought how they might destroy Him; but they could not find what they might do, for all the people were very attentive to hear Him. Doubtless many in the crowds that heard His words were brought to trust in Him eventually, and we may be sure that numbers of them were among that great throng on the day of Pentecost when many accepted Him as Saviour and owned Him as their Lord.

ADDRESS SIXTY-SEVEN

THE PARABLE OF THE VINEYARD

"And it came to pass, that on one of those days, as He taught the people in the temple, and preached the gospel, the chief priests and the scribes came upon Him with the elders, and spake unto Him, saying, Tell us, by what authority doest Thou these things? or who is He that gave Thee this authority? And He answered and said unto them, I will also ask you one thing; and answer Me: The baptism of John, was it from heaven, or of men? And they reasoned with themselves, saying, If we shall say, From heaven; He will say, Why then believed ye him not? But and if we say, Of men; all the people will stone us: for they be persuaded that John was a prophet. And they answered, that they could not tell whence it was. And Jesus said unto them, Neither tell I you by what authority I do these things. Then began He to speak to the people this parable; A certain man planted a vineyard, and let it forth to husbandmen, and went into a far country for a long time. And at the season he sent a servant to the husbandmen, that they should give him of the fruit of the vineyard: but the husbandmen beat him, and sent him away empty. And again he sent another servant: and they beat him also, and entreated him shamefully, and sent him away empty. And again he sent a third: and they wounded him also, and cast him out. Then said the lord of the vineyard, What shall I do? I will send my beloved son: it may be they will reverence him when they see him. But when the husbandmen saw him, they reasoned among themselves, saying, This is the heir: come, let us kill him, that the inheritance may be our's. So they cast him out of the vineyard, and killed him. What therefore shall the lord of the vineyard do unto them? He shall come and destroy these husbandmen, and shall give the vineyard to others. And when they heard it, they said, God forbid. And He beheld them, and said, What is this then that is written, The stone which the builders rejected, the same is become the head of the corner? Whosoever shall fall upon that stone shall be broken; but on whomsoever it shall fall, it will grind him to powder"—Luke 20: 1-18.

THE rejection of Christ by the world is what fixes the Christian's place in this scene. He to whom the believer owes everything for eternity has been spurned, cast out, and crucified by those who represented the present world-order;

for both Jew and Gentile united in refusing to acknowledge as Lord Him whom the Father sent into the world. This comes out clearly in the parable of the vineyard and in what follows here and in the twenty-first chapter. The world was tested by the personal presence of the Son of God, who had come in grace, seeking man's blessing and telling out the love of the Father's heart. This is the One of whom men said, "We will not have this Man to reign over us." Rejected by men, He has gone up to the Father's right hand, where He waits expectantly until His enemies shall be made His footstool (ver. 43). Meantime the world continues unchanged in its opposition to its rightful King, as manifested by its hatred of those who now are called to represent Him in this scene. When the restraints of Christian light are withdrawn, its true character will be manifested, as we see in many lands today, both in Europe and Eastern Asia, where for many years the cause of Christ seemed to be in the ascendant, but where new persecution has broken out as violently as in any past period.

In the first eight verses we have the controversy between Jesus and the chief priests, scribes, and elders of Israel. These leaders of the people, who had from the very first rejected the testimony of Christ, were now gathered about Him as He taught the people in the temple: that is, the outer court of the temple, where teachers met with their disciples. They put the question to Jesus, "Tell us, by what authority doest Thou these things?" They referred to the cleansing of the temple which had taken place shortly before. They asked a second question: "Who is He that gave Thee this authority?" They resented the thought that a mere carpenter from that mean village of Nazareth should have dared to enter the precincts of the temple and undertake to cleanse it by driving out those who sold doves, lambs, etc., for sacrifices, and they challenged Him in this way. Jesus replied, "I will also ask you one thing; and answer Me: The baptism of John, was it from heaven, or of men?" What did that have to do with their question? Well, it had everything to do with it. Declaring he was sent to prepare the way of the Lord, John had pointed the people to Jesus as the Messiah of Israel. He said, "I knew Him not: but He that sent me to baptize with water, the same said unto me, Upon whom thou shalt see the Spirit descending, and remaining on Him, the same is He which baptizeth with the Holy Ghost." John had directed the people to Jesus, exclaiming, "Behold the Lamb of God, which taketh away the sin of the world." How blessedly John preached the gospel! I have heard it said that John the Baptist never knew the gospel, that all he preached was legal instruction, pressing upon the people the guilt of their sins and calling upon them to be baptized in order that their sins might be remitted. But the records as given in Holy Scripture will show that statement to be false. John never promised forgiveness of sins through baptism; he did not preach that baptism could cleanse men of their guilt. Those who came down to John to be baptized were not justified through baptism. In their baptism they acknowledged their sins and need of remission, and John bore witness to the Christ as the Son of God, the Lamb of God, through whom alone sins could be put away. John was the forerunner of Jesus, and he pointed men to our Lord as the Messiah and the Saviour. If these leaders accepted John as a prophet they would know who gave to Jesus the authority to enter into the temple and cleanse it, for it was written in the Old Testament, "The Lord, whom ye seek, shall suddenly come to His temple, even the Messenger of the covenant, whom ye delight in" (Mal. 3:1). When the Lord put this question to these self-righteous legalists, "They reasoned with themselves, saying, If ye shall say, From heaven; He will say, Why then believed ye him not? But and if we say, Of men; all the people will stone us: for they be persuaded that John was a prophet. And they answered, that they could not tell whence it was. And Jesus said unto them, Neither tell I you by authority I do these things." Notice that our Lord never attempted to make things clear to these hypocrites; He never attempted to explain divine mysteries to men who were not genuine. If people came to Him as serious inquirers, who were honest and really wanted help, He gave gladly what they needed; but as to these men who had rejected deliberately His testimony and had refused to accept Him, He did as He had commanded His disciples: "Neither cast ye your pearls before swine, lest they trample them under their feet, and turn again and rend you" (Matt. 7:6), He never sought to answer their cavils.

"Then began He to speak to the people this parable; A certain man planted a vineyard, and let it forth to husbandmen, and went into a far country for a long time." It is God Himself who is here set forth under the symbol of the Owner of the vineyard, which represents the people of Israel (Isa. 5:1-7). The husbandmen were their rulers, temporal and spiritual. "At the season he sent a servant to the husbandmen, that they should give him of the fruit of the vineyard: but the husbandmen beat him, and sent him away empty." So they had treated the prophets who were sent to Israel in the name of God to call the people back in heart to His law; yet they not only turned deaf ears to their entreaties, but also persecuted them for telling the truth (Matt. 6:12). "And again he sent another servant: and they beat him also, and entreated him shamefully, and sent him away empty." Other messengers were sent from time to time, only to be treated with contempt and contumely (Acts 7:52). All this revealed the actual state of the hearts of Israel's leaders.

"And again he sent a third: and they wounded him also, and cast him out." For long centuries one prophet followed another, seeking fruit for God, but it became more and more evident that there was no desire to glorify Him on the part of those who had been blessed so greatly. As we look back in the Old Testament records we find that this agrees perfectly with the history of the prophets. They had been misused, ill-treated, and their testimony refused; some of them were actually put to death, and others treated most insolently.

Last of all we find the Lord of the vineyard saying, "What shall I do? I will send my beloved son: it may be they will reverence him when they see him." What an insight this gives us into the heart of God! We can see Him, as it were, looking down upon Israel, conscious of all the sinfulness, the waywardness of the people, yet saying, "I am going to send My Son to them. Surely, they will not treat Him as they have treated the prophets." Of course God knew exactly what would take place, but this is what theologians call an "anthropomorphism"—God represented as speaking and acting on the human plane. In the fulness of time He sent forth His Son (Gal. 4: 4). He who was the delight of the Father's heart was sent into the world, to the lost sheep of the house of Israel (Matt. 15: 24), to reveal the love of the God of their fathers. The people of Israel had misused God's messengers; they had put many of the prophets to death; but at last He sent His Son. Would they accept Him and yield obedience to His word? Instead of that, we are told that "When the husbandmen saw him, they reasoned among themselves, saying, This is the heir: come, let us kill him, that the inheritance may be our's." This was sinful man's response to the love of the Father. Instead of reverencing the Son, they were determined to get rid of Him, and they refused to acknowledge His authority.

"They cast him out of the vineyard, and killed him." Our Lord here anticipates that which He knew was soon to take place. He showed His enemies that He foresaw all that they were about to do. His death was foreordained of God, but their part in rejecting Him was the expression of their own wicked hearts, as Peter told them later on (Acts 2:23). The picture is clear. Now what will be the next step? Jesus puts the question to His hearers: "What therefore shall the Lord of the vineyard do unto them?" What should be done with a people who had enjoyed such privileges but had spurned all of them? The answer comes: "He shall destroy these husbandmen, and shall give the vineyard to others." These words were fulfilled literally some forty years after the crucifixion of our Lord Jesus Christ, when God in His governmental dealing, permitted the Roman army to overrun the land of Palestine, encircle the city of Jerusalem and utterly destroy it. Israel has been a nation of wanderers ever since. Her day of opportunity, for the present at least, is over, and God has given His vineyard to other husbandmen; and the Gentiles are enjoying the blessing Israel might have had. Having forfeited all claim upon God because of their attitude toward Christ, Israel after the flesh must be set aside and the vineyard be given to those in a later day who will turn to God in repentance. It is not exactly the call of the Gentiles that is here set forth, but the regenerated Israel of the last days. Some day there will be a remnant of Israel who will be brought back, when they will once again be gathered in the land promised to them in the covenant with Abraham, Isaac, and Jacob. During this age they are cast out because of their rejection of their Messiah. The Lord Himself makes the declaration that God will destroy these wicked husbandmen and give the vineyard to others.

"What is this then that is written, The stone which the builders rejected, the same is become the head of the corner?" Jesus drew the attention of His hearers to that same 118th Psalm from which the children sang as He rode into Jerusalem, where, in verses 22 and 23, both His rejection and His triumph are prophesied. According to Jewish tradition, Psalm 118 was written about the time of the completion of Solomon's Temple and may even have been sung at its dedication. It is said that the passage Jesus quoted may have reference to something that occurred during the building of the temple. It will be remembered that Solomon was seven years in constructing this glorious sanctuary, and that he had many thousands of workmen, who labored six months at a time and then were superseded by others; consequently very few who were in the early relays were engaged upon the building when it was about to be completed. From the Book of Kings we learn that the stones for the temple were all hewn and cut to order in the quarry below before being sent up to the great platform on the top of Mount Moriah.

The Jews say that these stones were practically all the same size and shape, but that one stone was sent up which was so different from the rest that they were at loss to know what to do with it. It did not seem to fit anywhere. After consultation they decided a mistake had been made, and so they placed it upon rollers and pushed it over to the edge of Mount Moriah and tumbled it down into the vale below. "The stone which the builders rejected!" But as time went on and the temple was nearing completion, the day drew near for the placing of the chief cornerstone. There was nothing suitable on the platform. Word was sent down to the quarrymen to send up this cornerstone, as they were now ready for it, but the answer came back, "We sent it to you long ago; you must have it there upon the temple site." But a thorough search failed to reveal it. Then an old workman said: "I remember now; there was a stone sent up when we first began to build, but we saw no place for it, and we hurled it down into the abyss. Go down below, and you will find it." And so they sent a searching party and eventually discovered it almost covered with debris and overgrown with moss. They raised it with great effort to the platform above and found it fitted exactly into the place prepared for it. Thus the rejected stone became the head of the corner.

"Whosoever shall fall upon that stone shall be broken." Israel fell upon the stone, and they have been broken to pieces nationally and scattered among the nations (Isa. 8:14). "But on whomsoever it shall fall, it will grind him to powder." When He comes the second time the Lord will fall, like the stone in Daniel 2:34, 35, 45, upon the great nations of the Gentiles and break them in pieces, in order that the kingdoms of this world may become the kingdom of our Lord and His Christ (Rev. 11:15).

The Lord Jesus said, practically, "I am that Stone, for I have come to you, but you do not know that I am the Corner Stone of the spiritual temple that God is now about to build." So they rejected Him. They cast Him out, but God the Father raised Him from the dead and has made Him the head of the corner. "Jesus Christ Himself," we are told, "being the chief Corner Stone" (Eph. 2:20).

"And the chief priests and the scribes the same hour sought to lay hands on Him; and they feared the people: for they perceived that He had spoken this parable against them. And they watched Him, and sent forth spies, which should feign themselves just men, that they might take hold of His words. that so they might deliver Him unto the power and authority of the governor." Unable to answer Him, and having wilfully rejected Him, they stooped to the meanest and most contemptible methods in order to discredit Him before the people, and to find some occasion against Him in order that they might accuse Him before Pilate.

Men are not lost because they do not know better; they are lost because they sin against the light which God gives them. These men had abundance of light, but they spurned it. He who is Himself the Light of the world stood in their midst, but their eyes were blinded by unbelief and self-righteousness, and they knew Him not. Nothing brings out the corruption and incurable evil of the heart of sinful man like the presence of Jesus. His holiness emphasizes man's unholiness. His righteousness throws into bold relief man's unrighteousness. His love stirs up man's hatred. It is a sad commentary on fallen human nature that when God Himself came unto His own creation in the Person of the Incarnate Son, men, instead of being melted by His grace, were hardened by His goodness, and were never satisfied until they saw Him nailed to a felon's cross. God has declared, "As in water face answereth face, so the heart of man to man" (Prov. 27:19). It is only the grace of God working in the soul that leads anyone to trust Christ and to repent of rejecting Him in the past.

Address Sixty-eight

JESUS CONFOUNDS HIS QUESTIONERS

✝ ✝ ✝

"And they asked Him, saying, Master, we know that Thou sayest and teachest rightly, neither acceptest Thou the person of any, but teachest the way of God truly: Is it lawful for us to give tribute unto Caesar, or no? But He perceived their craftiness, and said unto them, Why tempt ye Me? Show Me a penny. Whose image and superscription hath it? They answered and said, Caesar's. And He said unto them, Render therefore unto Caesar the things which be Caesar's, and unto God the things which be God's. And they could not take hold of His words before the people: and they marvelled at His answer, and held their peace. Then came to Him certain of the Sadducees, which deny that there is any resurrection; and they asked Him, saying, Master, Moses wrote unto us, If any man's brother die, having a wife, and he die without children, that his brother should take his wife, and raise up seed unto his brother. There were therefore seven brethren: and the first took a wife, and died without children. And the second took her to wife, and he died childless. And the third took her; and in like manner the seven also: and they left no children, and died. Last of all the woman died also. Therefore in the resurrection whose wife of them is she? for seven had her to wife. And Jesus answering said unto them, The children of this world marry, and are given in marriage: but they which shall be accounted worthy to obtain that world, and the resurrection from the dead, neither marry, nor are given in marriage: neither can they die any more: for they are equal unto the angels; and are the children of God, being the children of the resurrection. Now that the dead are raised, even Moses showed at the bush, when he calleth the Lord the God of Abraham, and the God of Isaac, and the God of Jacob. For He is not a God of the dead, but of the living: for all live unto Him. Then certain of the scribes answering said, Master, Thou hast well said. And after that they durst not ask Him any question at all. And He said unto them, How say they that Christ is David's son? And David himself saith in the book of Psalms, The Lord said unto my Lord, Sit Thou on My right hand, till I make Thine enemies Thy footstool. David therefore calleth Him Lord, how is He then his son? Then in the audience of all the people He said unto His disciples, Beware of the scribes, which desire to walk in long robes, and love greetings in the markets, and the highest seats in the synagogues, and the chief rooms at feasts; which devour widow's houses, and for a show make long prayers: the same shall receive greater damnation"—Luke 20: 21-47.

IN this section we have our Lord Jesus Christ in controversy with His enemies. Two questions were raised by the leaders of the Jews; and one by the Lord Himself, and a very solemn warning added.

The first question had to do with the tribute money. We are told in verse 19, "And the chief priests and the scribes the same hour sought to lay hands on Him." They were watching Him. They sent men as spies, and they wanted to find some fault in Him for which they might arrest Him. This was the reason for their questions, which were put to Him by men who desired to entrap Him. In the first instance they endeavored to get Him to say something that would put Him in opposition to the Roman Government. They themselves hated that government, and they would have been delighted if it had been overthrown and the Jews liberated as a nation. But they took this opportunity to try to put the Lord Jesus in apparent opposition to the representatives of that government: "And they asked Him, saying, Master, we know that Thou sayest and teachest rightly, neither acceptest Thou the person of any, but teachest the way of God truly." This was mere flattery. If they believed what they said they would have given heed to His words. They approached Him in this way in order to get Him to commit Himself, "We know that Thou sayest and teachest rightly, neither acceptest Thou the person of any, but teachest the way of God truly." Then they put the question, "Is it lawful for us to give tribute unto Caesar, or no?" In other words, they were saying, "This is the land of Israel! We know God gave this land to Abraham, our father, and to us, his descendants. Have the Romans the right to bear authority over us and to collect tribute from us? Is it lawful for us to meet their demands and pay taxes, to give tribute to Caesar?" "But He perceived their craftiness, and said unto them, Why tempt ye Me? Show Me a penny. Whose image and superscription hath it? They answered and said, Caesar's." The word translated "penny" refers to a much more valuable coin than either our penny, or an English penny, which is worth twice as much as ours. The word is "denarius." A denarius was a little smaller than our twenty-five cent piece but had far more purchasing value in those days. "Show Me a denarius," and someone handed Him one. Did He have none Himself? Probably not. He deigned to become poorer than the poorest in order to enrich us. You remember on another occasion a denarius was needed to pay the temple tax; so He sent Peter down to the seaside and commanded him to cast in his line and bring up a fish. He told him when he had taken the fish and opened his mouth he would find a denarius. When Peter obeyed, by casting in his line he drew up the fish and found the denarius. Evidently somebody had lost that coin overboard, and this fish, seeing it sinking in the water, darted over and swallowed it, and it lodged in the gullet of the fish; and there it was ready to pay the Lord's tax when the time came. He seems to have been without a penny this time, and He said, "Show Me a penny," and they handed Him one. He looked it over and asked, "Whose image and superscription hath it?" Many of those ancient Roman denarii, with the likeness of one of the Emperors upon them, are found today in different collections in our great museums. "They answered and said, Caesar's." He said, "Render therefore unto Caesar the things which be Caesar's, and unto God the things which be God's." They were willing to use Caesar's money; they were ready to profit thereby. Then they should pay such taxes to Caesar as he demanded. They were to recognize that "the powers that be are ordained of God."

The principle which the Lord set forth applies today. We as Christians know that it is God who puts up one ruler and puts down another; it is He who permits any particular government to exist. We are therefore to pay taxes as commanded by the rulers of the land in which we live. We are also to remember that we are heavenly citizens, that we are linked up with the God of heaven. We are to render unto Caesar the things that belong to Caesar, and we are to render unto God the things that belong to Him. Jesus knew well that these scribes were trying to get Him to commit Himself so that they might accuse Him, but His words silenced them. "They could not take hold of His words before the people: and they marvelled at His answer, and held their peace."

Having been silenced on this point they next came to Him with a doctrinal question: "Then came to Him certain of the Sadducees which deny that there is any resurrection." There were at this time several different sects among the Jews; two of them are specifically mentioned in Scripture, the Pharisees and the Sadducees. The Pharisees were the most orthodox party in Israel. The Sadducees did not believe in angels or spirits, or in the resurrection of the body. The Pharisees confessed all these things. And so there was constant strife between them because of their different doctrinal positions. It was a group of these Sadducees who put to the Lord what they thought was a very perplexing question. "They asked Him, saying, Master, Moses wrote unto us, If any man's brother die, having a wife, and he die without children, that his brother should take his wife, and raise up seed unto his brother." That was according to the law of Moses. If an Israelite married and he was taken away by death and left no children to inherit his estate, his brother, if free to do so, was responsible to marry the widow. If children were born as the result of that marriage, the first child would inherit the estate of the deceased husband as though the child were his own. The Sadducees supposed a case where seven brothers were married in turn to one woman and all died childless. Probably the whole story was fabricated in order to enable them to show, as they thought, the absurdity of a physical resurrection. So they put the question, "Therefore in the resurrection whose wife of them is she? for seven had her to wife." The Lord Jesus was not perplexed; He was not troubled about that. He turned to them and said, "Ye do err, not knowing the Scriptures, nor the power of God" (Matt. 22: 29). How often we err because we do not know the Scriptures and ignore the power of God! If we knew our Bibles better we would have fewer questions to ask. And if we recognized the power of God more definitely we would not be as confused as we often are. The Sadducees did not know the Scriptures, nor did they realize God's omnipotence. Jesus added, "The children of this world marry, and are given in marriage, but they which shall be accounted worthy to obtain that world, and the resurrection from the dead, neither marry, nor are given in marriage: neither can they die any more: for they are equal unto the angels; and are the children of God, being the children of the resurrection." When our Lord became Man He was made "a little lower than the angels." Man under the present order is lower than the angels which are greater in power and might; but in the resurrection the redeemed will be equal unto the angels. We will no longer be inferior to them, because we will be the children of God in a manifest sense, even the children of the resurrection. All this the Sadducees denied. The Lord continued to answer by saying, "Now that the dead are raised, even Moses showed at the bush when he calleth the Lord the God of Abraham, and the God of Isaac, and the God of Jacob. For He is not a God of the dead, but of the living: for all live unto Him." But where is there anything in that about resurrection? Well, Abraham, Isaac, and Jacob were not blotted out of existence; they had not become extinct through death; they are still living. God did not say to Moses that He was the God of Abraham, of Isaac, of Jacob when they were here in the world. He said, "*I am* the God of Abraham, Isaac, and Jacob." Jesus explained this clearly. So our dear ones in Christ who have left us are not utterly unconscious: they are living unto God; He knows them well and they know Him, and they have blessed fellowship with Him. It is necessary that there be a resurrection for Abraham, Isaac, and Jacob, because God had made a promise to them which had not been fulfilled. He promised to give them the land of Canaan that they might possess it to the end of the time, and they never possessed it while on earth. They dwelt in the land as strangers, but the promise will be fulfilled when God brings them back from the dead. Thus the Lord silenced these Sadducees. "Then certain of the scribes answering said, Master, Thou hast well said. And after that they durst not ask Him any questions at all."

He then put a question to them; one which they found it impossible to answer unless they were willing to bow before Him and accept Him as their Messiah and Saviour. "He said unto them, How say they that Christ is David's Son?" Why did the scribes say the Messiah is David's Son? Scripture says that in many places. In the 110th Psalm (ver. 1) we read, "The Lord said unto my Lord, sit Thou at My right hand, until I make Thine enemies Thy footstool." Now that passage admittedly referred to the Messiah, the coming Redeemer. David wrote it, and David there calls the Messiah his Lord. He says, "Jehovah said unto my Lord." "David therefore calleth Him Lord, how is He then his Son?" If they had been able to answer that question intelligently, the whole truth of His Messiahship would have been settled. The answer is this: He is David's Lord because He is the eternal God; He is David's Son because He became Man, and He chose to come into this world as born of a daughter of David's line, the blessed Virgin Mary. He is therefore both David's Son and David's Lord.

"Then in the audience of all the people He said unto His disciples, Beware of the scribes, which desire to walk in long robes, and love greetings in the markets, and the highest seats in the synagogues, and the chief rooms at feasts." They took their places as the religious leaders of the people. The Lord knew that many of them were downright hypocrites: they devoured widows' houses, and for a show they made long prayers. Many of them were money-lenders, who would take mortgages on the homes of widows at exorbitant interest, so that the poor women would have great difficulty in keeping up their payments; and then when they got in arrears these hypocrites would foreclose the mortgages and take everything from the helpless widows. Was not that legal? Yes; it was legal according to man's laws. But many things were legal according to man's law which were absolutely illegal according to the law of God, who had forbidden the very practices of which these hypocrites were guilty. Imagine one of these extortioners foreclosing on a widow's home on Friday night, and on the Sabbath standing up in the synagogue and making a long prayer! It may well speak to us today. God give us to be consistent, that our lives may answer to our profession, that we may be real in public and in private, as real before God in our business as in the affairs of the Church of God. The Lord said, "The same shall receive greater damnation." The day is coming when the Lord will deal with all hypocrites. Such hypocrites are found among those who profess Christianity, and many make this an excuse for rejecting Christ. But it does not alter the fact that if you are not saved at last you will have to answer for your own sins in the day of judgment. How much better to get right with God now than to wait until that day when He will judge every man according to his works!

ADDRESS SIXTY-NINE

OUR LORD'S GREAT PROPHETIC DISCOURSE

"And He looked up, and saw the rich men casting their gifts into the treasury. And He saw also a certain poor widow casting in thither two mites. And He said, Of a truth I say unto you, that this poor widow hath cast in more than they all: for all these have of their abundance cast in unto the offerings of God: but she of her penury hath cast in all the living that she had. And as some spake of the temple, how it was adorned with goodly stones and gifts, He said, As for these things which ye behold, the days will come, in the which there shall not be left one stone upon another, that shall not be thrown down. And they asked Him, saying, Master, but when shall these things be? and what sign will there be when these things shall come to pass? And He said, Take heed that ye be not deceived: for many shall come in My name, saying, I am Christ; and the time draweth near: go ye not therefore after them. But when ye shall hear of wars and commotions, be not terrified: for these things must first come to pass; but the end is not by and by. Then said He unto them, Nation shall rise against nation, and kingdom against kingdom: and great earthquakes shall be in divers places, and famines, and pestilences; and fearful sights and great signs shall there be from heaven. But before all these, they shall lay their hands on you, and persecute you, delivering you up to the synagogues, and into prisons, being brought before kings and rulers for My name's sake. And it shall turn to you for a testimony. Settle it therefore in your hearts, not to meditate before what ye shall answer: for I will give you a mouth and wisdom, which all your adversaries shall not be able to gainsay nor resist. And ye shall be betrayed both by parents, and brethren, and kinsfolks, and friends; and some of you shall they cause to be put to death. And ye shall be hated of all men for My name's sake. But there shall not an hair of your head perish. In your patience possess ye your souls. And when ye shall see Jerusalem compassed with armies, then know that the desolation thereof is nigh. Then let them which are in Judaea flee to the mountains; and let them which are in the midst of it depart out; and let not them that are in the countries enter thereinto. For these be the days of vengeance, that all things which are written may be fulfilled. But woe unto them that are with child, and to them that give suck, in those days! for there shall be great distress in the land, and wrath upon this people. And they shall fall by the edge of the sword, and shall be led away captive into all nations: and Jerusalem shall be trodden down of the Gentiles, until the times of the Gentiles be fulfilled" —Luke 21: 1-24.

"AND He looked up, and saw the rich men casting their gifts into the treasury. And He saw also a certain poor widow casting in thither two mites." There are two important things which we learn from a consideration of this incident. The first is that our blessed Lord is deeply interested in what we give to God. Sometimes there is a tendency, even on the part of Christians, to belittle the importance of giving; and there is a repugnance to taking up offerings in Christian services, as though it savors too much of worldly commercialism. But we need to remember that all through the history of God's dealings with His people, He has looked to them to give of their substance for the carrying on of His work. It is a recognition of our discipleship if we bring our offerings to Him from time to time. It was so in Israel of old; it has been so all through the centuries. Our Lord was sitting over against the treasury, taking note of what the people contributed. He is still observant of what His people give to Him; He knows whether or not it is out of love to Him that we give; He knows whether or not those who give do so sacrificially and with real self-denial.

In the second place, we learn from this passage that heaven's arithmetic—heaven's method of bookkeeping—is altogether different from ours. We generally judge people by the amount of money they give. If a rich man gives a large sum we say he has given much; but if one brings in little we may pay scant attention to it. God's way of reckoning is quite otherwise. He takes note, not so much of the amount given, as of what is left. A rich man might give thousands and have hundreds of thousands left; another person, in lowly circumstances, might give a very small amount, but because he had very little left for himself it would go down as a large contribution. The Lord Jesus saw the poor widow casting in two mites, a very small sum. Two mites, we are told, amount to a farthing, a very infinitesimal coin, even of less value than a British farthing. Yet Jesus said, "Of truth I say unto you, that this poor widow hath cast in more than they all: for all these have of their abundance cast in unto the offerings of God: but she of her penury hath cast in all the living that she had." I take it that was her whole day's pay. She worked all day and this was all she had for it, and she put it all into the treasury of the Lord. No one giving thus to God ever suffers because of it. God will reimburse him in His own way and time. He will be no one's debtor; He will make it up in some way for whatever we give to Him.

We must next turn to consider Luke's account of our Lord's great prophetic discourse: "And as some spake of the temple, how it was adorned with goodly stones and gifts." At that time Jerusalem was a great city, as cities were in the Orient. It was surrounded by a strong wall. Its large buildings were beautiful, particularly the glorious temple on which Herod had spent millions of dollars in his endeavor to make it as grand as the temple of Solomon before that was destroyed by Nebuchadnezzar's army. Naturally, the Jews were very proud of the temple and the other buildings; and the apostles evidenced the same spirit as they turned to Jesus and sought to impress Him with their architectural magnificence. But He saw it all with prophetic eyes in a way they could not see. He saw what was going to happen to these buildings. He declared, "As for these things which ye behold, the days will come, in the which there shall not be left one stone upon another, that shall not be thrown down." It must have appeared most unlikely that such words would ever be fulfilled. Yet within the next forty years the great temple and all the other buildings of the city were leveled to the ground. Every prophecy of Scripture either has been or will be fulfilled literally as written or spoken. When the Lord Jesus told His disciples of these things to come they were amazed, and they asked Him, saying, "Master, but when shall these things be? and what sign will there be when these things shall come to pass?" In order to get His complete answer we need to read the report of this entire discourse as given in the three Synoptic Gospels: Matthew 24, Mark 13, and here in Luke 21. Luke gives an account of the circumstances which should take place before and leading up to the destruction of Jerusalem; Matthew deals particularly with what was to take place afterward, leading on to the second coming of Christ. Luke tells us something of that, but does not give us nearly as full and complete a report as Matthew does. Mark's account is very much like that of Matthew's, though not quite so full. In the threefold report of these words from the lips of the Lord, we have a remarkable prophecy of the things that will take place after His death, resurrection, and ascension to heaven. The destruction of Jerusalem, the state of the world during all the present age, and the conditions that will prevail in the time of the end—the last unfulfilled seventieth week of Daniel (chapter 9)—and the second advent in glory, are all graphically portrayed. There is nothing here about the Church, the Body of Christ, or the rapture. These were truths yet to be revealed.

"And He said, Take heed that ye be not deceived: for many shall come in My name, saying, I am Christ; and the time draweth near: go ye not therefore after them." History tells us that there were many deceivers who rose up in Israel, making Messianic claims, during the forty years that elapsed after the cross. The true Messiah had been rejected. The greater part of Jerusalem refused to believe that Jesus was the promised One, and so they fell readily under the influence of these false prophets. Jesus gave a general description of conditions that would prevail in the world before Jerusalem met its doom. "But when ye shall hear of wars and commotions, be not terrified: for these things must first come to pass; but the end is not by and by." "By and by" is one word in the Greek original, translated into three words, and is generally rendered "immediately" or "forthwith." So what our Lord was saying is this: "There will be wars and rumors of wars, but you are not to be disturbed, because these things must happen and will happen, but the end is not yet." It is clear from a careful study of Matthew's report that such conditions will prevail until Christ comes back. But He never gives us these things as definite signs of the coming of the end; they are simply the natural result of the rejection of the Prince of Peace.

The better acquainted with history we become, the more we realize how literally fulfilled were the words of our Lord during that forty-year period. Then He said, "Before all these, they shall lay their hands on you, and persecute you, delivering you up to the synagogues, and into prisons, being brought before kings and rulers for My name's sake." We need only to read the Book of Acts to see how this prophecy had its fulfilment in connection with the early disciples of our Lord Jesus Christ. They were persecuted by the Jews in the synagogues and also by the Gentiles; many were put to death for His name's sake. The Lord encouraged the disciples by assuring them that they did not need to fear: their foes could not really harm them. At the worst they could but send the disciples home to the Father's house. Death is not evil for a child of God. They need not fear their adversaries. "Settle it therefore in your hearts, not to meditate before what ye shall answer: for I will give you a mouth and wisdom, which all your adversaries shall not be able to gainsay nor resist." Again we need but to turn to the Book of Acts and read how marvelously Peter, Stephen, and Paul were enabled to make their defence. We realize that the Lord Jesus did give them help by enabling them to speak just the right words at the right time under all circumstances. "And ye shall be betrayed both by parents, and brethren, and kinsfolks, and friends; and some of you shall they cause to be put to death. And ye shall be hated of all men for My name's sake." In those days people looked with more suspicion upon the Christian Church and individual Christians than upon any other institution or group of people in the world. Believers were thought of as the bitterest enemies of mankind, and yet they were the representatives of the God who so loved men that He gave His only Son to be their Saviour. "But there shall not an hair of your head perish." Did they not die? Yes. Did they not perish? No! For the moment that death came they were absent from the body and present with the Lord. So they lost nothing by being killed by their enemies; rather, death ushered them into the joys for which they had waited in hope. "In your patience possess ye your souls." Or it might be stated, "In patience win your souls": that is, in enduring persecution, in going through suffering for Christ's sake they would become stronger disciples. Growth in grace comes in times of persecution and severe trial.

Next He came directly to the question as to when these things should be of which He had spoken. When would Jerusalem be destroyed and its buildings cast down? These events occurred about A.D. 70. He foresaw all this and said, "When ye shall see Jerusalem compassed about with armies, then know that the desolation thereof is nigh." Many who were living when He spoke these words would see the armies of Titus beleaguering the city. Jesus gave instruction to them: "Then let them which are in Judaea flee to the mountains; and let them which are in the midst of it depart out; and let not them that are in the countries enter thereinto." Josephus is the authority for the statement that when the Christians saw Jerusalem compassed with armies they remembered the words of the Lord, and they left Jerusalem and fled to the city of Pella, where they were protected by the Roman Government, so that they did not have to endure the judgment that came upon Jerusalem and its guilty people who "knew not the time of their visitation."

"For these be days of vengeance, that all things which are written may be fulfilled. But woe unto them that are with child, and to them that give suck, in those days! for there shall be great distress in the land, and wrath upon this people. And they shall fall by the edge of the sword, and shall be led away captive into all nations: and Jerusalem shall be trodden down of the Gentiles, until the times of the Gentiles be fulfilled." See how clearly our blessed Lord looked down through the centuries and observed what would take place in connection with Israel, God's earthly people, and their city, Jerusalem. The city was destroyed. Thousands upon thousands were slaughtered; the most awful condition imaginable prevailed in Jerusalem during the time of the Roman siege. And when at last the armies of Titus entered the city—although he, himself, gave the command that the temple was not to be destroyed—we are told by Josephus that a drunken soldier flung a lighted torch into the temple area and within a little while the temple burst into flames, and it was destroyed completely. Today where that temple once stood there is a mosque; where the smoke of sacrifice once ascended to Jehohah, Mohammedans meet to join in the praise of their false prophet.

Those of the Jews who were not destroyed were led away captives into all nations. Moses long before had predicted that they should be sold into slavery to the Gentiles, until "no man shall buy you" (Deut. 28: 68); and history tells us that many thousands of Jews were thus sold. The slave-markets of the world were glutted; and strong able-bodied Jewish men were offered for sale in the great cities of the Roman Empire, in Alexandria, Corinth, Rome itself, and other cities, at prices so low that it was almost impossible to make a profit on them.

Jesus declared, "Jerusalem shall be trodden down of the Gentiles, until the times of the Gentiles be fulfilled." Notice, there is a limit to Jerusalem's degradation. The city shall not be trodden down forever; but just until the times of the Gentiles be completed. The expression "the times of the Gentiles," found only here, covers the entire period during which the Jews—Jerusalem and the land of Palestine—are under Gentile domination. This began with Nebuchadnezzar, about 606 B.C. It will go on until the Lord Jesus comes again to deliver His earthly election, at the close of the great tribulation. Meantime, the truth of the Church as the Body of Christ has been revealed; and while Israel is rejected nationally and their holy city dominated by the Gentiles, God is taking out from Jew and Gentile a people for His name. These constitute the Church of God, the fellowship of His Son, and must be removed from the earth ere the time of Jacob's trouble, the great tribulation, begins.

ADDRESS SEVENTY

THE BUDDING FIG-TREE

"And there shall be signs in the sun, and in the moon, and in the stars; and upon the earth distress of nations, with perplexity; the sea and the waves roaring; men's hearts failing them for fear, and for looking after those things which are coming on the earth: for the powers of heaven shall be shaken. And then shall they see the Son of Man coming in a cloud with power and great glory. And when these things begin to come to pass, then look up, and lift up your heads; for your redemption draweth nigh. And He spake to them a parable; Behold the fig tree, and all the trees; when they now shoot forth, ye see and know of your own selves that summer is now nigh at hand. So likewise ye, when ye see these things come to pass, know ye that the kingdom of God is nigh at hand. Verily I say unto you, This generation shall not pass away, till all be fulfilled. Heaven and earth shall pass away: but my words shall not pass away. And take heed to yourselves, lest at any time your hearts be overcharged with surfeiting, and drunkenness, and cares of this life, and so that day come upon you unawares. For as a snare shall it come on all them that dwell on the face of the whole earth. Watch ye therefore, and pray always, that ye may be accounted worthy to escape all these things that shall come to pass, and to stand before the Son of Man. And in the day time He was teaching in the temple; and at night He went out, and abode in the mount that is called the mount of Olives. And all the people came early in the morning to Him in the temple, for to hear Him"—Luke 21: 25-38.

THIS is the second part of our Lord's great prophetic discourse given to His disciples during His last week with them before His crucifixion. The first part of this prophecy carried us down to the destruction of Jerusalem. The Lord had told His disciples, as they were admiring the marvelous temple and other buildings in Jerusalem, "As for these things which ye behold, the days will come, in the which there shall not be left one stone upon another, that shall not be thrown down." He depicted conditions that would lead up to this, concluding with the declaration, "And when ye shall see Jerusalem compassed with armies, then know that the desolation thereof is nigh." Everything up to this point was fulfilled literally, and Jerusalem was destroyed in A.D. 70, as He predicted. But He put a limit on its being trodden down. He said, "Jerusalem shall be trodden down of the Gentiles," (not forever; not so long as the world lasts, but) "until the times of the Gentiles be fulfilled." We have seen that the expression "times of the Gentiles refers to the entire period during which the Jews are under Gentile dominion. Ever since Nebuchadnezzar's day this has been their condition. So the times of the Gentiles have continued considerably over two thousand years. Just when it will come to an end we dare not attempt to say. Many have tried to work out some kind of time system, but so far all these have failed. But we can be very sure that we are rapidly drawing near the end of the Gentile times.

A glorious event is going to take place for us before the end comes, of which the Lord said nothing in this great prophetic discourse, but which later He mentioned to His disciples as they were gathered together that evening in the upper room. He said, "I go to prepare a place for you. And if I go and prepare a place for you, I will come again, and receive you unto Myself." In the Epistles of Paul we find details unfolded concerning that event. Before the times of the Gentiles come to an end the Lord Jesus is coming in the air to take His heavenly people out of this scene. "The dead in Christ shall rise first: then we which are alive and remain shall be caught up together with them in the clouds, to meet the Lord in the air: and so shall we ever be with the Lord" (1 Thess. 4:16, 17). Now our Lord does not mention this here. The time had not come to reveal it. But He went on to explain what will take place when the times of the Gentiles shall be fulfilled. First He spoke of astronomical signs, "And there shall be signs in the sun, and in the moon, and in the stars." Now these signs have not begun to take place so far as we know; but we can be certain of this, that the people who will be living on the earth at the time these things begin to have their fulfilment will see these great signs in connection with the heavenly bodies. Jesus next spoke of conditions that will prevail on the earth, "And upon the earth, distress of nations, with perplexity; the sea and the waves roaring." In a limited sense we may say that these conditions are manifest now, "distress of nations, with perplexity." It has often been pointed out that this word "perplexity" means literally, "no way out": "Distress of nations and no way out." This is most significant. At this very time our statesmen and the rulers of the various countries are endeavoring to form a league to bring about a warless world and assure continued prosperity. But it is evident that they are at their wits' end as they face apparently insurmountable difficulties. We may be sure of this: conditions will not improve, and wars will continue until the Lord Jesus Christ comes in glory.

Jesus also mentions great natural convulsions. Elsewhere we read that not only will the earth be shaken but also heaven, "that those things which cannot be shaken may remain" (Heb. 12:27). So we may be sure, in the light of the prophetic Word, that this poor world is doomed so far as man's ability to help is concerned. When things are at their worst God will intervene. "And then shall they see the Son of Man coming in a cloud with power and great glory." He will take over the reins of government and set up the kingdom of God on the ruins of all earth's vaunted dominions. He says, "When these things begin to come to pass, then look up, and lift up your heads; for your redemption draweth nigh."

Surely His words can mean nothing else than the visible second advent of the Lord Jesus Christ. In the Book of Revelation (1:7) we read, "Behold, He cometh with clouds; and every eye shall see Him, and they also which pierced Him: and all kindreds of the earth shall wail because of Him." There are people who profess to accept the Bible and yet tell us that they do not believe in the literal second coming of Christ. They insist that all this will have only a spiritual fulfilment. But I remind you again that every prophecy having to do with the first coming of our Lord was fulfilled literally, and therefore we have every reason to believe that all the prophecies having to do with His second coming will be fulfilled just as literally. He is coming back in person to this earth, and the world that rejected Him will bow before Him, recognizing

His absolute authority. He tells them very definitely when these things will take place: at the end of the times of the Gentiles. The believers in the Lord Jesus Christ need not be in distress because of present world conditions. We know that God works everything according to the counsel of His own will, and we can trust Him and not be afraid. As these signs begin to come to pass they serve to tell us that the coming of the King draweth nigh, and so our hearts are encouraged as we look up and wait for our blessed Lord's return.

"And He spake to them a parable; Behold the fig tree, and all the trees." The fig tree as used in Scripture is a symbol of the nation of Israel. In the Book of Judges (in the parable of Jotham), there are four trees mentioned. These are the olive, the fig-tree, the vine, and the bramble. Now all these different trees are really types or symbols of Israel. The olive-tree speaks of Israel in covenant relationship with God: Abraham is the root, and the branches represent those who are his descendants after the flesh and after the Spirit. During the present time the national branches have been broken off from their own olive-tree because of unbelief, and Gentile wild branches have been grafted in. Some years ago I noticed an objection to this illustration. A learned doctor of divinity insisted that Paul was very ignorant of the first principles of horticulture, or he never would have spoken of grafting wild branches into a good olive-tree. He pointed out that the very opposite is what is done. Therefore it is folly to think that this was written by inspiration. God would not use such an absurd illustration as this to teach spiritual or dispensational truths. But if that good man had read his Bible a little more carefully he would have found that Paul said his illustration about grafting in the Gentiles was "contrary to nature." The apostle knew he was using an illustration which was contrary to nature, and he tells us so. But that is the way grace works. Grace is ever contrary to nature. When the end of this age comes the natural branches will be grafted in again, and Israel will enter into the new covenant blessing.

So the olive-tree speaks of God's covenant people. The fig-tree speaks of Israel, as a nation, set by God in Palestine to glorify Him. The vine speaks spiritually of Israel. God brought forth a vine out of Egypt and planted a vineyard, Jehovah's witnesses in the earth, and "He looked that it should bring forth grapes, and it brought forth wild grapes" (Isa. 5:2). Because of this, Israel has for a time been set aside. Jesus said, "I am the true Vine, My Father is the Husbandman" (John 15:1). He speaks of those who profess faith in Him as the branches of the Vine, who are to bring forth fruit unto God. But the day is coming, as we have seen, when the Church of God will be caught up, and a remnant of Israel will be left in the world to witness for God. The other symbol is the bramble. This speaks of Israel away from God, a curse instead of a blessing to the world. It was the Lord's intention that Israel should be a blessing to all nations, but because they turned away from God they became a curse instead of a blessing among the Gentiles. Some day that will be changed, and Israel will become a means of blessing to the whole world.

The symbol to which Jesus refers here is the fig-tree. For centuries Israel has been without national consciousness. At the end of the age the fig-tree will begin to bloom again. Israel will be brought back into her land and into relationship with God. There will be a new Israel, a regenerated people, who will lead all the nations in devotion to the Lord Jesus Christ. Already the fig-tree is beginning to bud. The day of deliverance is near. "When they now shoot forth, ye see and know of your own selves that summer is now nigh at hand. So likewise ye, when ye see these things come to pass, know ye that the kingdom of God is nigh at hand." It is as though He said, "Watch Israel, and watch the movements among the other nations." "All the trees" refers, undoubtedly, to the Gentile nations in the prophetic vision. As we see these conditions developing and note what is taking place among the nations, we can see the great combinations forming that will have a place in the final conflict ere the return of our Lord Jesus Christ. Israel will come again into a special place before God. Already they are beginning to think of themselves as a nation, not simply a scattered people; and many of them are turning to the Lord. The close of this age is drawing near. The end of the times of the Gentiles will soon come. One evidence of changing sentiment among the Jews is that many of their leaders now insist that the Gentiles are indebted particularly to them because of the teachings of Jesus Christ of Nazareth, who was one of their greatest Rabbis! They acknowledge that their fathers did not understand Him and made a great mistake in rejecting Him. But the sad thing is that they think of Him only as a great teacher instead of God manifested in flesh. Nevertheless, the eyes of many are being opened to Christ, their promised Messiah, the Son of God; and there have been more definite conversions in the last quarter of a century than during many centuries before. "So likewise ye, when ye see these things come to pass, know ye that the kingdom of God is nigh at hand." That kingdom has been making its way into the hearts of men ever since our Lord ascended into heaven and the Holy Spirit came down. He will soon be manifest openly.

"Verily I say unto you, This generation shall not pass away, till all be fulfilled." There has been a great deal of argument as to the exact meaning of these words. In my judgment, the Lord is simply saying that the race of Israel will not pass away until all these things have been fulfilled. God will preserve Israel in the world, though sadly enough the great majority will remain in their unbelief until these things begin to come to pass.

"And take heed to yourselves, lest at any time your hearts be overcharged with surfeiting, and drunkenness, and cares of this life, and so that day come upon you unawares. For as a snare shall it come on all them that dwell on the face of the whole earth." As the Lord warns His disciples so we may take the words to our hearts, even though we are waiting for the coming of our Lord Jesus Christ to gather us together unto Himself. We need to be careful lest we become so occupied with the things of this scene, with making a living and getting on in the world, that we fail to put Christ first in our lives and to live day by day as those who are waiting for His return. "Watch ye therefore, and pray always, that ye may be accounted worthy to escape all these things that shall come to pass, and to stand before the Son of Man." These words have a particular application to those who will be living on the earth in the days of the great tribulation. The coming of the Son of Man is the consummation, and is always distinguished from the coming of the Lord to receive His saints into the air.

The chapter concludes by telling us that during the last week He was on earth, "in the day time He was teaching in the temple; and at night He went out, and abode in the mount that is called the mount of Olives." Whether this refers to Bethany which is on the eastern slope of the Mount of Olives, or whether it means He lay in the open, we are not told; but at any rate, He left the city, where He was an outcast as far as Jerusalem and all its religion was concerned, but early in the morning many people came to Him in the temple to hear Him.

Address Seventy-one

THE LAST PASSOVER AND THE INSTITUTION OF THE LORD'S SUPPER

✝ ✝ ✝

"Now the feast of unleavened bread drew nigh, which is called the Passover. And the chief priests and scribes sought how they might kill Him; for they feared the people. Then entered Satan into Judas surnamed Iscariot, being of the number of the twelve. And he went his way, and communed with the chief priests and captains, how he might betray Him unto them. And they were glad, and covenanted to give him money. And he promised, and sought oportunity to betray Him unto them in the absence of the multitude. Then came the day of unleavened bread, when the passover must be killed. And He sent Peter and John, saying, Go and prepare us the passover, that we may eat. And they said unto Him, Where wilt Thou that we prepare? And He said unto them, Behold, when ye are entered into the city, there shall a man meet you, bearing a pitcher of water; follow him into the house where he entereth in. And ye shall say unto the goodman of the house, The Master saith unto thee, Where is the guestchamber, where I shall eat the passover with My disciples? And he shall show you a large upper room furnished: there make ready. And they went, and found as He had said unto them: and they made ready the passover. And when the hour was come, He sat down, and the twelve apostles with Him. And He said unto them, With desire I have desired to eat this passover with you before I suffer: for I say unto you, I will not any more eat thereof, until it be fulfilled in the kingdom of God. And He took the cup, and gave thanks, and said, Take this, and divide it among yourselves: for I say unto you, I will not drink of the fruit of the vine, until the kingdom of God shall come. And He took bread, and gave thanks, and brake it, and gave unto them, saying, This is My body which is given for you: this do in remembrance of Me. Likewise also the cup after supper, saying, This cup is the new testament in My blood, which is shed for you. But, behold, the hand of him that betrayeth Me is with Me on the table. And truly the Son of Man goeth, as it was determined: but woe unto that man by whom He is betrayed! And they began to enquire among themselves, which of them it was that should do this thing. And there was also a strife among them, which of them should be accounted the greatest. And He said unto them, The kings of the Gentiles exercise lordship over them: and they that exercise authority upon them are called benefactors. But ye shall not be so: but he that is greatest among you, let him be as the younger; and he that is chief, as he that doth serve. For whether is greater, he that sitteth at meat, or he that serveth? is not he that sitteth at meat? but I am among you as He that serveth. Ye are they which have continued with Me in My temptations. And I appoint unto you a kingdom, as My Father hath appointed unto Me; that ye may eat and drink at My table in My kingdom, and sit on thrones judging the twelve tribes of Israel. And the Lord said, Simon, Simon, behold, Satan hath desired to have you, that he may sift you as wheat: but I have prayed for thee, that thy faith fail not: and when thou art converted, strengthen thy brethren. And he said unto Him, Lord, I am ready to go with Thee, both into prison, and to death. And He said, I tell thee, Peter, the cock shall not crow this day, before that thou shalt thrice deny that thou knowest Me. And He said unto them, When I sent you without purse, and scrip, and shoes, lacked ye any thing? And they said, Nothing. Then said He unto them, But now, he that hath a purse, let him take it, and likewise his scrip: and he that hath no sword, let him sell his garment, and buy one. For I say unto you, that this that is written must yet be accomplished in Me, And He was reckoned among the transgressors: for the things concerning Me have an end. And they said, Lord, behold, here are two swords. And He said unto them, It is enough"—Luke 22: 1-38.

ʼ ʼ ʼ

WE now look at this lengthy section which deals with five distinct events: first, the treachery of Judas; second, the preparation and observance of the passover; third, the Lord's Supper instituted; fourth, the place which His disciples will occupy in the future kingdom; and last, the Lord's warning to Peter.

The Passover Lamb was slain on the night the children of Israel were delivered out of Egypt. For the Jews the passover was a memorial of that event, but it was also a type of something that was yet to take place. The day had now come when this was about to be fulfilled. In 1 Cor. 5: 7, 8 we read, "Purge out therefore the old leaven, that ye may be a new lump, as ye are unleavened. For even Christ our Passover is sacrificed for us. Therefore let us keep the feast, not with old leaven, neither with the leaven of malice and wickedness; but with the unleavened bread of sincerity and truth." In the Bible leaven is always a symbol of evil, as we have seen. So we are called upon to put away from our lives everything unclean, everything contrary to the Spirit of Christ.

For centuries Israel had kept this feast. Now the Lord Jesus Christ, the real Paschal Lamb, was in their midst and most of the people were utterly unaware of His presence. While He was preparing to keep the feast, the chief priests and scribes were conferring together how they might kill Him, little realizing that He was the antitypical Passover Lamb. "Then entered Satan into Judas surnamed Iscariot, being of the number of the twelve." He was doing only what God had foreseen should be done. The perfidy of Judas was prophesied centuries before it became a reality. The leaders were plotting to kill Jesus, and Satan took possession of one of His disciples, who offered to betray Him for money. Think of Judas, companying with the Lord and the other disciples for three-and-one-half wonderful years, now communing with the chief priests and captains how he might deliver Him into their hands! There are many today who associate with Christians and take active part in religious services but have never known Christ themselves. Such was Judas. So when the time came Satan found in him a ready instrument to carry out his will. "And he went his way, and communed with the chief priests and captains, how he might betray Him unto them." It would seem almost unbelievable were it not for the fact that the same kind of conduct has been repeated many times since. "And they were glad, and covenanted to give him money. And he promised, and sought opportunity to betray Him unto them in the absence of the multitude." Judas imagined that no other eye saw nor ear heard as he plotted with the chief priests; but Jesus, God manifest in Him, knew all about the transaction, as He later revealed.

Then the day came when the passover was to be killed. This involves a perplexing question for some people. We need to remember that the Jews' day began at sunset, and it was after sunset on the fourteenth of Nisan that the Lord kept the passover with His disciples. Before the next sunset, that is, in the afternoon of the day following, our Lord Himself died on the cross. So He kept the Passover on the first evening of the appointed day, and He Himself suffered and died as the true Passover before the next evening. According to the Jews' reckoning, therefore, both events took place on the one day.

Jesus sent "Peter and John, saying, Go and prepare us the passover, that we may eat." And they put the natural question to Him, "Where wilt Thou that we prepare?" He had no home in or about Jerusalem. But in those days it was customary for the Jews to have a special room set apart as a guestchamber where they might entertain travelers, especially at the passover time. Now Jesus knew of one in whose house He would be welcome, and where He could eat the passover with His disciples. So He said, "Behold, when ye are entered into the city, there shall a man meet you, bearing a pitcher of water; follow him into the house where he entereth in." We might think these directions were rather indefinite. He did not tell them the man's name nor anything else whereby to identify him; how were they to know when they met the right person? Well, you see it was a very unusual thing for a man to be found in the public streets bearing a pitcher of water. Ordinarily it was the women who went to the wells and carried the water, generally in earthen jars upon their heads. This is the common practice still in Oriental lands. So when Jesus said, "There shall a man meet you, bearing a pitcher of water," He indicated something distinctive. The water-bearer may speak to us of those who with joy draw water from the wells of salvation. "And ye shall say unto the goodman of the house, The Master saith unto thee, Where is the guestchamber, where I shall eat the passover with My disciples?" That was all that was necessary. The owner of the house was evidently a believer in the Lord. "And he shall show you a large upper room furnished: there make ready." It may be that this was the house in which John Mark lived, and that this large upper room was the same as that to which the disciples resorted after the resurrection of our Lord, and where the early Church held its first prayer-meetings. "And they went, and found as He had said unto them: and they made ready the passover." They set the table with the roasted lamb, the unleavened bread, the bitter herbs, and the passover wine. Then we read, "And when the hour was come, He sat down, and the twelve apostles with Him." It was a blessed scene of fellowship, save for one jarring note—the presence of Judas the traitor. "And He said unto them, With desire I have desired to eat this passover with you before I suffer." He had often participated in the passover feasts in the years that had gone. It was a picture of His own approaching death, and His love led Him to long to have His own with Him at the paschal table. He knew so well what was ahead of Him. He was the only One in Israel who knew that this passover prefigured His own death on Calvary and the salvation which He was to procure by the shedding of His precious blood. Now He had come to the last passover that God would ever recognize, the last passover of which He Himself would partake before fulfilling all He came to accomplish. He said, "I will not any more eat thereof, until it be fulfilled in the kingdom of God." The type was passing away, the antitype was seen to take its place. "And He took the cup, and gave thanks." This cup has nothing to do with the Lord's Supper; it concluded the passover. He said, "Take this, and divide it among yourselves: for I say unto you, I will not drink of the fruit of the vine, until the kingdom of God shall come." God had not commanded them to use the fruit of the vine in the passover, but this was a custom that had been practised for many centuries, and the Lord recognized this and accepted it. He Himself did not drink of it, for the fruit of the vine speaks of joy and gladness. He was going to death and sorrow: it was not His hour of gladness; He was to endure the cross before He entered into His joy.

Following the passover He established the beautiful ordinance which has been carried on by the Church of God for nineteen hundred years as a memorial of His death and suffering. "And He took bread, and gave thanks, and brake it, and gave unto them, saying, This is My body which is given for you: this do in remembrance of Me." He took one of the passover loaves, the flat unleavened cakes, which He brake. Strange that anyone should have ever supposed that what He meant here was that the bread was changed into His own physical body. It was a symbolic act. The bread remained as it was after His thanksgiving, but it now had a special character as a picture of His body about to be given up to death. He said, "This is My body which is given for you: this do in remembrance of Me." That is, do this from time to time to call Me to mind. "Likewise also the cup after supper, saying, This cup is the new testament in My blood, which is shed for you." The word for "testament" and "covenant" is the same. I prefer the word "covenant" here. This is the cup of blessing (1 Cor. 10:16) setting forth the *new covenant in His blood* about to be shed upon the cross for our redemption. As they drank of it they were expressing their fellowship as sinners redeemed to God by His blood. The day of the old covenant was passing away, and He was about to seal the new covenant by the shedding of His blood upon the cross.

The Lord's Supper (1 Cor. 11:20) is a feast of remembrance, which is intended to carry our minds back to the death of our Saviour and also to cause us to look on to His coming again (1 Cor. 11:26). It consisted, in the beginning, of a very simple meal, called the breaking of bread (Acts 2:46), and seems at first to have been observed daily or whenever a few Christians came together, possibly at the close of every ordinary meal. Later it appears to have been celebrated regularly on the first day of the week (Acts 20:7), though there is no hard-and-fast rule as to this. "As oft" as ye do this, seems to leave the question of time and frequency to the love and spiritual sensibilities of the disciples of Christ. In this service of remembrance the bread remains bread, and the fruit of the vine in the cup is unchanged in character, but the representative characters of both are insisted on. When Jesus said, "This is My body," and, "This . . . is . . . My blood," He sat in the midst of His followers, and His blood was still flowing in His veins and His body manifest among them. It was as if one held a photograph before a friend and said, "This is my mother." No one would think that the piece of cardboard had been actually changed into the flesh and blood of a woman! But these memorials were designed to bring before us vividly the Person of our adorable Lord, enabling us to call Him to mind with more than ordinary clarity. Because of this, and of the expressed desire of Jesus Christ that we should thus remember Him, it has been the joy of christian hearts down through the centuries to come together around the table of the Lord to think of His sufferings, to meditate upon His love, and to enjoy communion with Him.

In the celebration of the Lord's Supper we are to be occupied with Christ Himself, with the memories of His love and grace, recalling His sorrows, sufferings, and death, and bearing in mind His promise to come again and receive us unto Himself. It is a mistake to think of this blessed ordinance as a means of grace, in the sense of having to do with the salvation of the soul. It is intended to deepen in the heart of those already saved, the realization of the preciousness of Christ. We come together to remember Him, and as He fills the vision of our souls we feast in spirit upon all that He is and all that He has done.

Following this we have the treachery of Judas. "But, behold, the hand of him that betrayeth Me is with Me on the table." We read, "After the sop Satan entered into him. Then said Jesus unto him, That thou doest, do quickly." And he went immediately out and it was night—night not only outside but also in his own soul, never to be relieved by one ray of light. Jesus went on to say that the fact that the Son of Man had come into the world to die would not excuse those who deliberately sought to crucify Him. "And truly the Son of Man goeth, as it was determined: but woe unto that man by whom He is betrayed!" Actually, according to John 13:29, 30, Judas left the room before the Lord's Supper was instituted.

In verse 24 we read of a strife among the disciples as to which of them should be the greatest. The Lord was about to die; He had just given them the communion, a picture of His death, and now these who really loved Him began to quarrel among themselves as to who would have the chief place in the coming kingdom. Pride is so hard to root out. There they were with the shadow of the cross falling over them, striving among themselves as to who should be greatest. He gently rebuked them by indicating that although this ambitious spirit is common among the nations and is to be expected among sinful men, it should not be found among His own. "But ye shall not be so: but he that is greatest among you, let him be as the younger; and he that is chief, as he that doth serve." It was customary for worldly leaders to seek to hold their fellows in subjection, and those who did so were looked up to as benefactors if they seemed to govern righteously. But this lust for place and power is inconsistent for a disciple of Jesus. Greatness is shown by lowly service. The kingdom of God is the only kingdom ever known to man where the greatest are those who take the humblest place. "For whether is greater, he that sitteth at meat, or he that serveth? is not he that sitteth at meat? but I am among you as He that serveth." In this attitude Jesus has set the example which all His followers should emulate.

Then our Lord said, "Ye are they which have continued with Me in My temptations. And I appoint unto you a kingdom, as My Father hath appointed unto Me." When He comes again to reign in glory, those who share His rejection now will participate with Him in His triumph (Rev. 3:21). He refers not to the present age but to that which succeeds this, when His kingdom will be established over all this earth; and in that day those who have been identified with Jesus, His own people, who owned Him when He was mocked and rejected, will have a wonderful place of recognition. The twelve will sit on thrones and judge the twelve tribes of Israel. "That ye may eat and drink at My table in My kingdom, and sit on thrones judging the twelve tribes of Israel." The twelve (Matthias taking Judas' place, Acts 1:26) are to have a special place in the administration of the coming kingdom in connection with restored Israel. While of the Church, they will rule with Christ over Israel on earth.

The Lord says finally, "Simon, Simon, behold, Satan hath desired to have you, that he may sift you as wheat." The word translated "desired" is really a stronger term than our English word; it is better rendered "demanded." Just as Satan went before God and practically demanded to have the opportunity to test Job, accusing him before God, saying that Job loved God only for what God gave him, so Satan demanded to test Peter. But Jesus said, "I have prayed for thee, that thy faith fail not." You know when we get into the devil's sieve he can shake us up badly, but all that is left when he is through is chaff: the wheat falls through, and Satan has only the chaff. So do not be afraid of the devil's sieve; God is able to sustain us. Remember that Jesus has said, "I have prayed for thee, that thy faith fail not!" Peter failed sadly. He denied his Lord three times, but his faith was preserved, and we find him turning back to Jesus and able to say, "Lord, Thou knowest all things, Thou knowest that I love Thee." The Lord Jesus said, "And when thou art converted (when you are restored), strengthen thy brethren." Sometimes the Lord has to allow some of His best servants to fail terribly in order to show them their weakness, and that they may be more tender and sympathetic toward others. Not realizing his own weakness Peter said, "Lord, I am ready to go with Thee, both into prison, and to death." But the Lord said, "I tell thee, Peter, the cock shall not crow this day, before that thou shalt thrice deny that thou knowest Me." The Lord knew Peter far better than he knew himself, and He knows you and me better than we know ourselves.

Next our Lord warned His disciples of coming conflicts. He knew what would take place, and He said to them, "When I sent you without purse, and scrip, and shoes, lacked ye any thing?"—that is, when He sent them out into the cities of Galilee to give out the message of the gospel of the kingdom. "And they said, Nothing." Everything had been provided. He said to them, "But now, he that hath a purse, let him take it, and likewise his script: and he that hath no sword, let him sell his garment, and buy one." He did not mean literally that they should be armed with material swords; but we are taught elsewhere in Scripture that the Word of God is sharper than any two-edged sword (Heb. 4:12). When they were ready to leave the upper room they said to Him, "Lord, behold, here are two swords. And He said unto them, It is enough"—that is, no more talk about that. He was not speaking about actual defense; He was not interested in weapons. He wanted them to go forth armed with the sword of the Spirit that they might meet the enemies of the truth as they went forth to proclaim the gospel.

Address Seventy-two

THE AGONY IN GETHSEMANE

"And He came out, and went, as He was wont, to the mount of Olives; and His disciples also followed Him. And when He was at the place, He said unto them, Pray that ye enter not into temptation. And He was withdrawn from them about a stone's cast, and kneeled down, and prayed, saying, Father, if Thou be willing, remove this cup from Me: nevertheless not My will, but Thine, be done. And there appeared an angel unto Him from heaven, strengthening Him. And being in an agony He prayed more earnestly: and His sweat was as it were great drops of blood falling down to the ground. And when He rose up from prayer, and was come to His disciples, He found them sleeping for sorrow, and said unto them, Why sleep ye? rise and pray, lest ye enter into temptation. And while He yet spake, behold a multitude, and he that was called Judas, one of the twelve, went before them, and drew near unto Jesus to kiss Him. But Jesus said unto him, Judas, detrayest thou the Son of Man with a kiss? When they which were about Him saw what would follow, they said unto Him, Lord, shall we smite with the sword? And one of them smote the servant of the high priest, and cut off his right ear. And Jesus answered and said, Suffer ye thus far. And He touched his ear, and healed him. Then Jesus said unto the chief priests, and captains of the temple, and the elders, which were come to Him, Be ye come out, as against a thief, with swords and staves? When I was daily with you in the temple, ye stretched forth no hands against Me: but this is your hour, and the power of darkness"—Luke 22: 39-53.

LEAVING the upper room the Lord went with His eleven disciples across the brook Kedron to the Mount of Olives. It had been His custom, when in Judaea, to retire from time to time to a garden on the slope of this mountain, called, as we are told elsewhere, Gethsemane. To this retreat He pursued His way. Luke does not mention the fact that He left eight of His followers at the entrance but took Peter, James, and John with Him as He passed into the garden. Coming to the place where He was wont to engage in prayer He bade them, "Pray that ye enter not into temptation. And He was withdrawn from them about a stone's cast," going deeper into the shades of the olive-yard, for such it was.

There He fell on His knees and prayed. He was suffering intense perturbation of spirit. The very fact that He was the infinitely Holy One filled Him with deepest grief as He contemplated the full meaning of the cross. He could not have been who and what He was if He could contemplate with equanimity the awfulness of being made sin for a guilty world. His holy human nature shrank from this terrible ordeal. It was not death that He dreaded; but "with strong crying and tears" He prayed to "Him who was able to save Him *out of* death," as Hebrews 5: 7 should be translated. We are told there that He "was heard in that He feared," or literally, He "was heard for His piety"; that is, His reverence for God His Father.

In His soul's distress, He prayed, saying, "Father, if Thou be willing, remove this cup from Me: nevertheless not My will, but Thine, be done." What was the cup which He dreaded? I have heard many unworthy things said by those who have endeavored to explain this. Some have maintained that He was in such distress that He feared He might lose His reason and be unable to go on to the cross as a voluntary Substitute for sinners. But they who speak in this way lose sight of the fact that He was not only Man in all perfection, but also God with all power. Satan could do nothing against

Him save by divine consent; and nowhere in Scripture is it intimated that the devil might be permitted such an advantage as this over the Christ of God.

Others have taught that He feared the adversary would crush Him to death in the garden, and the plan of God be defeated which involved His hanging upon a tree. But this theory ignores His own declaration, "No man taketh it (His life) from Me, but I lay it down of Myself. I have power to lay it down, and I have power (authority) to take it again. This commandment have I received of My Father" (John 10:18). This absolutely contradicts any supposition as to Satan's ability to destroy Him before His time.

The cup He dreaded was not death as such. It was the cup of judgment which our sins had filled. In Psalm 75:8 we read, "In the hand of the Lord there is a cup, and the wine is red; it is full of mixture; and He poureth out of the same: but the dregs thereof, all the wicked of the earth shall wring them out, and drink them." This cup of the wrath of God against sin was that from which the Holy Soul of our Saviour shrank. There in the garden He prayed that if there were any other way whereby the sin question might be settled, it should be manifested. There was no opposition to the will of the Father, no conflict of wills. It was rather full acquiescence with the will of God, even though He dreaded the drinking of that chalice of judgment. It was the perfection of His humanity that was manifested in that hour of His spirit's agony. Luke alone of all the Evangelists tells us that, "There appeared an angel unto Him from heaven, strengthening Him." How this emphasizes the reality of His Manhood! He, the Creator of angels, now as Man, derived strength from the ministry of one of these glorious beings.

"Being in an agony He prayed more earnestly: and His sweat was as it were great drops of blood falling down to the ground." There was great significance in this for Dr. Luke, to whom alone we are indebted for this information. It indicated the severity of the pressure under which our Lord was suffering.

When the ordeal was over He arose in perfect calmness of spirit and came to His disciples, whom He found "sleeping for sorrow, and said unto them, Why sleep ye? rise and pray, lest ye enter into temptation." For them the supreme test was about to take place, when He would be taken from them and they left bewildered and frightened. Even as He spoke lights were seen, and a mob of soldiers, priests, and civilians approached, led by Judas the traitor, who "drew near unto Jesus to kiss Him." This was the prearranged signal which would indicate to the officers whom they were to arrest. "Jesus said unto him, Judas, betrayest thou the Son of Man with a kiss?" Apparently, the wretched traitor made no reply, and the soldiers proceeded to take Jesus into custody. The disciples were aroused by this act and exclaimed, "Lord, shall we smite with the sword?" One of them—Peter, as we know from other sources—began slashing about with his sword, and cut off the right ear of the servant of the high priest. But Jesus said, "Suffer ye thus far;" and He healed the wounded man. Someone has well remarked, "How busy we keep the Lord putting on ears that we in our mistaken zeal, cut off!"

Addressing the chief priests and other officials, Jesus said, "Be ye come out, as against a thief, with swords and staves? When I was daily with you in the temple, ye stretched forth no hands against Me: but this is your hour, and the power of darkness." It was a home-thrust. They had not dared attempt to arrest Him in the presence of the people, because many of them believed He was a Prophet even if they did not recognize in Him the promised Messiah. But in the dark these cowardly ecclesiastics and their henchmen laid hands on Him as He willingly surrendered Himself to them, and they led Him away for trial as a blasphemer and a seditionist. It was a sad manifestation of the incurable evil of the hearts of those outwardly pious priests and religious leaders.

Address Seventy-three

PETER'S FAILURE AND REPENTANCE

✓ ✓ ✓

"Then took they Him, and led Him, and brought Him into the high priest's house. And Peter followed afar off. And when they had kindled a fire in the midst of the hall, and were set down together, Peter sat down among them. But a certain maid beheld him as he sat by the fire, and earnestly looked upon him, and said, This man was also with Him. And he denied Him, saying, Woman, I know Him not. And after a little while another saw him, and said, Thou art also of them. And Peter said, Man, I am not. And about the sapce of one hour after another confidently affirmed, saying, Of a truth this fellow also was with Him: for he is a Galilean. And Peter said, Man, I know not what thou sayest. And immediately, while he yet spake, the cock crew. And the Lord turned, and looked upon Peter. And Peter remembered the word of the Lord, how He had said unto him, Before the cock crow, thou shalt deny Me thrice. And Peter went out, and wept bitterly"—Luke 22: 54-62.

✓ ✓ ✓

IN relating these life-stories it is characteristic of Holy Scripture to give us, not only the evidence of the love and devotion, but also something of the mistakes and sins of the friends of God in the Old Testament, and the disciples of our Lord Jesus Christ in the New. The reason is, I believe, that God would have us learn how to avoid their failures as well as to imitate their virtues, and follow them as they followed Christ. We might think that it would have been best to have told us only the good things and to have covered their blunders, but then we would be likely to come to the conclusion that these servants of God and our Lord Jesus Christ in past centuries were quite different from us; that they were men superior to us, and they did not fail as we do. So we get the whole story. Many souls have been warned and helped by the account of Peter's failure and, thank God, his repentance. The whole life of Peter as we learn it from our Bible is most interesting and instructive: this sturdy fisherman who, from the time he first met the Lord Jesus, lost his heart to Him. His first meeting with Jesus was on that occasion when, as we read in John 1:41, his own brother, Andrew, sought him out and brought him to the Lord after Andrew and John, the author of the fourth Gospel, had spent the afternoon with the Saviour. From that time on Peter's heart was won for Christ, but he did not immediately leave all for Him; he was not called to do so. Afterward the Lord was preaching on the shores of the Sea of Galilee, and the crowd thronged Him. Jesus looked about, and there was Peter's fishing-boat near the shore; the Lord asked for permission to enter it, and Peter gladly received Him. Jesus told him to thrust out a little from the land; and using Peter's boat as a pulpit He taught the people. This was easy to do. Anyone who has been there will recall how the land along the shore rises upward, forming an amphitheater. The throng could have stood or sat on the ground and looked at the Lord as He preached the Word. Possibly the message did not really reach the heart of this man Simon; but afterward when the crowd dispersed, Jesus turned to him and said, "Launch out into the deep, and let down your nets for a draught" (Luke 5:4). Peter was surprised at this, for the sun was shining; it was a most unlikely time for fishing, and he said, "Master, we have toiled all the night and have taken nothing." Now the day was no time for fishing, but Peter said, "At Thy word I will let down the net;" and immediately they enclosed a great multitude of fish. You know the rest of the story. The interesting thing is this: when Peter saw the fish they had caught at that time of day he knew he was in the presence of the Creator of the fish, and he fell down at the feet of Jesus and said, "Depart from me; for I am a sinful man, O Lord." And yet he took Him by the feet, as much as to say, "While I know I am not fit for Your company, Lord, You shall not get away from me if I can help it." The Lord never turns away from a sinner's confession. He spoke words of encouragement to Peter, assuring him of His confidence in him and saying, "Fear not; from henceforth thou shalt catch men" (Luke 5:10). Jesus called Peter into full-time association with Himself; so he left the fishing business to become a fisher of men. Later on Peter made his great confession of faith: "He asked His disciples, saying, Whom do men say that I the Son of Man am? And they said, Some say that Thou art John the Baptist: some, Elias; and others, Jeremias, or one of the prophets. He saith unto them, But whom say ye that I am?" Answering for all the disciples, Peter replied with holy enthusiasm, "Thou art the Christ, the Son of the living God. And Jesus answered and said unto him, Blessed art thou, Simon Bar-jona: for flesh and blood hath not revealed it unto thee, but My Father which is in heaven" (Matt. 16:13-17). It is always a divine revelation when one is brought to know the Lord Jesus Christ in the true mystery of His Person. Then the Lord said, "I say unto thee, That thou art Peter, and upon this rock (the rock of this confession) I will build My Church; and the gates of hell shall not prevail against it" (Matt. 16:18). I do not think Peter ever rose to a greater height in his experience while the Lord was with him on earth than at that time. But have you noticed that his backsliding began almost immediately afterward? We need to heed the important warning: "Let him that thinketh he standeth take heed lest he fall" (1 Cor. 10:12). The Lord had just spoken of the wonderful revelation given to Peter and then went on to tell them of His approaching death on the cross, to be followed by His resurrection; and Peter, exalted undoubtedly by the abundance of the revelation, turned to the Lord and dared to say to Him, "Be it far from Thee, Lord: this shall not be unto Thee" (Matt. 16:22). He was correcting, or attempting to correct Jesus for saying He was to be delivered to the Gentiles and be crucified. Peter declared that nothing like that should take place. The Lord immediately turned to him and said, "Get thee behind Me, Satan: thou art an offence unto Me: for thou savorest not the things that be of God, but those that be of men" (Matt. 16:23). What a rebuke to be given to the prince of the apostles, and that so soon after he had made his great confession! Evidently he had become exalted by spiritual pride, and Satan led him to say that which, if acted upon, would mean that we would have been left without a

Saviour and our sins unatoned for. It was only by going to the cross that the propitiation for sin could be made.

We do not read much concerning the experiences of Peter after that, but we do know that he never reached such a high spiritual point again. On the Mount of Transfiguration, when Jesus was speaking with Moses and Elias of His decease which He would accomplish at Jerusalem, Peter felt he must say something—though he knew not what to say—and so he blurted out, "Lord, it is good for us to be here: if Thou wilt, let us make here three tabernacles; one for Thee, and one for Moses, and one for Elias. While he yet spake, behold, a bright cloud overshadowed them: and behold a voice out of the cloud, which said, This is My Beloved Son, in whom I am well pleased; hear ye Him" (Matt. 17:4, 5). As much as to say, "Peter, do not put anybody on the level with My Son; He must have the pre-eminence in all things."

Scripture passes over the rest of Peter's history until the night of our Lord's betrayal. Then we see him with the rest of the disciples in the upper room. The Lord said, "All ye shall be offended because of Me this night: for it is written, I will smite the Shepherd, and the sheep of the flock shall be scattered abroad" (Matt. 26:31). Self-confident, yet loving the Lord and meaning every word, but failing to realize his own weakness, Peter said, "Although all shall be offended, yet will not I" (Mark 14:29). "I am ready to go with Thee, both into prison, and to death" (Luke 22:33). He was to go both to prison and to death in after years for Christ's sake, but he was not ready at this time. The Lord said to him, "I tell thee, Peter, the cock shall not crow this day, before that thou shalt thrice deny that thou knowest Me." And He who knew Peter so well, also said, "But I have prayed for thee, that thy faith fail not: and when thou art converted, strengthen thy brethren."

They went out to the garden of sorrow; and there Peter failed with the others: for the Lord took Peter, James, and John into the garden with Him. Ere He went a little farther to talk with His Father, He said to the three, "Watch and pray, that ye enter not into temptation: the spirit indeed is willing, but the flesh is weak" (Matt. 26: 41). And He went away and prayed, saying, "O My Father, if it be possible, let this cup pass from Me: nevertheless not as I will, but as Thou wilt" (Matt. 26: 39). And when He rose from His knees He found the three disciples sleeping for sorrow; it was the weakness of the flesh. Peter was asleep when he should have been alert, watching and praying. The Lord aroused them from their sleep and again bade them watch and pray; and He went away the second time, praying the same words, "Not My will, but Thine be done." When He came the third time and found that Peter was still asleep, He said, "Sleep on now, and take your rest: behold, the hour is at hand, and the Son of Man is betrayed into the hands of sinners" (Matt. 26: 45). Then came Judas and the rest, and Judas said, "Hail, Master; and kissed Him." They came and took Jesus, and Peter became enraged. He was alert now, and he turned and drew his sword and cut off the ear of one of the servants of the high priest. The Lord said, "Put up thy sword," and He healed the man. This was the energy of the flesh on Peter's part. He, who before had been asleep when he should have been alert, was now roused up and active when he should have been passive and quiescent. They took Jesus away, and we are told that "Peter followed afar off." This was a further evidence of his backslidden condition: instead of keeping close to Jesus and letting all see that he was identified with Him, he fell behind; his love would not let him leave entirely. Finally he reached the high priest's house. There in the court a fire was burning, for it was a cold night; and Peter went in and sat with others around the fire. Again we see him drifting: in company with the ungodly while his Lord was on trial. "A certain maid beheld him as he sat by the fire, and earnestly looked upon him, and said, This man was also with him. And he denied Him, saying, Woman, I know Him not. And about the space of one hour after another confidently affirmed, saying, Of a truth this fellow also was with Him: for he is a Galilean. And Peter said, Man, I know not what thou sayest." The more he opened his mouth the more he got into trouble. The Galileans had their own peculiar accent, so that the Judeans recognized Peter immediately as one from the northern province. His speech betrayed him. Evidently because he was overcome with fear, Peter began to curse and to swear, saying, "I know not the Man." "And immediately the cock crew." The Saviour's words came back to Peter as Jesus looked upon him. Peter had gone down, down, down, until he had denied all knowledge of Christ. But now, oh, how he wept as Jesus gazed sadly and reproachfully upon him! That was the beginning of the work of restoration. Repentance had commenced. If we follow the record we find that the Lord had a private interview with Peter after the resurrection. We are told that the women who arrived at the tomb early on the resurrection morning were instructed to "Go your way, tell His disciples *and Peter*" (Mark 16:7). I am sure Peter must have been greatly distressed during those three days and nights; he felt that he had lost all contact with Jesus. But the risen Lord acknowledged him as a disciple still. When the two Emmaus disciples returned to the Eleven, they said, "The Lord is risen indeed, and hath appeared to Simon" (Luke 24:34). Undoubtedly Peter was fully restored at the time of the Lord's private interview with him. His public restoration took place on the shores of Galilee shortly after, on that morning when the Saviour cooked Peter's breakfast and served him and his fellow-disciples after they had toiled all night and again had caught nothing. Three times the Lord put the question to Peter: "Lovest thou Me?" Peter was grieved that Jesus asked him this question three times, but he had denied his Lord three times. Having restored him, the Lord said to Peter, "Feed My lambs . . . feed My sheep."

Oh, the infinite grace of our blessed Lord! We have failed Him, but He never has failed us. I can call upon all who believe and trust in Him to bear witness. God grant that as we face the difficulties of the coming days we will lean more completely upon Him; that we will faithfully acknowledge Christ, our blessed, risen Lord. Let us be careful not to trust in our own strength, but distrusting ourselves to rely wholly on Him, that we may ever be true to the trust committed to us!

ADDRESS SEVENTY-FOUR

JESUS BEFORE THE PRIESTS

✝ ✝ ✝

"And the men that held Jesus mocked Him, and smote Him. And when they had blindfolded Him, they struck Him on the face, and asked Him, saying, Prophesy, who is it that smote Thee? And many other things blasphemously spake they against Him. And as soon as it was day, the elders of the people and the chief priests and the scribes came together, and led Him into their council, saying, Art Thou the Christ? tell us. And He said unto them, If I tell you, ye will not believe: and if I also ask you, ye will not answer Me, nor let Me go. Hereafter shall the Son of Man sit on the right hand of the power of God. Then said they all, Art Thou then the Son of God? And He said unto them, Ye say that I am. And they said, What need we any further witness? for we ourselves have heard of His own mouth"—Luke 22: 63-71.

✝ ✝ ✝

WE have considered the agony in Gethsemane and the arrest of our blessed Lord when He was taken to the high priest's house in the middle of the night. Then we noticed the failure, the denial of the apostle Peter; and as we looked a little farther on in the record we saw how graciously he was restored. Now we come back to the house of the high priest. It was directly contrary to Jewish law to conduct a trial in Jerusalem in the night-time, but all this was forgotten when the hatred of His enemies stirred their hearts to seek the condemnation and destruction of the Lord Jesus Christ.

As we consider this portion we find several things emphasized. One is this: in order to be saved it is not enough that a person be religious. I suppose these priests were as religious as anyone in all Israel at this particular time. They were the religious leaders of the people; they believed firmly in the revelation that Jehovah had given of Himself as the one true and living God. Some have the idea that if one believes in one God nothing more is required; but we remember the apostle James (2: 19) has said, "Thou believest that there is one God; thou doest well: the demons also believe, and shudder" (literal rendering). Demons recognize the truth of the unity of the Godhead, and they know that some day they are going to be called to judgment before Him; so they shudder at the very mention of His name. Mere faith, mere recognition rather, of the fact that there is one God does not save anyone. A man might turn from the worst kind of heathenism, fetishism, or any other form of paganism, and accept the idea that there is only one God and henceforth profess to serve Him, and yet not be saved at all. These priests believed in one God, but they were not saved. More than that, they believed in the inspiration of the Bible; they accepted the sacred writings as divinely given, and they believed in the prophetic character of those writings. They knew the Scriptures foretold the coming of the Messiah into the world. For centuries their forefathers had been studying the writings of the prophets; and they, themselves, had been looking forward to the coming of this Just One. Yet when the Lord Jesus Christ actually came in fulfilment of all that was written aforehand, they did not recognize Him. They refused to accept Him; they spurned Him, and turned Him over to Pilate that He might be crucified. There is something here that you and I may well take to heart. Many profess to accept the Bible as a revelation from heaven, at least to recognize the fact that God has spoken in it to mankind as in no other book. In that respect they are orthodox. But remember, one may believe all this and yet not know God's salvation. It is not enough to know the Scriptures in order to be saved. Years ago when I first visited the Jerry McAuley Mission in New York, I sat through a very interesting service, and at the conclusion a man pointed to an old Scotsman over in one corner of the room, and he said to me, "That is Old Chapter-and-Verse." I inquired what he meant by that. He replied, "Well, that is the name we have given him—Old Chapter-and-Verse. He is an alcohol addict; we never have known him to be sober. Yet every night he is at the meeting. He sleeps through most of it, but let anyone get up to give a testimony and misquote a scripture and Old Chapter-and-Verse wakes up at once. He has such a knowledge of the Bible from his Scotch bringing-up that it stirs him when he hears anyone misquote Scripture. The other night somebody got up and quoted that passage in Matthew 11:28 according to the old English prayer-book rendering, rather than from the Authorized Version: 'Come unto Me, all ye that are weary.'

Old Chapter-and-Verse jumped up at once and said, 'Haud on noo. Dinna ye be handlin' the Word o' God deceitfully. It does na' say, 'All ye that are weary,' it says, 'All ye that labor and are heavy laden;' then he dropped back to go to sleep until somebody else misquoted another scripture." Poor old man! He had a head full of Bible and a heart full of sin. The Bible says no drunkard shall inherit the kingdom of God. This man knew the Bible but not the Saviour of whom it speaks.

These priests knew their Bibles, and yet they rejected the Christ of the Bible. They knew the Bible so well that some thirty years before, when Herod had heard of the birth of the King and inquired where Christ should be born, the scribes and chief priests turned at once to the prophecy, and answered, "In Bethlehem of Judaea: for thus it is written by the prophet. 'And thou Bethlehem, in the land of Juda, art not the least among the princes of Juda: for out of thee shall come a Governor, that shall rule My people Israel'" (Matt. 2:6). They knew exactly where Messiah was to be born, and yet they did not receive Him for themselves. As He grew up to Manhood and went about ministering the Word among His own people, they actually fulfilled their own Scripture by condemning Him. So it is not enough to be acquainted with Scripture. One needs to open his heart to Christ and receive Him as his personal Saviour: for the Bible says, "There is none other name under heaven given among men, whereby we must be saved" (Acts 4:12).

The men who took Jesus mocked Him and smote Him. I suppose these were the riff-raff, the reckless mob. They realized their religious leaders were against Christ, so they turned against Him too. "And when they had blindfolded Him, they struck Him on the face, and asked Him, saying, Prophesy, who is it that smote Thee?" Our blessed, adorable Lord, who was led as a lamb to the slaughter and as a sheep before the shearers was dumb, answered not a word. "And many other things blasphemously spake they against Him."

As the first light appeared upon the horizon, the leaders, chief priests, and scribes came together and led Him into their council. This was the supreme council in Israel which was made up of seventy of their most noted elders. They were there to judge the Lord Jesus Christ; and we are told in another Gospel that they brought a great many false witnesses to testify against Him—men who declared they had heard Him say certain things which they pieced together with other sayings which they tried to prove He had said, but which He never had said at all. In this way they endeavored to convict Him of blasphemy. They asked Him, "Art Thou the Christ?" The Lord Jesus answered, "If I tell you, ye will not believe: and if I also ask you, ye will not answer Me, nor let me go." That is, if He were to assert Himself and say, "I am the Messiah," giving Scripture to show how the Word of God had been fulfilled in Him, they would not believe. He knew their hearts were set upon rejecting Him. There was no evidence of repentance, and there was no sense of their need of a Saviour. That is why men and women are lost today: they reject Christ; they imagine they can get along without Him; they have no realization of the innate deceitfulness of their hearts. I have known many persons who objected to the truth of the gospel, claiming they could not believe it; until at last, broken down under the convicting power of the Holy Spirit of God, they realized their lost condition and the sinfulness of their lives, and found that only Jesus could meet their need. They had no difficulty trusting Him then; for they saw, as John Hambleton, the converted actor, used to put it, that "Jesus Exactly Suits Us Sinners."

The Lord Jesus Christ never attempted to answer these objectors, because He knew they had no desire to understand the truth. He said on one occasion, "If any man will do His will, he shall know of the doctrine, whether it be of God, or whether I speak of Myself" (John 7:17). But these people had no desire to make such a test; they were not ready to face things honestly in the presence of God.

Jesus went on to make a marvelous declaration. He told them that though they spurned Him then, "Hereafter shall the Son of Man sit on the right hand of the power of God." To them this was the very height of blasphemy; it amounted to nothing less than a claim to actual Deity. They continued the examination by inquiring—though not with any desire to know the truth—"Art Thou then the Son of God?" Doubtless they remembered what was written by Daniel the Prophet, of one like the Son of Man who came to the Ancient of Days to receive power, and glory, and a kingdom. Did Jesus mean that this prophecy referred to Himself? Was He the Son of the Highest? He answered, "Ye say that I am." That is, they had spoken the truth in using that title when referring to Him. He was indeed the Son of God. They were full of indignation and cried, "What need we any further witness? for we ourselves have heard of His own mouth." So they put Him down as guilty of blasphemy. And they were right if, as many claim today, He were only a man, even though the best and greatest of humankind; because for any mere man to claim what Jesus claimed for Himself would rightly prove Him to be either self-deceived or a blasphemer. But the Word reveals our blessed Lord to be God the Eternal Son who came down to this world, taking humanity into union with Deity, in order that He might go to the cross to give His life a ransom for sinful men.

Address Seventy-five

PILATE'S PERPLEXITY

✝ ✝ ✝

"And the whole multitude of them arose, and led Him unto Pilate. And they began to accuse Him, saying, We found this fellow perverting the nation, and forbidding to give tribute to Caesar, saying that He Himself is Christ a King. And Pilate asked Him, saying, Art Thou the King of the Jews? And He answered him and said, Thou sayest it. Then said Pilate to the chief priests and to the people, I find no fault in this Man. And they were the more fierce, saying, He stirreth up the people, teaching throughout all Jewry, beginning from Galilee to this place. When Pilate heard of Galilee, he asked whether the Man were a Galilean. And as soon as he knew that He belonged unto Herod's jurisdiction, he sent Him to Herod, who himself also was at Jerusalem at that time. And when Herod saw Jesus, he was exceeding glad: for he was desirous to see Him of a long season, because he had heard many things of Him; and he hoped to have seen some miracle done by Him. Then he questioned with Him in many words; but He answered him nothing. And the chief priests and scribes stood and vehemently accused Him. And Herod with his men of war set Him at nought, and mocked Him, and arrayed Him in a gorgeous robe, and sent Him again to Pilate. And the same day Pilate and Herod were made friends together: for before they were at enmity between themselves. And Pilate, when he had called together the chief priests and the rulers and the people, said unto them, Ye have brought this Man unto me, as one that perverteth the people: and, behold, I, having examined Him before you, have found no fault in this Man touching those things whereof ye accuse Him: no, nor yet Herod: for I sent you to him; and, lo, nothing worthy of death is done unto Him. I will therefore chastise Him, and release Him. (For of necessity he must release one unto them at the feast.) And they cried out all at once, saying, Away with this Man, and release unto us Barabas: (who for a certain sedition made in the city, and for murder, was cast into prison.) Pilate therefore, willing to release Jesus, spake again to them. But they cried, saying, Crucify Him, crucify Him. And he said unto them the third time, Why, what evil hath He done? I have found no cause of death in Him: I will therefore chastise Him, and let Him go. And they were instant with loud voices, requiring that He might be crucified. And the voices of them and of the chief priests pre-

vailed. And Pilate gave sentence that it should be as they required. And he released unto them him that for sedition and murder was cast into prison, whom they had desired; but he delivered Jesus to their will"—Luke 23: 1-25.

↑ ↑ ↑

AS we consider the inspired account of the condemnation and crucifixion of our blessed Lord, we may well approach the subject with repentant hearts and broken spirits while we remind ourselves afresh that it was for our sins that He went to the cross. Apart from this solemn fact there was no power on earth or in hell that could have forced Jesus Christ to die as He did. He need not have died at all: He was the sinless Son of God. But He chose to die as our substitute. He voluntarily became our Surety and undertook in grace to pay the debt we owed. The pitiable thing is that men, led on by Satan, should have raised wicked hands against Him and heaped such shame and ignominy upon Him. But it only told out the vileness of the sinful heart of man and the malignity of Satan. As we follow our Lord in His mock trials before Pilate and Herod, and from Pilate's judgment-hall to Calvary with its bitter cross, it should surely break down our pride and subdue us as we reflect upon what sin really is, when we see the lengths to which men like ourselves could go when under its power.

We have four references to Pontius Pilate in other parts of the New Testament outside the Gospels. Of course, we read of the trial of Jesus in all the Gospels, and of Pilate's failure to stand for righteousness at a time when he knew the Prisoner before him was guiltless of the charges brought against Him. When the apostle Peter was addressing the people of Israel after Pentecost (Acts 3:13, 14), he said, "The God of Abraham, and of Isaac, and of Jacob, the God of our fathers, hath glorified His Son Jesus; whom ye delivered up, and denied Him in the presence of Pilate, when he was determined to let Him go. But ye denied the Holy One and the Just, and desired a murderer to be granted unto you." In Acts 4:27 we hear Peter speaking in prayer to God, saying, "For of a truth against Thy holy Child Jesus, whom Thou hast anointed, both Herod, and Pontius Pilate, with the Gentiles, and the people of Israel, were gathered together." Then in chapter 13:28, when Paul was preaching in the synagogue at Antioch of Pisidia, he said, "And though they found no cause of death in Him, yet desired they Pilate that He should be slain." In writing to his own convert, the young preacher Timothy, Paul reminds him, in 1 Timothy, of the faithful testimony of our Lord on the occasion of His trial. In 1 Timothy 6:13, he said, "I give thee charge in the sight of God, who quickeneth all things, and before Christ Jesus, who before Pontius Pilate witnessed a good confession; that thou keep this commandment without spot, unrebukable, until the appearing of our Lord Jesus Christ." Pontius Pilate's name stands out in the Word of God and on the pages of history for eternal infamy. I suppose there is no other mortal man whose name is mentioned as frequently as the name of Pontius

Pilate. Every Lord's Day and often on many other occasions, hundreds of thousands of professed Christians gathered together in various places, repeat the words found in the Apostles' Creed; "crucified under Pontius Pilate," and so Pilate's name is repeated and has been repeated all down through the centuries as the one who condemned the innocent Christ to death. And Pilate has not heard the last of it yet. When he stands finally at the great white throne he will see sitting on that throne the One who once stood as a Prisoner before him; the One whom he pronounced to be innocent of the charges against Him, and yet whom he delivered up to be crucified. The trouble with Pontius Pilate was this: he was so filled with selfish ambition, a desire to win the favor of the powers above him and even of the people whom he ruled, that he did not have the manhood, the conscientious principle, to stand up for what he knew to be right.

When Jesus Christ was brought before Pilate, He was not a stranger to him. Pilate had heard of Jesus before; he knew of His ministry in Israel; and he knew it was because of envy that the chief priests had delivered Jesus to be tried. Pilate should have dealt with Him as One who was falsely accused, but he was fearful he might be censured and so lose his position which he held by Caesar's favor.

The whole multitude were gathered together and led Jesus to Pontius Pilate to be charged with sedition against the Roman Government. They began to accuse Him, saying, "We found this fellow perverting the nation, and forbidding to give tribute to Caesar, saying that He Himself is Christ a King." Notice there was a certain element of truth in their charges, and yet the charges as a whole were false, for a half-truth is often a whole lie. It is true the Lord Jesus Christ proclaimed Himself to be a King, but He never declared Himself to be King over Israel at that time. He came in full accord with prophecy and knew He was to be rejected, and that His kingdom was yet to come. On the other hand, their charge of sedition was utterly false, because when He was asked, "Is it lawful for us to give tribute unto Caesar, or no?" Jesus replied by requesting them to show Him a penny, and He asked, "Whose image and superscription hath it? They answered and said, Caesar's. And He said unto them, Render therefore unto Caesar the things which be Caesar's, and unto God the things which be God's" (Luke 20:24,25). They heard Him say this; therefore, they lied when they came before Pilate and said He had forbidden them to give tribute to Caesar.

Pilate put the question definitely, "Art Thou the King of the Jews?" The Lord answered, "Thou sayest it." This may seem to be ambiguous, but it was as though He said, "You have said it; you said that by right, by divine title, I am King of the Jews." He had not stressed that as He went about ministering among the people, but the question was put to Him, and He confessed that He was indeed the One whom God had sent to rule Israel. Pilate turned to the chief priests and to the people and said, "I find no fault in this Man. And they were the more fierce." They would not listen to anything that could be said in behalf of Christ. They cried, "He stirreth up the people, teaching throughout all Jewry, beginning from Galilee to this place." When Pilate heard the word "Galilee," he thought he had found a loophole through which he might escape responsibility; so he asked whether the Man were a Galilean. When he learned that Jesus came from Galilee, he saw an opportunity to turn the judgment of Christ over to someone else. Herod was tetrarch, or governor of Galilee, who had come down to Jerusalem in order to keep the feast of the passover, and as soon as Pilate knew that Jesus belonged to that jurisdiction he sent Him to Herod, who, when he saw Jesus, was glad. He was delighted to see Him; he had heard so much of Him. He was always interested in wonder-workers and those whom the people lauded. He had been interested in John the Baptist until John faithfully said to him, as he pointed to another man's wife who was sitting by his side, "It is not lawful for thee to have her" (Matt. 14:4). In indignation Herod put John the Baptist in prison, and, later to satisfy that woman's desire for vengeance, Herod decapitated him.

Now here was a Man who was reported to have wrought great miracles, and Herod was glad to see Him, and hoped to see some wonder done by Him. "Then he questioned with Him in many words: but He answered him nothing." As always the Lord Jesus had nothing to say to those who were curious but who had no desire to know the truth. "And the chief priests and scribes stood and vehemently accused Him. And Herod with his men of war set Him at nought, and mocked Him, and arrayed Him in a gorgeous robe." It was evidently a robe of something like what we call changeable silk. One Gospel writer says it was purple; another says it was scarlet. The warp may have been of one color and the woof of another, so that it was indeed a gorgeous robe. They put it on Him; they bowed their knees, and put a reed in His hand, and mocked Him, crying, "Hail, King of the Jews." In the other Gospels we learn that the Roman soldiers platted a crown of thorns and pressed it upon His head, causing intense and bitter suffering.

We read in the next verse, "The same day Pilate and Herod were made friends together: for before they were at enmity between themselves." Here were two crafty politicians who hated and distrusted each other, but they could agree in rejecting the Lord Jesus Christ.

Herod sent Jesus back to Pilate. "And Pilate, when he had called together the chief priests and the rulers and the people, said unto them, Ye have brought this Man unto me, as one that perverteth the people: and, behold, I, having examined Him before you, have found no fault in this Man touching those things whereof ye accuse Him: no, nor yet Herod· for I sent you to him; and, lo, nothing worthy of death is done unto Him. I will therefore chastise Him, and release Him."

This was the second session in Pilate's courtroom. It took place after Jesus had returned from Herod, where He had been set at nought, but no charge sustained against Him. "I, having examined Him before you, have found no fault in this Man." Pilate's declaration should have meant the acquittal of Jesus, but that would not satisfy his relentless enemies, who were determined that He must die, little realizing that His death was predetermined by God for our salvation (Acts 2:23). "No, nor yet Herod." This godless king had not dared to condemn Jesus to death, for he well knew he was not guilty of the charges, either of blasphemy or sedition, which were brought against Him. Pilate said, "I will therefore chastise Him, and release Him." To inflict chastisement on an innocent man was preposterous, but Pilate evidently thought by this to placate the Jewish leaders and so he could release Jesus from any greater condemnation.

It had been the custom for some time, that a notable prisoner would be set free at the passover, and Pilate grasped at the thought that he might act upon that and release Jesus. There was a prisoner named Barabbas awaiting execution, and so he proposed, as recorded in another Gospel, "Whether of the twain will ye that I release unto you? They said, Barabbas" (Matt. 27:21). Barabbas was a notable rebel. He was in prison for sedition and murder. But the people cried all at once, "Away with this Man, and release unto us Barabbas." With one voice they chose for release this famous champion of Jewish nationalism who was condemned to die. They demanded instead the death of Jesus, the innocent One. It is written (Matt. 27: 22) that Pilate put the solemn question, "What shall I do then with Jesus which is called Christ?" This is the question which has come ringing down the ages to every man. "And they cried out all at once, saying, Away with this Man. . . . Crucify Him, crucify Him." Pilate felt he was helpless before the multitude if he was going to save his own reputation, for he was afraid that the Jews would bring a charge against him. "And he said unto them the third time, Why, what evil hath He done? I have found no cause of death in Him: I will therefore chastise Him, and let Him go. And they were instant with loud voices, requiring that He might be crucified. And the voices of them and of the chief priests prevailed." Pilate went against his own conscience; he went against his own best judgment; he went against the pleadings of his wife, who sent a message to him, saying, "Have thou nothing to do with that Just Man: for I have suffered many things this day in a dream because of Him" (Matt. 27: 19). And Pilate gave sentence that it should be as they required. "And he released unto them him that for sedition and murder was cast into prison, whom they had desired; but he delivered Jesus to their will."

In the choice that was made that day between Jesus and Barabbas, we find the choice not only of Israel, but also the choice that the nations have been making all down through the centuries. They have chosen a murderer, a malefactor, instead of the Lord of glory. If Christ had been received He would have brought peace and righteousness to the world; but because He was not chosen the nations have been dominated by men of the spirit of Barabbas, in a large measure, ever since that fatal day. The world, itself, has been soaked with the blood of millions of people who have died because of the awful conditions which have ensued through the rejection of the Prince of Peace.

The question comes to every one of us as individuals: "What shall I do then with Jesus?" You who have heard the story of Jesus all your lives, do you still vacillate just as Pilate vacillated? Though you know you should receive Christ, are you afraid as Pilate was afraid? Do you fear what man will say more than what God would say? If you have never yet trusted Christ Jesus, I plead with you to answer, "Not Barabbas, but this Man!" for "through this Man is preached unto you the forgiveness of sins: and by Him all that believe are justified from all things, from which ye could not be justified by the law of Moses" (Acts 13:38, 39).

Address Seventy-six

"WITH ME IN PARADISE"

ↄ ↄ ↄ

"And as they led Him away, they laid hold upon one Simon, a Cyrenian, coming out of the country, and on him they laid the cross, that he might bear it after Jesus. And there followed Him a great company of people, and of women, which also bewailed and lamented Him. But Jesus turning unto them said, Daughters of Jerusalem, weep not for Me, but weep for yourselves, and for your children. For, behold, the days are coming, in the which they shall say, Blessed are the barren, and the wombs that never bare, and the paps which never gave suck. Then shall they begin to say to the mountains, Fall on us; and to the hills, Cover us. For if they do these things in a green tree, what shall be done in the dry? And there were also two other, malefactors, led with Him to be put to death. And when they were come to the place, which is called Calvary, there they crucified Him, and the malefactors, one on the right hand, and the other on the left. Then said Jesus, Father, forgive them; for they know not what they do. And they parted His raiment, and cast lots. And the people stood beholding. And the rulers also with them derided Him, saying, He saved others; let Him save Himself, if He be Christ, the chosen of God. And the soldiers also mocked Him, coming to Him, and offering Him vinegar, and saying, If Thou be the King of the Jews, save Thyself. And a superscription also was written over Him in letters of Greek, and Latin, and Hebrew, THIS IS THE KING OF THE JEWS. And one of the malefactors which were hanged railed on Him, saying, If Thou be Christ, save Thyself and us. But the other answering rebuked him, saying, Dost not thou fear God, seeing thou art in the same condemnation? And we indeed justly; for we receive the due reward of our deeds: but this Man hath done nothing amiss. And he said unto Jesus, Lord, remember me when Thou comest into Thy kingdom. And Jesus said unto him, Verily I say unto thee, today shalt thou be with Me in paradise"—Luke 23: 26-43.

ↄ ↄ ↄ

We have followed our Saviour to Pilate's judgment-hall and witnessed His trial; we observed Pilate's cowardly conduct, and saw our Lord scourged cruelly and turned over to the soldiers to be put to death. Now we read that they led Him from the judgment-hall to the place which is called Calvary, and then we have the account of His crucifixion. Connected with that is wondrous grace in saving a poor, condemned sinner who hung by His side on one of the other crosses.

Notice what is written concerning the journey to Calvary: "They *led* Him away." We are told—not in the Bible but in church tradition—that He staggered and fell beneath the weight of His cross. We do not read that in the Scripture; it may be true, but we have no positive evidence of it. At any rate, it is clear that the soldiers must have observed that the cross seemed heavy for Him to carry after all He had suffered the night before and because of the cruel scourgings He had endured; for we are told that "They laid hold upon one Simon, a Cyrenian, coming out of the country, and on him they laid the cross, that he might bear it after Jesus." What a privilege this black man had! Simon was from Cyrene, a city of North Africa, and therefore he was undoubtedly a man of dark complexion. How honored was this colored man to be permitted to bear the cross of Jesus! There is another church tradition that Simon became one of Jesus' immediate disciples, and that the Rufus, mentioned in Rom. 16:13 is the same as the brother of Alexander, Simon's son, referred to in Mark 15:21. It seems to me that every colored person should feel grateful that one of his race had the opportunity of helping the blessed Lord as He went out to die upon that cross of shame.

As they pursued their way, there followed Him a great multitude of people: some in sympathy with Him, and others who were ridiculing and reviling Him. Of the sympathetic group there were a number of women who bewailed and lamented Him, but Jesus turned to them and said, "Daughters of Jerusalem, weep not for Me, but weep for yourselves, and for your children." With prophetic eye He beheld Jerusalem surrounded with the Roman army and undergoing awful horrors, when conditions should become so terrible on account of famine that even tender women would devour their own children. This awful cannibalism had been predicted by Moses (Deut. 28: 53-57). Our Lord foresaw that all this would come because the people had turned away from God and knew not the time of their visitation. This had been before His mind when He looked upon the city of Jerusalem, saying, "O Jerusalem, Jerusalem, which killest the prophets, and stonest them that are sent unto thee; how often would I have gathered thy children together, as a hen doth gather her brood under her wings, and ye would not! Behold, your house is left unto you desolate: and verily I say unto you, Ye shall not see Me, until the time come when ye shall say, Blessed is He that cometh in the name of the Lord" (Luke 13: 34, 35). It was all this that led Him to say to these women, "Weep not for Me." He was only carrying out the will of God. This was the express purpose for which He came into the world. "For the Son of Man is come to seek and to save that which was lost" (Luke 19: 10). "Weep for yourselves, and for your children," because of the judgment which they will have to undergo; for "the days are coming, in the which they shall say, Blessed are the barren, and the wombs that never bare, and the paps which never gave suck." This would be far better than seeing their children torn from them in death. He added, "Then shall they begin to say to the mountains, Fall on us; and to the hills, Cover us." He was speaking of Jerusalem. But these same words are used in the Book of Revelation regarding the great day of the wrath of the Lamb yet to come on them that know not God, when "the kings of the earth, and the great men, and the rich men, and the chief captains, and the mighty men, and every bondman, and every free man, (shall hide) themselves in the dens and in the rocks of the mountains; (and say) to the mountains and rocks, Fall on us, and hide us from the face of Him that sitteth on the throne, and from the wrath of the Lamb: for the great day of His wrath is come; and who shall be able to stand?" (Rev. 6:15-17.) If men and women refuse the salvation that God offers in Jesus Christ, then they must endure His wrath. And so our Lord warned these people of judgment soon to come upon Jerusalem. He referred to a passage in the Old Testament as He said, "For if they do these things in a green tree, what shall be done in the dry?" In Ezekiel (20:47) the prophet was told to prophesy against the forest of the south, "Hear the word of the Lord; thus saith the Lord God; Behold, I will kindle a fire in thee, and it shall devour every green tree in thee, and every dry tree:

the flaming flame shall not be quenched, and all faces from the south to the north shall be burned therein. And all flesh shall see that I the Lord have kindled it: it shall not be quenched." The blessed Lord Himself was pictured as the green tree: "In Him was life; and the Life was the light of men" (John 1:4). Rejecting Jesus and turning away from God, formal, religious Israel was represented by the dry tree. If they refused the only perfectly holy, sinless Man in all Israel and condemned Him to suffer upon the cross, what would be the doom of those who spurned Him, who were living in their sins and ignoring the salvation that He came to bring?

"And there were also two other, malefactors, led with Him to be put to death." These were two who, like Barabbas, had been cast into prison for evil. These men were to be crucified with the Lord Jesus: "He was numbered with the transgressors." "And when they were come to the place, which is called Calvary, there they crucified Him, and the malefactors, one on the right hand, and the other on the left." We have to go to each of the four Gospels to get the full account of what took place on Calvary; in fact, I probably should not have used that expression, "full account," for we will never know exactly what took place there until we stand in His presence and look upon His blessed face, and then we shall begin to understand what it really meant for Him, the holy One, to put away our sins. But we have to consult each of the four Gospels to get fuller details of what took place.

One writer tells some things; another gives additional details, and if we take them all we have a very comprehensive and graphic account. Here we are told of the prayer of the Lord Jesus as He hung on the cross. Think of Him extended there upon the tree: nails driven into His hands; the thorn-crown pressed upon His brow; the soldiers keeping guard around the cross; the multitude reviling and mocking Him, and blaspheming His name, crying out in ridicule, "If Thou be the King of the Jews, save Thyself." Matthew also tells us they cried out, "He saved others; Himself He cannot save." They did not realize the truth of that statement; if He was to save others He could not save Himself; He must endure the suffering in order that we might be delivered from the judgment that our sins deserved. So as He heard them, instead of any resentment in His heart, we hear Him praying, "Father, forgive them; for they know not what they do." In the Old Testament if a man slew his neighbor without intending to kill him, he was to flee to the city of refuge, and there he would be safe from the avenger of blood. For the actual murderer there was to be no escape from death. God said, "Whoso sheddeth man's blood, by man shall his blood be shed" (Gen. 9: 6). But He made a distinction between a wilful murderer and one who slew in ignorance. So Jesus by this prayer, "Father, forgive them; for they know not what they do," put them on the ground of manslaughter rather than of deliberate murder. After Pentecost Peter declared that "through ignorance ye did it" (Acts

3:17). In speaking of the rulers of the Gentiles, Paul said, "Which none of the princes of this world knew: for had they known it, they would not have crucified the Lord of glory" (1 Cor. 2:8). They did not understand; they did not know who Jesus was; they did not know what they were doing in delivering Him up to death on the cross. The Lord said, as it were, "Father, open the door to the City of Refuge, and let them flee from the avenger of blood." And, thank God, all who have fled to Jesus —who is Himself the City of Refuge—have found security from the judgment which sin deserves. Some say the prayer of our Lord was not answered. Yes, it was answered, in this way: God did not treat them as murderers, but He opened up the way of salvation for them. If men deliberately and wilfully spurn the offer of mercy which is through our Lord Jesus Christ, then they put Him to an open shame and crucify the Son of God afresh, and there is no hope for those who persist in rejecting Christ. They are adjudged guilty of the murder of the Son of God. If I am addressing any unsaved ones, any who do not know the Lord Jesus, I plead with you to come now to God through Christ; flee to the City of Refuge which God has provided. Receive Him as your Saviour and thus be assured of a glorious welcome.

The soldiers below the cross "parted His raiment, and cast lots." This had been prophesied many years before. In Ps. 22:18 we read, "They part My garments among them, and cast lots upon My vesture." That scripture was fulfilled that day when Jesus died in our stead on Calvary. We read, "The people stood beholding. And the rulers also with them derided Him, saying, He saved others; let Him save Himself, if He be Christ, the chosen of God." The Roman soldiers joined with His own people in ridiculing and mocking Him, "coming to Him, and offering Him vinegar, and saying, If Thou be the King of the Jews, save Thyself."

We are told that Pilate caused a superscription to be written and put over His head. In those days when a man was crucified it was customary to write his sentence on a tablet and nail it to his cross. This superscription was written in Greek, the language of culture; in Latin, the language of authority; and Hebrew, the language of religion: "THIS IS THE KING OF THE JEWS." All passing might see that He was crucified as an insurrectionist, which Pilate knew was not true. The rulers came to Pilate and said, "Write not, The King of the Jews; but that He said, I am King of the Jews" (John 19:21). By this time Pilate was out of patience with them, and he said, "What I have written I have written;" and he let the tablet stand. The last that those men saw of Jesus was as He hung on the cross with the superscription above Him, proclaiming Him to be King of the Jews: He was God's King, and God has said in Ps. 2:6, "Yet have I set My King upon My holy hill of Zion." And in time the Jews will gladly own Him as Lord of lords and King of kings.

We read that "one of the malefactors which were hanged railed on Him." Both of them railed on

Him at first and said, "If Thou be the Christ, save Thyself and us." But suddenly divine conviction laid hold of one of those men. As he gazed upon the holy Sufferer on that central cross, possibly as he heard Him pray for His enemies, he seemed to realize who it was who was there being crucified. He rebuked his fellow-malefactor saying, "Dost not thou fear God, seeing thou art in the same condemnation? And we indeed justly; for we receive the due reward of our deeds: but this Man hath done nothing amiss." He seemed to sense the perfect holiness of Jesus, and in vivid contrast he saw the sinfulness and wickedness of his own life and that of his companion. "But this Man hath done nothing amiss!" What a declaration at such a time! Years before Isaiah asked the question, "Who shall declare His generation? for He was cut off out of the land of the living" (Isa. 53:8). Someone has translated that question, "Who shall declare His manner of life?" Think of the declaration coming from a dying thief, hanging by His side: "This Man hath done nothing amiss!" He then turned to Jesus as he recognized in that thorn-crowned Sufferer, the One who is the King of glory, and he said, "Lord, remember me when Thou comest into Thy kingdom." It was real faith coupled with genuine repentance. So this man hanging there upon that cross was saved. Jesus said, as it were, "You will not have to wait till I come into My kingdom": "Today shalt thou be with Me in Paradise." I know there are some who would like to make us believe that what Jesus said was, "*Today* (not yesterday nor tomorrow) I say unto thee that some day shalt thou be with Me in Paradise." That does violence to the text as we have it both in the original and in the English Bible, and it would imply that our Lord did that thing which He condemns in us—used idle words. No; what He said was, "Today shalt thou be with Me in Paradise." And He was; for ere that day closed—according to Jewish reckoning of a day, from sunset to sunset—the Lord Jesus had dismissed His spirit to the Father, and the spirit of the thief had gone to be with Christ in Paradise: the firstfruit of His glorious redemptive work. An old writer has suggested that there is great danger in putting off our salvation until the end of life. In the Bible there is one man who was saved at the last moment. There is one, that none might despair; only one, that none might presume.

During a series of meetings years ago, an evangelist saw a young man who looked somewhat concerned. The evangelist went to him and asked if he were ready to die, and the lad replied, "No; I am not ready; I hope to come some day. Remember the dying thief?" The evangelist asked, "Which thief?" The young man looked up startled and said, "Oh, I had forgotten; there were two, weren't there?" "Yes," replied the evangelist; "and one went out, so far as we have any record, into eternity closing his heart to the Saviour and was lost forever. The other trusted Him and was saved forever. Which thief are you going to be like?" The young man said, "I'd better come now." And he closed with Christ that evening. Think of the grace of the Lord Jesus Christ to a dying thief, and remember that salvation is for you if you will fully trust Him.

ADDRESS SEVENTY-SEVEN

CHRIST CRUCIFIED AND THE VEIL RENT

✝ ✝ ✝

"And it was about the sixth hour, and there was a darkness over all the earth until the ninth hour. And the sun was darkened, and the veil of the temple was rent in the midst. And when Jesus had cried with a loud voice, He said, Father, into Thy hands I commend My spirit: and having said thus, He gave up the ghost. Now when the centurion saw what was done, he glorified God, saying, Certainly this was a righteous Man. And all the people that came together to that sight, beholding the things which were done, smote their breasts, and returned. And all His acquaintance, and the women that followed Him from Galilee, stood afar off, beholding these things. And, behold, there was a man named Joseph, a counsellor; and he was a good man, and a just: (the same had not consented to the counsel and deed of them;) he was of Arimathea, a city of the Jews: who also himself waited for the kingdom of God. This man went unto Pilate, and begged the body of Jesus. And he took it down, and wrapped it in linen, and laid it in sepulchre that was hewn in stone, wherein never man before was laid. And that day was the preparation, and the sabbath drew on. And the women also, which came with Him from Galilee, followed after, and beheld the sepulchre, and how His body was laid. And they returned, and prepared spices and ointments; and rested the sabbath day according to the commandment"—Luke 23: 44-56.

✝ ✝ ✝

THOSE who have followed carefully the various accounts of the death of our Lord Jesus Christ, know that there are certain details omitted in each of the Gospels which are given in the others, but all are in perfect agreement. You will have noticed that our blessed Lord hung for six awful hours on Calvary. He was nailed to the cross at the third hour: that is what we call nine o'clock in the morning; He was taken down from the cross after the ninth hour: that is, after three o'clock in the afternoon. During those first three hours the sun was shining; all nature seemed bright, as though utterly indifferent to what was taking place: the Creator of all things was dying upon a felon's gibbet, rejected by those whom He had not only brought into being but also come to bless and to save. At the sixth hour—this answers to our twelve noon—the sun was, as it were, blotted out of the heaven. This was not an eclipse. It was the passover time, and it was impossible that there should be an eclipse when the moon was at the full. It was a supernatural darkness that spread over all the scene, not only over the land of Judaea, but possibly, at the same time, over all parts of the known world. The early Christians tell us (whether on reliable authority or not I cannot say, but it is interesting that the story has come down from early times) that a Greek philosopher was giving a lecture in the city of Alexandria of Egypt at the very hour the darkness spread over the land, and he stopped in the midst of his discourse and exclaimed, "Either a god is dying or the universe is going into dissolution." He who is both God and Man was dying! He was dying at that awful hour for our sins. From the sixth to the ninth hour the darkness continued, and after it passed away the Lord bowed His head and died.

It is instructive to observe that during the first three hours Jesus never exhibited concern for Himself. He was perfectly calm, and though He was suffering excruciatingly He gave no evidence whatever of self-pity. He saw His blessed mother standing near the foot of the cross and John the beloved disciple near her; and He said to His mother, "Behold thy son!" and to John, "Behold thy mother!" And John led her away from the scene of her holy Son's dying agony; and, we are told in other records, cared for her for the rest of her life here on earth. Then our Lord looked upon the multitude, blaspheming, mocking, and ridiculing Him; and He recognized the wickedness of their hearts; yet He opened up for them a City of Refuge into which they might flee, as we have seen already, when He prayed, "Father, forgive them; for they know not what they do." He heard the plea of the penitent thief and assured him of a place in Paradise. Thus in those first three hours He exhibited no perturbation of spirit, no concern for Himself but only tender consideration for others.

From the time that the darkness overspread the scene no sound escaped the lips of Jesus, according to the record, until the three hours were drawing to a close; and then, we are told in two other Gospels, He cried out in agony, "My God, My God, why hast Thou forsaken Me?" In those first three hours of darkness He was suffering at the hands of man: He endured without a murmur all the shame and ignominy that man could heap upon Him. But during the last three hours of darkness He was suffering at the hand of God—the God who made His soul an offering for sin. There He drank the bitter cup of judgment that our sins had filled—the cup from which He shrank in Gethsemane, which if we had to drink could not be exhausted throughout eternity. God "hath made Him to be sin for us, who knew no sin; that we might be made the righteousness of God in Him" (2 Cor. 5:21).

In the first three hours He addressed God as "Father": "Father, forgive them; for they know not what they do." But in these last three hours He did not use the term "Father," until the darkness had passed. He address Him as God: *"Eloi, Eloi, lama sabachthani?* which is, being interpreted, My God, My God, why hast Thou forsaken Me?" (Mark 15:34.) For it was God as Judge who was there dealing with His holy Son on our behalf as Christ took the sinner's place. We read, "And the sun was darkened, and the veil of the temple was rent in the midst." One critic tells us that Luke links up the rending of the veil with the darkness rather than with the death of Jesus, and that he was in too much of a hurry to get to the climactic scene and announce Christ's victory, because the other Gospels record the veil as having been rent after Jesus gave up His spirit. Well, we do not blame Luke for being in a hurry to record the rending of the veil; but it was the Holy Spirit who was desirous to let us know that the veil has been rent! Throughout Old Testament times God had said, "I will dwell in the thick darkness." The veil of the temple signified that no man could pass into the presence of God except as in the case of the high priest on the day of atonement, and that, "not without blood." But when Christ died as the propitiation for sin the way was opened up into the Holy of holies. Now God can come out in unhindered love to man, and man can go into God's presence, accepted in Christ. The rent veil speaks of redemption accomplished. "Having therefore, brethren, boldness to enter into the holiest by the blood of Jesus" (Heb. 10:19). One of our hymn-writers has written:

"Through Thy precious body broken—
  Inside the veil.
Oh, what words to sinners spoken—
  Inside the veil.
Precious as the blood that bought us;
Perfect as the love that sought us;
Holy as the Lamb that brought us—
  Inside the veil!

"Lamb of God, through Thee we enter—
  Inside the veil;
Cleansed by blood we boldly venture—
  Inside the veil.
Not a stain; a new creation;
Ours is such a full salvation:
Low we bow in adoration—
  Inside the veil!

"Soon Thy saints shall all be gathered—
  Inside the veil;
All at home—no more be scattered—
  Inside the veil.
Nought from Thee our souls shall sever;
We shall see Thee, grieve Thee never;
'Praise the Lamb,' shall sound forever—
  Inside the veil!"

At the last Jesus prayed, saying, "Father, into Thy hands I commend My spirit: and having said this, He gave up the ghost." He dismissed His spirit. The work was done, and He went home to be with the Father. Our attention is next directed to the scene before the cross. We are told, "When the centurion saw what was done, he glorified God, saying, Certainly this was a righteous Man." He was a Roman; he was in charge of the soldiers who were there on guard; he saw and heard all that took place, and his heart was stirred. According to other Gospels he added also, "Truly this was the Son of God." Then we are told that, "All the people that came together to that sight, beholding the things which were done, smote their breasts, and returned." A great throng was gathered there, not only enemies but also friends; but these last were powerless to interfere as they stood looking on in grief and sorrow. It must have been hard for them to believe that Jesus had actually died. They thought it was He who should have redeemed Israel, but now their hopes were blasted, and they turned away and went to their homes sorrowing and bewailing. All His acquaintance stood afar off, beholding these things. They had been watching Jehovah's Anointed die like a felon upon a cross of shame; but oh, the joy that awaited them when they were to learn of His glorious resurrection!

You will notice that as long as the Lord Jesus was standing in the sinner's stead God allowed every kind of indignity to be heaped upon His blessed Son: they spat in His face; they slapped Him with the palms of their hands, a most insulting gesture; they flogged Him until His flesh was torn from His back and blood poured from every wound; they pressed a thorn-crown upon His head; and they put a gorgeous robe upon Him and knelt before Him, mocking Him, saying, "Hail, King of the Jews;" they took Him out to Calvary and nailed Him to the cross; and lastly, one of the soldiers pierced His side, but that was the final act of indignity that God permitted. "The very spear that pierced His side drew forth the blood to save." After that it was as though God said, "I gave My Son into your hands; you have shown all the hatred and bitterness of your hearts by the way you have treated Him. Now not another unclean hand shall touch Him." From that time on no enemy touched that sacred body.

"And, behold, there was a man name Joseph, a counsellor; and he was a good man, and a just: (the same had not consented to the counsel and deed of them;) he was of Arimathea, a city of the Jews: who also himself waited for the kingdom of God. This man went unto Pilate, and begged the body of Jesus." He and his servants tenderly and reverently took that body from the cross, washed away the blood-stains, wrapped the body in linen, and carried it to Joseph's new tomb and left it there, intending, after the sabbath had passed, to embalm it according to the Jewish custom. "And the women also, which came with Him from Galilee, followed after, and beheld the sepulchre, and how His body was laid." They then turned sadly away, intending to return and perform the last sacred rites after the sabbath. They "prepared spices and ointments; and rested the sabbath day according to the commandment." The Christ—who was born of a virgin; who had grown up as a tender plant in the garden of the Lord, and had gone forth, anointed of Jehovah, healing the sick, giving sight to the blind, proclaiming the gospel of the kingdom—had died at last on the cross for sinners; and now His body lay in the tomb, and no one on earth knew whether or not redemption was an accomplished fact. If He had not come forth from that tomb then there would have been no evidence that the sin question had been settled. But His resurrected body was to be the proof of the efficacy of His work. Now, thank God, "He is able also to save them to the uttermost that come unto God by Him, seeing He ever liveth to make intercession for them" (Heb. 7:25).

ADDRESS SEVENTY-EIGHT

THE EMPTY TOMB

"Now upon the first day of the week, very early in the morning, they came unto the sepulchre, bringing the spices which they had prepared, and certain others with them. And they found the stone rolled away from the sepulchre. And they entered in, and found not the body of the Lord Jesus. And it came to pass, as they were much perplexed thereabout, behold, two men stood by them in shining garments: and as they were afraid, and bowed down their faces to the earth, they said unto them, Why seek ye the living among the dead? He is not here, but is risen: remember how He spake unto you when He was yet in Galilee, saying, The Son of Man must be delivered into the hands of sinful men, and be crucified, and the third day rise again. And they remembered His words, and returned from the sepulchre, and told all these things unto the eleven, and to all the rest. It was Mary Magdalene, and Joanna, and Mary the mother of James, and other women that were with them, which told these things unto the apostles. And their words seemed to them as idle tales, and they believed them not. Then arose Peter, and ran unto the sepulchre; and stooping down, he beheld the linen clothes laid by themselves, and departed, wondering in himself at that which was come to pass"—Luke 24: 1-12.

UNBELIEVING scholars, who scoff at the story of the resurrection of our Lord Jesus Christ, have often tried to make it appear that the followers of the Lord were expecting Him to rise from the dead; that every shadow seen on the side of Calvary was taken to be the risen Saviour; and that His followers were in an exalted, emotional state of mind and imagined they actually saw Him; but that in reality His body never left the tomb. These critics further claim that when the followers of Christ went into the sepulchre and found it empty it was because, in their excitement, they entered the wrong tomb. Matthew Arnold has written, "The body of Jesus still sleeps in a Syrian tomb." Well, if the body of Jesus still sleeps in a Syrian tomb, then you and I are without hope so far as salvation is concerned, because, "If Christ be not risen, then is our preaching vain, and your faith is also vain" (1 Cor. 15: 14). We are not saved by the teaching of Jesus, wonderful as that was: "Never man spake like this Man." His teaching could not atone for sin; His teaching could not cleanse guilty souls; it could not make men and women fit for heaven. Neither are we saved by imitating the lovely life of Jesus. If our salvation depended upon our imitating that perfect life, we might everyone of us give up all hope and consider that we are just as good as eternally lost; because it is absolutely impossible for any sinful man to live a life such as Jesus, the holy Son of God, lived. It is true that after we are converted, after we have received a new nature through faith in Him, we are called upon to follow in His steps; but even then as we seek to imitate Him we realize day by day how much we fail. It is not the teaching of Jesus that saves us; it is not by imitation of His life that we are saved: we are saved by His death and resurrection! He "was delivered for our offences, and was raised again for our justification" (Rom. 4:25).

The Scriptures are clear and definite in regard to the great reality of His triumph over death. One witness after another is brought before us to testify to the fact that Joseph's new tomb was empty after the three days following the crucifixion. Angels appeared to say He was risen; He Himself appeared on one occasion after another during forty days ere He ascended into heaven in the sight of His apostles. Horace Bushnell has well said that the resurrection of our Lord Jesus Christ is the best attested fact of ancient history. If you are familiar with history I should like to put a question to you. Take any outstanding character or event in ancient history —by ancient history I mean that which has to do with persons who lived or events which took place before the Christian era—and try to think on the testimony of how many witnesses you accept the story which you have received concerning these persons or events. There was a man by the name of Socrates. How do you know he lived? Well, you have the testimony of Plato and Xenophon. Beyond that you do not have the testimony of any other eye- or ear-witness. Others referred to him in later days on the authority of these witnesses. God has given us abundant testimony of the death and resurrection of the Lord Jesus Christ. In order to get the full force of it we need to read what is recorded in all the four Gospels. In addition to that, we have the definite witness of the apostle Paul, and the testimony of the apostles James and Jude, who were related to Christ after the flesh, but who write of Him as the risen One who is now Lord of all. God saw to it that there was all-sufficient evidence of the resurrection that no honest soul need doubt.

"Now upon the first day of the week, very early in the morning, they came unto the sepulchre." The pronoun *they* refers to the women spoken of in verse 55 of the preceding chapter: that is, the women from Galilee. Actually, there were two groups of women, but Luke was not led to speak of two separate visits; so he simply says, "They came early in the morning." The other Gospels give certain particulars concerning their coming, all in full accord with what we have here: "They came early in the morning on the first day of the week." The first day of the week stands out from all other days, and will stand out until the time when our Lord Himself shall appear again. In Ps. 118, after saying, "The Stone which the builders refused is become the head stone of the corner" (ver. 22), the Psalmist cries out, "This is the day which the Lord hath made; we will rejoice and be glad in it" (ver. 24). This was the day of the Lord's triumph over death. The last Jewish sabbath that God ever recognized had ended. While the Jews were observing the day according to their law, the body of the Lord Jesus Christ lay cold in death in Joseph's tomb. They had refused and rejected Him. The sabbath speaks of rest, and the Lord said, "Come unto Me, all ye that labor and are heavy laden, and I will give you rest" (Matt. 11:28). The One who came to bring in the true sabbath of God had been rejected. But on "the morrow after the sabbath," as written in Leviticus, chap. 23, when the firstfruits were to be presented to God on the first day of the week, Jesus came forth—the first-fruits of the resurrection; and thus redemption was proved to be an accomplished fact.

Moved by their love for the One who had died, the women were bringing spices which they had prepared in order to properly embalm the body. They had no thought that Jesus had risen from the dead. It is absolutely absurd to contend that the followers of Christ expected Him to rise again; that it was easy for them to think they saw Him; that He had told them He would rise again, and so they were expecting Him. They expected nothing of the kind. All they knew was that He had died, and with Him died also their hopes of deliverance, for they had trusted He was the One who would free them from the Roman yoke. They brought the spices to perform the last acts of love, to show their respect for and interest in the One who had been with them for so long, but who was now taken away. We read in Mark's Gospel that when the women came to the tomb "they said among themselves, Who shall roll us away the stone from the door of the sepulchre?" It was really like a vast millstone. And when they looked they saw that it was already rolled back. At first they were afraid to enter; and upon doing so they were astonished to find that the body was gone. They never dreamed for a moment that He was risen, but thought that someone had broken the Roman seal and stolen the body. As they stood there wondering about it, "two men stood by them in shining garments." One of the angels asked, "Why seek ye the living among the dead?" That gave them the first intimation that the Lord had actually risen. "He is not here, but is risen: remember how He spake unto you when He was yet in Galilee, saying, The Son of Man must be delivered into the hands of sinful men, and be crucified, and the third day rise again." Many times He had told them of His approaching death and resurrection, but they had not understood what His rising from the dead could mean. The angels said, "Remember!" And all that Jesus had said came back to the minds. They remembered His words; and they returned from the sepulchre to carry the word of His resurrection to the disciples. On the way something happened that is not recorded here. Jesus personally appeared to Mary Magdalene, and later to all the women, but Luke does not stop to tell us this. Writing by inspiration of the Holy Spirit, he was so eager to tell how the news was carried to the disciples and how they came out to see for themselves, that he omits some of these beautiful and lovely details given in the other Gospels.

They "returned from the sepulchre, and told all these things unto the eleven, and to all the rest." There is something so pathetic about this expression: "Told all these things unto the *eleven*." Only a few days before there had been twelve, but now there are only eleven. One who had been with Jesus for three-and-one-half wonderful years, who had seen His works of power, beheld His wondrous deeds, and knew the perfection of His Person, had turned away and gone into eternal infamy as Judas the traitor. Oh, how we need to remind ourselves of that scripture which says, "Let him that thinketh he standeth take heed lest he fall" (1 Cor. 10:12).

Many have companied with God's people down through the years, going in and out among them and apparently giving every evidence of being real disciples of His, and yet have never definitely known the Lord, but at last have apostatized from the truth. They, like Judas, will go out into eternal darkness. These words speak to my heart every time I read them; God grant they may speak to yours.

Luke gives us the names of Mary Magdalene, out of whom Jesus had cast seven demons; Joanna, a wealthy woman who ministered to Jesus with her substance; Mary, the mother of James and Joses, intimately related to the Lord Himself, "and other women that were with them, which told these things unto the apostles." At first the disciples refused to believe the women, for "their words seemed to them as idle tales." Not one of the apostles expected Jesus to come back from the dead; not one had understood when He told them that He would rise again; therefore, when the women came with such a wonderful tale they listened in amazement, doubtless shaking their heads and saying, "These women are terribly excited, but we cannot credit their story: it is incredible that one should arise from the dead." Finally Peter was stirred—Peter, the one who had said, "Although all shall be offended, yet will not I;" and within another hour had failed his Lord! But Peter loved Jesus devotedly. He determined to go and see for himself, and away he went. John tells us in his Gospel that he followed also and reached the tomb before Peter, but he did not go in. Peter stooped down—he had to stoop because the door of the sepulchre would be very low—and he entered in and saw the empty crypt, and the linen clothes lying by themselves in exactly the same form as they had been when wrapped around the body of Jesus. It was the custom of the Jews to wrap the body in long linen bands, beginning with the extremities and coming up to the torso, binding the lower limbs together, and the arms to the side, and putting a turban on the head. When the body was wrapped in these linen clothes it would be impossible for a person to free himself without disturbing them; as in the case of Lazarus when the Lord cried, "Lazarus, come forth." He came forth bound hand and foot, and Jesus said, "Loose him, and let him go." As Peter looked at those linen clothes he must have known that only the power of God could ever have taken the body out of them. He "departed, wondering in himself (he was amazed) at that which was come to pass."

Yes, Jesus lives! He has been raised from the dead; and because He lives, we shall live also. This is the rock foundation of our faith.

ADDRESS SEVENTY-NINE

THE MYSTERIOUS STRANGER

ᛘ ᛘ ᛘ

"And, behold, two of them went that same day to a village called Emmaus, which was from Jerusalem about threescore furlongs. And they talked together of all these things which had happened. And it came to pass, that, while they communed together and reasoned, Jesus Himself drew near, and went with them. But their eyes were holden that they should not know Him. And He said unto them, What manner of communications are these that ye have one to another, as ye walk, and are sad? And the one of them, whose name was Cleopas, answering said unto Him, Art thou only a stranger in Jerusalem, and hast not known the things which are come to pass there in these days? And He said unto them, What things? And they said unto Him, Concerning Jesus of Nazareth, which was a Prophet mighty in deed and word before God and all the people: and how the chief priests and our rulers delivered Him to be condemned to death, and have crucified Him. But we trusted that it had been He which should have redeemed Israel: and beside all this, today is the third day since these things were done. Yea, and certain women also of our company made us astonished, which were early at the sepulchre; and when they found not His body, they came, saying, that they had also seen a vision of angels, which said that He was alive. And certain of them which were with us went to the sepulchre, and found it even so as the women had said: but Him they saw not. Then He said unto them, O fools, and slow of heart to believe all that the prophets have spoken: ought not Christ to have suffered these things, and to enter into His glory? And beginning at Moses and all the prophets, He expounded unto them in all the Scriptures the things concerning Himself. And they drew nigh unto the village, whither they went: and He made as though He would have gone further. But they constrained Him, saying, Abide with us: for it is toward evening, and the day is far spent. And He went in to tarry with them. And it came to pass, as He sat at meat with them, He took bread, and blessed it, and brake, and gave to them. And their eyes were opened, and they knew Him; and He vanished out of their sight. And they said one to another, Did not our heart burn within us while He talked with us by the way, and while He opened to us the Scriptures? And they rose up the same hour, and returned to Jerusalem, and found the eleven gathered together, and them that were with them, saying, The Lord is risen indeed, and hath appeared to Simon. And they told what things were done in the way, and how He was known of them in breaking of bread"—Luke 24: 13-35.

WE turn now to Luke's account of the appearance of Christ following the resurrection. There is a delightful simplicity and straightforwardness about the various narratives of these great events as given in the four Gospels, which forbids all thought of untruthfulness or of an insane obsession. The writers knew whereof they spoke. They were assured, beyond any doubt, that Jesus, who had died on a malefactor's cross and whose body lay entombed for three days, had risen in triumph and appeared to so many different witnesses that they could not question the reality of His resurrection. Luke evidently was not one of those who saw the Lord after He rose from the dead, but he was a scientific man, a physician of inquiring mind, who did not rest satisfied until he had examined all the evidence with meticulous care, as a result of which he was convinced of the truthfulness of the testimony given by those who declared they had seen and talked with the risen Saviour (Luke 1: 1-3).

Among the many manifestations of our Lord to His disciples during the forty days between the resurrection and ascension is this incident, which I have always considered to be one of the most tender and interesting of all His appearances. It concerns two disciples, Cleopas and another. I believe this other was his wife. We do not know much about Cleopas; some think he is the same as Cleophas (John 19: 25). Cleopas is a Hebrew name, however, and the other is Aramaic; but whether the two are identical we do not know. At any rate, these two disciples had loved Jesus; they believed He was the Messiah; and perhaps they were in that throng that watched Him die. Now, in deep perplexity, they were wondering whether their hope was in vain, and whether He was deceived or a deceiver in presenting Himself as the Messiah of Israel, which they had believed He was. They were walking along the way from Jerusalem to Emmaus. It is not a long distance. I have ridden over the road myself, and as I did so I thought of these two as they sauntered along the way speaking of those things which had happened so recently, and I felt as I know they must have felt when that blessed, wondrous Stranger drew near and interrupted their conversation in such a sweet way. "And it came to pass, that, while they communed together and reasoned, Jesus Himself drew near, and went with them." There is something very comforting about that: Jesus was there! But they did not know it; they did not realize it, and I think oftentimes the same is true with us. Sometimes we are going through trials, bewilderments, sorrow, disappointments, and we feel so utterly alone, we feel as though no one cares, but if our eyes could only be opened—like the eyes of that servant of Elisha in Dothan, so long ago, when he saw the angels of the Lord encamped around them to protect them from their enemies—we might have a similar experience. The eyes of these two disciples were holden so that they did not know who the Stranger was. They were not expecting Him, and did not recognize Him. That He was marvelously changed there can be no doubt. He was no longer the Man of Sorrows, but the triumphant Christ, every trace of care and grief having vanished from His face. They thought, perhaps, He was a visitor, a mysterious Stranger, walking close to them. Drawing nearer He put the question to them, "What manner of communications are these that ye have one to another?" He knew well, but He would draw them out, have them express themselves in order that He might open to them the truth of the Word of God in regard to the great matters of His death and resurrection. They had overlooked in the Bible the very things they were wondering about. The prophets had testified beforehand of the sufferings of Christ, and the glory that should follow His resurrection. Our Lord would have us bring to Him our griefs and our burdens; He delights to have us come to Him and tell Him everything that is on our hearts, and He is ever ready to comfort, lead, instruct, and help. Cleopas, who took the lead, inquired, "Art Thou only a stranger in Jerusalem, and hast not known the things which are come to pass there in these days?" As this was the season of the Passover and there were many visitors in Jerusalem, they supposed this Stranger might be one of them, and had not heard of what had taken place. It might be that He was not in that throng who gazed upon the three hanging on those crosses at Calvary; perhaps He had never heard of this Jesus, the supposed Messiah, who had performed such wondrous works, and so had never learned of His marvelous deeds and teaching. They supposed

Jesus to be just a stranger, and indeed He was a Stranger in this world; yet He was the Central Figure in all that had happened in these days. He again put a question to them, "What things?" They answered, "Concerning Jesus of Nazareth, which was a Prophet mighty in deed and word before God and all the people: and how the chief priests and our rulers delivered Him to be condemned to death, and have crucified Him. But we trusted that it had been He which should have redeemed Israel: and beside all this, today is the third day since these things were done. Yea, and certain women also of our company made us astonished, which were early at the sepulchre; and when they found not His body, they came, saying, that they had also seen a vision of angels, which said that He was alive." This news had spread among all who loved the name of Jesus; but they were not sure that what the women said was true. Perhaps they were misled; perhaps some optical illusion had dazzled their eyes, or perhaps they were excited and had been deceived into thinking that they had actually seen Him. "And certain of them which were with us went to the sepulchre, and found it even so as the women had said: but Him they saw not." "Certain of them" refers to Peter and John. They found the tomb empty, the linen clothes lying as they had been wrapped around the body, but they did not see Jesus; and they were not yet clear as to just what had taken place. Jesus undertook to answer them. "O fools, and slow of heart to believe all that the prophets have spoken." The word rendered "fools" is not an opprobrious term. It means "simple ones." They were like children who failed to understand, and so did not believe the prophetic declarations concerning Christ. In other words, there was nothing in all that they had related which was contrary to what was taught in the Word of God; there was nothing opposed to what was written by the prophets. If these two disciples had weighed carefully everything, and had studied the prophecies that speak of the Redeemer of Israel and of His glorious coming kingdom, they ought to have seen how definitely the Scriptures predicted the rejection of the Saviour, His crucifixion, His death and burial; yes, and His resurrection, for it is written in Isa. 53: 10, "When Thou shalt make His soul an offering for sin, He shall see His seed, He shall prolong His days."

"Ought not Christ to have suffered these things, and to enter into His glory?" The cross must come before the crown. There was no other way by which the divine plan of redemption for the individual soul and for the world at large could be carried out. The Lord proceeded to give them a running exposition of practically the whole Old Testament. How one would have delighted to have been in their company that day and heard the blessed Christ of God unfold the Scriptures, referring to His whole life, His rejection, His death on the cross, and resurrection, and even His ascension to God's right hand, for in Ps. 110: 1 we read, "The Lord said unto my Lord, Sit Thou at My right hand, until I make Thine enemies Thy footstool." He went through the prophecies of the whole Old Testament, beginning with

Moses. Our Lord never cast any doubt on the authorship of the first five books of the Bible. Unbelieving critics today may question it. They go so far as to deny that Moses wrote those books, but our Lord had no such doubt. He said, "Had ye believed Moses, ye would have believed Me: for he wrote of Me" (John 5:46). He knew that Moses was the writer of the early books. "And beginning at Moses and all the prophets, He expounded unto them in all the Scriptures the things concerning Himself." What a Bible-reading that was! Their hearts were thrilled as the Lord Jesus showed how He was the theme of all phophecy, and so He gave them the key that opens up the Scriptures as nothing else can. Who has ever been able to expound the Word of God and give such a wondrous unfolding of divine truth as our Lord gave that day! If only we had a record of it, how it would enrich our lives; but He chose that we should not have such a record, in order that we might be stirred up to study the Word for ourselves, and search it daily in dependence upon the Holy Spirit. We are to begin with Moses and go on through all the prophets, and with the light that the New Testament throws on these books, we can see the things which they have to teach us concerning Him, for Christ Himself is the theme of the entire Old Testament as truly as the New.

As our Lord walked on with these two, "they drew nigh unto the village whither they went." They dwelt at Emmaus, and as they turned to go into their home "He made as though He would have gone further." The Lord Jesus never presses Himself upon anybody; He always waits for an invitation. He will pass on if we allow Him to do so. If He is not invited to come in we will be left without the spiritual help that we might have experienced. "They constrained Him, saying, Abide with us." So interested were they in what this heavenly Stranger had unfolded that they urged Him to become their Guest for the night. Thus pressed, He went in to tarry with them. Oh, how He appreciated their invitation! He loves to be welcomed; He never turns away when He is invited. He went in to tarry with them. They soon prepared the evening meal, and this wondrous Stranger was asked to recline at the table with them. It might have been a very simple meal; there might not have been very much variety, but they were prepared to share what they had with Him. He took His place at the table, but not simply as a guest; He took the place of the Host. Instead of waiting for Cleopas or the other disciples to ask the blessing, He took one of the wafers of bread and looked up to heaven and gave thanks. They thought they were inviting Him as their Guest, but they found that they were His guests, and He was the Host. Suddenly, as they looked upon His hands when He was about to break the bread, a revelation came to them. We read, "And their eyes were opened, and they knew Him; and He vanished out of their sight." How did they know Him? They told the disciples afterward in Jerusalem, "He was known of us in breaking of bread." These two were not at the Lord's Supper. At that time there were the eleven, the apostles of the Lord Jesus Christ. These two were but disciples who, otherwise, were unknown. So they did not recognize Him because of something they had seen Him do in the Upper Room. But as they gazed upon those hands, no doubt they saw the print of the nails, as Thomas was shortly afterward to see; and they said, "Oh, this is He! Look at those hands! This is the One who was nailed to that cross." They recognized Him and they knew Him now to be the Christ, the Redeemer of Israel. But when they looked again, He was gone; He had vanished out of sight. His resurrection body was no longer subject to earthly order. A little later we find Him entering a room with the doors shut. He could manifest Himself and vanish from them at any time. "And they said one to another, Did not our heart burn within us, while He talked with us by the way, and while He opened to us the Scriptures?" They had never heard Scripture unfolded like that. Now as they looked back they felt they might have known who He was who had revealed the truth in such a heart-warming manner. "And they rose up the same hour, and returned to Jerusalem, and found the eleven gathered together, and them that were with them." They knew just where to find the eleven. As these two disciples came to the door they heard someone say, "The Lord is risen indeed, and hath appeared to Simon." Simon! the one who had denied Him, taken an oath that he did not even know Jesus; yet somewhere on that resurrection day the Lord had sought him out, and He had revealed Himself to him; and Simon knew that he was forgiven. Peter must have felt, of all the apostles, the most forlorn and wretched, as he recalled in bitterness of spirit his sad failure to stand the test in the hour of trial. What a relief to his heart when Jesus appeared to him alone, to restore his soul and console his spirit! It is but one sample of the grace He ever manifests toward His erring followers. A little later we find the Lord giving Peter the commission, "Feed My lambs . . . feed My sheep."

"And they told what things were done in the way, and how He was known of them in breaking of bread." And so the two disciples added their testimony. What an experience they had and what joy must have been theirs as they knew for certain that He who had died was alive again. And, thank God, He lives to die no more!

At the risk of some repetition let me emphasize the truth that apart from the physical resurrection of our Lord Jesus Christ, the Church of God has no foundation upon which to rest, and there would be no basis for the gospel message. Therefore God has emphasized this great truth in a very remarkable way. In the Old Testament it was plainly predicted that the Saviour was to die for our sins and that He would rise from the dead and take His seat on the right hand of God in Heaven. For Him the path of life lay through the regions of death, but His soul was not to be left in Sheol, the unseen world, nor His body see corruption (Ps. 16: 9-11). After His soul was made an offering for sin, He was to "see

His seed," and "prolong His days, and the pleasure of the Lord" should prosper in His hand (Isa. 53: 10.) In the prophets we have prediction; in the Gospels, fulfilment. Christ is risen. He has "become the firstfruits of them that slept" (1 Cor. 15: 20). Through His name, the name of the One who was dead and is alive again (Rev. 1:18), mighty signs and wonders have been wrought during all the centuries since He vanquished death and "brought life and immortality to light through the gospel" (2 Tim. 1:10).

ADDRESS EIGHTY

OUR LORD'S LAST INSTRUCTIONS AND ASCENSION

✝ ✝ ✝

"And as they thus spake, Jesus Himself stood in the midst of them, and saith unto them, Peace be unto you. But they were terrified and affrighted, and supposed that they had seen a spirit. And He said unto them, Why are ye troubled? and why do thoughts arise in your hearts? Behold My hands and My feet, that it is I Myself: handle Me, and see; for a spirit hath not flesh and bones, as ye see Me have. And when He had thus spoken, He showed them His hands and His feet. And while they yet believed not for joy, and wondered, He said unto them, Have ye here any meat? And they gave Him a piece of a broiled fish, and of an honeycomb. And He took it, and did eat before them. And He said unto them, These are the words which I spake unto you, while I was yet with you, that all things must be fulfilled, which were written in the law of Moses, and in the prophets, and in the psalms, concerning Me. Then opened He their understanding, that they might understand the Scriptures, and said unto them, Thus it is written, and thus it behoved Christ to suffer, and to rise from the dead the third day: and that repentance and remission of sins should be preached in His name among all nations, beginning at Jerusalem. And ye are witnesses of these things. And, behold, I send the promise of My Father upon you: but tarry ye in the city of Jerusalem, until ye be endued with power from on high. And He led them out as far as to Bethany, and He lifted up His hands, and blessed them. And it came to pass, while He blessed them, He was parted from them, and carried up into heaven. And they worshipped Him, and returned to Jerusalem with great joy: and were continually in the temple, praising and blessing God. Amen"—Luke 24: 36-53.

✝ ✝ ✝

CHRIST'S commissions to His apostles in regard to carrying His gospel to the world were not given all at one time. In Acts 1: 2, 3 Luke tells us that during the forty days between His resurrection and ascension the Lord gave commandment regarding their future service, and spoke of many things "pertaining to the kingdom of God."

The present section is divided into two portions: Verses 36 to 49 give the first appearance of the Lord Jesus Christ in the upper room in Jerusalem, as referred to in John, chap. 20. The last four verses take us to the slopes of Mount Olivet, from which the Lord ascended to heaven.

We read, "As they thus spake." That is, while the two who came back from Emmaus were telling of their remarkable experience with the risen Lord, Jesus suddenly appeared standing "in the midst," having entered the room without opening the closed doors. In His resurrection body He was no longer subject to the laws that He submitted to during His humiliation. "And as they thus spake, Jesus Himself stood in the midst of them, and saith unto them, Peace be unto you." He said, "Peace be unto you," for He had made peace by the blood of His cross (Col. 1:20). He had told them long before, "Where two or three are gathered together in My name, there am I *in the midst*" (Matt. 18:20). This is always true: wherever there are two or three, or a great gathering met in His name, He is *in the midst*. I think if Christians realized this more fully we would not be found absent so often from meetings for prayer and worship. We would take every opportunity to meet with our blessed Lord. We would go, not just to meet one another, nor merely to hear the preaching of the Word, nor to enjoy the singing of the hymns, but to be in His holy presence and be occupied with Christ Himself. When He hung on the tree there were two thieves crucified with Him, and Jesus was *in the midst*. There He took the place of the sinner and bore the judgment that we so richly deserved. And when His disciples were gathered together He appeared *"in the midst"* of them. When the apostle John beheld the heavenly home he tells us, *"In the midst* of the throne and of the four beasts, and *in the midst* of the elders, stood a Lamb as it had been slain" (Rev. 5:6). His place is always *in the midst.*

The disciples had heard of the testimony of His resurrection from a number of the others; yet it seemed so utterly impossible that some were filled with terror rather than gladness. They supposed they had seen a spirit, that is, a ghost; they thought a phantom had appeared to them. "They were terrified and affrighted." They could not credit the testimony of their own senses, so little did they understand about His rising from the dead. They thought they beheld a wraith, and that it boded some evil rather than good. Jesus said, "Why are ye troubled? and why do thoughts arise in your hearts?" He checked their disordered thoughts and rebuked them for their distress, which was caused by unbelief. Had they paid careful attention to His words before His arrest, they would not have been troubled now, but would have rejoiced that they were so gloriously fulfilled. He added, "Behold My hand and My feet, that it is I Myself: handle Me, and see; for a spirit hath not flesh and bones, as ye see Me have." He bade them grasp His arms firmly to feel for themselves that it was no phantom that had appeared to them, but one in a real body of flesh and bones. He did not say "flesh and *blood.*"

The life of the flesh is in the blood (Lev. 17:11). The resurrection body is apparently bloodless. But it is a material body nevertheless—of flesh and bone—though of a character different from the present body. Then He showed them His hands and His feet. John mentions His hands and side and omits His feet. He directed attention to His wounds, for He bore in His resurrection body the scars that told of His suffering, and He will bear them forever as the supreme reminder of His love.

Recently I was preaching in an eastern city, and I went down to visit a mission with the brother in charge. He told me, as we stood by the pulpit, of a remarkable experience he had there a short time before. He said he was standing in the pulpit, and as he looked down the aisle the door opened, and a strange-looking figure entered, clothed in a long white robe. Coming to where my friend stood, the stranger looked up at him and said, "I have come to take possession. I am the Lord Jesus Christ." My friend looked at him for a moment; at first he thought perhaps the man was a maniac, and he had better leave him, but instead he asked, "You say you are the Lord Jesus Christ?" "Yes," was the reply, "and I have come back as I promised I would." "Let me see your hands," said the mission man. The visitor held out his hands. "Oh, no; you are not my Saviour; my Saviour has the prints of the nails in each hand." The man looked hard at him and turned and left. Jesus bears the marks of identification in His wounded hands and feet. He said, "Behold My hands and My feet, that it is I Myself:

handle Me, and see; for a spirit hath not flesh and bones, as ye see Me have." The natural thing to have said is "A spirit hath not flesh and *blood*." But our Lord had poured out His precious blood on Calvary to make atonement for us, and His resurrection body had no need of blood to sustain it. "He said unto them, Have ye here any meat? And they gave Him a piece of a broiled fish, and of an honeycomb. And He took it, and did eat before them." They were still incredulous; so He undertook to eat before them, so that they might know beyond all doubt that He stood there in a true human body. Thus He made it clear that He was actually present with them in His resurrection body, not simply a glorified spirit.

"And He said unto them, These are the words which I spake unto you, while I was yet with you, that all things must be fulfilled, which were written in the law of Moses, and in the prophets, and in the psalms, concerning Me." The risen Lord here authenticates the entire Old Testament by declaring without any equivocation that all things written in the law, the prophets, and the psalms, concerning Him must be fulfilled. This goes on to His second coming and kingdom. Nothing is to be cancelled. All must take place as written. This is our authority for believing in the literal fulfilment of prophecy. It is a great mistake to spiritualize the prophecies and suppose that God is going to go back on His word.

Then the Lord Jesus Christ did something for the disciples that we would have Him do for us, "Then opened He their understanding, that they might understand the Scriptures." It is only as the Lord, through His Spirit, opens the understanding of men and women that they can comprehend the truth that God has revealed in His Word. In this chapter, ver. 31, we read, "And their eyes were opened, and they knew Him." Here we are told that the Lord opened their understanding; and after He had disappeared from the room, the Emmaus disciples said one to another, "Did not our heart burn within us, while He talked with us by the way, and while He opened to us the Scriptures?" Link these three together: He opened the *Scriptures,* their *eyes,* and their *understanding.* It is only in this way that we can learn the mind of God. It is a great thing to go back to what is written in the Scriptures. We get so occupied with human theories that we fail to depend on what is written in the Word. "And He said unto them, Thus it is written, and thus it behoved Christ to suffer, and to rise from the dead the third day: and that repentance and remission of sins should be preached in His name among all nations, beginning at Jerusalem. And ye are witnesses of these things." Jerusalem at that time was the guiltiest city on the face of the earth. Its people had gone so far as to crucify their own blessed, adorable King. One might have wondered if God in His wrath would not wipe that city off the face of the earth; but it was there that He was to begin showing the exceeding riches of His grace. Within a short time three thousand persons were led to accept Christ as Saviour and having accepted Him, were baptized in His Name; that is, by His authority. After beginning in Jerusalem, the apostles were to be witnesses to His resurrection through the entire world. In Acts 1: 8 we read, "And ye shall be witnesses unto Me both in Jerusalem, and in all Judaea, and in Samaria, and unto the uttermost part of the earth."

Notice that in the commission as given here there are two things that God has joined together: personal repentance and remission of sin. What is repentance? It is nothing meritorious; it is the recognition of the disease that is destroying us. When we acknowledge our sinfulness we are glad to avail ourselves of the salvation God has provided. Then one is ready for the message which tells him that Christ has done for him that which he cannot do for himself. When he puts his trust in Christ he receives remission of sins. To believe in Him is to put your trust in Him, and when you do that you receive remission of sins. How do you know when your sins are forgiven? You must take God at His word; believe it because He says so. It is not because of a happy feeling that you know you are forgiven, but because you know that God cannot lie.

Our Lord added, "And, behold, I send the promise of My Father upon you: but tarry ye in the city of Jerusalem, until ye be endued with power from on high." They were not to go at once, however. The promised Comforter must come first, whom the the Father was to send in His name (John 14: 26). He would empower them to preach so as to carry conviction to the hearts of their hearers. They were to wait in Jerusalem until this promise was fulfilled. After ten days the Spirit of God came upon them in an absolutely new way. This was their power for testimony. The reason why much of our witnessing does not amount to more than it does is that we witness in our own strength and not in the power of the Holy Spirit.

Following these instructions, "He led them out as far as Bethany, and He lifted up His hands, and blessed them." In order to reach Bethany one must climb up the Mount of Olives, and then go down a little on the eastern side. The Lord Jesus often visited in Bethany at the home of Mary, Martha, and their brother Lazarus, whom Jesus raised from the dead. On the mountain-side near this town He lifted up His hands and blessed His disciples, and then ascended to heaven, and a cloud received Him and hid Him from their view. His work on earth was finished, and He returned to the Father and to the glory that He had with Him before the world began.

We are told that they "worshipped Him, and returned to Jerusalem with great joy." All questions as to the mystery of His Person were now at an end. They adored Him as the Eternal Son of the Father, and then, in obedience to His word, "returned to Jerusalem with great joy" to await the descent of the Holy Spirit. "They were continually in the temple, praising and blessing God." During the tarrying period they seem to have dwelt together in one common home, where they spent time in prayer

(Acts 1: 13, 14), but during the greater part of the days they were found in the temple courts, "praising and blessing God." It was not, as some have concluded without proper evidence, that a prayer-meeting went on continually for the ten-day period.

The one great fact which is brought before us in this lesson is that we who know Christ as Saviour are responsible to carry the gospel to all the people of the world. It is not for us to enjoy the goodness of the Lord ourselves, while forgetting the need of lost souls all about us, and those in distant lands who are still sitting in darkness and the shadow of death. Nor are we cast upon our own resources in the carrying out of our commission. He who sends also empowers. By the Holy Spirit He fits His servants to go forth, as His anointed heralds, to make known the riches of His grace to men of every nation. Increased blessing comes to the Church at home as her members reach out into the regions beyond. With this Luke closes this account to take it up again in the first chapter of the Book of Acts.

Nothing is more pitiable than to hear Christians arguing about the application of the great commission, while neglecting to obey it. We are responsible to give our generation the opportunity of hearing the gospel. In a future day God will have His witnesses to the nations, but this does not relieve us of present accountability to make known the grace of God everywhere, so far as it is in our power. He who knows the blessing of salvation is called to make Christ known to others even though his circle be a very limited one. All are not gifted preachers or evangelists, but all saved ones can tell someone else of the Lord Jesus and the way of life. If we know Christ for ourselves, are we doing all we can to extend this knowledge to those who are still in their sins? Repentance and remission of sins go together, for when one owns his lost condition, he is prepared to trust the only Saviour. Have we done this?